Woolf Studies Annual

Volume 19, 2013

PACE UNIVERSITY PRESS • NEW YORK

Copyright © 2013 by
Pace University Press
41 Park Row, Rm. 1510
New York, NY 10038

All rights reserved
Printed in the United States of America

ISSN 1080-9317
ISBN 978-1-935625-12-4 (pbk: alk.ppr.)

Member

Council of Editors of Learned Journals

♾ Paper used in this publication meets the minimum requirements of
American National Standard for Information
Sciences–Permanence of Paper for Printed Library Materials,
ANSI Z39.48–1984

Editor

Mark Hussey — Pace University

Editorial Board

Tuzyline Jita Allan	Baruch College, CUNY
Eileen Barrett	California State University, East Bay
Morris Beja	Ohio State University
Kathryn N. Benzel	University of Nebraska-Kearney
Pamela L. Caughie	Loyola University Chicago
Wayne K. Chapman	Clemson University
Patricia Morgne Cramer	University of Connecticut, Stamford
Beth Rigel Daugherty	Otterbein College
Louise DeSalvo	Jenny Hunter Endowed Scholar for Literature and Creative Writing, Hunter College, CUNY
Anne Fernald	Fordham University
Amanda Golden	Georgia Institute of Technology (Book Review Editor)
Sally Greene	Independent Scholar
Leslie Kathleen Hankins	Cornell College
Suzette Henke	Thruston B. Morton, Sr. Chair of Literary Studies, University of Louisville
Karen Kaivola	Stetson University
Karen Kukil	Special Collections, William Allan Neilson Library, Smith College
Jane Lilienfeld	Lincoln University
Jane Marcus	Distinguished Professor, CCNY and CUNY Graduate Center
Toni A. H. McNaron	University of Minnesota
Patricia Moran	University of Limerick
Vara Neverow	Southern Connecticut State University
Annette Oxindine	Wright State University
Beth Carole Rosenberg	University of Nevada-Las Vegas
Bonnie Kime Scott	San Diego State University
Brenda R. Silver	Dartmouth College
Susan Squier	Brill Professor of Women's Studies and English, Pennsylvania State University
Peter Stansky	Stanford University
Alex Zwerdling	University of California, Berkeley

Woolf Studies Annual is indexed in *Humanities International Complete, ABELL* and the *MLA Bibliography.*

> *we can't wait to speak until we are wholly clear and righteous*
> —Adrienne Rich, "Split at the Root"

In the fall of 2011, I suggested to the editorial board a special issue on Woolf and Jews and/or Jewishness. I had been struck by how frequently a submitted article on this topic was withdrawn rather than being revised and resubmitted following readers' reports. With the editors' encouragement, I issued a call in early 2012 for contributions of either full-length articles or short commentary. "We are less interested," the special issue description explained, "in the question of whether or not Woolf herself was or was not anti-Semitic ... than in how the figure of the Jew operates within her work."

During that summer, short commentaries contributed to a "Forum" were shared with a number of scholars, and with each of their writers, with an invitation to forward them at will and to respond. Over the ensuing months, the Forum took shape as writers engaged with each others' arguments, and other voices added their responses. These in turn were shared, and the comments and responses further revised. The advantage of this format is that the contributions suggest many avenues of further inquiry and argument that might be pursued, without closing off discussion.

Although our process has not resulted in a whole volume devoted to the topic, I am hopeful that the discussion in the Forum and the two fine articles published herein will prompt a wider discussion of Jews and antisemitism within Woolf studies, connecting that discussion with the work that has been done on other modernist writers and antisemitism.

I want particularly to thank the editorial board for its support and, especially, the readers for this issue who often worked within a timeframe quite different than what is typical for a scholarly journal.

—Mark Hussey, Editor

Many thanks to readers for volume 19 (in addition to the Editorial Board): Judith Allen (Writers House, U of Pennsylvania); Jessica Berman (U of Maryland Baltimore County); Stuart N. Clarke (Independent Scholar); Jane DeGay (Leeds Trinity U); David Eberly (Independent Scholar); Brenda S. Helt (Independent Scholar); Molly Hite (Cornell U); Emily Hinnov (Granite S C); Maggie Humm (U of East London); Michael Lackey (U of Minnesota Morris); Cheryl Mares (Sweet Briar C); Gabrielle McIntire (Queens U); Patricia McManus (U of Brighton); Eleanor McNees (U of Denver); Jeanette McVicker (SUNY Fredonia); Marlowe Miller (U of Massachusetts Lowell); Mary Beth Pringle (Wright S U); Steven Putzel (Penn S U); Natania Rosenfeld (Knox C); Urmila Seshagiri (U of Tennessee Knoxville); Paul Saint-Amour (U of Pennsylvania); Anna Snaith (King's C London); Helen Southworth (U of Oregon); Alice Staveley (Stanford U); Lara Trubowitz (U of Iowa); Julie Vandivere (Bloomsburg U); Janet Winston (Humboldt S U); Tory Young (Anglia Ruskin U).

Contents

Woolf Studies Annual

Volume 19, 2013

ix   Abbreviations

VIRGINIA WOOLF AND JEWS

FORUM

Maren Linett	1	"What'll He Gobble Next?" Jews, Nazis, and Bodily Excess in Virginia Woolf's 1930s Writing
Denell Downum	4	Seeing People Singly
Lara Trubowitz	6	Virginia Woolf and Antisemitism, or Sailing South with the Jews
Beth C. Rosenberg	7	The Belated History of Woolf and Jews
Patricia Laurence	9	*One wanted fifty pairs of eyes*: Virginia Woolf and the Jews
Christina L. Svendsen	12	In the Family: Representations of Jewishness by Virginia Woolf and Julia Margaret Cameron
Lara Trubowitz, David Eberly, Alice Keane, Maren Linett, Beth C. Rosenberg, Christina L. Svendsen, Natania Rosenfield	16	Forum Responses

Leena Kore Schröder	27	"A question is asked which is never answered": Virginia Woolf, Englishness, and Antisemitism
Phyllis Lassner and Mia Spiro	58	A Tale of Two Cities: Virginia Woolf's Imagined Jewish Spaces and London's East End Jewish Culture

ARTICLES

Michèle Barrett	83	Virginia Woolf's Research for *Empire and Commerce in Africa* (Leonard Woolf, 1920)
John McGuigan	123	The Unwitting Anarchism of *Mrs. Dalloway*
Jamie Horrocks	147	"Little Accidents": Virginia Woolf and the Failures of Form in "The Moment: Summer's Night"
Diane F. Gillespie	171	Wedding Rituals: Julia Strachey, Virginia Woolf, and Viola Tree
Monica Latham	195	Variations on *Mrs. Dalloway*: Rachel Cusk's *Arlington Park*

GUIDE

	215	Guide to Library Special Collections

REVIEWS

Beth C. Rosenberg	235	*Civil Antisemitism, Modernism, and British Culture, 1902-1939* by Lara Trubowitz
Emily Kopley	238	*A Russian Jew of Bloomsbury: The Life and Times of Samuel Koteliansky* by Gayla Diment

Emily James	243	*Virginia Woolf and the Migrations of Language* by Emily Dalgarno
Bryony Randall	246	*Virginia Woolf: The Patterns of Ordinary Experience* by Lorraine Sim
Morris Beja	249	The Cambridge Edition of *The Waves* by Virginia Woolf. Michael Herbert and Susan Sellers, eds.
Pamela L. Caughie	254	The Cambridge Edition of *Between the Acts* by Virginia Woolf. Mark Hussey, ed.
Maria DiBattista	256	*The Essays of Virginia Woolf*, volumes 5 and 6
Mark Hussey	259	*Modernist Commitments: Ethics, Politics, and Transnational Modernism* by Jessica Berman
Kristin Czarnecki	262	*In the Hollow of the Wave: Virginia Woolf and Modernist Uses of Nature* by Bonnie Kime Scott
Michael Lackey	266	*Thinking in Literature: Joyce, Woolf, Nabokov* by Anthony Uhlmann
Rachel Trousdale	269	*The Web of Sense: Patterns of Involution in Selected Works of Virginia Woolf and Vladimir Nabokov* by Irena Ksiezopolska
Teresa Prudente	271	*Language, Time, and Identity in Woolf's* The Waves. *The Subject in Empire's Shadow* by Michael Weinman
Amy Elkins	274	*Visuality and Spirituality in Virginia Woolf's Fiction* by Savina Stevanato

Kelly Walsh	278	*Mourning Modernism: Literature, Catastrophe, and the Politics of Consolation* by Lecia Rosenthal
Mary Wilson	281	*Virginia Woolf and the Theater* by Steven D. Putzel
Erwin Rosinberg	285	*Bloomsbury, Modernism, and the Reinvention of Intimacy* by Jesse Wolfe
Sarah Cornish	288	*Contradictory Woolf: Selected Papers from the Twenty-First Annual International Conference on Virginia Woolf* Derek Ryan and Stella Bolaki, Eds.
Tamar Katz	291	*A Sense of Shock: The Impact of Impressionism on Modern British and Irish Writing* by Adam Parkes; *At the Violet Hour: Modernism and Violence in England and Ireland* by Sarah Cole
Amanda Golden	295	*Virginia Woolf and the Literary Marketplace* Jeanne Dubino, ed.
Jessica Berman	297	*Modernism and the New Spain: Britain. Cosmopolitan Europe, and Literary History* by Gayle Rogers
Victoria Rosner	301	*Charleston and Monk's House: The Intimate House Museums of Virginia Woolf and Vanessa Bell* by Nuala Hancock
Patricia Moran	304	*On Being Ill* by Virginia Woolf
Helane Levine-Keating	309	*Dying for Time: Proust, Woolf, Nabokov* by Martin Hägglund
Notes on Contributors	313	
Policy	324	

Abbreviations

AHH	*A Haunted House*
AROO	*A Room of One's Own*
BP	*Books and Portraits*
BTA	*Between the Acts*
CDB	*The Captain's Death Bed and Other Essays*
CE	*Collected Essays* (4 vols.)
CR1	*The Common Reader*
CR2	*The Common Reader, Second Series*
CSF	*The Complete Shorter Fiction*
D	*The Diary of Virginia Woolf* (5 vols.)
DM	*The Death of the Moth and Other Essays*
E	*The Essays of Virginia Woolf* (6 Vols.)
F	*Flush*
FR	*Freshwater*
GR	*Granite & Rainbow: Essays*
JR	*Jacob's Room*
L	*The Letters of Virginia Woolf* (6 Vols.)
M	*The Moment and Other Essays*
MEL	*Melymbrosia*
MOB	*Moments of Being*
MT	*Monday or Tuesday*
MD	*Mrs. Dalloway*
ND	*Night and Day*
O	*Orlando*
PA	*A Passionate Apprentice*
RF	*Roger Fry: A Biography*
TG	*Three Guineas*
TTL	*To the Lighthouse*
TW	*The Waves*
TY	*The Years*
VO	*The Voyage Out*

VIRGINIA WOOLF AND JEWS

FORUM

"What'll He Gobble Next?" Jews, Nazis, and Bodily Excess in Virginia Woolf's 1930s writing

Maren Linett

Although Herbert Marder suggests that Woolf's antisemitism decreased as the Nazis consolidated their power in Germany (9), a survey of references to Jews in her letters and diaries alongside her antisemitic scene in *The Years* (1937), her short story "The Duchess and the Jeweller" (1938), and her depiction of Ralph Manresa in *Between the Acts* (1941), shows her antisemitism intensifying during this period.[1] The fact that Woolf was simultaneously antisemitic and antifascist is not particularly surprising.[2] Many antifascists in Britain continued to engage in "drawing-room antisemitism."[3] But why did her antisemitic output *increase* as she became more aware of Nazism's threat? Could there have been some link in Woolf's mind between her distaste for Jews and her disgust with fascism?

---

[1] See Linett, *Modernism*; Trubowitz, "Concealing"; Lassner; & Schröder.

[2] But this congruence, jarring from our post-Holocaust viewpoint, has led other critics to read her portrayals of Jews as self-reflexive, demonstrating her awareness of her own antisemitism (see, e.g., Lee 310; about *The Years* see Marcus 64 and Bradshaw 182-3). I rebut some of these claims about *The Years* in *Modernism, Feminism, and Jewishness* (52-9); moreover, there is too much similarity between Woolf's private references to Jews and her fictional portrayals to make such claims convincing.

[3] In *Varieties of Anti-Fascism*, Andrzej Olechnowicz points out that many anti-fascists did not make anti-semitism "a prominent feature (or at all) of [their] analysis of fascism" (16). He concludes that "Britain's political culture was 'liberal' enough not to prove fertile ground for the BUF's brand of anti-semitism, but not 'liberal' enough to condemn Nazi anti-semitism incessantly and unequivocally" (17). Todd Endelman describes the pervasive anti-Jewish discrimination of British culture in the interwar period as "common enough that few Jews avoided it altogether" (199). In his essay "Jew-Consciousness" (1939) E. M. Forster writes that "[p]eople who would not ill-treat Jews themselves, or even be rude to them, enjoy tittering over their misfortunes; they giggle when pogroms are instituted by someone else and synagogues defiled vicariously" (13). Close to home for Woolf, we find antisemitic comments being made by Clive Bell, Vanessa Bell, John Maynard Keynes, Lytton Strachey, Bertrand Russell, and others. See Quentin Bell (38-39), Nina Paulovicova, Frederic Spotts (470), and Natania Rosenfeld (47-48). About antisemitism in left-wing writers George Bernard Shaw and H. G. Wells, see Cheyette (94-149).

If there is such a link, could it be the voracious bodiliness Woolf attributed to both Jews and Nazis? There are, indeed, similarities in her depictions of Jews and fascists as excessively bodily and as impeding intellectual freedom.[4] In her diaries and letters, Jews are portrayed as physically over-vital, constantly eating cake and erupting in speech, while Nazis—in a sort of caricature of the already-caricatured figure of the bodily Jew—gobble and howl. Although it seems counterintuitive, it is worth considering the extent to which Woolf viewed Jews and fascists in similar ways and why she might have linked them.

In her private writings, Woolf continually connects what she perceives as her in-laws' Jewish vulgarity with having to buy and eat cake.[5] She complains that they "talk incessantly" (*L6* 58; see also *L5* 209). In the famous letter where Woolf admits "what a snob" she was to "hate" marrying a Jew, she links Jews to money, sexuality, and physical vitality. Their "nasal voices" round out her portrayal of "incessantly" talking Jews.[6] Their "noses and their wattles" conjure a fleshiness common to antisemitic stereotypes. Woolf concludes that she was "a snob" not because she's decided these descriptions aren't true, but because she has learned to appreciate this "vitality": "They cant die...their flesh dries on their bones but still they pullulate, copulate, and amass...millions of money" (*L4* 195-6). The word "pullulate" best sums up Woolf's view of Jews. The OED defines it as "to sprout, to germinate...to spring up abundantly; to teem, to swarm."

Such bodiliness is sharply opposed, for Woolf, to the mind. To take just one example: in 1933 Woolf wrote, "Tonight I...dine with 22 Jews and Jewesses to celebrate my mother in laws 84th birthday.... And it'll be as hot as the monkey house. And tomorrow I shall have a headache and shan't be able to write" (*L5* 239).[7] Woolf links Jews to the grotesque body and casts the combination as an obstacle to intellectual work.

---

[4] That intellectual freedom is of paramount importance for Woolf is made clear in *A Room of One's Own*, particularly in the narrator's claim that her aunt's legacy gave her the "freedom to think of things in themselves" (39). She describes mental freedom variously in other works: in *Three Guineas* she calls it "freedom from unreal loyalties" (95-96); in the drafts of *The Pargiters* she describes a Jewish character "breaking into the privacy of the mind, violating solitude" (75).

[5] See *L4* 222 & 241-42; *L5* 258; *L6* 106. Lara Trubowitz points out Woolf's association of the Jewish Victor Rothschild with meat imagery ("Concealing" 283-84), a link that adds to her portrait of animalistic Jews.

[6] Sander Gilman describes stereotypes of the Jewish voice in *The Jew's Body* (10-37), and provides further information about representations of Jewish bodies in "The Jewish Nose" (169-193).

[7] Further discussion of Jewishness as an obstacle to creative work in *The Years* scene with the "Jew in the bath" and in her private writings can be found in Linett, *Modernism* (50-58; 187-8).

Woolf portrays Nazis, too, as voraciously bodily: they are animalistic, they lick and suck sweet paper, they gobble and howl.[8] About Nazi soldiers she writes, "[L]ook at the masks these men wear—the brutal faces of baboons, licking sweet sweet paper" (*D4* 224). She describes Hitler as a "great mould" shaping his "slaves," whom she pictures as "brown jelly" (*D4* 304). She imagines him consuming Europe: "When the tiger, ie Hitler, has digested his dinner he will pounce again" *(D5* 132). And a bit later, "All Europe in Hitler's keeping. What'll he gobble next?" (*D5* 173). There are also several mentions of Nazis howling and baying: "Hitler boasted and boomed.... A savage howl like a person excruciated; then howls from the audience..." (*D5* 169; see also *D5* 178 & 243).

It is clear that one of the prime evils of fascism for Woolf is the way it precludes mental privacy and freedom. In *Three Guineas* Woolf denounces "the creature, Dictator we call him when he is Italian or German, who believes that he has the right...to dictate to other human beings how they shall live; what they shall do" (*TG* 65). And "without private there can be no public freedom" (*TG* 142).

Is there an association, then, between Woolf's depictions of grotesquely bodily, mind-endangering Jews and Nazis? If so, what prompted this association? Was Woolf feeling contaminated by the proximity of Leonard's Jewish body as a Nazi invasion loomed? Did she displace her fears of fascism onto the thing that brought the Nazi threat home—Leonard's Jewishness? Perhaps it would be more surprising if Woolf, steeped in British social antisemitism, did *not* show signs of resenting the new liability of being married to a Jew "while the knives sharpen[ed] for the operation" (*D5* 299).

---

[8] Insect imagery adds to the animalistic portrait. In *Three Guineas* she describes fascists as dangerous caterpillars who "spit" their poison (65). And in her diary she connects Hitler to a wasp who will sting (*D5* 278). Many scholars discuss Woolf's broader responses to fascism; see for example Carlston and Pawlowski.

Seeing People Singly
Denell Downum

A thin line of grease runs the length of Virginia Woolf's career, tracing a vein of antisemitic expression present in her work from her earliest apprentice sketches to her last fully completed novel, *The Years*. Woolf draws repeatedly on a stock stereotype prevalent in her time and social class, associating Jews with oil or grease. That a writer of Woolf's subtlety and originality made use of such tired clichés has long disconcerted critics. It is my aim to suggest that while such stereotyping is undoubtedly offensive, it is not entirely out of keeping with Woolf's writing practice, and in fact it is associated with a habit of thought that in another form produces some of her most original polemical work.

Toward the end of her life, Woolf recorded in her diary a difference between her husband Leonard and herself: "L. sees people in the mass. I singly"(*D5* 332). This self-assessment rings true for anyone who has appreciated the complexity and individuality of many of Woolf's characters. Her arguments about character-making in "Mr. Bennett and Mrs. Brown," together with her conscientious efforts to see her characters whole in "A Sketch of the Past," reveal a writer deeply invested in capturing the individual spark of life animating her characters, whether fictional or biographical. The strength of this impression is such that it can obscure the fact that Woolf is simultaneously quite disposed toward identifying people by "type," often making use of thoroughly banal stereotyping in the process. Thus her recollection of Jack Hills in "A Sketch of the Past" draws heavily on Woolf's perception of him as a member of "the English country gentleman type" (*MOB* 101). She writes, for instance, "He was *of course* very fond of dogs" (103; emphasis mine), the "of course" delineating the extent to which this trait is associated with his "type." Because Hills belongs to a privileged group that Woolf views as "a desirable type" (101), that "of course" and the assumptions that it encompasses appear harmless, and do not figure in any tally of the "offensiveness" of Virginia Woolf. The same rhetorical move, however, seems less innocent when applied to Jewish characters.

We know we're in for trouble when, opening the collection of early sketches published in 2003 as *Carlyle's House*, we find one entitled "Jews." This brief depiction of the wealthy Mrs. Loeb, Woolf's hostess for an apparently uncongenial dinner, drips with condescension and malice. That Woolf does not see her hostess singly, but rather as an exemplar of a type, is apparent in the title. Mrs. Loeb, though a rich woman, seems inveterately middle class: "She might be behind a counter" (*Carlyle's* 14). Her skin, like her palate, is "coarse"; even her kindness is "vulgar." She is a flatterer and a fawner, and "her food, *of course*, swam in oil and was nasty" (14; emphasis mine). The "of course" here lays bare Woolf's assumptions, rooted in prejudice, about her Jewish hostess. The mental operation involved is not so different than the one we already saw at work in the depiction of Jack Hills, as both are instances of seeing people not singly but as part of a mass with predetermined attributes. This mode of thinking at times allows Woolf to seem to grasp quickly the essence of character, but it also leads to lapses that are as much aesthetic as moral.

The interesting point here is that seeing people as a mass, rather than individually, may have been a flaw in Woolf's creative writing, but it is also the precondition that made her political writing possible. When Woolf views her servant Nelly singly, she is often scathing and unsympathetic; it is only when she considers her as a member of the class of uneducated women that she is able to see that "the fault lies in the system" *(D*3 220). Perceiving "the immense forces society brings to play upon each of us," encompassing the "invisible presences" that shape gender, class, and race (*MOB* 80) Woolf is able to construct her arguments in *A Room of One's Own* and *Three Guineas* because of this habit, incorrectly ascribed exclusively to Leonard, of seeing people in the mass.

Following the greasy trace of antisemitic expression through Woolf's career, we come to the "Present Day" section of *The Years*, in which Sara Pargiter complains that her neighbor Abrahamson, "the Jew in [her] bath," leaves a line of grease in the bathtub they share (323). This same stereotypical slur is deployed more thoughtfully here than in the earlier sketch. By noting Abrahamson's work in the tallow trade, Woolf seems to be probing the relationship between two different ways of seeing people in the mass. The stereotypical association of Jews with grease is partially displaced by a class-based analysis that finds cause for his bodily state in the material conditions of his work. The gesture, however, is vestigial. Had Woolf carried out her initial plan of making *The Pargiters* a "novel-essay," this scene and the ideas it embodies would doubtless have been more fully explored. As it stands, it is a jarring moment of seeing people in the mass, rather than singly, that sits uncomfortably in the novel. Nevertheless, it does create a link with Woolf's overtly political writing, raising a number of important questions: What is the relationship between stereotyping and the collective mode of thought endemic to politics? Is "seeing people singly" necessary to the novelist's art? If so, what are the implications for the political possibilities of the novel as a genre?

Virginia Woolf and Antisemitism, or Sailing South with the Jews
Lara Trubowitz

Until recently, scholars have tended to approach antisemitism in the work of modernist writers (and of Virginia Woolf specifically) as either an expression of ambivalence about Jews or as the product of individual prejudice. Diverging from these essentially psychological diagnoses, I consider the ways in which antisemitism in the modernist period operates as a form of productive rhetoric or argumentation. In short, I assume that antisemitism serves a purpose, despite, and often because of, its distastefulness, and that such purpose may be political, social, or, in the case of Woolf and her Bloomsbury compatriots, stylistic. To interrogate more precisely how this plays out in Woolf, let me examine two letters Woolf writes to her friend Violet Dickinson in 1905 as she journeys through Portugal and Spain with her half-brother Adrian. I will then turn briefly to her 1915 novel *The Voyage Out*. I focus on these works to demonstrate how, in the very earliest stages of her career, Woolf is already conceiving of antisemitism as material to be composed and reworked.

On April 5th, Woolf writes from "somewhere off the Coast of Spain," telling Dickinson that she and Adrian have had a "splendid journey"; they "stayed a day at Havre, and went to Rouen, and saw the 3 churches, and then set sail again" *(L*1 184). But she adds that the ship on which they are traveling has been temporarily stranded due to engine trouble, and that she is now "a little bored," a sentiment she attributes "mainly ... to [her] fellow passengers" *(L*1 183). Soon after she laments that she "[has] been cut adrift from the world altogether"; the other guests, specifically one old man, are "a burden to her" *(L*1 184). To "escape," she and Adrian find a secluded spot from which they see "the loveliest sight of Cornwall, and the Lands End, passing so close that we saw the houses and the people" *(L*1 184). This envisaging of England is, however, interrupted by an apparent non sequitur that seems to intrude as if without forethought or craft: "There are a great many Portuguese Jews on board, and other repulsive objects, but we keep clear of them" *(L*1 184). Yet the assertion proves useful, enabling Woolf to simultaneously express and elide her distress at being trapped with "bores," nearing, as she shall later write, "the most Southern place [she has] seen" *(L*1 185).[9] In short, Jews are the fodder, the *objects*, through which she establishes an impression of her fear of the South and, in broader terms, a story about what it means to turn away from England or home. Five days later, worried about the return journey and the fact that the boat is full,

---

[9] Letter to Dickinson (10 April 1905).

she writes to Dickinson: "I am afraid I shall have to sleep with a Portuguese Jew" *(L*1 186).

This kind of improper or unwanted intimacy—with the South, with foreignness, with Jews (all of which effectively amount to the same thing)—finds a parallel in *The Voyage Out*, also the story of a first trip South, here South America. In a scene midway through the book, the protagonist, Rachel, is at a dance, in conversation with the brusque St. John Hirst: "Rachel felt herself surrounded, like a child at a party, by the faces of strangers all hostile to her, with hooked noses and sneering, indifferent eyes" (155). Pages later, Woolf extends the allusion to "hooked noses" with a form of apophasis by aligning Hirst's impropriety and Jewish biology/physiognomy, thus obliquely attributing his failure to impress Rachel in the earlier scene to his "Jewish" (ill)-breeding, a state that will also preclude him from being a progenitor of a "new" English race (205-06). Linking the "hooked noses" with Hirst, it thus becomes possible, through a complex metaleptical chain, to read Woolf as bewailing (through the Jew and in the novel as a whole) all that is erotically repulsive and threatening but also, ironically, infecund or unfertile. The chain is reinforced if we consider Woolf's figuration of "Jewish blood" (206) in *The Voyage Out* as a transposition and stylistic refinement of her comments in her 1905 letters. Only by tracing this transposition from work to work can we fully understand how Woolf's antisemitism operates: as technique rather than sentiment, which is to say, as productive style. To put it another way, for Woolf, Jews (qua Jews) may or may not be useful as people, friends, or lovers (or, later, as husbands), but they are decisively significant as material. As I argue elsewhere, by the time she writes *The Years* and "The Duchess and the Jeweller" in the 1930s[10]—works with identifiable Jewish characters—Woolf will have learned more fully to translate prejudice from the realm of the social parlor to the page; this does not mean that her own bigotry had tempered or dissipated, but rather that she had learned with greater authority how to employ "the Jew in the text."

The Belated History of Woolf and Jews
Beth C. Rosenberg

Woolf Studies, like modernist studies in general, has come late to the study of history. By this I do not refer to the study of archives or influence, nor the digitization

---

[10] Critics such as David Bradshaw, Steven Connor, Leena Kore Schröder, Phyllis Lassner, Karen Leick, Maren Linett, and Natania Rosenfeld have written at length about these works. See also my book, *Civil Antisemitism, Modernism, and British Culture*, 1902-1939 (reviewed in this volume 235-238).

of primary sources, but to our investigations of historical method and our assumptions regarding the construction of historical narrative, something Woolf herself was concerned with. Renaissance, eighteenth-century, and Victorian studies crossed this threshold decades ago, opening the way for various interpretations of representation and culture. Michel Foucault's theories and the New Historical method that followed have become alternatives to positivistic models of history. Foucault has allowed scholars in these other fields to understand history not only through event, but through language. My claim here is that Woolf Studies, if it is to fully articulate the impact of Jews and Jewishness on Woolf's writing and modernism as a whole, must allow for this alternative method. It must move beyond a reading that holds Woolf solely accountable for her self-determined aesthetic and ethical choices, for her published and unpublished antisemitic language, without considering the cultural history that contributed to her intellectual growth and development.

In regard to Woolf and Jews, scholars have focused on or grounded their arguments in historical events and personalities, such as World War II, the rise of Hitler, British fascist movements, and political activism (Bradshaw, Hargreaves, Lassner, Leick, Linett). Criticism begins with Woolf's work of the 1930s, particularly *The Years* and "The Duchess and the Jeweller," or deals with her marriage to the Jewish Leonard Woolf and her complicated relationship with him (Rosenfeld, Schröder, Wilson). If her early life is considered at all, it is to develop a narrative that leads teleologically to the 1930s and 40s (Trubowitz).

However, Woolf's 1912 letters demonstrate Woolf had already configured a notion of the Jew and how the Jew functions within her society and culture. For example, her letters to Violet Dickinson, Madge Vaughan, and Janet Case, upon her engagement to Leonard, reflect a full awareness of the cultural response to the "penniless" Jew. She writes that she must "insist upon [Dickinson's] liking him too," and that she "couldn't bear it if" her friends "disapproved" of her husband *(L*1 500); to Vaughan she writes that she doesn't mean "there to be any lapse in [their] friendship" *(L*1 500), and to Case she comments, "I want you to like him" *(L*1 501). It is clear her engagement to the Jewish Leonard caused Woolf a great deal of anxiety. These early and brief utterances, even though private and not meant for public presentation, are embedded in a thick context of discussion surrounding Jews and Jewishness in fin de siècle Britain.

Just three years earlier, in 1909, Woolf's tone and perspective were far less apologetic and far more self-assured. Her sketch "Jews," also not intended for public view, outlines what appears to be Woolf's notion of the typical Jew: Mrs. Loeb is "fat . . . coarsely skinned, with drooping eyes, and tumbled hair" (*Carlyle's* 14). She describes Loeb as lacking class and as a groveling fool who "flattered" and "wheedled" her guests, who "wished to ingratiate herself" and "expected to be kicked" by those she served (14). Woolf's tone is one of disdain and disgust, and she notes Loeb's utter lack of aesthetic sense.

Woolf's notions about Jews began at her birth and an excavation of the discourse of Jewishness at the end of the nineteenth and beginning of the twentieth centuries reveals a great deal about what contributed to her identity as a writer and thinker. If we look at medical, scientific, journalistic, economic, and/or political texts during that time, we find that the cultural expression of Jewishness is overdetermined and is so forcefully engrained in cultural discourse as to almost go unnoticed. An example of this is the debates over alien immigration that took place during the1890s. While the final Aliens Restriction bill of 1905 contains absolutely no reference to Jews, the debates that preceded the bill are full of explicit reference to Jewish health and hygiene and their association with pollution and disease. The bill was motivated by British concern over massive Jewish immigration from Eastern Europe and Russia, and it reflects the perception of Jews as the antithesis of British character. The language is, in fact, the same language Woolf uses to describe Mrs. Loeb.

The time has come for critical discussion of Woolf's relation to Jews and Jewishness to turn to the earlier years of Woolf's intellectual development, the years before her marriage to Leonard and the onslaught of fascism. Rather than limit our interpretations to diachronic views of history, we must stop to analyze the synchronic moment in depth. One cannot escape the circulation of discourse during one's time, and it can be demonstrated that Woolf's world view was part and parcel of her cultural network, whether she was conscious of it or not.

One Wanted Fifty Pairs of Eyes: Virginia Woolf and the Jews
Patricia Laurence

A knowing critic can only acknowledge that individual writers will sometimes reify, reflect upon or resist racial stereotypes—like antisemitism—that permeate the history of the West. Though Jews share the oppressed history of other peoples enslaved or subjected to colonialism,[11] it is an important moment for Woolf studies and modernist critics to reflect upon Virginia Woolf's writing and her relation to the particularity of Jewish historical experience.

What is it that readers of different identifications and nationalities "read" when Woolf writes about Jews in her diary and letters before the war? What do humanist critics read now? What do those who focus on her biting views of Leonard

---

[11] See Cheyette and Marcus.

Woolf's family perceive? Those who focus on Woolf's treatment of Jews in her fiction? These issues have been discussed in the field, and new methodologies and approaches continue to be developed in order to answer such questions responsibly.

The most important thing to remember in any approach to Woolf and the Jews is to contextualize. One must be aware of Woolf's historically and personally specific circumstances and not just cherry pick antisemitic statements. Or as Beth Rosenberg ably argues in this volume, we must seek alternative approaches and analyze "the cultural history that contributed to her intellectual growth and development." Another approach, as Maren Linett demonstrates in this forum, is to pay close attention to Woolf's language of the body in her depictions of Jews.

But though Woolf's personal, cultural and historical circumstances might inform her views of Jews as well as of other outsiders, the transformation of these views into fiction or a sketch is another matter. For her representation of Jews must also be considered in the context of her preoccupations as a writer and a feminist. She was concerned always with women's lives and their exclusions in society as well as the customs and thinking that contributed to this. In an early piece, "Jews and Divorce," Woolf sketches an unabashedly biting representation of a Jewish woman. It was written in 1909 when she was twenty-seven, in a state of discontent with her marital situation, having just been proposed to by Lytton Strachey (who quickly realized his error and withdrew the proposal). It is not only Jews but women's roles, money, class and marriage that are on her mind. Her representation of the vulgarity of Mrs. Loeb, a modern day Jewish matchmaker, must be acknowledged, yet it cannot be ignored that it is embedded in her ideas about marriage and divorce. Mrs. Loeb, a wealthy meddling woman is seen in this sketch mainly from the outside as "fat…coarsely skinned, with drooping eyes, and tumbled hair" (Woolf, *Carlyle's House* 14). She irks the reader and Woolf in that she "wheedles" her guests to "ingratiate" herself and advance her "poor relations" through marriage. Importantly, she is described as "perhaps, kind, in her vulgar way" (14). Her coarseness leads her to press a single, young woman, Miss T., based on a talented harpist —"a chocolate box young woman, a business woman, used to protecting herself" (14)—upon the attentions of men in the orchestra.

David Bradshaw tells us in his notes that Mrs. Loeb is based upon a Jewess, Mrs. Annie Loeb, the wife of Mr. Sydney Loeb, a stockbroker with a passion for music. "How," the narrator in the sketch asks, did Mrs. Loeb become a rich woman? It is an accident of marriage as she belongs "behind a counter." This early sketch, then, is not only about Jews and class as it poses a very important question that Woolf will return to in her polemics and fiction: why must women marry? Eighteen years later she will again pose it in *To the Lighthouse* through Lily, the single artist, and her relation to the more attractive but equally domineering Mrs. Ramsay who wants her to marry. All pay tribute to the beauty of Mrs. Ramsay—unlike the ugly

Mrs. Loeb—but she manipulates Lily and Mr. Bankes at her dinner party just as Mrs. Loeb of the earlier sketch "wheedles" her guests to arrange Miss T.'s introductions. One of the main differences in narration and Woolf's more developed skill as a novelist eighteen years later is the revelation of Lily, the single woman's mind and thoughts of resistance, as she tries to experiment with "not being nice" to the young man next to her—to Mrs. Ramsay's dismay. Mrs. Ramsay is subject to the same "misjudgments" attributed to Mrs. Loeb, as they "arise," according to Lily, "from some need of her own rather than of other people's" (87). "Women must marry," they both say. This is a sentiment to which Woolf personally and culturally responds, and her criticism of this dictum infuses her sketch of Mrs. Loeb as well as her more developed characterization of Mrs. Ramsay.

It is useful then to contextualize this sketch, "Jews and Divorce Courts," at two points of reading or reception. Woolf penned the portrait of Mrs. Loeb in 1909, before the Great War, and before she met Leonard Woolf and his family; indeed, before knowing many Jews or experiencing the historical upheaval of fascism that would later provoke her to write *Three Guineas*. In 1909, what must not be lost is that both marriage and "conceiving of antisemitism as material to be composed and reworked" (as Lara Trubowitz perceptively notes above) are on Woolf's mind. What piques her about Mrs. Loeb in the context of the other stories in this notebook is her "common" aspiration for herself and other women through the convention of marriage; and what interests her in the second part of the sketch is the divorce of a couple, as she continues her ruminations on the perils and comforts of marriage.

In our search for new approaches, then, we must encourage readers, editors and critics to contextualize Woolf's representations of Jews at different personal, historical and fictional moments. The editor of *Carlyle's House* chose to separate "Jews and Divorce Courts" into two separate sketches, "Jews" and "Divorce Courts," viewing the title as "purely functional" (38). This separation implies that the two sketches are unconnected in theme, giving the sketch "Jews" greater prominence as commentary on Jews than as Woolf's view of Jews *and* marriage and divorce. The sketch, "Jews," was used as the story to highlight *Carlyle's House* in the *Guardian* in 2003 upon its publication, earning the sketch more attention. Critics pounced upon this newly separated portrait of Mrs. Loeb, a common aspiring Jewess, to attack Woolf's antisemitism. It is a negative portrait and the accent falls differently on Mrs. Loeb's "foreignness," but it is to be understood in the context of Woolf's evolution as a novelist, feminist and social and political thinker. We need, as this Forum represents, sensitive readers and editors with at least fifty pairs of eyes to see round Virginia Woolf and to fairly assess her evolving views of Jews in her writing.

In the Family: Representations of Jewishness By Virginia Woolf and Julia Margaret Cameron

<u>Christina L. Svendsen</u>

Virginia Woolf's characterizations of Jewishness have often awakened dismay. In her polemical long essay of 1938, *Three Guineas*, Woolf energetically denounces antisemitism and relates it to the gender discrimination she experienced in her own life. Yet her short story "The Duchess and the Jeweller," composed during an interval between revisions of *Three Guineas*, displays embarrassingly crude stereotypes about Jews. Woolf's private life further complicates the picture. In her diaries, affection for her husband, Leonard Woolf, alternates with distaste for his middle-class family and his sister Flora's "Jewish laugh" (Schröder, 303). How should we understand this contradiction between the public figure who spoke out early against Nazi antisemitism, and the novelist and private diarist who stoops to easy stereotypes, without succumbing to post-1945 historical hindsight? A novel angle of vision will shed new light: the art created by her great-aunt, Julia Margaret Cameron.

Woolf was ambivalently entwined with Cameron, seeing her as both a role model and an example to be avoided of the domestic traps of Victorian mores. She wrote a parodic play about her great-aunt, *Freshwater: a comedy*, as well as an affectionate biographical introduction to the Hogarth Press edition of Cameron's work, *Victorian Photographs of Famous Men and Fair Women*. Woolf was indebted to her great-aunt for early introductions into literary circles (her aunt photographed Alfred Tennyson, Charles Darwin, Henry Wadsworth Longfellow, and Robert Browning, among others) as well as for knowledge of her mother Julia; some of Cameron's most important photographs are portraits of her beloved niece. Cameron also connected her to the society of startlingly multicultural individuals. The Pattle sisters were descendants of French and British ancestors who had lived in India for generations. Even when they inhabited the Isle of Wight, Cameron and her husband named their home Dimbola Lodge after the coffee plantations where they sometimes lived in Ceylon. Cameron had cosmopolitan interests, befriending and photographing a range of people including the exiled child prince Alemayehu of Abyssinia. She reverently photographed Jewish iconography, asking Sir Henry Taylor to pose for a portrait of King David (Fig. 1) and creating large-scale tableaux such as "Daughters of Jerusalem" (Fig. 2) or "Queen Esther before King Ahasuerus." Her portraits tend to interest us most today—for example, a lost photograph rediscovered in 2002 of Hannah de Rothschild (Fig. 3).

Cameron was a narrative photographer, often choosing titles that suggest a hidden plot, whether directly (as in the series requested by her friend Alfred Tennyson to illustrate his *Idylls of the King*), or more allusively. Her portraits' highly subjective soft focus was another means of representing the sitter's inner state of mind. Her 1871 portrait of Hannah de Rothschild sympathetically reveals the subject's contemplative mood. Dressed in a medieval gown that may be one of Cameron's many props, Hannah is shown with one elbow leaning against a reading stand. Her gaze moves beyond the frame of the photograph. Her half-smile reacts to something beyond our vision, while light pours down on her from above through a small skylight. The only written documentation comes from a letter by Hannah's mother, Charlotte: "Hannah spent a day with the lady of Freshwater and was, I believe, amused" (Ford 35). Yet the women were clearly acquainted and shared friends. A photograph of Hannah's Mentmore House studio shows multiple Cameron photographs hanging on the wall, including a portrait of Woolf's mother, Julia (Ford 33).

Rothschild was married to the Earl of Rosebery and, like Woolf, in a mixed-religion marriage. In both pairings, spousal love was mixed with anxiety about Jewishness expressed in jokes, such as Virginia referring to Leonard as "my Jew" (Schröder 298) and Lord Rosebery allegedly remarking that "le Jew est fait" upon his son's birth (Trevelyan 305). An intimate unease marks both comments, suggesting an Enlightenment-style tolerance towards Jewishness. This attitude is certainly not unprejudiced, but it is also very far from the pseudo-scientific racial fundamentalism of Social Darwinist and Nazi theories common at the time. Woolf's aristocratic reaction to Jewishness seems based on perceptions of taste and manners (that improper "Jewish laugh") rather than on notions of race. This distinction makes it easier to understand the noble portraits of Jews created by her great-aunt as well. Woolf's bias was originally based on class, and therefore "casual, unsystematic" (Briggs 310). When she wrote *Three Guineas*, she was in the process of shifting from an inherited attitude towards a more self-conscious stance, and her conception of Jewishness shifts from cultural to political and racial.

Fig. 1

Fig. 2

Fig. 3

RESPONSES

Lara Trubowitz

In her analysis of Virginia Woolf's 1933 satirical novel *Flush*, Karen Leick illuminates the ways in which Jewishness appears as a central issue despite the fact that "the figure of the ... Jew is absent from [the] bestselling [novel]" (124). Rather than describing Jewish identity explicitly, Woolf establishes what Leick calls "Jewish-inflected" characters, for instance the thief, Mr. Taylor, who abducts Elizabeth Barrett Browning's dog. "Taylor of course is not a Jewish name," Leick notes. "[I]nstead Woolf relies on the stereotype of the Jewish tailor to identify his ethnicity" (124). Such techniques by which Jewish history and identity are obfuscated and simultaneously made visible are, I suggest, a principal way in which Woolf introduces Jewishness into her texts, a circumvention of subject matter in keeping with the broader evolution of her work. We find evidence of this as early as 1915 in *The Voyage Out*, with the oblique reference to "hooked noses" that I discuss above. To neglect such stylistic machinations has crucial consequences for Woolf scholarship: if we look only for what Woolf directly says about Jews, or seek primarily to evaluate whether she is representing Jews well or badly, we risk negating Jews' use-value as figures for Woolf, and may miss the most provocative expressions of her antisemitism.[12] Indeed, extending Denell Downum's thoughtful observations about Woolf's emphasis on "type" and her tendency to "see ... people in the mass," I would add that Woolf's views of Jews—along with her "Jewish" types—remained relatively static over the course of her career, even as her techniques for representing Jewishness evolved.[13]

---

[12] Recall for instance Woolf's descriptions of Mrs. Manresa in her 1941 novel, *Between the Acts*. Mrs. Manresa, while not identified as Jewish herself, is married to the Jewish Ralph Manresa, a character who never actually appears in the novel. Woolf portrays Mrs. Manresa as "[v]ulgar ... in her gestures, in her whole person, over-sexed, over-dressed for a picnic" (41), traits she also associates with Mrs. Loeb, the "fat Jewess" in "Jews," as Patricia Laurence notes. But here Mrs. Manresa's vulgarity allows sentiments to be uttered that otherwise could not be said; those around her "follow [her] like leaping dolphins in the wake of an ice-breaking vessel" (41).

[13] I would characterize most of these "types" as archival figures, meaning that they are primarily wanderers, biblical figures, and turn of the twentieth century ethnographic subjects in the Charles Booth vein. Consider for example Abrahamson from *The Years*—son of Abraham—or the class-climbing jeweller in "The Duchess and the Jeweller," whose roots in the East End are recollected throughout the story. As I discuss at greater length in *Civil Antisemitism, Modernism, and British Culture*, Woolf's attentiveness to such types often results in the preclusion of Jews as contemporary political subjects.

FORUM: VIRGINIA WOOLF AND JEWS

David Eberly

Recently I bought a copy of *Salute to Roy Campbell* published by Typographeum Press. I was attracted by the association of many of its contributors with British modernism and with Bloomsbury, and drawn to its fine printing. As I began to read Richard Aldington's opening essay, I found him favorably quoting from Campbell's *Talking Bronco*: "Through Africa, huge reefs of quartz/ Grind like the gilded teeth of Jews." "Campbell," Aldington enthuses, "shows a mastery of English verse equal to Dryden himself" (Kershaw 16). Reading it was like being hit with a pail of dirty water.

Dryden and Blake, Anthony Julius writes in *Trials of the Diaspora*, conceived of Israel in allegorical relation to England. "These forms of identification could lead in several directions, toward positions hostile or sympathetic to Jews, or unstable combinations of both" (433). That instability may account for the contradictory characterizations of Woolf's antisemitism among these forum papers. Maren Linett claims Woolf's antisemitism intensified during the late thirties, even as, Christina Svendsen notes, she "energetically denounces" it in *Three Guineas*.

Several authors remark on Woolf's historically and culturally inflected antisemitism, which Hermione Lee notes could be "blithely unselfconscious" throughout her milieu (308). Together these papers point to a troubling persistence in Woolf's antisemitism from "Jews" (1909) to "The Duchess and the Jeweller" (1938) that needs emphasis. Julius, discussing Woolf's antisemitism in the context of her society's overall prejudice, states that in writing about the "fat Jewess" Mrs. Loeb, Woolf "does not merely find herself in the presence of a Jew, she is *unwillingly* in the Jew's presence" (360) and notes her "experience of recoil and suffocation," which surpasses the "faint contempt" Noel Annan attributed to her Bloomsbury relations, an observation that contradicts some of the more benign opinions that seek to minimize Woolf's prejudice.

Lara Trubowitz suggests that critics consider "ways in which antisemitism in the modernist period operates as a form of productive rhetoric or argumentation." In doing so, however, one must not forget the historical fact of prejudice, telegraphed in 1938: "COULD YOU CHANGE RACE OF JEWELLER SINCE THERE IS TERRIFIC RACIAL PREJUDICE IN AMERICA" (Lee 668). Interestingly, that cable from Woolf's erstwhile New York agent reinforces the need for contextualization of Woolf's antisemitism, as argued by several of this forum's authors. Seen by one American publisher as a "psychological study of the Jew" (Lee 668), Woolf's story nevertheless is drenched in anti-Semitic stereotype. "Isadore" is erased for Oliver to cross the Atlantic at a time when Jews fleeing Europe were embargoed from the United States.

In his "salute" to Roy Campbell, who "thrashes decadent England, the pommies, the Lesbians, the nancyboys, the Jews, and all who weep that they were born" (92), Alan Paton writes, "I do not think for a moment that he understood the true nature of fascism, though I think he should have done. Campbell lived; he did not think" (Kershaw 96-97). Woolf lived *and* thought, leaving her readers a complex and contradictory record of a prejudice enacted, observed, and challenged, as these contributions collectively show.

Alice Keane

Maren Linett's analysis of Woolf's intensifying antisemitic animal imagery in the 1930s calls to mind not only fellow Bloomsbury member John Maynard Keynes's troping of "animal spirits" in the *General Theory of Employment, Interest and Money* (1936)[14] but also his own occasional "drawing-room antisemitism."[15] Might there be commonalities here between Woolf and Keynes in the late 1930s? Writing to Franklin Delano Roosevelt in 1938, Keynes figures *homo economicus* as a non-rational creature: "surly, obstinate, terrified" when fear-driven. "You could do anything you liked with them," Keynes advises Roosevelt of business leaders, "if you would treat them (even the big ones), not as wolves and tigers, but as domestic animals by nature…" (CW XXI: 438). Keynes characterizes the French government's representative at the 1919 Versailles peace conference as "a short, plump, heavy-moustached Jew….prating of his 'goold'" (CW X: 422). As late as 1941, in a letter to Britain's chancellor of the exchequer, he both praises and disparages junior United States government employees as "exceptionally capable and vigorous (with the very gritty Jewish type perhaps a little too prominent)" (CW XXIII: 107).

Keynes's economic theorizing about "animal spirits," insofar as it draws upon modernist conceptions of irrationality, uncertainty and the unconscious, owes a debt to Freud, albeit one of uncertain scope[16]—as do Woolf's innovations in modern fiction. Keynes's use of animalistic imagery is vivid and rhetorically resonant chiefly because it calls upon indeterminate empirical intuition rather than

---

[14] Keynes defines "animal spirits" in the *General Theory* as "the characteristic of human nature that a large proportion of our positive activities depend on spontaneous optimism rather than on a mathematical expectation" (161).

[15] For more information on Keynes's antisemitism, see Chandavarkar and Paulovicova.

[16] Addressing Bloomsbury's Memoir Club in 1938, Keynes employs disturbing language: the Edwardian influence of philosopher G. E. Moore, he contends, "was a purer, sweeter air by far than Freud cum Marx" ("My Early" 58). But Keynes is not always so disparaging of Freud. In a 1925 pseudonymous review of the Hogarth Press's translations of Freud, he avoids such overtones of reflexive revulsion, recommending "the most patient and unprejudiced examination" of Freud's ideas (Dostaler 107; "Siela" [John Maynard Keynes] 643-44).

exact scientific proof. But as Linett's examples from Woolf's writings compellingly demonstrate, Bloomsbury's metaphors of animalistic irrationality, necessarily and powerfully vague, also could and did lend themselves too easily to misuse and co-opting by antisemitic forces in the late 1930s.

Maren Linett

In his valuable response to the forum, David Eberly points out differing assessments of Woolf's antisemitism in the late thirties. "Maren Linett claims Woolf's antisemitism intensified during the late thirties, even as, Christina Svendsen notes, she 'energetically denounces' it in *Three Guineas*." It is true that in *Three Guineas* Woolf links Jews to women as victims of fascist/patriarchal oppression when she writes "You are feeling in your own person what your mothers felt when they were shut out, when they were shut up, because they were women. Now you are being shut out, you are being shut up, because you are Jews, because you are democrats" (102-3).[17] But as I mention in my contribution to the forum, Woolf and her contemporaries could abhor "Jews beaten up" or locked up while retaining their distaste for Jews and expressing that distaste in everyday comments and in fiction. Consider the American scenario at the same time, where there would have been millions of Euro-Americans who would sincerely condemn lynchings while nevertheless viewing African-Americans as inferior human beings. E. M. Forster makes a similar distinction in "Jew-Consciousness" when he writes "I do not think we shall go savage. But I do think we shall go silly" (13). Prejudice has degrees of intensity.

Woolf's distaste for Jews, contrary to what Christina Svendsen asserts in her discussion of class, applied to upper-class Jews such as Victor Rothschild[18] as well as to middle-class Jews such as Mrs. Loeb (from the early sketch) or her mother-in-law Marie Woolf and to poverty-stricken Jews such as the man "glaring out of his misery" in "Street Haunting" (251). Her antisemitic responses were, however, inflected by class, resulting in fascinatingly different varieties of literary and social antisemitism. It is time to move beyond the apologies and excuses that pepper the forum and continue the important work of exploring what her antisemitism meant to Woolf, and how it functioned for her personally, politically, and as Lara Trubowitz stresses in her contribution, aesthetically.

[17] I trace, however, ways in which Jewishness lingers as a danger even within *Three Guineas* in *Modernism, Feminism, and Jewishness*, 67-70.
[18] See Trubowitz, "Concealing Leonard's Nose."

Beth C. Rosenberg

David Eberly's response to this forum astutely points to the "instability . . . [and] contradictory characterizations of Woolf's antisemitism" in Woolf studies. Though I find no attempts in this forum to apologize for Woolf, I do find two tendencies: the first is to conflate the reference and meaning of the Jew with antisemitism, two very different terms, and the second is the insistence on using a positivistic notion of history that moves toward the fascism of the 1930s as its end point. Eberly does argue for contextualization, as does Patricia Laurence, and this seems to be the most reasonable way to understand both Woolf's and her critics' ambivalence toward the Jewish figure. Natania Rosenfeld asks, "Is there more to be said about Woolf and Jews in 2012?" The answer is undoubtedly yes. The question now is where to turn our attention. It is not, as Maren Linett suggests, that we see Woolf's "antisemitism intensifying during" the 1930s, but that her antisemitism gets more explicit and clearly articulated during this period. Woolf's views and responses toward Jews were formed and existed decades before the fascist turn, and in some ways the latency of her earlier response can be viewed as more subversive and intense. Our attention need not be spent so much on what "antisemitism meant to Woolf, and how it functioned for her personally" (something which I believe is impossible to determine), but rather on the cultural influences that contributed to her development as an artist and writer and the ways those influences are inflected in her work—that is, what Linett terms the political and aesthetic.

Patricia Laurence rightly asserts that "it is an important moment for modernist critics to reflect upon Virginia Woolf and her relation to the particularity of Jewish historical experience." To do this we must approach our study from a new methodological perspective, and Lara Trubowitz's rhetorical analysis of Jews and Jewishness opens up the most productive possibilities. There is always an over-determined discourse regarding Jews; the "metaleptical chain" that Trubowitz refers to connects the 1880s and the birth of British modernism to the 1930s and fascism. The political and aesthetic discourses surrounding Jewishness influenced Woolf's aesthetic as a writer and modernist from the beginning of her development. This includes the discourse of photography that Christina Svendsen comments on; Svendsen's distinction between a Jewishness "based on perceptions of taste and manners . . . rather than on notions of race" is correct—the Jew of the Victorian period exists within a distinct context and carries different cultural meanings than the Jew of 1930.

The Jew in history has never maintained a static and stable meaning, and the one way to understand both our own and Woolf's ambivalence toward Jews and Jewishness (and by extension Woolf's antisemitism) is within the context of language and discourse. If we do so we shall find that many aspects of Woolf's Jew in the 1930s existed long before her ability to articulate them, and that her very earliest works contain many of the references and connotations of the fascist years.

Christina L. Svendsen

In response to Maren Linett's critique, I would like to point out my agreement with David Eberly and Beth Rosenberg in their discussion of Virginia Woolf's antisemitism, and in particular the need to historicize it. Woolf's deepest associations with Jewishness appear to be related to the Victorian stereotype of the Jew, which she retains implicitly even as she explicitly rejects Nazi racialized and pseudo-scientific hateful theories of Jewish identity. As Rosenberg states, the earlier Victorian prejudice shares some strands and historical connections with the prejudice of the 1930s, since the prejudice of the 1930s developed out of it, but they are not the same. Woolf's case is particularly interesting and disturbing because we see these different antisemitisms interact in her writing.

There is a field in German literary studies devoted to tracing the history of concepts—not words, but concepts—which shift even more subtly than words do, since concepts depend on social and cultural context and cannot be directly recorded at different moments in time in as direct a way as words can. This field, *Begriffsgeschichte*, which has been awkwardly translated into English as "conceptual history" but is really "the history of concepts" and has been pioneered by Reinhard Koselleck, is a useful framework for understanding historical shifts in antisemitism.

My contribution to the forum states that Woolf's bias is expressed in terms of "perceptions of taste and manners" rather than of race. Although Linett interprets that to mean that I argue Woolf's anti-Jewish sentiment was only directed against one class, that's simply not the case, since I cite disturbingly biased comments by Woolf herself and by Lord Rosemont, a British peer, in regards to his own offspring. In fact, in my contribution I agree with Linett in believing, instead, that Woolf's antisemitic prejudice was "inflected by class," just as Linett writes in her response.

Historicizing antisemitism is not the same thing as making excuses for it. In fact, it can be precisely the opposite, because instead of isolating antisemitism of the 1930s, it shows its historical kinship with other more familiar forms of bias. Furthermore, as psychologists such as Mahzarin Banaji have shown over the past decade in studies inaugurated by Banaji's article "The consciousness of social beliefs: A program of research on stereotyping and prejudice,"[19] implicit bias against

[19] Banaji, M. R., & N. Dasgupta, "The consciousness of social beliefs: A program of research on stereotyping and prejudice." In V. Y. Yzerbyt, G. Lories, & B. Dardenne, eds., *Metacognition: Cognitive and social dimensions*. London: Sage Publications, 1998: 157-70

stigmatized groups can coexist with a conscious desire to be unprejudiced, as seems to have been the case with Virginia Woolf in the 1920s and 1930s. Rather than excusing Woolf, I hope that this forum will have the opposite effect of reminding all of us how pervasive bias is, including, surely, in ourselves.

Natania Rosenfeld

"An intimate unease"—I like this phrase in Christina Svendsen's contribution to the forum. It suggests restlessness, stimulation, even homelessness, tropes connected with Jews in Europe from medieval times through the Shoah. It evokes Freud's idea of the narcissism of minor differences. It even suggests the very thing a writer needs most: to feel, beneath her skin, a driving discomfort. And Leonard Woolf was good for Virginia's writing. Was Virginia's writing always good for Leonard/the Jews? On the one hand, the more she experimented, the more she moved away from English gentility and propriety (and, perhaps, in Beth C. Rosenberg's words, "the perception of Jews as the antithesis of British character"—or an embrace of them for that very reason). *Between the Acts* champions misfits and outsiders. On the other hand, there is that problem of "The Duchess and the Jeweller" and the Jew in the bathtub in *The Years*, of which Maren Linett and Lara Trubowitz have both written. Is there more to be said about Woolf and Jews in 2012? I am most intrigued by Linett's counter-intuitive (or too-deeply-intuitive-for-comfort) notion that Woolf elided Nazis and Jews in her complex, brilliant and troubled mind. Did she feel that her husband's identity as a Jew might bring the Nazis down on them and resent him for this? Perhaps, but I would say that somewhere, in the hardened deposits of her brain created by early acculturation, the Jews represented an offense against manners, against Civilization itself. And that is fascinating. We have seen throughout history that Jews can be made to represent just about anything the representer despises: for instance, the worst excesses of capitalism; the worst of communism. Why not Jews as Nazis? Even brilliance is not immune to such inversions; sometimes, indeed, brilliance may be particularly susceptible to them.

Works Cited

Bradshaw, David. "Hyams Place: *The Years*, the Jews, and the British Union of Fascists." *Women Writers of the 1930s: Gender, Politics, and History*. Ed. Maroula Joannou. Edinburgh: Edinburgh UP, 1999. Print.
Bell, Quentin. *Bloomsbury Recalled*. New York: Columbia UP, 1995. Print.
Briggs, Julia. *Virginia Woolf: An Inner Life*. New York: Harcourt, 2005.

Carlston, Erin G. *Thinking Fascism: Sapphic Modernism and Fascist Modernity.* Stanford: Stanford UP, 1998. Print.

Cheyette, Bryan. *Constructions of 'the Jew' in English Literature and Society: Racial Representations 1875-1945.* New York: Cambridge UP, 1995. Print.

Cheyette, Bryan and Laura Marcus, eds. *Modernity, Culture and the Jew.* Cambridge, UK: Polity Press, 1998. Print.

Chandavarkar, Anand. "Was Keynes Anti-Semitic?" *Economic and Political Weekly* 35.19 (May 6-12, 2000): 1619-1624. Web. 20 August 2012.

Connor, Steven. "Virginia Woolf, the Baby and the Bathwater." In *The Years*, by Virginia Woolf. London: Vintage, 2004. xi–xxx. Print.

Dostaler, Gilles. "Keynes, Art and Aesthetics." *Keynes's General Theory After Seventy Years.* Ed. Robert W. Dimand, Robert A. Mundell and Alessandro Vercelli. Basingstoke: Palgrave Macmillan, 2010. 101-118. Print.

Endelman, Todd M. *The Jews of Britain, 1656 to 2000.* Berkeley: University of California Press, 2002. Print.

Ford, Colin. "Hannah, Charlotte…and Julia." *The Rothschild Archive: Review of the Year April 2001-March 2002.* London: Rothschild Archive, 2002. Print.

Forster, E. M. "Jew-Consciousness." *Two Cheers for Democracy.* London: Edward Arnold, 1972. 12-14. Print.

Gilman, Sander. *The Jew's Body.* New York: Routledge, 1991. Print.

Hargreaves, Tracy. "I Should Explain He Shares My Bath: Art and Politics in *The Years*." *English* 50 (Autumn 2001): 183-90. Print.

Julius, Anthony. *Trials of the Diaspora: A History of Anti-Semitism in England.* Oxford: Oxford UP, 2010. Print.

Kershaw, Alister, ed. *Salute to Roy Campbell.* Francestown, New Hampshire: Typographeum, 1984. Print.

Keynes, John Maynard. "Dr Melchior: A Defeated Enemy." *The Collected Writings of John Maynard Keynes X: Essays in Biography.* Ed. Donald Moggridge. London: Macmillan, 1972. 389-429. Print.

——. *The General Theory of Employment, Interest and Money. With a New Introduction by Paul Krugman.* 1936. Basingstoke and New York: Palgrave Macmillan, 2007. Print.

——. "My Early Beliefs." 1938. *The Bloomsbury Group: A Collection of Memoirs, Commentary and Criticism.* Ed. S. P. Rosenbaum. Toronto and Buffalo: U of Toronto P, 1975. 48-64. Print.

——. "To Franklin Delano Roosevelt." 1 February 1938. Letter. *The Collected Writings of John Maynard Keynes XXI: Activities 1931-1939.* Ed. Donald Moggridge. London: Macmillan, 1982. 434-439. Print.

———. "To Sir Kingsley Ward." 2 June 1941. Letter. *The Collected Writings of John Maynard Keynes XXIII: Activities 1940-1943*. Ed. Donald Moggridge. London: Macmillan, 1979. 103-113. Print.

Lassner, Phyllis. "'The Milk of Our Mother's Kindness Has Ceased to Flow': Virginia Woolf, Stevie Smith, and the Representation of the Jew." *Between Race and Culture: Representations of 'the Jew' in English and American Literature*. Ed. Bryan Cheyette. Stanford: Stanford UP, 1996. Print.

Lee, Hermione. *Virginia Woolf*. New York: Alfred A. Knopf, 1997. Print.

Leick, Karen. "Virginia Woolf and Gertrude Stein: Commerce, Bestsellers, and the Jew." *Virginia Woolf and the Literary Marketplace*. Ed. Jeanne Dubino. NY: Palgrave Macmillan, 2012. 121-33. Print.

Linett, Maren Tova. "The Jew in the Bath: Imperiled Imagination in Woolf's *The Years*." *Modern Fiction Studies* 48.2 (Summer 2002): 341-61. Print.

———. *Modernism, Feminism, and Jewishness*. New York: Cambridge UP, 2007. Print.

Marcus, Jane. *Virginia Woolf and the Languages of Patriarchy*. Bloomington: Indiana UP, 1987. Print.

Moore, George Edward. *Principia Ethica*. 1903. London: Cambridge UP, 1922. Print.

Olechnowicz, Andrzej. "Introduction: Historians and the Study of Anti-Fascism in Britain." *Varieties of Anti-Fascism: Britain in the Inter-war Period*. Eds. Nigel Copsey and Andrzej Olechnowicz. Basingstoke: Palgrave Macmillan, 2010. Ebook Library. Web. 6 June 2012.

Paulovicova, Nina. "The Immoral Moral Scientist: John Maynard Keynes." *Past Imperfect* 13 (2007): 24-55. Web. 20 August 2012.

Pawlowski, Merry M., ed. *Virginia Woolf and Fascism: Resisting the Dictator's Seduction*. New York: Palgrave, 2001. Print.

Rosenfeld, Natania. *Outsiders Together: Virginia and Leonard Woolf*. Princeton: Princeton UP, 2000. Print.

Schröder, Leena Kore. "Tales of Abjection and Miscegenation: Virginia Woolf's and Leonard Woolf's 'Jewish' Stories." *Twentieth-Century Literature* 49.3 (Fall 2003): 298-327. Print.

"Siela" [John Maynard Keynes]. Letter. *The Nation and Athenaeum*. Vol. 35. 29 August 1925. 643-644. Print.

Spotts, Frederic, ed. *Letters of Leonard Woolf*. New York: Harcourt Brace Jovanovich, 1989. Print.

Trevelyan, Raleigh. *Princes Under the Volcano*. NY: Morrow, 1973. Print.

Trubowitz, Lara. *Civil Antisemitism, Modernism, and British Culture, 1902-1939*. Palgrave Macmillan, 2012. Print.

———. "Concealing Leonard's Nose: Virginia Woolf, Modernist Antisemitism, and 'The Duchess and the Jeweller.'" *Twentieth-Century Literature* 54.3 (Fall 2008): 273-306. Print.

Wilson, Jean Moorcroft. *Virginia Woolf and Anti-Semitism*. London: Cecil Woolf, 1995. Print.

Woolf, Virginia. *Between the Acts*. London: Harcourt, 1941. Print.

———. *The Diary of Virginia Woolf*. 5 Vols. Ed. Anne Olivier Bell. New York: Harcourt, 1977. Print.

———. "Divorce Courts." *Carlyle's House*. Ed. David Bradshaw. Foreword by Doris Lessing. London: Hesperus Press, 2003. 16-18. Print.

———. "The Duchess and the Jeweller." 1938. *The Complete Shorter Fiction of Virginia Woolf*. Ed. Susan Dick. 2nd ed. New York: Harcourt, 1989. 248-53. Print.

———. *Flush*. London: Hogarth, 1933. Print.

———. "Jews." *Carlyle's House*. Ed. David Bradshaw. Foreword by Doris Lessing. London: Hesperus Press, 2003. 14-15. Print.

———. *The Letters of Virginia Woolf*. Ed. Nigel Nicolson and Joanne Trautmann. 6 Vols. New York: Harcourt Brace Jovanovich, 1975-1980. Print.

———. "Modern Fiction." *The Common Reader*. New York: Harcourt, 1925. 207-218. Print.

———. *The Pargiters*. The Virginia Woolf Manuscripts from the Henry W. and Albert A. Berg Collection of the New York Public Library. Woodbridge, CT: Research Publications, 1993. Microfilm.

———. *A Room of One's Own*. New York: Harcourt Brace & Company, 1989. Print.

———. "A Sketch of the Past." In *Moments of Being*. Ed. Jeanne Schulkind. New York: Harcourt, 1985. 61-159. Print.

———. "Street Haunting." *The Virginia Woolf Reader*. Ed. Mitchell A. Leaska. New York: Harcourt, 1984. 246-259. Print.

———. *Three Guineas*. New York: Harcourt Brace & Company, 1966. Print.

———. *To the Lighthouse*. 1927. Orlando: Harcourt, 2005. Print.

———. *The Voyage Out*. 1915. New York: Harcourt, 1920. Print.

———. *The Years*. 1937. New York: Harcourt, 2008. Print.

"A question is asked which is never answered": Virginia Woolf, Englishness and Antisemitism
Leena Kore Schröder

1. Making the Jew

The attention of late twentieth-century literary and cultural studies to discourses of ideological power, in the interests of recovering what has been marginalized and silenced, has found a rich subject in Virginia Woolf. In the process of revisionary readings she has rightly emerged as a twentieth-century feminist icon whose radical social vision is *almost* beyond doubt. It is in the qualification of that "almost" that this edition of *Woolf Studies Annual* finds its critical space, and in which this essay poses the question: in what sense is Virginia a "bad Woolf"? I play, of course, with the title given by Douglas Mao and Rebecca Walkowitz to their edited collection of essays, *Bad Modernisms*, which takes modernism's acknowledged claims for subversion and disruption, and explores what such so-called "bad behavior" can mean in widely different cultural contexts. The closer one looks, the more the idea of "being bad" ceases to exhibit uniform insubordination. One woman's avant-garde radicalism can be another's snobbery and elitism: that response was already there in Woolf's own lifetime (one thinks of Queenie Leavis, for example), but Woolf wasn't publicly called an antisemite until the early 1990s, when Tom Paulin dared to accuse her on British television in the Channel Four program *J'Accuse*. His charge always was rather naïvely put, but since then there has been an increasingly steady stream of scholarship attempting the rather difficult maneuver of discussing Woolf as a writer who can be both "good" *and* "bad."

My own contribution to that stream has framed Woolf's intermittent racism in Julia Kristeva's psychoanalytic terms of abjection.[1] Ten years later, neither as supplement to, nor contradiction of my previous analysis, Woolf's antisemitism intrigues me for different reasons, for in seeking to understand the wider ideological implications of her antisemitism, the intersubjective formations of her Englishness are what concern me now. Perhaps, like Lara Trubowitz in her recent *Civil Antisemitism, Modernism, and British Culture, 1902-1939*, I have independently come to the same decision to "resist these psychologically informed diagnoses, not because they are inherently false or misleading, but rather because they tend, for my purposes, to draw too heavily on notions of pathology and psychosis" (17). Certainly, I would agree with Trubowitz's trenchant observation that "what we discover in

---

[1] See my "Tales of Abjection and Miscegenation: Virginia Woolf's and Leonard Woolf's 'Jewish' Stories" in *Twentieth-Century Literature* 49.3 (Fall 2003): 298-327.

early twentieth-century configurations of antisemitism is a continual series of entirely social and civic pressures to present virulent prejudices in the guise of legitimate discourse, a rhetorical rather than psychological or theological response both to changing demographics in Britain and to newly emerging definitions of what it means to be 'civil' in the postempire era" (18). My own interest in what it means to be English in the first half of the twentieth century also addresses a kind of "legitimate discourse," not least because the unstated yet rigorous codes of politeness and gentility which the class system assumes are an integral part of how Englishness is perceived. In some ways, then, my reading of Englishness shares Trubowitz's concern with "civil antisemitism": that is, how notions of manners and respectability promote antisemitism "as a polite or reasonable pastime, an acceptable, even at times laudatory, component of mainstream civil discourse" (10). But where she performs a necessarily historicized analysis, mine is not always so. I do not want to keep to her strict distinction between "collective or individual 'states of mind'" and "structural formulations of a civil or civic impulse" (12)—indeed, to me the two seem necessarily interdependent. It is Sartre's more existentially-inflected exploration of antisemitism that helps me to tease out these interrelations and follow them through. In his 1946 *Anti-Semite and Jew* he declares that antisemitism is "a comprehensive attitude that one adopts not only toward Jews but toward men in general, toward history and society; it is at one and the same time a passion and a conception of the world" (17). I argue that Trubowitz's sense of "civil or civic discourse" is not at odds with Sartre's "conception of the world," and therefore it is the fundamental interrelations of these two seemingly conflicting positions which drive my discussion of Woolf, antisemitism and Englishness.

The fact of the matter is that for as much as scholars may not want Virginia Woolf to be a racist, they find her writing marked uncomfortably by racism. Neither marriage to a Jew nor even the Second World War changed her attitude. What she does not hide about Portuguese Jews and "other repulsive objects" encountered on her 1905 trip to Spain at the age of twenty-three (*L*1 184), remains pronounced to the end of her life. In 1940, even as Woolf enjoys the company of a highly educated woman whose politics chime with her own, Jewishness will out: "she shrivelled in her hard high hat into the common, the lemon on steel acid vulgarity of the obvious, the cheap hard Jewess, which at lunch I hadn't seen" (*D*5 265). These reflections on Dr. Rita Hinden—a socialist South African-born economist who was currently helping to set up the Fabian Colonial Bureau—reveal Woolf's prejudices in all their irrational fullness. She is happy to discuss questions of race with her luncheon guest when they share the same visceral response that George Orwell observes is standard to middle-class British upbringing in general, which teaches that "race hatred, religious hatred, differences of education, of temperament, of intellect, even differences of moral code, can be got over; but physical repulsion cannot":

famously, as he declares in *The Road to Wigan Pier*, "*the lower classes smell*" (119, his italics). Orwell may know the lower classes to be clean, as for instance a personal servant, but nonetheless "the smell of their sweat, the very texture of their skins, [are] mysteriously different" (120). It is the same gut reaction which unites Woolf and Rita Hinden over the "mysteriously different" qualities of race and class: "Natives smell she [Hinden] said. Native servants rooms smell very strong. We discussed how nice ordinary people are. Then why are they so repulsive in the mass?" But retrospectively, in a sly metaphoric shift, Woolf assigns Dr. Hinden, with her commonness, vulgarity and cheap hardness, to the very same masses which they had *both* earlier agreed were so "repulsive." Now she is a "swarthy hooknosed red cheeked racy Jewess," who looked more "Frau" than "Dr." (*D5* 264-5). The issue, of course, is not whatever characteristics of race or class Dr. Hinden may or may not have possessed. Whether or not she was the "racy Jewess" whom Woolf describes is irrelevant. The cast of her skin, the shape of her nose, the color of her cheeks are simple physical features that in themselves carry no significance. It is Woolf herself who makes these the signs of Jewishness. In this diary account of a lunch, as we follow the course of Woolf's initial *identification with* Dr. Hinden through their mutual cultural prejudices, to *differentiation from* her along the axis of that selfsame response, we are witness to nothing less than the process by which Virginia Woolf makes the Jew.

We may not like to see Woolf making Rita Hinden into a Jew, but it provides us with a relevant English example of cultural processes which Sartre observes of French society in *Anti-Semite and Jew*. His argument is in many ways a deliberately a-historicizing one, which at the same time acknowledges its own moment in 1940s France. In placing Sartre beside Woolf not only can we read both against the larger contemporaneous context of European responses to the effects of Hitler's policies, but we can also see that a stereotype such as that which Woolf forms out of the raw material of a female South African economist is *not* entirely the result of historical circumstance. Antisemitism does not occur because, to take Woolf as an example, the socio-cultural balance of British society in the late 1930s was suddenly thrown out of kilter by an overly prominent Jewish presence. Such a ridiculous suggestion serves only the kind of historical explanation which would seek to account for (and, in extreme cases, to justify) the rise of Hitler by pointing to the dominance of Jews in influential cultural, political and financial positions in early twentieth-century German society. Antisemitism would thus be linked to a pre-existing historical given. It is important to realize, therefore, that Sartre wields a conscious a-historicism intended to refute the expectation that there *should* be a correlation between racism and historical situation: it is the same expectation which makes us wish that Woolf the hostess would have behaved otherwise, and have welcomed Dr. Hinden to her table in full sympathetic awareness of what was happening across Europe to Jewish people under fascism at that moment. After all, it is what Woolf is able to register in the novel that she was writing at the time, *Between the Acts*, where concerned voices ask "what about the Jews? The refugees . . . the Jews . . . People like ourselves, beginning life again" (74). Rita Hinden, however, is not "like ourselves." She is "mysteriously different," as Orwell observes of the abject lower classes, and that is where the problem lies. What possible reason could Woolf have had to portray her with such meanness? *There is no reason*, and that is exactly Sartre's point: history does not give rise to ideas so much as it is ideas which shape history.

Antisemitism, as I quoted from Sartre at the beginning, is "a comprehensive attitude that one adopts not only toward Jews but toward men in general, toward history and society; it is at one and the same time a passion and a conception of the world" (17). The breadth of what this implies is both far-reaching and considerable. For Sartre antisemitism, at least in its manifestation in 1940s France, is not some passing phase of history, or a set of opinions that can be taken up by some, and rejected by others. Indeed, antisemitism is an inseparable part of French identity, nothing less than the "great explanatory myth" upon which rests all sense of Frenchness itself (148). By this argument, one does not have to espouse antisemitic opinions in order to be an antisemite: it is always already part of one's cultural and political unconscious. Antisemitism is cultural blindness, and is as true of England as it is of France. It is for this reason, therefore, that to unmask Woolf's own cultural blindness we must examine primarily how she expresses her sense of Englishness before we tackle the more conspicuous instances of antisemitism in her work.

2. Moments of blindness

How, then, can Virginia Woolf be both "good" *and* "bad"? As already acknowledged, her commitment to social and political equality is beyond question, and it would not serve my purpose to undermine it. When Jane Marcus states in a ringing declaration that "Virginia Woolf's most important work as a public intellectual was in the struggle against the fascism of the 1930s in Europe" (194), I agree with her entirely. But I agree as well with Rebecca Walkowitz that:

> writers seeking to resist social conformity must develop strategies of critique that exceed homogeneous or merely pious styles of expression. They must accept, if not embrace, the profanity of conflicting sensibilities—beautiful metaphors and ugly events, acts of kindness and scenes of cruelty, suicide in the afternoon and a party in the evening—and they must accept the ethical discomfort that this profanity may evoke. (140)

"Ethical discomfort": does *that* describe how we feel about Woolf's treatment of Rita Hinden in her diary? "The profanity of conflicting sensibilities": does *that* reconcile Woolf's radical politics and social commitment with how she writes about Jews? Before we can answer, we need to follow Walkowitz's logic a little further. She calculates the ideological geometry of post-First World War British culture in terms of "positive" and "negative" axes (the mathematical simplification is mine), by which to explore the moral compass of the novel *Mrs. Dalloway*. To take one of her own examples, in the way that the ambulance which passes Peter Walsh is at once an index of "English society at its most humane" (139), and of the very medical establishment itself that drives Septimus Smith to suicide, the compromised ethics of the novel's world are revealed. The value of Walkowitz's analysis lies in its recognition that these are not the operations of simple juxtaposition. It is not that Woolf is able to show how the novel's social, political and ideological world contains both the good and the bad, but rather, that they are aspects fused one with the other which, as Walkowitz reminds us, is also the point of Benjamin's conflation of civilized documents with the barbaric (141). The real interest, however, of Walkowitz's reading lies in her argument that such fusion or conflation is the result of a systemic *blindness* or *evasion* that works in the novel at many levels. In other words, to return to the example of the ambulance, it is directly *because* Peter Walsh takes it as the positive sign of social care and responsibility (the "good") that he is unable to realize how it feeds into the larger negative agenda of Britain's imperial civilizing mission (the "bad"). Nevertheless, this is a blindness or evasion of understanding that is in some sense unavoidable and even necessary in order for civilization to continue. To argue that Peter Walsh (or anyone else) should recognize the ambulance in *Mrs. Dalloway* as an instrument of patriarchal domination and colonial power would be absurd, if not downright perverse: Woolf would no more have denied the importance of ambulances in relieving suffering and saving lives in contemporary battlefields and civilian streets, than we would wish to deny the Syrians the ambulances and medical help they so desperately need at the moment of my writing (January, 2013). Nevertheless, the point to be made is that the absolute moral necessity for the endorsement of such humanist values will always hide, or detract attention from, the way in which those same values underpin a dominant ideology, and it is in that moment of distraction and forgetting—when we take our eyes off the ideological ball, as it were—that ideology receives its strongest support. One can have the best intentions in the world, and still be racially prejudiced.

Some of these moments of distraction or blindness in *Mrs. Dalloway*, Walkowitz argues, are found in the novel's use of euphemism, the business of "making words mean as little as possible." "The point of euphemism," she explains, "is to make what it has replaced and the act of replacement invisible" (137)—taking one's eye off the ball. In rhetoric euphemism is the mechanism by which unpleasant ideas are expressed in more palatable terms, made palatable precisely because what would otherwise be objectionable has been substituted and rendered safe by the anodyne. So, for example, in *Mrs. Dalloway* when Sir William Bradshaw refers to insanity, he couches it in the euphemism of lacking "a sense of proportion" (106). If Peter Walsh's mistaking of the ambulance for the imperial mandate is an act of evasion which shores up the power of Empire, then here Bradshaw's use of euphemism shows the effects of evasion from another direction, but one which nevertheless still works to sustain the ideology of power. Both Walsh and Bradshaw enact moments of distraction and forgetting, and as such they help us to understand (but not condone, or explain away) the nature of our "ethical discomfort" when we read how Woolf writes about Jews in her letters and diaries, in which she forgets and evades so much.

Unlike Bradshaw's skirting around the issue of madness, Woolf's descriptions of Rita Hinden in terms of her hooked nose, or Portuguese Jews in terms of their smell and sweat, are not instances of euphemism: they magnify and distort, rather than hide. However, as examples of antisemitic cultural cliché and stereotype I would argue that they work in ways that are still similar to Walkowitz's explanation, and that they can therefore be understood in parallel. Like euphemism, both stereotype and cliché are also operations of figurative substitution which work to evade and forget, and in so doing they offer an oblique access to the irrationalities of the political unconscious. Moreover, it is precisely because in Woolf's case the workings of stereotype and cliché reveal themselves most often in the processes of national idealization and nostalgia that, if we want to confront the nature of her antisemitism then—as Sartre does with the French—we must first look to her sense of nationhood, her sense of Englishness. For it is here that we find Woolf at her most stereotypical and forgetful. Moments of being can also be moments of blindness, allowing for states of mind and attitudes which, from another angle, can be read as part of the antisemitic discourses of exclusion.

3. The Amnesia of Englishness

A good place to start is *Three Guineas*, with Woolf's arresting statement that "as a woman, I have no country. As a woman I want no country. As a woman my country is the whole world" (313). Critical elaboration usually continues along lines of feminine identity and radical politics, under the general heading of patriarchal critique: nothing could be further from antisemitism. All this is well and good, but Woolf's addendum is often left out of the discussion:

> And if, when reason has said its say, still some obstinate emotion remains, some love of England dropped into a child's ears by the cawing of rooks

> And if, when reason has said its say, still some obstinate emotion remains, some love of England dropped into a child's ears by the cawing of rooks in an elm tree, by the splash of waves on a beach, or by English voices murmuring nursery rhymes, this drop of pure, if irrational, emotion she will make serve her to give England first what she desires of peace and freedom for the whole world. (313)

Woolf takes back as much as she gives away: for all its radicalism, read as a whole this is still a deeply conservative patriotic affirmation. Indeed, Woolf herself concedes as much with her admissions of "obstinate" and "irrational" emotion. Why is such emotion so irresistible? Why does she allow herself to be pulled back from the liberating and expansive spaces of the "whole world" to the island home surrounded by splashing waves, and withdraw yet further into the childhood nursery with its reassuring rituals and rhymes? And what is forgotten in the process? When the myth of rural England is thus doubled by nostalgia for childhood the result is a powerful combination, and Woolf may well confess to its obstinate and irrational hold. For, what she invokes here is something profoundly unintellectual that emerges only *after* "reason has had its say," and is therefore accessed solely through sight, sound and memory: all conditions of remembered vagueness rather than reasoned political analysis.

It is useful to think of Woolf's slide from radical to reactionary Englishness in the terms which Patrick Wright in *On Living in an Old Country* assigns to a kind of nationhood that is invoked whenever the idea of "heritage" is at stake: "Deep England."[2] Deep England refers to a country that lies beyond constitutional definition, whose appeal is overwhelmingly emotional, and rests upon a perceived subjective base that is at once specifically personal while reaching back into shared immemorial experience. It is at heart nostalgic and romantically rural. What Wright implies by Deep England is yet another way of explaining Sartre's "passion and a conception of the world," by which identity is understood as "a comprehensive attitude that one adopts not only toward Jews but toward men in general, toward history and society" (17)—in other words, it is a state of mind. It is no coincidence, then, that such "passion" is active typically during wartime. This is not of the same order as propaganda: the active threat of the alien enemy demands a corresponding expression of national identity as something intrinsically conceived in a nation's culture and geography. Woolf's *Three Guineas* is as much an English expression of this intrinsic "passion" on the eve of the Second World War as Sartre's *Anti-Semite and Jew* is a French expression just after. But both texts also speak beyond

---

[2] I am greatly indebted to Patrick Wright's fascinating analysis of the operations of nostalgia in twentieth-century England, and especially the section "The Vagueness of Deep England," pp. 77-83 of *On Living in an Old Country*.

the politics of their specific historical moment. More tellingly, they show the *narcissism* of such "passion," which Patrick Wright observes is also a feature of the "deep" nation:

> Deep England also speaks to other experiences. Beyond the favoured images, in other words, it is also formally expressive of some of the basic conditions of modern everyday life, almost regardless of the social situation in which it is lived. Just about anyone who, in the developing turmoil of modern society, has ever had cause to look back and wonder about old forms of security will surely be able to find meaning in Deep England, just as will anyone who has ever fallen under the spell of his or her own intersubjective formation—for there is a narcissism in this love of the green moments underpinning and resonating at the incommunicable heart of the "inner-most being." (82-3)

"Falling under the spell of her own intersubjective formation" is one way in which to describe what is going on in *Three Guineas* when Woolf reconfigures her internationalism to an inward-looking sense of her own Englishness. Its "narcissism" becomes yet more apparent when we notice that it follows exactly the same movement as the extended biographical meditation that opens Woolf's "A Sketch of the Past," in which the account of her early childhood on the Cornish coast is achieved in terms that are as "elastic" and "gummy" as what is being described. While being attractively evocative, this late-life memoir is also extremely vague, and this vagueness is deliberate because it is *necessary*: this is a sense of Englishness that can be expressed *only* in so far as the rational political certainties of "I have no country" have blurred into the irrational sense memories (or "green moments") of rural childhood. The amnesiac nature of processes which are abbreviated in *Three Guineas* is thus played out fully by the performance of somnolent memory in "A Sketch of the Past," where things lack "clear outline":

> Everything would be large and dim; and what was seen would at the same time be heard; sounds would come through this petal or leaf—sounds indistinguishable from sights. Sound and sight seem to make equal parts of these first impressions. When I think of the early morning in bed I also hear the caw of rooks falling from a great height. The sound seems to fall through an elastic, gummy air; which holds it up; which prevents it from being sharp and distinct. . . . The rooks cawing is part of the waves breaking—one, two, one, two—and the splash as the wave drew back and then it gathered again, and I lay there half awake, half asleep, drawing in such ecstasy as I cannot describe. (66)

All the markers of that "obstinate emotion," the "love of England" that Woolf admits to in *Three Guineas*, are placed in this memory: the cawing of rooks, the waves splashing onto a beach, the security of childhood and the nursery, conjured up together through "sounds indistinguishable from sights." The same markers are there in *Mrs. Dalloway*, which begins only to recede into the past—"fresh as if issued to children on a beach"—complete with "the flap of a wave" and "rooks rising, falling" (3). They are there, too, at the start of *To the Lighthouse* where six-year-old James Ramsay, sitting with his mother in their holiday home by the sea, hears the "rooks cawing" (7). And they are established through all the sights and sounds registered by the six child-speakers in the first pages of *The Waves*, as they listen to the birds and waves of the seaside world outside their nursery. Such image-clusters, we should remind ourselves, are always symptomatic of what Sartre calls "a conception of the world": "a comprehensive attitude that one adopts not only toward Jews but toward men in general, toward history and society" (17).

These examples are as "large" and "dim" as what Woolf remembers of her own moment of waking up in the nursery at Talland House. Together, they comprise the fundamental components of her sense of Englishness, demonstrating how often it is something experienced not simply as nostalgia, but also and more importantly, as synesthesia. This mixing-up of senses is significant, because the "obstinate" and "irrational" precipitate that remains after "reason has had its say"—this synesthetic sensory confusion—is precisely why the remembered moment of being is always also a moment of forgetting and evasion, invariably working to mystify rather than clarify what Englishness can be. Take waves and rooks, for example: there is nothing necessarily English about them; they are common the world over. The magic which gives them their potency, their Englishness, is an intuitive and atavistic impulse, something that arises seemingly from pure instinct. This is not so much *ir*rational as *pre*-rational, for which reason it could even be described as a kind of cultural pre-Oedipalism. It is not for nothing that Englishness appeals so strongly to nostalgia—the state of childhood and a pre-civilized green world—for these represent nothing so much as sense of belonging which shades personal memory into the communal unconscious.

As readers we are invited to partake of this vision. Of course none of us can claim to have stood in the gardens at Talland House and seen *exactly* what Woolf describes in "A Sketch"; we have not felt how "the buzz, the croon, the smell, all seemed to press voluptuously against some membrane" (66). But we are not excluded. By yielding to the attractions of such overwhelming synesthesia while at the same time lapsing into the correspondingly fluid rhythms of Woolf's prose style, we are also initiated into an experience that is ancestral rather than learned, and invited to share in its "conception of the world." The canonically modernist "stream-of-consciousness" with which Woolf is popularly associated (she is, of course, a more varied writer) encourages a "dreamy" kind of reading. Anything more analytic or precise would not elicit the necessary instinctive sense of identification and belonging which makes it seem so familiar: the sense, quite literally, of having been here before, of coming *home* (hence nostalgia). This may even explain why so many readers recognise themselves in Woolf's prose style and feel that she speaks to them directly, which indicates that reading too can be as much a narcissistic act of "intersubjective self-formation" as anything else in Deep England. Home, whether one finds it in landscape, language, text or even a favourite author, is always also an ideological place, and what it takes for granted rests on certain cultural values. These values assume attitudes which can be identified with antisemitism.

Such typical markers for Woolf as rooks and waves, therefore, are signs which Sartre would associate with "a type of primitive ownership of land based on a veritable magical rapport, in which the thing possessed and its possessor are united by a bond of mystical participation" (23-4)—and, to make my long story short, for Woolf the Jew is not a mystical participant. For her, each moment of being, each act of appreciation in which a fleeting quality of light or sound becomes suddenly and specially significant, is thus a redemptive affirmation of wholeness, a renewal of the contract between the self and the world of imagined inheritance. But as Sartre would observe, this is an abstract "conception of the world." In reality there is nothing ancestral about Woolf's seaside childhood in Cornwall. Talland House was not inherited property; indeed, it was not even bought, but leased by Leslie Stephen for summer holidays. The moments of rapture and ecstasy which his daughter would experience growing up by the sea were thus made possible through rental agreement, the precariousness of which became apparent when the annual St. Ives holidays ceased at her mother's death. And yet, in Sartre's sense of "magical rapport," Woolf's "primitive ownership" of the place endured throughout her life. She never gave up the lease. Little wonder, then, that Woolf cannot rid herself of an obstinate "love of England," for the more she conjures up such signal images as rooks and waves, the more she ties herself back into a Deep England which she never possessed in the first place. But that too is part of the magic, for this is not a real England; it is, as Sartre puts it, "a conception of the world" (17).

This "conception of the world" can make for strange bedfellows. It allows for alignments of disposition between people who otherwise hold different views. I am thinking, for example, of Herbert Fisher, not because he was an antisemite (he was not), but because he reveals how Woolf's Englishness is able to carry an ideological agenda that is not always necessarily radical: it can, and does, have a reactionary message. Fisher is the cousin whom Woolf offers up in "A Sketch of the Past" as the best specimen of her family's masculine ideal. Cabinet Minister and Warden of New College, Oxford, he belongs squarely in the patriarchal political and academic establishments that are subjected to scathing critique in *Three Guineas*, and yet when he comes to express his love for England his memory spools back into sense impressions just as Woolf's does. The following extract from his essay "The Beauty of England," saturated with rural detail, makes it amply clear that his patriotism is as firmly rooted in the countryside and the past as Woolf's is in the seaside and childhood. Just as for Woolf in "A Sketch," "all these colour-and-sound memories hang together in St Ives" (66), so too for Fisher:

> The unique and incommunicable beauty of the English landscape constitutes for most Englishmen the strongest of all ties which bind them to their country. . . . As the scroll of memory unwinds itself, scene after scene returns with its *complex association of sight and hearing*, the emerald green of an English May, the carpet of primroses in the clearing, the pellucid trout-stream, the fat kine browsing in the park, the cricket matches on the village green, the church spire pointing upwards to the pale-blue sky, the fragrant smell of wood fires, the butterflies on chalk hills, the lark rising from the plough into the March wind, or the morning salutation of blackbird or thrush from garden laurels. These and many other notes blend in a harmony the elements of which we do not attempt to disentangle, for each part communicates its sweetness to the other. (15, my emphasis)

For all that they are cousins Woolf and Fisher are no soul-mates, but they are tugged by the same emotion, and both feel strongly that it is something beyond reach of explanation: in Woolf's case it is "such ecstasy as I cannot describe," and in Fisher's, an "incommunicable beauty" which he cannot "attempt to disentangle." Significantly, both writers appeal to sights and sounds rather than reasoned argument because Englishness, understood in this way, *requires* obfuscation. Patrick Wright also comments on the tendency for Englishness to display "this interpretative stress on the senses, on the experience of meanings which are vitally incommunicable and undefinable," and explains it in no uncertain terms, quoting Hermann Glaser, as the "deadening of thought through mythicizing vagueness" (79). "Deadening of thought" is a somewhat harsh way of accounting for the rural nostalgia of Fisher and Woolf (Glaser himself is talking about National Socialism), but it is a scaled-up idea of what I have been referring to as evasion and forgetting. By this interpretation Woolf's observation in *Three Guineas* that "this drop of pure, if irrational, emotion she will make serve her to give England first what she desires of peace and freedom for the whole world" (313) begins to sound more like a form of colonisation: Deep England has gone global. Is this any different from Peter Walsh's faith in the civilizing mission of a benign Empire? Not really: Englishness, when it deals thus in synesthetic stereotype and nostalgia, always runs the risk of blindness and amnesia, and it is in the operations of such oversight that antisemitism gains access.

4. The snobbery of antisemitism

There is a disturbing "clubbiness" about the kind of Englishness that I have been discussing in *Three Guineas* and "A Sketch of the Past": by its very nature Deep England can only be truly appreciated and understood if one is already a part of it. Like a joke that doesn't work if you have to explain it, you either "get" such Englishness or you don't. Those who don't are "bedint," to use the word coined by the Sackville-Wests and taken up by Vita and Harold Nicolson (defined by David Cannadine as meaning "lower or middle class, vulgar or undistinguished": 217). The Woolf who writes from within this position reveals herself when she tells Vita that she has been lecturing to "200 betwixt and betweens"—and the phonetic similarity with "bedint" may not be coincidence (*L*6 394). It is not pleasant to learn that she is referring to her audience at the Worker's Educational Association in Brighton to whom she read a paper in April 1940. She rewrote this as the essay "The Leaning Tower," in which the expression "betwixt and between" does occur, referring to language which is neither the "rich speech of the aristocrat" nor the "racy speech of the peasant" (E6 272)—I will be returning shortly to the far more frequent use of this phrase in the essay-letter "Middlebrow." Together with *Three Guineas*, "The Leaning Tower" belongs to those writings of the 1930s that Jane Marcus distinguishes as most trenchantly political: it is the mission of literature, Woolf argues, to democratize, and make commoners of us all. If in *Three Guineas*, as a woman, she has no country, in "The Leaning Tower" she is also the "outsider" who gets her accent wrong (as, presumably, do the "betwixt and betweens" to whom she was lecturing). In "The Leaning Tower" the Outsiders' Society is a fellowship of "common readers" united in the freedom of literature: "Literature is no one's private ground; literature is common ground. It is not cut up into nations; there are no wars there. Let us trespass freely and fearlessly and find our way for ourselves" (E6 278). In this we hear the unmistakeable voice of Woolf the radical feminist, but exactly how "common" is the "ground" which she urges us to claim?

Any company of mass trespassers needs must also include the "betwixt and betweens": the "bedint" bourgeoisie who had been invading the sacred rural spaces of the English countryside as ownership of motor cars increased from the 1920s onwards. While Woolf may invite us in "The Leaning Tower" to "trespass freely and fearlessly," her rhetoric is considerably more qualified when such intrusion is enabled by the growing availability of cars for the masses. "The cheapening of motor-cars is another step towards the ruin of the country road" she writes in a short column in the *Nation & Athenaeum* in 1924, and duly invokes the familiar rural stereotype (we've seen it, for example, in Fisher's account): "The English road, moreover, is rapidly losing its old character—its colour, here tawny-red, here pearl-white; its flowery and untidy hedges; its quiet; its ancient and irregular charm" (E3 440). Three years later Woolf herself would acquire the first of a number of cars, which allowed her and Leonard to drive regularly between their homes in London and East Sussex, yet it seems to be a different matter entirely when the countryside is taken over by hordes of weekending motorists: no "magical rapport" with the land for them. Freedom of access, it seems, is more readily granted to some than to others.

The fact that it is Vita Sackville-West to whom Woolf complains of the "betwixt and betweens" is therefore significant. Such opinions so blithely expressed prove how far she is from being "bedint" herself: she includes herself with Vita, on Vita's own ground, as one of the chosen. This is the unattractive face of Englishness, and it demonstrates the truth of Sartre's observation that antisemitism is "a poor man's snobbery" (26); only, the upper classes think in terms of the "bedint." As for Woolf, her word is "middlebrow." In the 1932 essay-letter of that title the middlebrow is the "betwixt and between": "mixed indistinguishably, and rather nastily, with money, fame, power, or prestige" (E6 472)—in short, a philistine who is not capable of appreciating *real* English art and culture. I do not mean that the middlebrow is Jewish, but it is out of such snobbery that antisemitism is born.

In "The Leaning Tower" Woolf takes the ideological argument of *Three Guineas* and reworks it into the register of literature and reading. But once again, if we look more closely across her work at how this reading metaphor operates as social critique we find the same movement from international expansion to insular contraction that we traced in *Three Guineas*: a withdrawal from the democratic public library of "The Leaning Tower," into the exclusive private library of the English country house in the essay "Reading." Jed Esty in his study *A Shrinking Island* has called this action an "anthropological turn," and recognizes it as a general movement backwards from the values of "imperial Britishness" to those of "immemorial Englishness" (39). He finds signs of greenness and nostalgia typical of late-modernist 1930s English literature and culture generally, partly agreeing with Patrick Wright that a resurgence of patriotism is always to be expected whenever a nation is threatened by war, but mostly arguing this as a specific response to the loss of Empire: "Shrinking back to its original island center, England would no longer be a world-historical nation, but it might recapture the humanist, aesthetic, and pastoral values that had been eroded or degraded by imperial capitalism" (39). The action of Woolf's "shrinking back" is precisely what we have been following from the introductory discussion of her lunch with Rita Hinden onwards, but there is also something of Peter Walsh's blindness about this interpretation which puts Esty's claims for recaptured "humanist, aesthetic, and pastoral values" into question.

If Woolf's point is that blindness such as Peter's is what actually maintains the imperial system, then it begs the question to what extent "true" English values could ever be recovered at all in the way that Esty suggests. For, if this is the currency of Englishness in which one deals, then the problem is that it is tainted from the start.

Let us look more closely at how *Mrs. Dalloway* places Peter Walsh into the familiar English stereotype. As he walks through London streets, thinking how he "dislik[es] India, and empire, and army" (60), he cranes to look through open doors, to catch glimpses of the interiors of typically upper-class English townhouses: "Admirable butlers, tawny chow dogs, halls laid in black and white lozenges with white blinds blowing, Peter saw through the opened door and approved of. A splendid achievement in its own way, after all, London; the season; civilisation" (60). These are interiors whose cliché we would recognize from any episode of *Downton Abbey* or *Upstairs, Downstairs*, yet they are not rendered entirely ironic through Peter Walsh's benignly appreciative eye: "there were moments when civilisation, even of this sort, seemed dear to him as a personal possession; moments of pride in England; in butlers; chow dogs" (60). Peter Walsh's vision of England as a nation of elegant Georgian houses filled with admirable butlers and tawny chow dogs is reconfirmed later that day when Richard Dalloway and Hugh Whitbread take their leave of Lady Bruton in her hall. Had Peter been passing as Lady Bruton opened her front door he would again have glimpsed an elegant hallway with malachite table and "her chow stretched behind her" (122). What Peter notices of upper-class London houses may well be a stereotype of interior decoration (its rural counterparts are the remembered country childhoods of Clarissa at Bourton and Lady Bruton in Devonshire), but this is the world that the novel itself invokes as its chronotope, and this makes its Englishness rather more than just ironic. An unironic "conception of the world" is problematic, for often it is only irony that keeps prejudice at bay.

In the way that the novel constructs him Peter Walsh is not "bedint," although perhaps it would be better to use Woolf's term "middlebrow." He is as comfortable a flâneur in London as Clarissa is on her way to Bond Street. Clarissa's enjoyment of the moment is well known, but its wealth of cliché bears repeating for details that we will be taking up—and here too we find the requisite fuzzy dogs:

> And everywhere, though it was still so early, there was a beating, a stirring of galloping ponies, tapping of cricket bats . . . the whirling young men, and laughing girls in their transparent muslins who, even now, after dancing all night, were taking their absurd woolly dogs for a run . . . and the shopkeepers were fidgeting in their windows with their paste and diamonds, their lovely old sea-green brooches in eighteenth-century settings to tempt Americans (but one must economise, not buy things

rashly for Elizabeth), and she, too, loving it as she did with an absurd and faithful passion, being part of it, since her people were courtiers once in the time of the Georges, she, too, was going that very night to kindle and illuminate; to give her party. (5)

Why exactly did Woolf include the detail about Americans? Is it because, unlike Clarissa (who is affluent enough) rich Americans could afford to buy expensive things? Englishness could certainly be bought, as William Randolph Hearst was actually doing at the time on a colossal scale, acquiring not just jewellery but the architectural features of entire houses complete with their black-and-white chequerboard hall floors.[3] Hearst was not known for his discriminating taste—he bought anything and everything—and this too is part of the disparaging meaning of "Americans": they are the middlebrows whom the essay-letter identifies as being preoccupied with only "money, fame, power, or prestige" (E6 472). The Englishness of Clarissa's and Peter's world, therefore, is bought into by Americans in order to project stereotyped commodity as inheritance (which today we find in something like the Ralph Lauren brand, whose very logo invokes the "stirring of galloping ponies"). To be sure, it is still "ownership," but ownership of the desirable "primitive" kind that Sartre marks out, by which "the thing possessed and its possessor are united by a bond of mystical participation" (23-4). Do Jews participate? As we will see, no more than Americans do.

The real mystical participants in *Mrs. Dalloway* are not the Americans, but characters like Clarissa, Peter and Lady Bruton. The wealth of what that novel conjures up is not just offered for the temptation of Americans, but is universally seductive and deeply familiar: butlers and chow dogs (60), bowls on malachite tables (121), "sea-green brooches in eighteenth-century settings" (5), silver two-handled Jacobean mugs and Spanish necklaces (like his wife, Richard Dalloway also window-shops: 124), and "one roll of tweed in the shop where her father had bought his suits for fifty years; a few pearls; salmon on an iceblock" (11). In the way that the novel presents commodity, when Clarissa's father buys things it is an activity that is entirely different from the shopping of Americans. He has bought tweed suits for fifty years, but it might as well be centuries, or at least since "the time of the Georges": this is an act of birthright rather than mere exchange, financial transaction as mystical participation. Of all this Clarissa thinks "no splash; no glitter"

---

[3] See Woolf's short 1925 vignette, "Coming Back to London..." in which she expresses her surprise at seeing the demolition of Devonshire House in Piccadilly, and in particular "the marble stairs, which, for all we know, may already be halfway across the Atlantic" (*E4* 4). John Harris's *Moving Rooms: The Trade in Architectural Salvages* puts Woolf's remark into context.

(11); this is not conspicuous consumption, but the epitome of good taste. If we now turn to Woolf's comments in "Middlebrow," we can see why the recognizable English stereotype of *Mrs. Dalloway* is not entirely ironic. There is a difference between "living" and "buying," as Woolf explains:

> We highbrows [she is speaking in genuine first-person] . . . have to earn our livings; but when we have earned enough to live on, then we live. When the middlebrows [i.e. the "bedints" and the Americans], on the contrary, have earned enough to live on, they go on earning enough to buy—what are the things that middlebrows always buy? Queen Anne furniture (faked, but none the less expensive); first editions of dead writers—always the worst; pictures, or reproductions from pictures, by dead painters; houses in what is called "the Georgian style"—but never anything new, never a picture by a living painter, or a chair by a living carpenter, or books by living writers, for to buy living art requires living taste. (E6 475)

"Living taste": this is what defines Clarissa and Richard Dalloway, as one admires eighteenth-century brooches and the other, even as he "doubted his own taste" draws "the tray of old jewels towards him . . . taking up first this brooch then that ring" (125). Richard should have more self-confidence: he is looking at the right things (jewellery does not have to be new, apparently), and more importantly, doing it in the right way. Clarissa and Richard appreciate the novel's many exclusive and expensive "things" as initiates. These things are part of their inheritance as much as waves and rooks are part of Woolf's. Jean-Paul Sartre has this to say about "things," substituting Frenchness for what I have been discussing as English (and with apologies for the length—my interjections will give critical perspective, but the italics are his):

> In a bourgeois society it is the constant movement of people, the collective currents, the styles, the customs, all these things, that in effect create *values*. The values of poems ["fear no more the heat 'o the sun"], of furniture [malachite tables], of houses [real Georgian ones], of landscapes [waves and rooks] derive in large part from the spontaneous condensations that fall on these objects like a light dew; they are strictly national and result from the normal functioning of a traditionalist and historical society ["her people were courtiers once in the time of the Georges"]. To be a Frenchman is not merely to have been born in France, to vote and pay taxes; it is above all to have the use and the sense of these values ["What a lark! What a plunge!"]. And when a man [*sic*] shares in their creation, he is in some degree reassured about himself; he has a justification for

existence through a sort of adhesion to the whole of society. To know how to appreciate a piece of Louis Seize furniture [or Queen Anne], the delicacy of a saying by Chamfort [or Shakespeare], a landscape of the Ile de France [or Cornwall], a painting by Claude Lorrain [or the Dalloways' Reynolds engraving], is to affirm and to feel that one belongs to French [or English] society; it is to renew a tacit social contract with all the members of that society. At one stroke the vague contingency of our existence vanishes and gives way to the necessity of an existence by right. Every Frenchman who is moved by reading Villon [I will be arguing that for Woolf it is Chaucer] or by looking at the Palace of Versailles [or Buckingham Palace] becomes a public functionary and the subject of imprescriptible rights. (80-1)

It is Sartre's next sentence that achieves the point: "a Jew is a man who is refused access to these values on principle" (81). When, therefore, Woolf invokes values of Englishness through stereotype and cliché, she too refuses access to the Jew and what he or she represents.

5. Bruton v. Loeb: the prejudice of cliché

When cultural values are made visible they become stereotypes, for which reason I have devoted so much critical attention to Woolf's stereotypes and clichés of Englishness. Let us now look at two personified stereotypes. On the one hand there is Lady Bruton—the latter-day Britannia of *Mrs. Dalloway* ("she had . . . acquired from her association with that armoured goddess her ramrod bearing, her robustness of demeanour" [198])—and on the other hand, there is the real-life Mrs. Annie Loeb of the 1909 sketch "Jews," who hosted a party in 1909 to which she invited Virginia Woolf (or Stephen, as she then was): "She is a fat Jewess, aged 56 (she tells her age to ingratiate herself) coarsely skinned, with drooping eyes, and tumbled hair" (14). Both Lady Bruton and Mrs. Loeb are society hostesses; both are rich; and both are subjected, to greater or lesser degree, to criticism. But what kind of criticism? First, Lady Bruton: women like her maintain the patriarchal and imperial status quo, gathering politicians and civil servants round themselves at lunch parties in order to flatter and cajole:

> Lady Bruton often suspended judgement upon men in deference to the mysterious accord in which they, but no woman, stood to the laws of the universe; knew how to put things; knew what was said; so that if Richard advised her, and Hugh wrote for her, she was sure of being somehow right. So, she let Hugh eat his soufflé; asked after poor Evelyn. (120)

Mrs. Loeb's gatherings are also occasions for tactical social maneuvering, as Patricia Laurence recognizes in "One Wanted Fifty Pairs of Eyes." Annie Loeb, too, gathers talented people around her—after all, Woolf herself was there. In 1909 she may have been a fledgling writer, but she was preceded by her impeccable intellectual pedigree, and her fellow guest, Miriam Jane Timothy, was a celebrated harpist of the day. Mrs. Loeb's socializing was aided by her grown son, whose extensive knowledge of classical music gained her access into musical high society (this is "Syd" in the sketch, but otherwise he was Sydney Loeb, a highly-respected Wagnerian who married the daughter of the conductor Hans Richter). But compared to Lady Bruton's smoothly orchestrated power lunch, according to Woolf Mrs. Loeb can manage only this:

> She fawned upon us, flattered us and wheedled us, in a voice that rubbed away the edges of all her words and had a falling cadence. . . . at dinner she pressed everyone to eat, and feared, when she saw an empty plate, that her guest was criticising her. . . . She adjusted her flattery, to suit me, whom she took to be severe and intellectual, and Miss Timothy whom she thought lively and flirtatious. (14)

Both women are also busybodies and pullers-of-strings. If Lady Bruton has schemes such as "that project for emigrating young people of both sexes born of respectable parents and setting them up with a fair prospect of doing well in Canada" (119), then the real-life Mrs. Loeb also hatches plans: "'young people' tickle her coarse palate; she wishes to be popular, and is, perhaps, kind, in her vulgar way, ostentatiously kind to poor relations. The one end she aims at for them, is the society of men and marriage" (14-5). For that matter—again, Patricia Laurence makes the same point—Mrs. Loeb's manipulations are no different from those of Mrs. Ramsay in *To the Lighthouse*. But these women are nevertheless fundamentally different. Where Mrs. Ramsay can bring people together round her dining-table to partake of an unctuous *boeuf en daube*, and Lady Bruton serves a sumptuously elegant lunch whose description rivals that of the celebrated Oxbridge meal in *A Room of One's Own* ("saucers of red fruit; films of brown cream mask turbot; in casseroles severed chickens swim" [MD 114]), Mrs. Loeb can only provide food that '*of course*, swam in oil and was nasty' (14).[4] And while Mrs. Ramsay and Lady Bruton preside like generous goddesses over occasions of geniality and wellbeing, putting people at their ease (here is Hugh Whitbread, for example, "feeling at peace with the entire universe and at the same time completely sure of his standing" [114-15]), Mrs. Loeb

---

[4] My italics. David Bradshaw's notes provide a full commentary on the antisemitism of this sketch: a reading with which I entirely agree.

"seemed as though she wished to ingratiate herself with her guests and expected to be kicked by them," and makes food into an issue of embarrassment and guilt (14). Nothing so dirty as money or work ever touches Lady Bruton: her lunch has lost its connection to the marketplace ("this profound illusion in the first place about the food—how it is not paid for" [114]) and requires no labour ("the table spreads itself voluntarily with glass and silver" [114]). Mrs. Loeb, however, is firmly identified with money and work from the very start, and even though she is rich enough to support her comfortable lifestyle, the sketch denies her even that security by immediately blurting out "One wonders how Mrs. Loeb became a rich woman. It seems an accident; she might be behind a counter" (14): more Frau indeed, than Lady.

Admittedly, I am not comparing like with like, and on this point Laurence's reading of "Jews" reminds me that context is important. It is necessary to remember that, written in 1909, the sketch pre-dates both World Wars and the Holocaust, and is even sufficiently early to pre-empt Virginia's marriage to Leonard, and subsequent familiarity with the Jewish Woolfs. Both personal and public history, therefore, would argue for "Jews" as a special case. Then, too, Lady Bruton is a fictional character, where Annie Loeb is real. *Mrs. Dalloway* is a polished novel; "Jews" is a rough sketch written some fifteen years earlier, never revised nor meant for publication. Besides, it may even be pointed out that Mrs. Loeb does not necessarily suffer in comparison to Lady Bruton: anybody who could think "To be not English even among the dead—no, no! Impossible!" (198) is surely in her way as lampooned as Mrs. Loeb is made to seem crass. But the conditions of contextual specificity do not disallow the fact that both women are stereotypes of their kind (it did not take either Hitler or Marie Woolf to "awaken" Woolf, as it were), and to read them as such is not an irresponsible act if we keep in mind that Sartre has shown us how stereotypes carry value. Mrs. Loeb, by "Middlebrow" standards, merely earns money and buys, while Lady Bruton *lives*. Even though she does not read poetry, Lady Bruton is no philistine. Poetry is part of her heritage, and defines who she is: Lovelace or Herrick has sat underneath the vine that still flourishes at her country house (115). The very fact that it could be one or the other poet, and it doesn't matter which, demonstrates how easily and familiarly the Bruton family tree has intertwined with English literary history (like their vine). This is a history which lives in them to the degree that they do not even have to read it; they *own* it, in the relationship Sartre explains as "magical rapport," whereby "the thing possessed [poetry] and its possessor [Lady Bruton] are united by a bond of mystical participation" (23-24). Whenever Woolf invokes English literary history in this way, and she does so regularly, as for example in the essay "Reading" and related passages in *Between the Acts*, it is always a kind of homage. The values of some stereotypes are better than those of others: Annie Loeb and what she represents never stand a chance.

6. In an English country library

"Reading" (1919) is one of Woolf's formally and thematically more recalcitrant essays. It is difficult to identify a consistent register and tone, and indeed even to establish a uniform subject: it moves from reading in a library in a country house setting, to a selective survey of English literary history, to an autobiographical account of children hunting for moths at night, and finishes with a discussion of Sir Thomas Browne. Woolf never published it in her own lifetime, but elements from it crop up regularly (particularly moth-hunting and the library motif) in essays and fiction from *Jacob's Room* to *Between the Acts*, making it a kind of "work in progress" whose ideas she was still shaping in her late-life unfinished "Anon." The question with which "Reading" opens—"Why did they choose this particular spot to build the house on?" (E3 141)—is still unanswered some twenty years later in *Between the Acts* regarding the problematic site of Pointz Hall: "this whitish house with the grey roof, and the wing thrown out at right angles, *lying unfortunately low* on the meadow with a fringe of trees on the bank above it so that smoke curled up to the nests of the rooks" (my italics and, yes, the rooks are significant: 7). But the question we might ask is: why did Woolf choose this particular spot to set her reading in? Moreover, why did a woman who was able to argue so comprehensively for a democratization of class and gender through the metaphor of the public library in "The Leaning Tower" (E6 276-7) place herself as reader into another metaphoric library that looks like this?:

> The house had its library; a long low room, lined with little burnished books, folios, and stout blocks of divinity. The cases were carved with birds pecking at clusters of wooden fruit. A sallow priest tended them, dusting the books and the carved birds at the same time. (E3 141)

Responding to what is, essentially, the stereotype of an English country house library, Julia Briggs notices the problems: "It translates the activity of reading into an idyll, a world of leisured privilege that had traditionally been the prerogative of men, deliberately ignoring the gender and class divisions Woolf had identified in the practices of reading and writing" (114). Although Briggs does not specifically point it out, a slope as slippery as this can easily lead to antisemitism as well. She is thus considerably more sceptical than Jed Esty, and does not regard this as an "anthropological turn": "Its celebration of Englishness was also suspect, out of step with a post-war mood of internationalism, and a contempt for patriotism and national pride" (114).

So, why *did* Woolf write herself into such a reactionary and, as we shall see, antisemitic space? She did so because it is situated within the English country house itself: the kind of house where one would have come upon poets like Herrick or Lovelace sitting in the garden, the seductions of which Woolf was never able to resist.[5] The discrepancy of subject matter in "Reading" may not be so problematic after all, therefore. If we read the essay along the familiar axis of the rural world and childhood, not only do the library setting and children's bug-hunting adventure suddenly match up, but the essay's other concerns with reading and literature also fall into place. The narrator is no visitor or intruder in this exclusive private library: she is there as a matter of birthright. The English country house and its landscape, English literary history, and the narrative "I" of the (English) reader all partake of one another in a mystical bond that is at once nature writing, literary criticism and autobiography:

> ...the windows being open, and the book held so that it rested upon a background of escallonia hedges and distant blue [this is Talland House], instead of being a book it seemed as if what I read was laid upon the landscape not printed, bound, or sewn up, but somehow the product of trees and fields and the hot summer sky, like the air which swam, on fine mornings, round the outlines of things. (*E*3 142)

We have seen this place before: it is the sacred geography of Woolf's ur-memory, constructed of "curved shapes, showing the light through, but not giving a clear outline" ("Sketch" 66). In other words, this country house with its library is situated in Deep England. And Deep England has its poet. His counterpart in Deep France is Villon, whose work a Frenchman has only to read in order to have his Frenchness confirmed, which Sartre recognizes as nothing short of an act of interpellation: "Every Frenchman who is moved by reading Villon . . . becomes a public functionary and the subject of imperceptible rights" (81). In France Villon's voice carries a "genuineness" which in England is assigned to that of Chaucer.[6] He

---

[5] For an extended discussion of how the English country house stereotype figures in Woolf's work see my article "'The Lovely Wreckage of the Past': Virginia Woolf and the English Country House."

[6] Steve Ellis's study of the modern uses of Chaucer recognizes Woolf's interest, without going into much detail. Given this, his views are surprisingly critical: "It must be admitted that Woolf's estimation of Chaucer in *The Common Reader* is hardly progressive; indeed it partakes of many of the commonplace and even patronizing attitudes toward him that feature in the popularizing commentaries we looked at in chapter 2, and it is no surprise to discover that her critical preparation for the Chaucer essay did not go much beyond such Victorian stalwarts as Matthew Arnold and James Russell Lowell" (68).

makes a cameo appearance in "Reading," standing at the back of the company of English writers: if one peers past Shakespeare one can just about make him out: "some shapes of men in pilgrims' dress emerged, Chaucer perhaps, and again—who was it? Some uncouth poet scarcely able to syllable his words" (*E3* 142). When Woolf recreates this library at Pointz Hall in *Between the Acts* ("the library's always the nicest room in the house" [14]) Chaucer takes center stage in the drafts. The library receives its back-story in typescript, where the room and its contents are discussed at great length. The draft library composes itself around Chaucer, materially as interior arrangement, figuratively in terms of character relations, and conceptually as origin of English literary history. What Chaucer represents wields great ideological clout:

> What Chaucer had begun was continued with certain lapses from his day to this very morning. There were books on chairs, on tables, on hollow-backed settees. . . . Chaucer, the great originator of this still-continuing conversation or argument or song, faced the window. . . . Could pure understanding be achieved between Bartholomew and Chaucer, Giles and Chaucer, Alice Swithin and Chaucer, Haines and Chaucer, Perry and Chaucer? . . . . each of those who actually took Chaucer down, and did not pass a feather broom or duster over his back, or consider him part of the decorative scheme of the wall, believed that they were in contact with something or other . . . . some felt, "This is my England. This is visible to me; I am padding along the road; I am the Clerk; I am the Nun; I am the Knight." . . . somebody had bought the Paston letters by way of a background; had bought that plot of ground with the cottages and the manor house; the Church, the village green all complete; and set it beside the Canterbury Tales opposite the window. . . . The Paston letters did very well side by side with Chaucer. (*Pointz Hall* 48-50, *passim*)

Chaucer is thus placed at the center of all English history: architectural, social and literary. He is synonymous with Englishness itself just as Villon is with Frenchness for Sartre, and for this reason it is no coincidence that both poets are medieval, for the "deep" nation is always founded on the far borders of a past that is traditionally associated with anonymity and communality: conditions which in European culture are usually identified with the Middle Ages. Woolf's medieval representative is Anon and, as we shall see, in the period when she was closely working with ideas of communality, orality and anonymity in texts such as "The Leaning Tower," *Between the Acts* and "Anon" this figure was very specifically historicized in ways that not only mark the origins of prejudice, but also exemplify how the radically feminist identifications of anonymity in *A Room of One's Own* can at the same time harbor a deeply conservative impulse. "Good" and "bad" are never mutually exclusive categories.

7. Anon the Aryan

Chaucer stands shoulder-to-shoulder with his half-brother Anon, who completes the greenwood stereotype: "He is the common voice singing out of doors, He has no house. He lives a roaming life crossing the fields, mounting the hills, lying under the hawthorn to listen to the nightingale" (*E6* 582). Anon's oral significance has often been noted, but what has not been recognized is the way in which this tradition was understood at the time as part of a larger history of so-called Aryan culture (now more broadly known as Indo-European). What did Woolf know of this Aryan history? Much of it would have come from H. G. Wells's 1920 *Outline of History*—and the clue is in the fact that in *Between the Acts* the title of the book that Lucy Swithin reads throughout is *The Outline of History*.[7] Although Wells is never directly quoted in the novel, he exerts a visual influence upon *Between the Acts*, as his book is copiously illustrated with the paleontological line drawings which inspire Mrs. Swithin to imagine an England populated by iguanodons, mastodons and mammoths. Not only does the narrative draw attention to the fact that her history book has pictures (129), but the pictures themselves as commented upon by Wells encourage precisely those connections which Lucy Swithin makes between the pre-historic English landscape and the Piccadilly and Strand of her present-day London. His caption for a sketch of a scene from the Early Paleozoic

---

[7] There are two main sources for Mrs. Swithin's history book, both of which are usually acknowledged in the reference notes of any good scholarly edition of *Between the Acts*. Following the careful scholarship of Brenda Silver, G. M. Trevelyan's *History of England* (1926) is commonly given priority over Wells: the relevant text is "For many centuries after Britain became an island the untamed forest was king" (Trevelyan 3). Silver points out that this line, which also serves Woolf for her opening sentence in "Anon" (E6 581), was only paraphrased into the late draft of *Between the Acts* after 26 October, 1940—the date on which we know that she began to read Trevelyan's book (see p. 129 of the novel). This fact, together with the concurrent relevance of "Anon" in the later stages of writing the novel, has privileged Trevelyan over Wells. Earlier typescripts, however, still refer to Mrs. Swithin's reading material as the "Outline of Science," which retains the format of Wells's title and combines it with his known scientific interests. These early drafts also already draw attention to the fact that the book is illustrated (as Wells's is): "the pictures seduced her; she looked at pictures" (*Pointz Hall* 187). I would propose, therefore, that Woolf worked with both of Wells's history books before supplementing them with Trevelyan, and that despite her low opinion of Wells as novelist, there is no reason to assume that she thought similarly of him as a historian. Wells's significance for Woolf is important, because his is the first popular history of its kind to begin its narrative from geological, paleontological and anthropological origins: in particular, see *The Outline of History* chapters 1-7, 3-29.

Age, for example (Fig. 1), draws attention to trilobites and sea-scorpions depicted in the prehistoric sea, and exhorts us to "Note its general resemblance, except for size, to the microscopic summer ditchwater life of today" (7). Similarly, the book's many drawings of various reptiles and mammals of prehistoric ages regularly place the figure of a modern-day man into the picture, inviting us to conceive of these strange animals in our own physically familiar terms (14, 20, 21, 26, 27).

Fig.1 *The Outline of History,* 7.

The *Short-title Catalog* of the Woolf library does not have a record of H.G. Wells's *Outline of History*. This does not mean that Woolf was unaware of the book; indeed, it was impossible not to be aware, as its success was phenomenal. In Woolf's lifetime *The Outline of History* was published in multiple translations and regularly updated by Wells in new editions (his last appeared in 1937, but others continued the work until the final edition in 1971). It made him very wealthy, selling more than two million copies over the years. What Woolf's library *does* contain, however, is the book that Wells wrote in the wake of the popularity of his first history: an abridged version which he published two years later in 1922 as *A Short History of the World*.[8] This second version retains all the attention to evolution

---

[8] The Woolfs' copy is a reprint of the 1922 edition: H. G. Wells, *A Short History of the World* (London, Labour Publishing, 1924).

and palaeontology that was a feature of the original and also, like the first one, it devotes an entire section to the "Aryan-speaking peoples." This is important, because as interpretation it puts human social and cultural history upon a natural base, in a continuous, deterministic evolution of life on earth. Aryan history is thus seen as part of the natural and anthropological development of the world.

Wells's explanation of how the world has come to be was as popular in the 1920s and 30s as the television programs of David Attenborough are today.[9] Mrs. Swithin is reading a bestseller and is therefore anything but eccentric in her interests: this is emphatically popular history. The novel's final image of cave-dwellers among rocks reaffirms the interdependence of anthropology and literary culture as it was very much seen at the time: the rhododendrons in Piccadilly (8) lead directly to the greenwood of Anon. Deep England is thus not simply cultural myth, but is also scientific fact. It originates from La Trobe's fertile mud, what H. G. Wells describes in *Outline of History* as "the slime of the tidal beaches" (67). In the way that Wells presents it, therefore, the Aryan is a scientifically true category, but because he mixes it up with social and cultural history, it necessarily assumes values which are ideological rather than scientific. These are the values which feed into the antisemitism of the time, and touch upon Woolf's work as well. It should not be thought that I am directly linking Woolf with how the concept of the Aryan was taken up by the Nazis, but nonetheless what Hitler went on to expound in Germany in the 1930s grew out of a popular interest in race and origin which Wells reflected in England. Nothing illustrates this better than Wells's account of Neolithic Man in *The Outline of History*, alongside which he places the image of a swastika (73; see Fig. 2), following the observation that "this odd little symbol spins gaily round the world; it seems incredible that men would have invented and made a pet of it twice over" (73). Wells alludes to the contemporary political popularity of the symbol (it had just been officially adopted by the German Nazi party in 1920) in a chapter that is otherwise devoted to charting the development of the main "races of mankind," and accompanies its explanation with illustrations of the various human "types" (67-74 *passim*). In the "Caucasian" panel the blonde "Nordic" head gazes out past the reader's shoulder towards the horizon, flanked by two "Mediterranean" representatives who turn deferentially towards him in profile (Fig. 3). This, we read, is an "Englishman," while on the left we see a "Jew of Algiers," and on the right, a "Berber" (71): the very visual arrangement itself of these three faces already suggests that there is an implicit ideological hierarchy in scientific observation.

---

[9] David Attenborough's 60-year involvement with natural history programs has received international recognition and they are the established benchmark for wildlife documentaries today. Examples of his most famous work are the *Life on Earth* (1979) and *The Living Planet* (1984) television series for BBC.

THE RACES OF MANKIND 73

"belt of brown-skinned men," and extend it far to the east across the stepping-stones of Polynesia. There are, we may note, some very striking resemblances between early Japanese pottery and so forth and similar Peruvian productions.) This peculiar development of the Neolithic culture, which Elliot Smith called the *heliolithic* [1] culture, included many or all of the following odd practices: (1) circumcision, (2) the very queer custom of sending the *father* to bed when a child is born, known as the *couvade*, (3) the practice of massage, (4) the making of mummies, (5) megalithic monuments [2] (*e.g.* Stonehenge), (6) artificial deformation of the heads of the young by bandages, (7) tattooing, (8) religious association of the sun and the serpent, and (9) the use of the symbol known as the swastika (see figure) for good luck. This odd little symbol spins gaily round the world; it seems incredible that men would have invented and made a pet of it twice over. Elliot Smith traces these practices in a sort of constellation all over this great Mediterranean-India Ocean-Pacific area. Where one occurs, most of the others occur. They link Brittany with Borneo and Peru. But this constellation of practices does not crop up in the primitive homes of Nordic or Mongolian peoples, nor does it extend southward much beyond equatorial Africa. For thousands of years, from 15,000 to 1,000 B.C., such a heliolithic Neolithic culture and its brownish possessors may have been oozing round the world through the warmer regions of the world, drifting by canoes often across wide stretches of sea. And its region of origin may have been, as Elliot Smith suggests, the Mediterranean and North-African region. It must have been spreading up the Pacific Coast and across the island stepping-stones to America, long after it had passed on into other developments in its areas of origin. Many of the peoples of the East Indies, Melanesia and Polynesia were still in this heliolithic stage of development when they were discovered by European

The Swastika

[1] "Sunstone" culture became of the sun worship and the megaliths. This is not a very happily chosen term. It suggests a division equivalent to palæolithic (old stone) and neolithic (new stone), whereas it is a sub-division of the neolithic culture.

[2] Megalithic monuments have been made quite

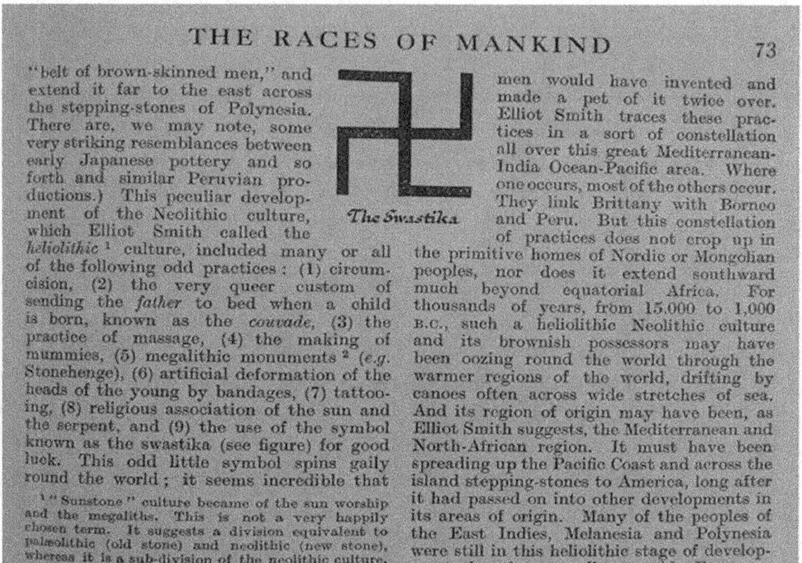

Fig.2 *The Outline of History*, 73.

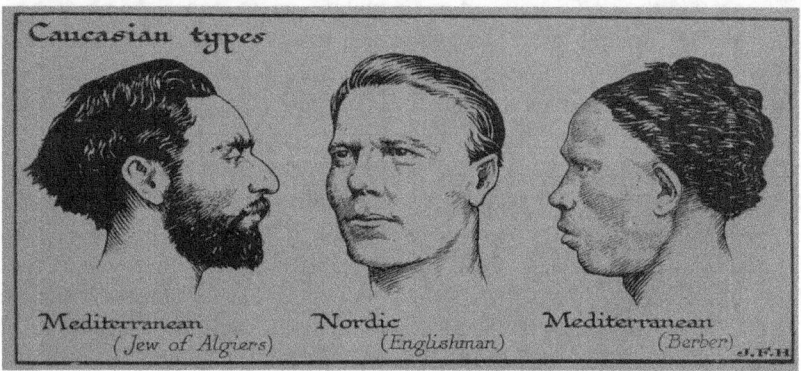

Fig.3 *The Outline of History*, 71.

How Woolf develops the idea of Anon and the oral tradition, therefore, necessarily absorbs these contemporary theories of evolution and race. As explained by Wells in his *Short History*, the book which Woolf possessed, Aryans (tribes of central and south-eastern Europe at around 2000 BC) "were destined to play a very important part indeed in the world's history":

They were a people of the parklands and the forest clearing. . . . [they] raised crops of wheat, ploughing with oxen. . . . They were a very vocal people. They enlivened their wanderings by feasts, at which there was much drunkenness and at which a special sort of man, the bards, would sing and recite. They had no writing until they had come into contact with civilization, and the memories of these bards were their living literature. This use of recited language as entertainment did much to make it a fine and beautiful instrument of expression, and to that no doubt the subsequent predominance of the languages derived from Aryan is, in part, to be ascribed. Every Aryan people had its legendary history crystallized in bardic recitations, epics, sagas and Vedas, as they were variously called. (Wells, ch. XIX, pars. 2-4)

The Aryan bard in Wells's *Short History of the World* is synonymous with Woolf's Anon, the free spirit of England before literature was inscribed in books, "who gave voice to the old stories, who incited the peasants when he came to the back door to put off their working clothes and deck themselves in green leaves" (*E6* 583). By placing Anon in alignment with the Aryan bard, we can discern an alternative story behind the Deep England of orality and communality; a conception of nation which also contains deep spaces of implicit antisemitism.

8. Voicing English

Anon as bard is primarily a singer. In the eponymous essay it is a *voice* which breaks "the silence of the forest" (*E6* 581), and can be heard "murmuring" as Woolf follows the progress of literature through the ages (*E6* 583). Even as literature evolves away from song into speech and the written word, still Woolf employs the criterion of *voice*: "It is not a learned voice; it is not a courtly voice; it is the voice of a plain man" (*E6* 587). Thus Woolf stresses that the developing writer, even though he is no longer the bard or minstrel, nevertheless retains an aural sensitivity: "his ear is stimulated by the sound of words spoken aloud. He must make words sonorous, rhythm obvious, since they are to be read out in company" (*E6* 589).

So much of Woolf's love for the English language responds to this oral quality: shapes of sound and rhythm that can run, dance, get stuck, or be rolled around in the mouth like sweets. Her beloved native tongue, even when it ventures into the foreign, does so with an unmistakeably English lilt: "the less we enquire into the past of our dear Mother English the better it will be for that lady's reputation. For she has gone a-roving, a-roving fair maid" (*E6* 626). It is important that this line, which so strongly recalls the way in which "The Leaning Tower" defines both the "rich speech of the aristocrat" and "racy speech of the peasant" against the humdrum voice of the "betwixt and between" (*E6* 272), originally was written to be read out in the BBC radio broadcast "Craftsmanship," for it is in the speaking voice that we can still hear the cadences of English oral tradition.[10] Like rooks and waves and sea-green brooches, voice, too, engenders that sense of "magical rapport," so that the very act of speaking, of *voicing English*, performs a reaffirmation of the social contract and re-inscribes the speaker into age-old Englishness. Love of England, we should remember, is "dropped into a child's *ears*," aroused not only by the sounds and rhythms of the natural world, but more importantly by "*English voices* murmuring nursery rhymes" (*TG* 313, my emphasis). Thus does Anon whisper to children in the nursery, and thus, too, can his voice be heard eddying on the breeze in *Between the Acts*, beckoning towards the shared green world of Deep England: "The King is in his counting house . . . Hark hark, the dogs do bark . . . As they listened and looked—out into the garden—the trees tossing and the birds swirling seemed called out of their private lives, out of their separate avocations, and made to take part" (70-71). Not all voices, however, stimulate such "magical rapport." After a visit from Leonard's sister Flora, Woolf declares "I do not like the Jewish voice" (*D1* 6), while Mrs. Loeb offends, with her "voice that rubbed away the edges of all her words and had a falling cadence" ("Jews" 14). Even by sound alone is Englishness able to delineate the Jew.

    I will finish with another shopping trip, this time in the essay "Street Haunting" (1927), which invites us to indulge in the commodities of the world of *Mrs. Dalloway*. In leisured window-shopping we can furnish our own front halls to look like that of Lady Bruton: "That rug will do for the hall. That alabaster bowl shall stand on a carved table in the window" (*E4* 485). Like Richard Dalloway we can dabble in a little speculative jewellery shopping: "let us indulge ourselves at the antique jewellers, among the trays of rings and the hanging necklaces" (*E4* 485). And like Clarissa, we can revel in all the luxury that London's exclusive shops have to offer: "sofas which are supported by the gilt necks of proud swans; tables inlaid with baskets of many coloured fruit, sideboards paved with green marble the better to support the weight of boars' heads, gilt baskets, candelabra" (*E4* 485). Shall we buy, or shall we *live*? Perhaps we can decide when we turn the corner and "come upon a bearded Jew, wild, hunger-bitten, glaring out of his misery" (*E4* 484). In the midst of all this wealth of Englishness is the Jew, who makes "the nerves of the spine . . . stand erect" and blinds us with a sudden flare: "a question is asked which is never answered" (*E4* 484-5). Who exactly is to answer this question: the

---

[10] Woolf's recording can be heard. The approximately seven-and-a-half minute excerpt of her BBC broadcast from 29 April 1937 is now available on multiple websites which can be readily found by internet search. It strikes me that Woolf's voice gives marked emphasis to "a-roving fair maid," but I leave it to listeners to come to their own conclusions about her intonation and accent.

narrator; the implied reader; we ourselves; or the Jew? No answer is forthcoming, for the language that is available in which to answer—the voice, the images, the literature, the culture of Englishness—is the very language by which Jewishness is silenced, evaded, forgotten and written out.

My thanks to Carol Macarthur of United Agents, London, U.K. for permission from H. G. Wells's estate to reproduce text from the 1920 revised and corrected edition of The Outline of History, *and for advice on the reproduction of images.*

Works Cited

Briggs, Julia. *Virginia Woolf: An Inner Life*. London: Penguin, 2005. Print.

Cannadine, David. "Portrait of More Than a Marriage: Harold Nicolson and Vita Sackville-West Revisited." *Aspects of Aristocracy: Grandeur and Decline in Modern Britain*. London: Penguin, 1995. 210-241. Print.

Ellis, Steve. 'English *Chaucer.' Chaucer at Large: The Poet in the Modern Imagination*. Minneapolis: University of Minnesota Press, 2000. 58-79.

Esty. Jed. *A Shrinking Island: Modernism and National Culture in England*. Princeton: Princeton University Press, 2003. Print.

Fisher, H. A. L. "The Beauty of England." *The Penn Country of Buckinghamshire*. Campaign to Protect Rural England, 1948. 9-15. Print.

Harris, John. *Moving Rooms: The Trade in Architectural Salvages*. New Haven: Yale University Press , 2007. Print.

King, Julia, and Laila Miletic-Vejzovic, eds. *The Library of Leonard and Virginia Woolf: A Short-title Catalog*. Pullman, Washington: Washington State University Press, 2003. Web. 18 August 2012 http://www.wsulibs.wsu.edu/holland/masc/onlinebooks/woolflibrary/woolflibraryonline.htm.

Laurence, Patricia. "'One wanted fifty pairs of eyes': Virginia Woolf and the Jews." *Woolf Studies Annual* 19 (2013): 00-00. Print.

Marcus, Jane. "Afterword." *Virginia Woolf and Fascism: Resisting the Dictator's Seduction*. Ed. Merry M. Pawlowski. Basingstoke: Palgrave, 2001.194-5. Print.

Mao, Douglas and Rebecca Walkowitz, eds. *Bad Modernisms*. Durham, North Carolina: Duke University Press, 2006. Print.

Orwell, George. *The Road to Wigan* Pier. London: Penguin, 1989. Print.

Paulin, Tom. *J'Accuse: Virginia Woolf*. Dir. and prod. Jeff Morgan. Fulmar Productions for Channel Four, London. 29 January 1991.

Sartre, Jean-Paul. *Anti-Semite and Jew*. Trans. George J. Becker. New York: Schocken, 1974. Print.

Schröder, Leena Kore. "Tales of Abjection and Miscegenation: Virginia Woolf's and Leonard Woolf's 'Jewish' Stories." *Twentieth-Century Literature* 49.3 (Fall 2003): 298-327. Print.

——. "'The Lovely Wreckage of the Past': Virginia Woolf and the English Country House." *English* 66.213 (Autumn 2006): 255-80. Print.

Silver, Brenda. "Introduction and Commentary" for "'Anon' and 'The Reader': Virginia Woolf's Last Essays." *Twentieth Century Literature* 25.3/4 (Fall/Winter 1979): 356-441. Print.

Trevelyan, G. M. *History of England*. London: Longmans, Green and Co., 1926.

Trubowitz, Lara. Civil *Antisemitism, Modernism, and British Culture*, 1902-1939. Basingstoke: Palgrave Macmillan, 2012. Print.

Walkowitz, Rebecca L. "Virginia Woolf's Evasion: Critical Cosmopolitanism and British Modernism." *Bad Modernisms*. Eds. Douglas Mao and Rebecca L. Walkowitz. Durham, North Carolina: Duke University Press, 2006. 119-144. Print.

Wells, H.G. *The Outline of History: Being a Plain History of Life and Mankind*. Rev. ed. London: Cassell and Co., 1920. Print.

Wells, H. G. *A Short History of the World*. London: Cassell and Co, 1922. Web. 15 August 2012 < http://www.bartleby.com/86/19.html>.

Woolf, Virginia. "Anon." *The Essays of Virginia Woolf*. Vol. 6. Ed. Stuart N. Clarke. London: The Hogarth Press, 2011. 581-99. Print.

——. *Between the Acts*. London: Penguin, 1992. Print.

——. "The cheapening of motor-cars." *The Essays of Virginia Woolf*. Vol. 3. Ed. Andrew McNeillie. London: The Hogarth Press, 1988. 440. Print.

——. "Coming Back to London. . . ." *The Essays of Virginia Woolf*. Vol. 4. Ed. Andrew McNeillie. London: The Hogarth Press, 1994. 3-4. Print.

——. "Craftsmanship." The Essays of Virginia Woolf. Vol. 6. Ed. Stuart N. Clarke. London: The Hogarth Press, 2011. 625-7. Print.

——. *The Diary of Virginia Woolf*. Vols. 1, 3, 5. Ed. Anne Olivier Bell. London: The Hogarth Press, 1977, 1980, 1984. Print.

——. *The Flight of the Mind. The Letters of Virginia Woolf*. Vol. 1. Eds. Nigel Nicolson and Joanne Trautmann. London: The Hogarth Press, 1975. Print.

——. "Jews." *Carlyle's House and Other Sketches*. Ed. David Bradshaw. London: Hesperus, 2003. 14-5. Print.

——. "The Leaning Tower." *The Essays of Virginia Woolf*. Vol. 6. Ed. Stuart N. Clarke. London: The Hogarth Press, 2011. 259-83. Print.

——. *Leave the Letters Till We're Dead. The Letters of Virginia Woolf*. Vol 6. Eds. Nigel Nicolson and Joanne Trautmann. London: The Hogarth Press, 1980.

——. "Middlebrow." *The Essays of Virginia Woolf*. Vol. 6. Ed. Stuart N. Clarke. London: The Hogarth Press, 2011. 470-9. Print.

——. *Mrs. Dalloway*. London: Penguin, 1992. Print.
——. *Pointz Hall: The Earlier and Later Typescripts of* Between the Acts. Ed. Mitchell A. Leaska. New York: University Publications, 1983. Print.
——. "Reading." *The Essays of Virginia Woolf*. Vol. 3. Ed. Andrew McNeillie. London: The Hogarth Press, 1988. 141-61. Print.
——. *A Room of One's Own* and *Three Guineas*. Oxford: Oxford World's Classics, 1992. Print.
——. "A Sketch of the Past." *Moments of Being*. Ed. Jeanne Schulkind. New York: Harcourt Brace Jovanovich, 1976. 64-137. Print.
——. "Street Haunting." *The Essays of Virginia Woolf*. Vol. 4. Ed. Andrew McNeillie. London: The Hogarth Press, 1994. 480-91. Print.
——. *To the Lighthouse*. London: Penguin, 1992. Print.
Wright, Patrick. *On Living in an Old Country: The National Past in Contemporary Britain*. Oxford: Oxford University Press, 2009. Print.

1899 map drawn to scale 6cm: 0.25 mile showing the density of London's East End Jewish population from Hackney Road and Old Ford Road to north, Burdett Road and Bloomfield Road to east, St George Street and High Street, Shadwell to south and Bishopsgate Street Without and Curtain Road to west. Created by George Arkell. Printed in The Jew in London: A Study of Racial Character and Present-day Conditions by Charles Russell and Harry Samuel Lewis for the Toynbee Trustees (New York: Thomas Y. Crowell and Co., 1901). Courtesy of the Jewish Museum of London.

A Tale of Two Cities: Virginia Woolf's Imagined Jewish Spaces and London's East End Jewish Culture

Phyllis Lassner and Mia Spiro

> "'But I don't need a country!' ... 'The whole world is my country!'"
> Simon Blumenfeld, *Jew Boy* (1935)

In "Street Haunting" Virginia Woolf's *flâneuse* narrator wanders the streets of Holborn and Soho on a winter's eve on the pretext of hunting down a lead pencil. "This is London," the speaker thinks to herself as she passes shops, houses, the "army of human beings," and the "oddities, sufferings and sordidities" of the city at dusk (156). Woolf captures the world of the Other — the twisted and deformed, the disabled and the poor who live in the abject conditions of urban misery. Similar to an ethnographer encountering the "hobbling grotesque dance" (156) of the foreign street, the speaker characterizes this mysterious, haunted encounter in ethnographic and racialized terms.[1] This is evident in the language and tone when both speaker and reader "come upon a bearded Jew, wild, hunger-bitten, glaring out of his misery." It is the sight of the Jew, more than any other character, which makes "the nerves of the spine seem to stand erect; [...] a question is asked which is never answered" (159). As the language and tone of the quote suggest, through this self-reflexive moment the narrator uncovers what for her is the most eerie, dangerous aspect of writing: the peril of becoming immersed in the retrograde foreign spaces of the self, the city, and the degenerate aspects of modern English civilization as a whole. It is an engagement with urban squalor that encapsulates Woolf's critique of modern English society evident in many of her portrayals of London. It is also an engagement that is often linked with Jews and imagined Jewish spaces in the city.

This essay uncovers how intersections among Woolf's spatial politics, her critique of modern English society, and her role as a social and political writer are complicated by the problematic terms in which she portrays "Jewish space" in her work. We define Woolf's "Jewish space" as her construction of imagined environments that Jews occupy as opposed to mappable places that identify the

---

[1] Carey Snyder similarly describes Woolf's method as the "self narrativizing" gaze of an ethnographer who "regards one's own culture" through "'participant observation'" (84).

places where Jews lived, worked, and produced Jewish culture in London.² By highlighting Jewish social and cultural contributions that Woolf's depiction of Jewish spaces obfuscates, this distinction will add important cultural and historical contexts to current discussions of Woolf's narrative constructions of the city. After all, if Woolf uses Jewish spaces in London thematically, as a tool to negotiate the borders of Englishness and political and economic oppression, how do scholars undo the erasure of Jewish historical reality and experience in London in the 1930s? For this reality is not only missing from Woolf's works, but also from various critical

---

² One of our readers noted that "it is not possible to talk about the 'Jewish people' in any meaningful or coherent sense. 'Jewish' as a cultural identity and way of life mean different things in any one decade, as well as a variety of individual and collective engagements with the world." To respond, we consulted experts in the field. Shlomo Avineri, the eminent political theorist, wrote: "Of course there is variety and fluidity in Jewish culture, as there are in Italian, or German or English cultures. By referring to culture one does not imply that it is uniform, one-dimensional or never changing, but that there are a number of phenomena which are in one way or another common to various sub-groups within the wider term of Jewish culture. Sephardi and Ashkenazi groups, for example, use an almost identical prayer book which is certainly different from the Anglican Book of Common Prayer and this does create a linkage between various groups which can be subsumed under an umbrella term like Jewish culture [...] The question of the existence of any identifiable human group is not just an issue of external taxonomical definition, but has also to address the question of whether a group (Jewish or Palestinian or Basque) or a significant part of it views itself as a people" (personal email 12/6/12: 3:18 PM). Sander L. Gilman, author of *Jewish Frontiers: Bodies, Histories, and Identities* and *The Jew's Body*, wrote that a definition of Jewish identity "needs to incorporate a range of variables" including "*a belief* in a biological or genetic identity along with religious, ethnic, cultural, class, gender, national qualifiers dynamically changing over time and place. It is the mix that defines a Jew at any given moment that is the base line of an identity and that simultaneously permits other mixes and variables to contest that identity. BUT such a definition must also include the lived experience that a Jew at any given moment may see his or her identity as fixed, inalterable, and historically and religiously unchanging. It is not sufficient to argue a purely relativistic definition of Jewish identity without recognizing that any and all of these mixes may well be experienced as transhistorical and fixed" (personal email 12-10-12: 8:49AM). Barry Wimpfheimer, Director of the Crown Center for Jewish Studies at Northwestern University and author of *Narrating the Law: A Poetics of Talmudic Legal Stories:* "Jews in the early twentieth century are marked both by shared cultural (including religious) patrimony and by their marginal standing in modern society. There are thus both a self-defined and an other-defined sense in which Jews can be spoken of as a meaningful and coherent entity. Like any ethnic group Jews are united by a set of practices, habits, beliefs, ideas, languages, and narratives. Within the ethnic formation there is understandable variety, disagreement and even fracturing. But there is no doubt that two Jews encountering each other on a British street in the 1920s would have been aware not only of their different positions within the Jewish landscape but of their common characterization as Jews" (personal email 12-11-12: 6:50AM).

interpretations that underscore negative Jewish portraiture and that emphasize Jewish alterity and difference. Such emphasis omits the experiences of a multifarious community that identified as Jewish and individuals who affiliated themselves with Jewish groups in London.[3] The extant discourse circulating around Woolf's imagined "Jews" and the urban space they occupy positions the social "place" of interwar Anglo-Jewry in a void that virtually obliterates Jewish self-determination and individual histories and experiences.

In effect, the marginalization of British Jewish cultural history within modernist literary discourses obscures the variations and vibrancy of Jewish traditions, as well as the social, political, and cultural activities that characterized London's Jewish neighborhoods. While important work on Jewish writers and artists proliferates, there is little integration of Jewish cultural traditions and production into modernist literary history and theory despite the expansion and inclusiveness of the field. To explore what implications such inclusion might have, one might ask, what difference does Kafka's, Benjamin's, or Modigliani's experience as Jews make to the parameters and issues with which Modernist Studies is concerned?[4] To fill in this lacuna in literary scholarship and highlight Anglo-Jewish cultural production and spatial historiography sets an important agenda for current and future research.

The distinction between "place" and "space" is key to analyzing Woolf's literary depiction of London neighborhoods. As Henri Lefebvre argues, space is socially and culturally constructed, but it is also a product of a specific historical "moment" (15). Although obviously related, place has different resonances than space for human geographers. Its significance is created more by individual imagination and as a product of individual and communal experience.[5] Anna Snaith and Michael Whitworth observe accordingly that rather than "locatable, material places," Woolf depicts "spaces" that in her essays and novels link "the bodies that inhabit space" with "the symbolic meanings that govern and regulate that habitation" (4, 5). In this symbolic conception, urban environments inhabited by Jews in Woolf's London similarly act as "spatial metaphors" that frequently evolve into conflated representations of character and environment. In works like "Street Haunting" or *The Years*, narrators' and characters' epiphanies occur in and are inspired by "foreign" environments within the city, destabilizing the "knowable"

---

[3] Scholars who analyze Jewish representation in British literature include Lassner, Spiro, Linett, Rosenfeld, Schröder, Trubowitz, Cheyette, Lowenstein, Panitz, and Surette.
[4] One of our readers noted the omission of some scholars who consider Jewish cultural history in relation to modernism. We fully appreciate the work of Kate McLoughlin, David Glover, and others on Jewish authors, but our concern here is more with the lack of integration of Jewish cultural production into discussions of non-Jewish modernism.
[5] See Hubbard *et al;* David Cesarani, M. Shain and T. Kushner eds., *Zakor V'Makor*.

within the home, nation, and country. The disintegrating fragments of the modern condition and the chaff of imperialist capitalism are symbolically located in London's most horrifically poor neighborhoods. In turn, the figure of "the Jew" associated with those neighborhoods unveils a gothic-like terror that a Mr. Hyde lurks in the crevices and alleyways of London—ready to reveal, as the narrator of "Street Haunting" muses, "the heart of the forest where live those wild beasts, our fellow men" (165). Woolf's positioning, however, does not grant Jews their own place or identify a milieu where they define or express themselves politically or culturally.

In response to these abject portraits, our critical survey of Jewish contributions to British culture and society will situate Woolf's representations of Jews and Jewish spaces in relation to Simon Blumenfeld's 1935 novel *Jew Boy*.[6] We maintain that this little known novel redraws the modernist map by opening its borders to include the Jewish East End. Far removed from Mayfair, Bloomsbury, and country house fêtes, the social and economic turbulence of London Jewish immigrant society in an identifiably Jewish "place" represents a dual challenge: to Virginia Woolf's characterization of Jewish spaces and to her scholarly reception. With a social landscape and narrative experiments of his own as complex as *Mrs. Dalloway*, *The Years*, *Three Guineas*, and *Between the Acts*, Blumenfeld's novel offers a Jewish left wing analysis of Britain's politically and economically fraught decade. The epicenter of this analysis is an immigrant island and its tense social and economic interdependence with the island nation. Born and bred on this island, Alec, the novel's protagonist, feels an urgent need to breach the social and economic constraints that have defined him. In response, the novel stages a cultural rebellion against the captivity that real and imagined abject Jewish spaces represent: "His whole life was turning into a sort of Odyssey, a painful search for a way of living" (Blumenfeld 125).

Blumenfeld's spatial politics not only underscores the multi-voiced dynamics of a London Jewish cultural milieu on the verge of transformation, it also puts Woolf's focus on London's human geography into context. Woolf's attention to the movement of narrators and characters across London's various economic and social spaces has been well noted by recent critics.[7] In essays such as "Street Haunting" and those sketches collected in *The London Scene*, as well as in novels like *Mrs. Dalloway* and *The Years*, narrators and characters move through London

---

[6] Given how much space we devote to Blumenfeld in this essay, we would like to emphasize that our purpose is to read his work within a consideration of Woolf's London spatial politics to extend understanding of her representations of Jews and Jewish culture.

[7] See, for example, Anna Snaith and Michael Whitworth, eds., *Locating Woolf: The Politics of Space and Place*, as well as the theoretical Introduction. See also Susan Squier, Jeanette McVicker, Tamar Katz, and Elizabeth Evans and Sarah Cornish, eds., *Woolf and the City*.

neighborhoods in a manner that signals their ever changing social and economic mobility. Snaith and Whitworth argue how Woolf's works "act as an encyclopedia of the city's streets and landmarks" in a way that provided "essential fuel for her writing" (1, 2). What is more, urban encounters in Woolf's work are shaped by the characters' layers of psychological and ideological attitudes and prejudices. Works by Woolf in the 1930s, such as *The Years*, *Between the Acts*, and her short story "The Duchess and the Jeweller," however, feature characters encoded as Jewish and linked to urban corruption, London's crass consumer culture, and a problematic modernity. They are notably absent as thinking, feeling, experiencing individuals, nor are they portrayed as connected with London Jewish cultural life or as part of self-defining communities engaged in meaningful traditions.[8]

Woolf's personal prejudices against Jews are made patent in a number of her diary entries and letters. As Natania Rosenfeld points out, when Virginia announced her engagement to Leonard, all her letters described him first as "a Jew" (59). Other letters and diaries in which Woolf often neglects to name individuals she meets at dinners or teas except to label them as "a Jew" also expose her prejudice. A list of examples from diary entries gathered by Leena Kore Schröder includes Woolf reading the French novel *Et Cie* "by a Jew" instead of by Jean-Richard Bloch (*D*1 134); she remembered the famous conductor Bruno Walter as "a swarthy fattish man ... a little Slav, a little semitic" (*D*4 153); and called journalist and political activist Dr. Rita Hinden, who had visited Monk's House (and whose name she forgets as soon as Hinden leaves), "a cheap hard Jewess" (*D*5 264–65). The view disclosed in the diaries and letters reflects what is ordinarily understood as the typical British upper middle class attitude toward Jews between the two world wars. Likewise, David Bradshaw has argued that in her fiction Woolf confronts and challenges prejudices by shedding light on British conceptions of the Jew.[9] Such optimistic defenses of her work would perhaps be more credible if they did not ignore the fact that there is no alternative to this view of Jews in any of Woolf's works.

---

[8] For analysis of Woolf's portrayal of "the Jew" and its rhetorical and political effects, see Phyllis Lassner, "'The Milk of Our Mother's Kindness" and *British Women Writers*, and Mia Spiro 174-86. For narrative and biographical analyses of Woolf's portrayal of Jews, see Maren Linett, Natania Rosenfeld, Leena Kore Schröder, and Lara Trubowitz.

[9] For example, David Bradshaw's commentary on *Carlyle's House* and *Other Sketches*—which contains a shockingly offensive sketch of a "fat Jewess"—rationalizes Woolf's representations of Jews by situating them among "attitudes [that] were endemic among [the] English upper middle class in Woolf's time" and claims that she would later "go out of her way in *The Years* to contest the anti-Semitism of the British Union of Fascists" (45).

Many British intellectuals who were outspoken about discrimination of society's Others still considered Jews vulgar or ill-bred—especially those Jews who had emigrated from Eastern Europe to escape persecution and had settled in London's East End toward the end of the nineteenth and beginning of the twentieth centuries. Jews were popularly perceived as being "un-British" or a threat to British culture. A Mass Observation survey taken in 1942 revealed that "up to one-tenth of the population was actually worried about the supposed Jewish power in society," and British culture in general maintained toward Jews "a tradition of intolerance in society" (Kushner, "Paradox" 79, 84). As Tony Kushner notes, "Historians and observers of modern antisemitism have often assumed that Britain, like the United States, is 'different'" ("Impact" 192). Kushner suggests that antisemitism in Britain was not necessarily violent, but by the time Woolf was writing in the 1930s, "government policy toward Jewish refugees from the Nazis...was not as generous as has been suggested" ("Paradox" 79). Common attitudes towards Jews as corrupt or overly powerful did affect government policies towards Jewish refugees escaping Nazism and British acceptance of Jewish immigrants. The function of antisemitism among the elite in British society, then, did not create violence, but reaffirmed a sense of Englishness that excluded minorities and bolstered anti-alien sentiment.[10] Woolf's depictions of "the Jew" as associated with crass commerce, exploitation of others, and the impoverished, squalid parts of London reveal how Jews were alienated through discourse in contrast to expressions of belonging in 1930s Britain.

The work of delineating the material geography of Jewish London by Raymond Kalman, associates the city's East End with the general area bounded by Shoreditch High Street and Kingsland Road to the west, the River Lea and Bow Creek to the east, and the Thames river to the south; in other words, what in the 1930s was considered the Borough of Tower Hamlets, which include Aldgate, Whitechapel (the "Jewish Ghetto"), Spitalfields, Ratcliff, Shadwell, Wapping, Mile End, and Limehouse.[11] These were areas characterized by poverty, crime, and racial tensions that centered on the high number of Jewish immigrants who settled there to escape persecution in Russia, Poland, and Galicia between 1881-1914. According to census information, in 1914 the Jewish East End at its peak had a population of approximately 80,000 Jews within a two mile radius in its central core, about two thirds of the Jewish population of London. By 1929-33, only a third of London's

---

[10] Our spelling of "antisemitism" accords with current scholarship in linguistics, anthropology, and Near Eastern Studies that rejects the traditional spelling, "anti-Semitism," because it falsely assumes the existence of a distinctive Semitic people. The designation Semitic refers only to Near Eastern languages. See the 2012 Program of the Association for Jewish Studies Conference.

[11] For more on the geography of London's Jewish East End, see Raymond Kalman (6-7).

estimated 234,000 Jews lived in the East End and 70 percent of those were British born (Lipman 37-38).[12] And while the East End by then was not synonymous with London Jewry as a whole, as a psychological concept it was considered "Jewish space" and symbolized a London environment on the verge of change due to Jewish commercial interests and immigration.

While literary depictions of the Jewish East End in the interwar years stress the squalid living conditions, studies of Jewish London show a far more complex picture.[13] As Geoffrey Alderman, David Cesarani, and Tony Kushner all emphasize in their studies of Anglo-Jewry, one neither wants to distort the depiction of Jewish London with nostalgic portrayals of an "authentic" vibrant Jewish culture, nor malign it with a narrow view of sweatshops, homelessness, filth, and radicalism. At the time Woolf was writing her major works, the Jewish East End could claim a lively cultural life, including twenty-seven synagogues, six Jewish schools, eight Almshouses, twenty-one charitable organizations and at least twenty-six Benevolent societies and seventy-four social groups (or "friendly societies"). Political activity was also profuse, with different Zionist societies representing various strands of political and religious Zionism, fourteen trade unions, and ardent support for socialist causes.[14] Culturally, Jewish London was also home to a host of writers and artists, including Mark Gertler, Isaac Rosenberg, and Simon Blumenthal; there was an active Yiddish theater, which in its heyday in 1934-35 presented nine performances a week, a Jewish art gallery on Whitechapel Road, the first and oldest English Jewish press, *The Jewish Chronicle*, and a number of Yiddish newspapers.[15] Moreover, neighborhoods outside the borders of the East End were also home to vital Jewish communities, including Soho, near the encounter of Woolf's street haunter with her "wild Jew," as well as Hendon, Golders Green, Hampstead, St Johns Wood, and the West End, West Kensington, Hackney, and Dalston.[16]

In spite of its multi-layered geographic and cultural history, Woolf's modernist literary tropes represent Jewish London as the irredeemable essence of a disintegrating English culture. The Jewish East End, as Judith Walkowitz notes, also suggests a "creepy space" where Jack the Ripper may have stalked his victims

---

[12] Surveys and census data about Jewish residents of the East End are found in V. D. Lipman, "Jewish Settlement in the East End – 1840-1940," and "The Booth and New London Surveys as Source Material."

[13] Cf. Geoffrey Alderman, *Modern British Jewry*, and essays on Anglo-Jewish history in Tony Kushner, ed. *The Jewish Heritage in British History*; David Cesarani, ed., *The Making of Modern Anglo-Jewry*; Aubrey Newman, ed., *The Jewish East End*; William Fishman, *East End Jewish Radicals*; and Todd Endelman, *The Jews of Britain, 1656 to 2000*.

[14] See Kalman 9-12 and Alderman 195-97, 211.

[15] See Bernard Mendelovitch's depiction of the Yiddish theater scene in *Memories of London Yiddish Theatre*.

[16] Soho, with its Jewish school and several synagogues, was home to a significant number

This is an "alien place, a center of cosmopolitan culture, and entrepot for [Jewish] foreign immigrants and refugees" (Walkowitz 193).[17] Unfortunately for those who found this space "distasteful," its Jews and their cultural and economic habits threatened to spread beyond the borders of the East End to other parts of London. A clear example of this appears in Woolf's *The Years*.

The depiction of Jewish space in the "1880" section of *The Years* becomes a sensory experience leading to Eleanor Pargiter's recognition of her suffocating condition within a Victorian patriarchal upper middle class environment. Death and illness link the urban spaces of the Grove district, where Eleanor does charitable work and visits "old Mrs. Levy" and the Pargiter home on Abercorn Terrace in St. John's Wood. In *The Pargiters*, Woolf names "the Grove" as Lisson Grove, near Marylebone Station (32, 37), in the west part London, not far from the "Street Haunting" Jewish space. Although most poor Jewish families at the time lived in the East End, it is important to any interpretation of Woolf's portrayal of Jewish women that the Levy women occupy a non-Jewish geographical place. As a psychological space, it is nonetheless claustrophobic and stagnant, thus functioning as a narrative device in Woolf's comment on the changing nature of Englishness.[18]

Eleanor's moment of revelation associated with creativity and narrative method resembles that in "Street Haunting." As the narrator relates, although Eleanor "did not like talking about 'the poor' as if they were people in a book" (*Y* 28), she does just that when she tells her sister Milly about Mrs. Levy, who is dying from cancer, and her daughter. In a rare depiction of the conditions of Jewish women at the turn of the century, Eleanor describes Mrs. Levy in her impoverished "hot little room," and her daughter, Lily, with stereotypical markers of Jewish consumerism and excess:

---

of Jews escaping Eastern European persecution who settled around Berwick Street Market. By the 1930s, 70 percent of shops and businesses on Berwick Street were owned by Jews. See Rory Lalwan, "Soho Jewish Community."

[17] Paul Newland similarly emphasizes that the East End as an "imaginative" space reflects the stigmatized bodies therein, tied to correlating concepts of "degeneration and regeneration" (15). The East End is both "mythical and mystical" but also the "terra incognita" of the foreign, uncivilized "eastern" Other (Newland 18-20).

[18] We thank our reader for this detail. In the 1880s, English Jews lived in North, West, and South London. Statistics show a majority of "poor Jews" living in East London and most Jewish communal anti-poverty work at the end of the nineteenth century were centered in these neighborhoods (Endelman 94-95, 128, Alderman 104). From 1851-1881, the Jewish population in London was approximately 46,000. Due to the influx of Jewish immigrants fleeing Russian persecution after 1881 that number grew to 135,000 by 1900; roughly 120,000 of them lived in the East End (Alderman 117-18). For the Levy women to live

> 'Mrs. Levy had her rent ready, for a wonder,' she said. 'Lily helps her. Lily's got a job at a tailor's in Shoreditch. She came in all covered with pearls and things. They do love finery—Jews,' she added.
> 'Jews?' said Milly. She seemed to consider the taste of the Jews; and then to dismiss it. (*TY* 29-30)

Although Eleanor is said to have "a great admiration for Mrs. Levy," one wonders what Eleanor admires. Evidently not the Levys' ability to support themselves without a man or to pay their rent on a meager tailor's assistant salary. The correlation between the "taste" of Jews and their unsavory materialism, however, is part of a network of contradictory metaphoric associations that link Woolf's thematic concerns with the disintegrating Victorian British household and Eleanor's imaginative self-revelation. Both Eleanor and Lily are saddled with the responsibility of taking care of sick mothers; but Eleanor's recognition of the similarity between "Canning Place; Abercorn Terrace; this room; that room" (*TY* 29) does not lead to understanding or empathy with her Jewish counterpart, but rather a meditation on the self. "Eleanor was ashamed," the narrator tells us:

> [S]he always was irritable for some reason when she came back from the Grove—so many different things were going on in her head at the same time: Canning Place, Abercorn Terrace; this room; that room. There was the old Jewess sitting up in her bed in her hot little room; then one came back here, and there was Mama ill; Papa grumpy;[...].... But she checked herself. She ought to say something to amuse her sister. (*TY* 29)

---

outside this support system is nevertheless possible. According to Anne Summers, a specialist in British women's history and author of "Gaps and Bias in the Records: Researching Christian-Jewish Charitable Collaborations, 1880s-1920s," *Archives* 36. 123-4 (2011): 26-35 and "False Start or Brave Beginning? the Society of Jews and Christians, c.1924-1944," *Journal of Ecclesiastical History* (forthcoming 2013): "A seamstress living in or near Lisson Grove would probably work in Soho. Lily Montagu ran a Jewish working girls' club in the West End from 1893 through to the Blitz, indicating there were poor Jewish families in the area" (personal e-mail: 12-8-2012). It is somewhat anomalous, however, that the Levy family would turn to a Christian charity, such as Eleanor Pargiter's volunteer group, when synagogues in the West End offered support, including the Central Synagogue in Great Portland Street; the West London (Reform) in Upper Berkeley Street, the Western Synagogue, or the West End Talmud Torah in Soho. See also Gerry Black *Living Up West: Jewish Life in London's West End*; and Summers, "Gender, Religion and an Immigrant Minority: Jewish Women and the Suffrage Movement in Britain, c. 1900-1920," *Women's History Review* 21.3 (2012): 399-418.

The claustrophobic Jewish space prompts Eleanor to reflect on her own unbearable social positioning as the responsible, selfless "Angel in the House." As Tamar Katz argues, anticipation for an end to the unbearable stasis of the Victorian social structure reiterates metaphorically throughout *The Years* and raises key questions: "Where are we going? When will this New World come? When shall we be free?" (Katz 9-10). Jewish spaces that allude to disabling change interrupt the flow of events to unveil those troubling questions. And yet, this discontinuous condition of Jewishness remains static throughout the novel, even with the passage of time from Victorian patriarchal culture to the "present day" in 1936.

An episode of *The Years* that continues the assaulting claustrophobia associated with Jewish space occurs when North visits his cousin Sara Pargiter's flat on Milton Street. The encounter with Jewish space—Sara's building and the bathroom shared with her upstairs neighbor Abrahamson—once again invites a character's critical meditation on the deleterious effects of British economic and social constraints: "'What a dirty,'" North thinks when he pulls up to Sara's building, "'sordid,' he added, 'low down street to live in'" (*TY* 295). The foreign names next to the building's doorbells and "curious smell" in the hall, however, remind him that he used to write poetry, "now the mood had come again as he stood there waiting" (*TY* 295). Like North's inspiration, Sara Pargiter's epiphany responds to the degenerate city slum and the Jew in her building: "Polluted city, unbelieving city, city of dead fish and worn-out frying pans!'" she cries. This observation immediately follows a description of "the Jew" who snorts as he sponges himself and leaves behind a line of grease in the bathtub (*TY* 323). Similar to the narrator's encounter with the Jew in "Street Haunting" and Eleanor's musings on the Levy women, Sara and North question their roles within a society corrupted by a parasitic capitalism. Milton Street, previously known as "Grub Street," was notorious for its hack writers and commercial literary pursuits. Sara agonizes over her need to "sell" her writing and "join the conspiracy" of a modern British society that dehumanizes its workers, the faceless "servile innumerable army" in London's commercial and industrial center (*TY* 323). "Must I join your conspiracy" she demands, "and sign on, and serve a master; all because of a Jew in my bath, all because of a Jew?" (*TY* 323). The Jew in Sara's building thus becomes a catalyst for exposing the repulsive aspects of literary production in "the present day" and its dependency on the crude appetites of the marketplace and exploitation of labor. This comment was surely one with which Woolf could relate.[19]

---

[19] Maren Linett, "The Jew in the Bath," finds that Sara uses her Jewish neighbor as a "metatextual scapegoat" who threatens both Sara's "mental freedom" and Woolf's, "who assigned Sara a version of her own fear of intellectual prostitution" (349). We emphasize the political effects of Woolf's scapegoating.

The Years correlates the destitution of Jewish spaces with the vexed social relations of a post-Victorian era that align the "daughters of educated men" like Sara Pargiter with tailors' assistants such as Lily Levy and Abrahamson's fiancée. All are tainted with residues of capitalist exploitation, including Abrahamson's filth, sweated labor, and the sea of foreign workers who "prostitute" their time and skills in exchange for money. To be sure, Woolf's negotiations among sordid Jewish spaces in *The Years* and civilized "English" homes critique the culture of modern British society. Jewish space nevertheless appears as an imaginative locale that only serves to clarify the "I" of the observer, confirming that actual Jewish "places" like the East End of London are intractably alien. Jewish figures and the Jewish city in works like *The Years* consequently exploit an image that displaced Jewish communities and social realities from the "we" of British culture. This was not incidental or benign. It was a racialist and gendered discourse that ironically resembled that which is integral to the very imperialism Woolf opposed.[20] This was an imaginary Jew that legitimized politically and psychologically damaging Jewish stereotypes.

If Woolf portrays Jewish space as a metaphor for avarice and squalor connected with the evils of Empire, a far different picture emerges when examining the critical contribution of Anglo-Jewish women and men. Jewish women reformers campaigned for political and economic rights, organizing women's trade unions and social equity projects in London from the Victorian period the 1930s and 1940s. As Linda Gordon Kuzmack outlines in her study of the Jewish women's movement in England and the U.S., influential figures like Louise Lady Rothschild organized philanthropic societies in 1840 to help families not unlike the fictional Levys in the poorer districts of the East End, and in 1885 she also established the first Jewish working girls' club (12-13). Jewish women activists were also central in the campaign for the passage of the 1857 Married Woman's Property Bill and the Divorce Bill and in establishing education opportunities for women (Kuzmack 15). Louisa Lady Goldsmid, for instance, was a key figure in establishing a women's college at Cambridge University, campaigning with Emily Davies to open professions for women. Notably, Lady Goldsmid was on the first board of Emily Davies's College for Women (established in 1869), which later became Girton College at Cambridge University, where Woolf gave one of the lectures that formed *A Room of One's Own* (1929). Many of the "educated daughters" of immigrants had significant political impact in the campaigns against sweated labor in the 1880s, in the suffrage movement, and in socialist unions.[21] Miriam Moses, for

---

[20] See David Feldman, "Jews and the British Empire c. 1900."
[21] See Linda G. Kuzmack, *Woman's Cause*, for the formation of England's Jewish League for

instance, born in Whitechapel to immigrant parents, became the first female mayor of Stepney in 1931, worked to open economic prospects for under-privileged youth, served on school boards and juvenile courts, and during both WWI and WWII volunteered as a nurse and air raid officer in London's Mile End, for which she was awarded the Order of the British Empire in 1945.[22]

Another particularly influential woman was Dr. Rita Hinden, the very same one who Woolf describes as "a cheap hard Jewess" (*D5* 264–65). In fact, Hinden (*née* Gesundheit), was more often described as "sensitive," with "a passion for social justice" by her many admirers, and recognized as an influential journalist and pioneering campaigner for social and economic reform in the colonies ("In Appreciation" 17-19).[23] Hinden, who was fluent in Hebrew and English, entered the London School of Economics and Political Science (LSE) in 1928, gained a degree in economics in 1931 and a doctorate in 1939. She became Leonard Woolf's assistant in 1939 and was a key figure in the Fabian investigative committee on the colonies, the League of Nations, and postwar reconstruction that advised the Labour party. Her publications on controversial colonial issues and work on economic development provide an important gloss to Virginia Woolf's depiction of the role of women—and especially Jewish women—in commodity driven London. As opposed to a generalized critique of colonial exploitation, Hinden's essays argue for economic independence, education, and the alleviation of poverty through enterprises such as cooperative farming and marketing. Her constructive solutions to improve the living and work conditions for colonial inhabitants of the Empire's fifty territories as they transitioned to post-imperial economies are still recognized as significantly progressive.[24]

Woman Suffrage in 1912 as well as many social justice movements supported by the Jewish Woman's Movement in England.

[22] Miriam Moses (1884–1965), awarded an Order of the British Empire in 1945 for her wartime bravery, also founded and served as president of the League of Jewish Women, on the Jewish Board of Guardians, and as vice-president of the Association of Jewish Youth. See the *Oxford Dictionary of National Biography*.

[23] Of the many political and social activists and government officials who offered tribute to Rita Hinden in *Socialist Commentary* upon her death in 1972, no one fails to mention her remarkable sense of honor, spirit, and dedication to promoting freedom, and her warmth and modesty. See "In Appreciation of Rita Hinden,"15-19. See also the *Oxford Dictionary of National Biography*. Hinden's numerous publications include: "Economic Plans and Problems in the British Colonies"; *Empire and After: A Study of British Imperial Attitudes*; 'Human Rights in Africa"; *Local Government and the Colonies: Fabian Colonial Essays*; *A World of Peace and Plenty*; *No Cheer for Central Africa;* and *The Radical Tradition: Twelve Essays in Politics, Education and Literature*, edited with Richard Henry Tawney.

[24] Hinden is discussed in Janet M. Manson's "Margery Perham, the Fabians, and Colonial Policy" in Chapman and Manson, eds. *Women in the Milieu of Leonard and Virginia Woolf*.

Perhaps equally pioneering were the literature, theater, art, and rallies that created a critical social, cultural, and political bridge from the far reaches of Eastern Europe to mainstream London, such as Simon Blumenfeld's *Jew Boy*. David Cesarani reports that *Jew Boy* was the first in what became a genre of East End-based "proletarian" novels. It deals largely with the experiences of second-generation Jews, the children of the immigrants, who grew up in a milieu from which they feel increasingly estranged while, at the same time, they find themselves rebuffed by the majority society around them" ("East End" 46).[25] As "an act of cultural defiance, taking a term of abuse and turning it into a badge of honour," *Jew Boy* represents a significant intervention in debates about modernism's multicultural promises and about antisemitic images and portraits in Woolf's writing and that of other high modernists such as T. S. Eliot and Ezra Pound (Worpole 7).[26]

Representing the struggle for cultural integration and economic equality, the novel features a Jewish flaneur, a wandering Jew.[27] Alec, a young garment worker, exploited like so many by the coercive economic structure of Britain's textile industry and hierarchical machinery of the East End rag trade, resists its inevitable objectification, his fate as "a limp, screwed-out rag," one of the "automata" (Blumenfeld 29, 21). The site of resistance, however, is neither interior nor collective consciousness; moreover, it does not interweave mutually affirming images of the struggle for selfhood.[28] Instead, the social and psychological epiphanies that mark Alec's outward bound journey chart his conflicted relationship with the cultural, political, and material dynamism of the Jewish East End. The

---

[25] Simon Blumenfeld (1907-2005), born in Whitechapel and an avowed Communist, became a celebrity journalist, reporting on a wide range of cultural events. Although he wrote three other novels, he is best known for his play *The Battle of Cable Street*. Aside from Ken Worpole's introduction to *Jew Boy*, Cesarani's article, and several obituaries, Blumenfeld is absent from contemporary scholarship.

[26] Recent scholarship and debates on the subject include Lassner and Trubowitz, eds. *Antisemitism and Philosemitism*, Anthony Julius, and Bryan Cheyette. One of our readers objected to our listing Anthony Julius as a scholar of antisemitic literary representation, because he is "a known Zionist," begging the following questions: should a scholar who supports the existence of the State of Israel be discounted, and should scholars who identify as Israeli Jews and/or as Zionist be maligned?

[27] For the origins of the term "Wandering Jew," see Joseph Gaer and Galit Hasan-Rokem, and Alan Dundes.

[28] This overtly political intervention by a writer in a cultural tradition that has not been included even in the New Modernist Studies positions the novel in a different literary history that Kristin Bluemel theorizes as "Intermodernism," which creates a critically stable but fluid position for writers who don't share the "values that shaped the dominant English literary culture of their time because they have the 'wrong' sex, class, or colonial status [or, we would add, ethnic or cultural identity]. They remain on the margins of celebrated literary groups" (*George Orwell* 5).

creative potential of this tension for Alec's adventure and Blumenfeld's narrative experiments is also self-critical, for the novel does not avert its gaze from the disintegrative forces of the Jewish East End, with its tenuous hold on religious identity and traditions and abusive emotional and economic manipulations.

The novel's critical perspective is highlighted by the tense nature of Alec's odyssey. In one perspective, it suggests the possibility of escape from two constraining forces: the lingering and claustrophobic fears emanating from the community's anxious memories of European persecution and pogroms and the hopelessness of the economically depressed East End, with its grime pitted tenements and greasy sweat shops. Although the novel's graphic descriptions of East End poverty and foul working conditions can easily be interpreted as dramatizing Blumenfeld's Marxist commitments, the novel is driven less by economic determinism than by historical and social psychological contingency. Through a cacophony of conflicting voices, each asserting its presence and perspective, the novel contravenes stereotypes of a self-enclosed Jewish society whose atavistic rituals oppose Western progress and its ideals of reason. Together, in their dissonance, these voices make it clear that despite the immigrants' shared history and self-defined cultural distinctions, London's Jewish East End is not a self-appointed ghetto. Nor is it a self-abusing, self-deceiving victim of unbridled craven impulses, the collective character formed by antisemitic images of a decadent Jewish culture. Instead, the novel analyzes the human geography of the Jewish East End as a collective yearning for individual integrity and self-expression amidst a daily struggle against family tensions produced by the oppressive, unrelieved long hours of joblessness or some kind of "filthy" work, including, for women, unrewarded domestic drudgery or prostitution (Blumenfeld 21). Indeed, no woman among the novel's striving populace, including Olive, a non-Jewish domestic worker and prostitute, or Sarah, the housekeeper for her working class Jewish family, bears any resemblance to Mrs. Levy's daughter in *The Years* who, like Alec, works for a tailor and who "wore pearls as big as hen's eggs; she had taken to painting her face; she was wonderfully handsome..." (*TY* 29).

Jew Boy creates a complicated relationship between the second generation's desire for subjectivity and self-expression, material compensation, and mimicry of or disdain for the upwardly mobile classes.[29] In one narrative perspective, to aspire to social and economic mobility requires the denial of individual and distinctive cultural expression. Sarah's sister, known only as Mrs. Saunders, who desires nothing more than to assimilate to gentile suburban respectability, expresses her subjectivity by submerging it in her indistinguishable, generic home far away from the East End. The home's "catholic taste" and "whole library of escape," guaranteed

---

[29] Using the word "mimic" and its variants, as derived from the work of Homi Bhabha, shows connections and marked differences between the Jews' conflicted struggles for assimilation into British society and those of postcolonial subjects.

to make you forget "there were such mundane things on earth as employment queues [...] and labour colonies, and filthy East End slums," armor her against the desire for anything more than to immobilize her desire (Blumenfeld 106). In rebuttal, the narrator joins Alec in thinking that "At least the Jewishness she had discarded, for all its faults, its turbulent excitable people and habits, had life and colour, throbbed with vitality. He couldn't for the life of him understand how any intelligent person could exchange that for the anaemic narrow-minded dreariness of suburbia" (Blumenfeld 113). As Alec's wandering takes him across London, the novel creates a critical link between the accoutrements and manners that define Mrs. Saunders's insecure home and those of the watering holes in the self-assured West End.

Privileging political and cultural critique as its intermodern narrative armature, Alec's observations assume a satiric register, mocking the cultural signs of Mrs. Saunders's assimilation to non-Jewish middle class moderation: "the usual stuff, middle to three-quarter brow," including "Warwick Deeping, Ethel Mannin, David Garnett, [...] Bernard Shaw [or] HG Wells" as "ready-made guides to the Universe" (Blumenfeld 106).[30] If, however, the temperate clime of middlebrow culture provides no critically creative inspiration for the Jewish upstart, neither does the more radical frisson of modernist culture.[31] Alec's initiation into London's modernist nighttown is at the behest of Elspeth, a post-debutante with enough rooms of her own to guarantee a comfortable border crossing from Mayfair to Bohemia. As Alec observes, however, despite their apparent social and cultural differences, these two worlds share a self-righteously exclusionary élitism. The novel's depiction of modernist culture is executed with parodic élan and its foil is a Jewish modernist wannabe named Leopold. Unlike Joyce's modernist creation of a complex Jewish everyman, the individualized Jewish character of Blumenfeld's Leopold has disappeared into a parody of a modernist poet, complete with "stooping" posture, "a sparse, gingery beard," Magdalen accent, and "echoes from the Palestinian waste land," Ezra Pound, and T.S. Eliot. "The next step was utter incomprehensibility, and Gertrude Stein ..." (Blumenfeld 126, 129). Of course this parody can easily be read as reflecting Blumenfeld's left wing élitism. From the perspective of Alec's odyssey, however, modernist culture, like that of the middlebrow, highlights the untraversable distance between British cultural values and the desire for self-expression of second generation Jewish immigrants.

Within all the novel's more and less privileged social contexts, the desire for individual self-expression embeds destructive romantic illusions and ultimately

---

[30] Mary Grover analyzes Deeping's wide popularity as an example of middlebrow culture, including his antisemitic references, in *The Ordeal of Warwick Deeping*.
[31] For critical analysis of middlebrow culture and reception, see Mary Grover and Erica Brown.

rejects romance in any narrative form. Although Woolf, too, rejects romance plots, Blumenfeld reveals its critical limitations across a spectrum of assumptions based on social and economic class. Like Woolf, Blumenfeld also proffers a gendered analysis. For example, if Alec's pungent observations emphasize the political import of London's different cultural styles, the narrative structure reveals his blindness to an equally disquieting politics, the sexual politics associated with romance plots. As with other male characters in *Jew Boy*, Alec's reliance on the romantic promises of sexual desire to achieve subjectivity and emotional freedom is as self-deceptive as the sublimated pleasures of filling one's bookshelves with "A Dickens set (probably from *The Daily Mail*)" or masquerading as a modernist icon (Blumenfeld 106). The novel's searing depictions of sexual manipulation and abuse confirm that there can be no romance in sexual desire so long as it remains tethered to a social and gendered pattern of exclusionary self-interest that economic wealth and social stability only exacerbate. Nowhere is this correspondence more apparent than in the way the characters' sexual relationships mirror each other. This narrative intricacy provides a multifaceted dissection of unequal power relationships in a world dominated by economic exploitation and rigid social and cultural boundaries. For example, Alec's attempted seduction of and disregard for Sarah's feelings and welfare as well as his dishonest treatment of Olive are reflected and critiqued in Elspeth's assumption that she can toy with Alec's feelings because she is his social superior. At first, Elspeth and Alec both enjoy his attraction to her, but then his "repressed hatred" for her wealth and privilege erupts, giving the battle of the sexes new ammunition:

> 'And where did you get all that money? [...] Do you work for it?'
> 'I don't have to!' she said. 'I have an income from my father. Isn't that good enough?' 'No, it isn't! he retorted. 'It isn't honest. That money comes from us, it's stolen from us, from the workers!'
> [...] 'I'm afraid you've made a mistake,' she said aloofly. 'My father is a landowner; our money comes from the earth, the English earth, my country. "Stolen from us!" – Why, you should be the last to speak. You and your people are only guests here!'(Blumenfeld 191)

This bitter contest and Elspeth's final accusation confirm the novel's analytical connections between gendered and economic exploitation and the antisemitic component of social exclusion. But it is Alec's response to Elspeth's ultimate antisemitic barb—"'Now you're talking like a Jew' [...] 'One who has no country'"—that forges a startling critical gloss on Woolf's *cri de coeur* in *Three Guineas* (Blumenfeld 192). He exclaims:

> 'But I don't need a country! [...] 'The whole world is my country! Isn't it time they threw overboard the old barbaric superstitions? Up to this line it's my country, beyond this line it's yours. Away with all that mumbo-jumbo. Every country belongs to us! – to the workers. Only to us!' (Blumenfeld 192).

The striking similarity between Alec's exhortation and Woolf's calls critical attention to their differences. Woolf's impassioned declaration is a response to women's exclusion from the political, cultural, and economic institutions dominated by British patriarchy. But her brief extends beyond the island nation whose citizenship she would renounce. Confirming the venomous character of British patriarchy, her polemical analysis in *Three Guineas* links it to British imperialism and ultimately to European fascist dictators/tyrants. That Woolf's diatribe against political oppression includes the Jews is salutary. That her list of victims creates an equivalency between the Jews' suffering and that of communists and women elides anything distinguishable about the Jews' historical and continuous persecution. In fact, by 1937, when Woolf was writing *Three Guineas*, Hitler's antisemitic ideology and Nuremberg Laws were already singling out the Jews for racialized persecution.

When *Jew Boy* was published in 1935, two years after Hitler came to power, word had already spread, as Alec puts it, that the "Jews were being ill-treated in Germany" (Blumenfeld 41). In 1936, inspired by European antisemitism, the threatening rhetoric of Oswald Mosley's Black Shirts was activated in their march on the East End. The Jews responded in the Battle of Cable Street about which Blumenfeld wrote a play with that title. Ken Worpole notes that "*Jew Boy* contains lively descriptions of several trade union demonstrations and political marches, based on real events, which foreshadowed the 1936 rout of Mosley's Fascists, and sealed the reputation of the radical East End" (Blumenfeld 13).[32] As a Jew, as a Communist and manual laborer, as an outsider everywhere, with no country he can claim as his own, Alec represents a battle against "the mumbo jumbo" of exclusionary boundaries that deny his humanity. After experiencing but not necessarily recognizing the full brunt of sexual and social disillusionment, Alec finds emotional and cultural expression in political action.

Propelling this action are several mass demonstrations for workers' rights, acts of desperation after the rejection of trade union demands and the failure of strikes. Despite their threats to dismiss those who leave their machinery to demonstrate, workshop managers and owners are not targeted as the perpetrators of economic oppression. Instead, they too are harassed by the pressure of fulfilling the demands of insatiable markets. Confronting the source of economic inequality, the workers

---

[32] See Fishman for detailed historical analysis of the political climate in the Jewish East End.

embark on a four hour march through the streets of Whitechapel, Spitalfields, Clerkenwell, and Stepney Green to Hyde Park, the heart of the wealthy and powerful West End. With no external economic or political sanction or support, this is no leisurely stroll that awakens and expresses the modernist yearning of a fragmented individual consciousness for mythical wholeness or empathetic communion. Instead, support emanates only from the narrator who gives coherent voice to a collective demand by thirty thousand Jewish workers and communists, Black and White, for a living wage and humane working conditions.

The novel creates a distinctive Jewish voice through Alec's observations and confirms its cultural value by merging it with that of the unidentified narrator. Rather than subsuming one voice within the other, creating an elliptical style, or gesturing towards the ambiguity and universality of Woolf's free indirect discourse, Blumenfeld's vocal fusion produces a historically grounded polemic. For example, during one of the demonstrations, Alec hears antisemitic and anti-Communist whispers from the sidelines. The voices of Alec and the narrator unite to politicize free indirect discourse by imagining a workers' communal countervoice:

> Jews wouldn't be lumped together as financiers and Bolsheviks. Nor would they be pointed out like tame zoological specimens by tolerantly superior Anglo-Saxons. "See here – these are our Jews. They've got black hair, dark skins and long noses, but they're quite harmless. They're different, but they can't help it." (Blumenfeld 48)

While politically urgent fictions are a hallmark of the thirties, responding to the rise of Fascism and Nazism as well as economic and social inequality,[33] *Jew Boy's* polemic targets the discriminations of modern British culture that marginalize or ignore the productive ferment of individual and collective Jewish subjectivity.

Several scenes in the novel dramatize Jewish cultural expression and appreciation of both classical and popular culture. The narrator's voice, merged with Alec's response, tells us that the audience "clapped wildly" at the Workers' Circle classical music concerts and that Alec "wouldn't miss the *lieder*" (Blumenfeld 78, 74). Nor would he miss films by Réné Clair, and if "Eisenstein and other Russian films were banned" except for expensive private showings, there was "Mickey Mouse and a Silly Symphony thrown in for full measure" (Blumenfeld 82). The pleasures of cultural reception are no match, however, for the social critique of Jewish cultural expression.

---

[32] See Naomi Mitchison's 1935 novel *We Have Been Warned*, Phyllis Bottome's 1937 *The Mortal Storm*, and Storm Jameson's 1936 *In the Second Year*.

Returning to the scene at Mrs. Saunders', we find both parody and protest at work. As in eighteenth or nineteenth century fiction, Sarah, the ingénue "on show," provides the parlor entertainment by playing the piano; Mrs. Saunders requests "that thing from *The Mikado*" (Blumenfeld 110, 111). Fulfilling his role of unsuitable suitor, Alec breaks in with two outré requests, first, "a couple of [...] Hebrew songs," and then, upstaged by Mrs. Saunders's insistence on a Mozart minuet, he sings "'Der Rebbe Hat Geheison Froelich Sein," a Chasidic ditty in Yiddish, translated as "The rabbi has commanded that we be merry" (Blumenfeld 110, 112). If Mrs. Saunders is appalled by this performance, Mr. Saunders is curious: "He'd look it up in the *Encyclopaedia Britannica*" (Blumenfeld 112).

The novel's multivocal and narrative shifts between outrage, protest, and satire map the conflicted desires and struggles of a second generation Jewish immigrant to achieve economic and cultural parity within an inhospitable British society, a conflict that intensifies the radical changes faced by an already destabilized Jewish East End community. At the end of the novel Alec occupies a transformed liminal position that represents a critical perspective on Virginia Woolf's Outsider Society and inclusion in intermodern literary history. He is already an outsider to mainstream British culture, and by both choice and exclusion. His solution is to find cultural and political self-expression by integrating his Jewish identity and history of oppression into a "worldwide fellowship" of workers (Blumenfeld 256). If in this otherwise hard hitting novel the "rhetoric of revolution" seems naïve and sentimental, David Cesarani offers a significant context: "In another type of novel this exclusion and humiliation would have led to Zionism. However, in the East End inhabited by the youthful Blumenfeld, the dominant political ideology was socialism; nationalism of all forms was widely dismissed" ("East End" 47).

Examining Woolf's works in relation to *Jew Boy* reveals that Jewish London is a vibrant and productive cultural and political space that belies stereotypical images of Jewish material decadence and moral degeneracy, the combination of which has been represented as the breakdown of the so-called "English" cultural character of London. To ignore the political and cultural implications of casual typecasting ends in distorting and silencing the achievements, experiences, culture, traditions, and contributions of the Jews who lived, worked, and raised families in London between the two world wars. *Jew Boy*'s multivalent Jewish voices and multicultural political solution should be considered in dialogue with Virginia Woolf's Society of Outsiders. To do so intervenes in scholarly debates about her antisemitism by including the complex presence of Jewish men and women as they represent themselves, their own history, and their culture.

Works Cited

Alderman, Geoffrey. *Modern British Jewry*. Oxford/New York: Oxford UP, 1992. Print.
Bhabha, Homi. *The Location of Culture*. New York: Routledge, 1994. Print.
Black, Gerry. *Living Up West: Jewish Life in London's West End*. London: London Museum of Jewish Life, 1994. Print.
Blumenfeld, Simon. *Jew Boy*. 1935. Introd. Ken Walpole. London: London Books, 2011. Print.
Bluemel, Kristin. *George Orwell and the Radical Eccentrics: Intermodernism in Literary London*. London: Palgrave, 2004. Print.
———. *Intermodernism: Literary Culture in Mid-Twentieth-Century Britain* Edinburgh: Edinburgh UP, 2009. Print.
Bottome, Phyllis. *The Mortal Storm*. 1938. Evanston, IL: Northwestern UP, 1998.
Bradshaw, David. Introduction. *Carlyle's House and Other Sketches*. Virginia Woolf. London: Hesperus, 2003. xiii-xxv. Print.
———. "Hyams Place: *The Years*, the Jews and the British Union of Fascists." *Women Writers of the 1930s: Gender, Politics and History*. Ed. Maroula Joannou. Edinburgh: Edinburgh UP, 1999. 179-91. Print.
Cesarani, David. "The East End of Simon Blumenfeld's *Jew Boy*." *London Journal* 13.1 (1987-1988): 45-53. Print.
———, ed. *The Making of Modern Anglo-Jewry*. Oxford: Blackwell, 1990. Print.
Cesarani, David, M. Shain and Tony Kushner, eds. *Zakor V' Makor: Place and Displacement in Jewish History and Memory*. London: Vallentine Mitchell, 2008. Print.
Cheyette, Brian. *Constructions of "the Jew" in English Liberalism and Society: Racial Representations, 1875-1945*. Cambridge: Cambridge UP, 1993. Print.
Feldman, David. "Jews and the British Empire c. 1900." *History Workshop Journal* 63 (2007): 70-89. Print.
Endelman, Todd M. *The Jews of Britain, 1656 to 2000*. Berkeley: U of California P, 2002. Print.
Evans, Elizabeth and Sarah Cornish, eds. *Woolf and the City: Selected Papers of the Nineteenth Annual Conference on Virginia Woolf*. Clemson: Clemson Digital Press, 2010. Print.
Fishman, William. *East End Jewish Radicals*. Nottingham: Five Leaves, 2004. Print.
Gaer, Joseph. *The Legend of the Wandering Jew* New York: Mentor Books, 1961. Print.

Grover, Mary. *The Ordeal of Warwick Deeping: Middlebrow Authorship and Cultural Embarrassment*. Madison, N.J.: Fairleigh Dickinson UP, 2009. Print.

Grover, Mary and Erica Brown, eds. *Middlebrow Literary Cultures: The Battle of the Brows, 1920-1960*. New York: Palgrave, 2011. Print.

Hasan-Rokem, Galit and Alan Dundes, eds. *The Wandering Jew: Essays in the Interpretation of a Christian Legend*. Bloomington: Indiana UP, 1986. Print.

Hinden, Rita. "Economic Plans and Problems in the British Colonies." *World Affairs* 112.3 (1949): 77-79. Print.

——. *Empire and After: A Study of British Imperial Attitudes*. London: Essential Books, 1949. Print.

——. "Human Rights in Africa." *Patterns of Prejudice* 21.1 (1968): 29-32. Print.

——. *Local Government and the Colonies: Fabian Colonial Essays* London: Allen & Unwin 1950. Print.

——. *No Cheer for Central Africa*. London: Fabian Commonwealth Bureau, 1958. Print.

Hinden, Rita and Richard Henry Tawney, eds. *The Radical Tradition: Twelve Essays in Politics, Education and Literature*. London: Allen & Unwin, 1964 Print.

Hubbard, Phil., Rob Kitchin and Gill Valentine, eds. *Key Thinkers on Space and Place*. London: Sage, 2004. Print.

"In Appreciation of Rita Hinden." *Socialist Commentary* (January 1972): 15-19. Print.

Jameson, Margaret Storm. *In the Second Year*. New York: Macmillan, 1936. Print.

Julius, Anthony. *Trials of the Diaspora: A History of Anti-Semitism in England*. Oxford: Oxford UP, 2010. Print.

Kadish, Sharman. "Moses, Miriam (1884–1965)." *Oxford Dictionary of National Biography*. Oxford University Press, 2004; online edn, Jan 2011. Web. 5 July 2012.

Kalman, Raymond, "The Jewish East End. Where Was It?" Newman, 6-7. Print.

Katz, Tamar. "Pausing, Waiting, Repeating: Urban Temporality in *Mrs. Dalloway* and *The Years*." Evans and Cornish, 2-16. Print.

Kushner, Tony. "The Impact of British Anti-semitism, 1918-1945." Ceserani, *Modern Anglo-Jewry*, 191-208. Print.

——, ed. *The Jewish Heritage in British History: Englishness and Jewishness*. London/ Portland, OR: F. Cass, 1992. Print.

——. "The Paradox of Prejudice: The Impact of Organised Antisemitism in Britain During an Anti-Nazi War." *Traditions of Intolerance: Historical Perspectives on Fascism and Race Discourse in Britain*. Ed. Tony Kushner and Kenneth Lunn. Manchester: Manchester UP, 1989. 72-90. Print.

———. *The Persistence of Prejudice: Antisemitism in British Society during the Second World War*. Manchester: Manchester UP, 1989. Print.

Kuzmack, Linda Gordon. *Woman's Cause: The Jewish Woman's Movement in England and the United States, 1881-1933*. Columbus: Ohio State UP, 1990. Print.

Lalwan, Rory. "Soho Jewish Community." *sohomemories.org.uk*. City of Westeminster Archives, n.d. Web. 20 July 2012.

Lassner, Phyllis. *British Women Writers of World War II: Battlegrounds of Their Own*. Basingstoke: Macmillan, 1998. Print.

———. "The Milk of our Mother's Kindness Has Ceased to Flow." *Between "Race" and Culture: Representations of "the Jew" in English and American Literature*. Ed. Bryan Cheyette. Stanford, CA: Stanford UP, 1996. 129-44. Print.

Lassner, Phyllis and Lara Trubowitz, eds. *Antisemitism and Philosemitism in the Twentieth and Twenty-first Centuries: Representing Jews, Jewishness, and Modern Culture*. Newark: U Delaware P, 2008. Print.

Lefebvre, Henri. *The Production of Space*. Trans. D. Nicholson-Smith. Oxford: Blackwell, 1991. Print.

Lipman, V. D., "Jewish Settlement in the East End – 1840-1940." Newman, 17-40. Print.

———. "The Booth and New London Surveys as Source Material." Newman, 41-50. Print.

Linett, Maren Tova. "The Jew in the Bath: Imperiled Imagination in Woolf's *The Years*." *Modern Fiction Studies* 48.2 (Summer 2002): 341-61. Print.

———. *Modernism, Feminism, and Jewishness*. Cambridge: Cambridge UP, 2007. Print.

Lowenstein, Andrea Freud. *Loathsome Jews and Engulfing Women*. New York: New York UP, 1993. Print.

Manson, Janet M. "Margery Perham, the Fabians, and Colonial Policy." *Women in the Milieu of Leonard and Virginia Woolf: Peace, Politics, and Education*. Ed. Wayne Chapman and Janet M. Manson. NewYork: Pace UP, 1998. 170-90. Print.

McVicker, Jeanette. "'Six Essays on London Life': A History of Dispersal, Part I." *Woolf Studies Annual* 9 (2003): 143-65. Print.

———. "'Six Essays on London Life': A History of Dispersal, Part II." *Woolf Studies Annual* 10 (2004): 141-72. Print.

Mendelovitch, Bernard. *Memories of London Yiddish Theatre*. The Seventh Annual Avrom-Nokhem Stencl Lecture in Yiddish Studies. 14 August 1989. Oxford: Oxford Centre for Postgraduate Hebrew Studies, 1990. Print.

Mitchison, Naomi. *We Have Been Warned.* London: Constable, 1935. Print.

Newland, Paul. *The Cultural Construction of London's Jewish East End: Urban Iconography, Modernity, and the Spatialisation of Englishness.* Amsterdam/ New York: Rodopi, 2008. Spatial Practices 5. Print.

Newman, Aubrey, ed. *The Jewish East End 1840-1939.* London: Jewish Historical Society of England, 1981. Print.

Panitz, Esther. *The Alien in Their Midst: Images of Jews in English Literature.* East Brunswick, NJ: Assoc. UP, 1981. Print.

Pugh, Patricia M., "Hinden, Rita (1909–1971)." *Oxford Dictionary of National Biography.* Oxford University Press, 2004; online edn, Jan 2011. Web. 5 July 2012.

Rosenfeld, Natania. *Outsiders Together: Virginia and Leonard Woolf.* Princeton: Princeton UP, 2000. Print.

Schröder, Leena Kore. "Tales of Abjection and Miscegenation: Virginia Woolf's and Leonard Woolf's 'Jewish' Stories." *Twentieth-Century Literature* 49.3 (Fall 2003): 298-327. Print.

Snaith, Anna and Michael Whitworth. Introduction. *Locating Woolf: The Politics of Space and Place.* Ed. Snaith and Whitworth. Basingstoke: Palgrave, 2007. 1-28. Print.

Snyder, Cary. "Woolf's Ethnographic Modernism: Self-Nativizing in *The Voyage Out* and Beyond." *Woolf Studies Annual* 10 (2004): 81-108. Print.

Spiro, Mia. *Anti-Nazi Modernism: The Challenges of Resistance in 1930s Fiction.* Evanston, IL: Northwestern UP, 2013. Print.

Squier, Susan. *Virginia Woolf and London: The Sexual Politics of the City.* Chapel Hill: U of North Carolina P, 1985. Print.

Surette, Leon. *Pound in Purgatory: From Economic Radicalism to Anti-Semitism.* Chicago: U of Illinois P, 1999. Print.

Trubowitz, Lara. "Concealing Leonard's Nose: Virginia Woolf, Modernist Antisemitism, and 'The Duchess and the Jeweller.'" *Twentieth-Century Literature* 54.3 (Fall 2008): 273-306. Print.

Walkowitz, Rebecca. *City of Dreadful Delight: Narratives of Sexual Danger in Late-Victorian London.* Chicago: U of Chicago P, 1992. Print.

Woolf, Virginia. *The Diary of Virginia Woolf.* Ed. Anne Olivier Bell. 5 vols. New York: Harcourt Brace, 1977-84. Print.

——. "The Duchess and the Jeweller." *The Complete Shorter Fiction of Virginia Woolf.* Ed. Susan Dick. London: Hogarth, 1989. 248-53. Print.

——. *The Letters of Virginia Woolf.* Ed. Nigel Nicolson and Joanne Trautmann. 6 vols. New York: Harcourt Brace Jovanovich, 1975-80. Print.

——. *The Pargiters, the Novel-Essay Portion of the Years.* London: Hogarth, 1977. Print.

———. "Street Haunting. A London Adventure." 1930. *Collected Essays*. Vol. 4. London: Hogarth, 1967. 155-66. Print.
———. *The Years*. 1937. Introd. Eleanor McNees. Orlando, FL: Harcourt, 2008. Print.
Worpole, Ken. Introduction. Simon Blumenfeld. *Jew Boy*. London: London Books, 2011. 7-17. Print.

Virginia Woolf's Research for *Empire and Commerce in Africa* (Leonard Woolf, 1920)

Michèle Barrett

> "*I copied out the notes, have put them all in order on your table (this is a lie but I will do so) and sent the book off*" (*L*2 191).

Virginia Woolf's note to her husband, of October 29, 1917, is not her first reference to taking notes. In March 1914 she had written to him, saying "All the morning I typewrite — then read your Co.op: books, and make futile notes I expect" (*L*2 44). In January 1915 she noted in her diary that after buying cod's roe in the fishmongers she had "made carbon copies of some notes of L's about Arbitration," adding that "one may now hope he will get started, which is the main thing" (*D*1 24). The research she referred to in the 1917 note, however, was of an altogether larger order, and more systematic. Virginia Woolf read extensively, making copious detailed notes, mainly by hand, which have been preserved in Leonard Woolf's papers at Sussex University. This work was for a book he had intended to write on International Trade, and for one that he did write, on *Empire and Commerce in Africa*.

These research notes run to a total of 783 folios, approximately 8" x 5" in size. They shed light on Virginia Woolf's relationship with her husband, and the critical intellectual and political ideas they shared about British imperialism. They also reveal Virginia Woolf as a meticulous, even slightly pedantic scholar. The research notes include an enormous amount of empirical information about international trade, mainly in the form of hand-drawn tables from the pen of Virginia Woolf. They throw light on her facility with factual data, a facility often disguised in her fiction but informing her handling of several characters. These research notes, made at the same time that she was writing *Night and Day*, cast a different light on the subject matter of that novel. This paper will present the notes and reflect on some of these issues.

Leonard Woolf's *Empire and Commerce in Africa*

Virginia Woolf's notes were made to provide research assistance to Leonard Woolf for a book he had contracted to write for the Fabian Society. He had been invited to write a book for them on international trade, but had been unwilling. On December 24, 1916, Sidney Webb wrote to him, saying that "Your letter demurring to undertaking International Trade" was a disappointment, "after I had got the project through a series of Committees!" and adding, "Could you not come and talk to me?"[1] Virginia Woolf was keen to lessen the influence of the Webbs on Leonard[2] but on this occasion she failed. In February 1917 Leonard Woolf signed a contract with the Fabian Society for a book on "International Trade," which he was to deliver "within the next year, or thereabouts" for which he was to be paid £100 in four installments (I/L/6). Sidney Webb had initially proposed the book in a Fabian and Labour framework, suggesting "eg the development of international dealing between the Cooperative Wholesale Societies."[3] It was just as well that he later wrote to Woolf, saying "please take your own line, & have a free hand"[4] as the book that emerged in 1920 was very different: it was a blistering criticism of economic imperialism in Africa.

The materials for a general work on international trade were found, read and analyzed but the book that was published was much narrower, being a study of imperialism in Africa and focusing on the northern and eastern parts of the continent. The extensive international research undertaken provided a global context for the study of Africa. Leonard Woolf's book was published by the Labour Research Department and George Allen and Unwin. The book's subtitle was *A Study in Economic Imperialism*. At 368 pages of text it is a substantial volume, and is divided into three parts. The first outlines Woolf's approach to the international policies of the major European powers, and he argues that during the last decade of the nineteenth century the policies of European states as regards Africa were entirely motivated by economic gain rather than any civilizing mission. The opening section is trenchant in its style, and a model of clarity of argument.[5] Of the UK, Woolf argues that "Mr Chamberlain's State and his Government Offices and his Secretaries of State and his Policy will all be of a particular kind, because he believes

---

[1] Leonard Woolf Papers, University of Sussex Library, Work Life Section, I/L/6. Where possible, further references to the Leonard Woolf Papers are embedded in the text. My thanks to the University of Sussex and the Society of Authors as the literary representative of the Estate of Leonard Woolf for permission to quote unpublished material in this article.
[2] On 22 February, 1915, Virginia Woolf wrote to Margaret Llewelyn Davies about the excitement of their printing press "I think there's a chance of damaging the Webb influence irretrievably, (which is my life's ambition)" (*L*2, 59).
[3] Sidney Webb to Leonard Woolf, 9 November 1916, Leonard Woolf Papers, I/L/6.
[4] Sidney Webb to Leonard Woolf, 27 January 1917, Leonard Woolf Papers, 1/L/6.
[5] Oddly, in light of the contributions of two women to the book, the image used on the opening page contrasts the reader of the book as a "a gentleman" who is to question the lessons imparted by his mother "or, more probably, at a kindergarten table under the worried eye of a most ill-informed lady" (*Empire and Commerce* 3).

that the promotion of commercial interests is the greatest of political interests, the chief function of the State" (*Empire and Commerce* 9).

Virginia Woolf's diary contains several references to the book her husband was writing, albeit very few to her own work on it. In March 1918 she commented that "We both notice that lately we've written at a terrific pace: L. 40,000 words & as yet hasn't touched the book itself" (*D*1 127). He had presumably been writing Part 1 on "International Economic policy". The "book itself," the meat of the empirical argument, was Part II of Leonard Woolf's book, the part that concerned "Economic Imperialism in Africa" in the late nineteenth century. This consisted of seven sections, mainly focused on northern and east Africa, including a section on Algeria, one on Tunis, another on Tunis and Tripoli, one on Abyssinia and the Nile and one on Zanzibar and East Africa. Finally, departing from the main focus of the book, there was a section on the Belgian Congo, designed to present a factual account of King Leopold II's brutalities there. The third part of the book, entitled "Reflections and Conclusions," considered the effects of economic imperialism and the future of Africa. It was to the second part of the book that Virginia Woolf's research notes made an extensive contribution.

In developing the research for the book, Leonard Woolf set up a team of three people. After himself, the second member of the team was Alix Sargant-Florence. Following the title page of the published book, Leonard Woolf has added a "Note": "I have to thank Miss Alix Sargant-Florence, who has given me valuable help in research for Part II. of this book." Among Leonard Woolf's papers for *Empire and Commerce in Africa* are the notes made by Alix Sargant-Florence, along with many of her covering letters to him: she read and summarized many of the "blue books" published by the UK government on trade issues, and she went through parliamentary papers and reports for him. Alix was later to marry James Strachey, and had by this time tried and quickly given up working for the Woolfs at the press. Wayne Chapman's informative paper about her takes its title from one of many lukewarm diary entries made by her employer's wife: "We went to the London Library, as usual; coming out ran in to the hatless dusky figure, L.'s dame secretaire: Alix; on her way to grope for facts, which L.'s eye finds a good deal quicker" (*D*1 71; Chapman 33-57).

The third member of the research team was Virginia Woolf. Wayne Chapman and Janet Manson have analyzed an earlier co-operation between Leonard and Virginia Woolf, a paper on International Relations which was eventually published under Leonard Woolf's name but for which a draft exists in her handwriting (58-78). Chapman and Manson provide a careful account of the development of that paper on International Relations, and the "complexly reciprocal" influence the Woolfs had on each other (77). Chapman, in writing about Alix Sargant-Florence's work on the *Empire and Commerce* project, briefly describes the filing system and notes that Virginia Woolf made for the book and the main texts she studied (38). Janet Manson touches again on *Empire and Commerce* in a paper on colonial scholar Marjorie Perham, itemizing some of the sources she consulted and concluding that Virginia Woolf thus "became acquainted...with the intense rivalry over Africa which drew France and Britain to the brink of war" (186).

Virginia Woolf's notes were largely made by hand, in ink (usually turquoise ink, although occasionally royal blue or violet), and they take the form of index cards, albeit made of thin paper rather than thick card. There are several stacks of these note cards in the archive at Sussex. Some of the material is typed, often corrected in her distinctive hand. The notes fall into two main categories.

The first category is that of materials that found their way into the text of *Empire and Commerce in Africa*. These consist of a pile of notes an inch or so high, mainly of quotations from the books that Virginia Woolf consulted. These include works such as the *Memoirs of Francesco Crispi* (in three volumes); F. D. Lugard's *The Rise of Our East African Empire* (in two volumes); P. L. McDermott's *British East Africa*; and Augustus Wylde's *Modern Abyssinia*. In addition to works such as these in English, Virginia Woolf made extensive notes (in French) from a book by Jean Darcy about Anglo-French conflict in the African sphere, *France et Angleterre: Cent Années de Rivalité Coloniale*, and from Alfred Rambaud's book on Jules Ferry. She also made notes in Italian from Lincoln de Castro's *Nella Terra Dei Negus: pagine raccolte in Abissinia*. These notes made in Virginia Woolf's longhand were then organized into regional and thematic classifications, added in the top right hand corner in Leonard Woolf's handwriting.

The second category, larger than the substantial pile of notes that were to be used in *Empire and Commerce*, consists of the notes that Virginia Woolf made from British Consular Reports around the world when the project was defined broadly as "International Trade." These begin with "the Argentine" (as it then was) and end with Zanzibar, and include lengthy quotations and very detailed reproductions of information in tabular form, covering imports and exports, immigration and other subjects. In total there are 666 pages, in Virginia Woolf's own hand, of notes from these British Consular Reports on international trade.

Empire and Commerce in Africa was published in January 1920, on the same day as the second London printing of Virginia Woolf's second novel, *Night and Day*.[6] Although the book itself acknowledges the research of Alix Sargant-Florence, it does not (perhaps unsurprisingly) acknowledge that of the author's wife. However, there can be no doubt that Virginia Woolf's extensive reading and research contributed to the distinctive factual ambition of this book. When the book

---

[6] According to Julia Briggs the first edition of *Night and Day* had been published on 20 October 1919 in the UK (52).

was published, reviewers made much of the empirical bases of the argument, and Leonard Woolf's coverage and grasp of the materials. *The Nation* said that Leonard Woolf had carried the anti-Imperialism argument "a great deal further" than previous exponents, and had given it "a definitely Socialistic statement, and driven it home with a tremendous battering-ram of historical knowledge." This reviewer concluded that "His mastery of facts is more than impressive, it is even at times a little overwhelming" (I/L/6). The *Glasgow Herald* described it as "a most fascinating book, packed full of information, brilliantly written and sound alike in statistics and judgment" (I/L/6). The Dublin-based *Freeman's Journal* referred to it as an "imposing and invaluable work of research" (I/L/6).

Reviewers were united in their admiration for the research that went into the book. *Common Sense* noticed the book twice, declaring that "no such profound, searching and fully documented study of economic Imperialism in action has yet happened," and later that "the whole rests on a masterly marshaling of indisputable fact" (I/L/6). The *Ceylon Daily News* explained the importance of the empirical approach that Leonard Woolf had taken: "Mr Woolf…lets the stern facts, supported by chapter and verse, speak for themselves. This testimony is far more illuminating and appalling than any rhetoric would be" (I/L/6). The reviewer for the *TLS* made the point with a more critical edge, noting that "the merits of the book are that it bears evidence of much research, though always on the one side and directed to proving what the author wants to prove" (I/L/6).

Virginia Woolf's research for the book

Virginia Woolf's research notes on sources used in Leonard Woolf's *Empire and Commerce in Africa* run to a total of 117 sides of notecards. Of these, sixty-seven are in her handwriting and approximately fifty of the typed notecards can also be attributed to her. Virginia Woolf's reading notes are mainly in the form of carefully referenced quotations rather than summaries of arguments.

Part II of *Empire and Commerce in Africa* begins with a cartographical comparison of Africa in 1880 and 1914. The first map is virtually blank, with a few territories such as Portuguese Angola, French Senegal or British Natal marked on the coastal margins. By sharp contrast, the 1914 map, showing the "scramble for Africa" of the intervening period, has the continent completely blocked out, including extensive areas of hinterland, owned by the colonial powers of Europe: for example Italian Tripoli, French Sahara, German Kamerun, Belgian Congo, British East Africa and German East Africa, and the huge tract of land from Northern Rhodesia down to Cape Colony in the hands of the British. The map is completely colored in, covering even the most interior parts of Africa.

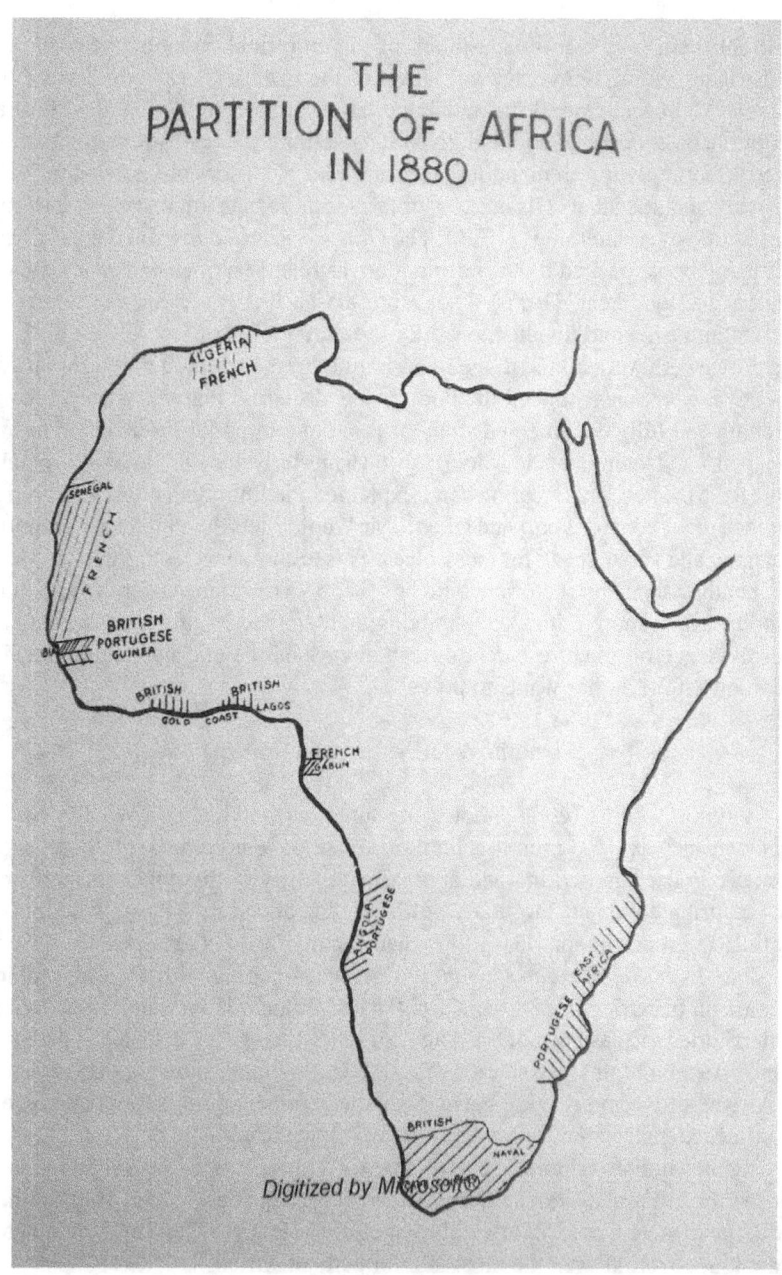

Fig. 1 Africa, 1880 (*Empire and Commerce* 52)

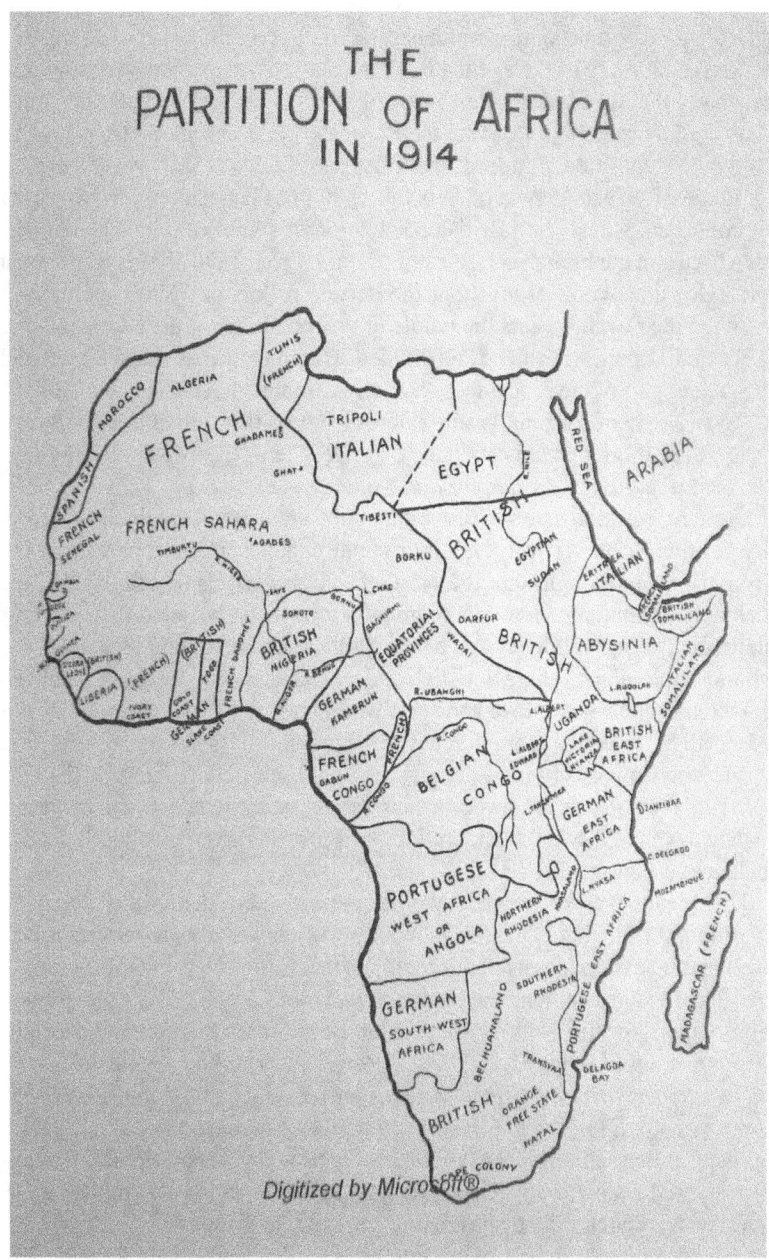

Fig. 2 Africa, 1914 (*Empire and Commerce* 52)

Leonard Woolf accompanies these stark images with a statistical digest and a discursive summary of the events. In 1815, Europe's claims on Africa amounted to less than 500,000 square miles, most of which was not "actually occupied or administered." From 1815 to 1880, the European penetration of Africa began, but it was "vague, spasmodic and, for the most part, feeble" (55). Woolf's argument is that in the fifty years between 1830 and 1880 this changed only in two specific, albeit important, ways— the British occupation of some 130,000 square miles in South Africa and the French conquest of Algeria. From 1880 all this was to change dramatically, and Woolf argues that the decade following 1880 was the crucial one: "In the next twenty years the whole of the remainder of the continent, except Morocco and Tripoli, was seized and divided up among the European States, and by far the greater part of the process was actually completed in the ten years following 1880" (56). Many of Virginia Woolf's notes from British Consular Reports, as we will see, focus on trade statistics during the decade of the 1880s, the key decade for the central argument of *Empire and Commerce in Africa.*

Leonard Woolf goes on to argue that a different ethos obtained in European policy on the North African Mediterranean coast from the operations in the rest of Africa. He thought that the Northern coast was historically folded into a gentlemanly, militaristic view of foreign policy, as was associated with Wellington or Metternich. What followed was a new political and national ideology of naked economic imperialism, characteristic of Cecil Rhodes and Joseph Chamberlain. Thus the statesmen who played for and won and lost Egypt, Tunis, Tripoli, and Morocco all believed that commerce was the greatest of political interests, and on the Niger, the Congo, and the Zambezi they put their beliefs into practice: but in Egypt, Tunis, Tripoli, and Morocco their economic imperialism was never pure; it was always mixed with considerations of European strategy and alliances and the balance of power. (58)

This means that for Leonard Woolf "the history of the northern coast" was "very different from that of the rest of Africa" (58). It was, he suggests, particularly the western and eastern coasts of the continent that European economic imperialism "seized and divided up among the predatory States of Europe" (59). Among Leonard Woolf's papers for the book is a typed list of the titles that he was considering for it: *Empire and Commerce in Africa; Power Policy and Commerce in Africa; Economic Imperialism in Africa; African Imperialisms*; and *The Capitalist State in Africa* (1/L/6). *Empire and Commerce in Africa*'s main section then begins with three chapters on Mediterranean Africa: on Algeria, Tunis and Tripoli. Then follow two substantial chapters on "Abyssinia and the Nile" and on "Zanzibar and East Africa", with a concluding discussion of the Belgian Congo.

One of Leonard Woolf's main sources of evidence was a book by the French historian Jean Darcy, *France et Angleterre: Cent Années de Rivalité Coloniale:*

L'Afrique (1904). Darcy had previously published *La Conquête de l'Afrique*, which Leonard Woolf had also read, and quotes from in *Empire and Commerce*; his frequent references to Darcy's *Cent Années* draw on Virginia Woolf's reading notes, of which there are 23 sides of handwritten notecards in the collection. Jean Darcy's *Cent Années* was, according to Leonard Woolf, with de Constant's book *La Politique francaise en Tunisie* (1891), "chosen for the facts because they are fervid supporters of the policy of imperialism, and their evidence is therefore unimpeachable" (*Empire and Commerce* 83, note 1). Darcy's book ran to over 470 pages. The organization of the book must have to some extent inspired Leonard Woolf's book, for Darcy begins with Algeria and Tunis and "les côtes barbaresque" before tackling the Niger, the Congo and the Nile. Virginia Woolf's extensive notes from Darcy include some where she has embarked on an altogether scholarly style of footnoting. One quotation from Darcy is embellished with two footnotes, in superior script and underlined in the text, in French, citing such mundane British sources as the *Daily Chronicle* and *The Times*, suggesting that Virginia Woolf was perhaps enjoying her work of transcription.

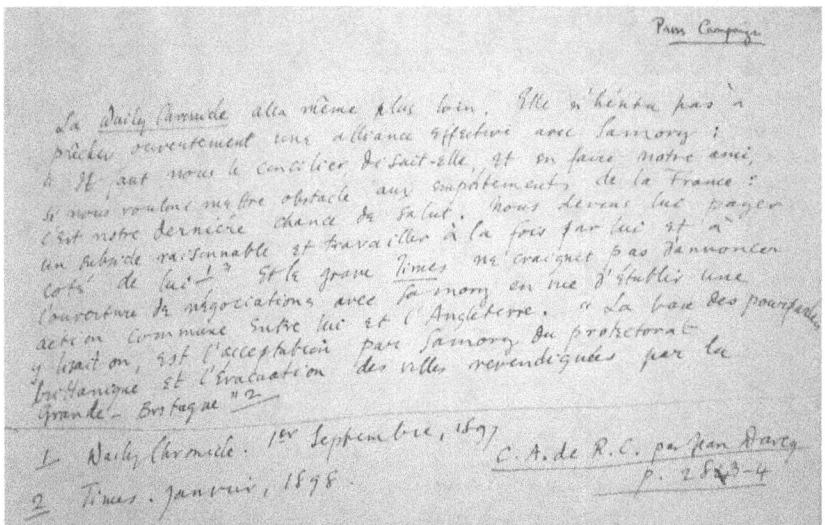

Fig. 3 Virginia Woolf: Notes from Jean Darcy, *France et Angleterre: Cent Années de Rivalité Coloniale*

The Woolf notes include many on Britain and her colonies. Under "Br. Policy Egypt Suez Canal" are two pages, handwritten by Virginia Woolf, being notes in French from Jean Darcy's *France et Angleterre*. Virginia Woolf has faltered on the word isthmus in French, and the transcription has corrections to it in her own, and some annotations in Leonard Woolf's hand about Disraeli and the House of Commons.

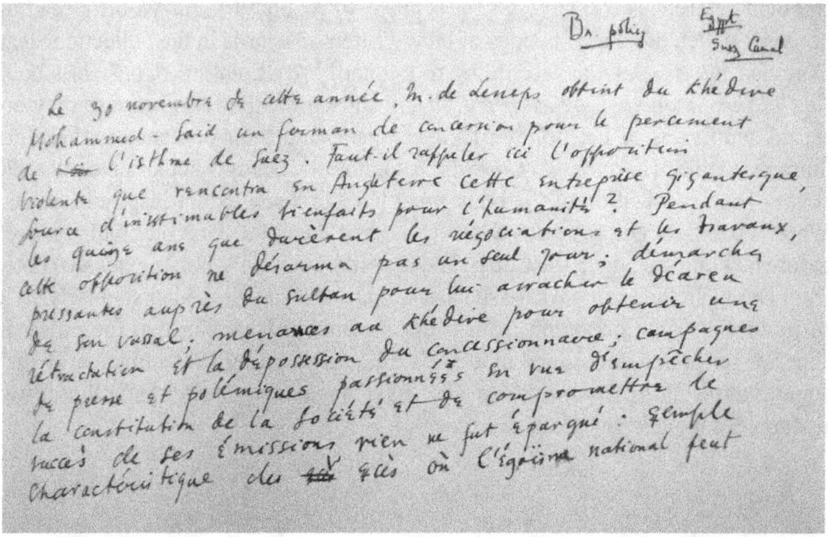

Br. policy Egypt Suez Canal

Le 30 novembre de cette année, M. de Leseps obtint du khédive Mohammed-Saïd un firman de concession pour le percement de ~~l'is~~ l'isthme de Suez. Faut-il rappeler ici l'opposition violente que rencontra en Angleterre cette entreprise gigantesque, source d'inestimables bienfaits pour l'humanité? Pendant les quinze ans que durèrent les négociations et les travaux, cette opposition ne désarma pas un seul jour; démarches pressantes auprès du sultan pour lui arracher le décret de son vassal; menaces au khédive pour obtenir une rétractation et la dépossession du concessionnaire; campagnes de presse et polémiques passionnées en vue d'empêcher la constitution de la société et de compromettre le succès de ses émissions rien ne fut épargné: exemple characteristique des excès où l'égoïsme national peut

Fig. 4 Notes from Jean Darcy, *France et Angleterre: Cent Années de Rivalité Coloniale*

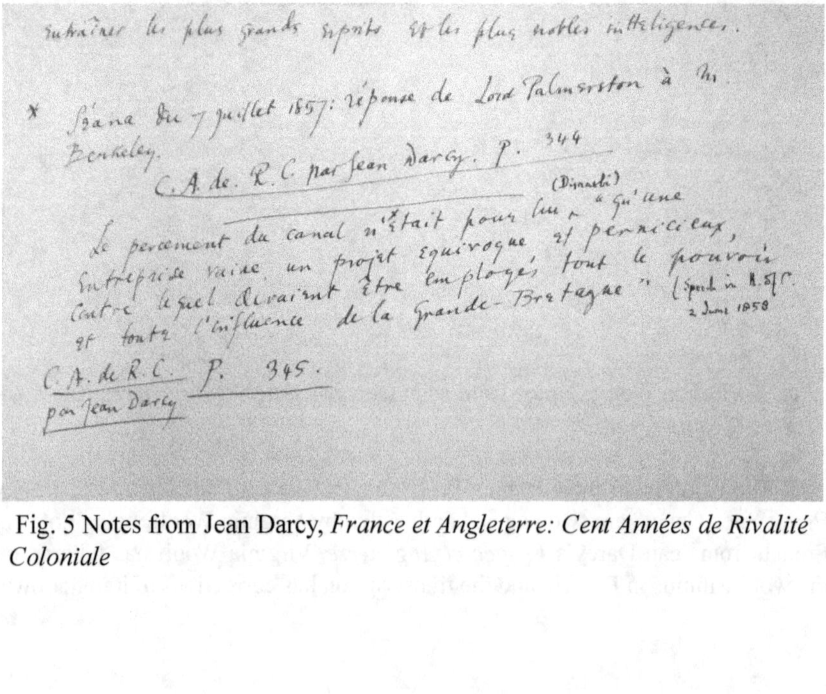

entraîner les plus grands esprits et les plus nobles intelligences.

* Séance du 7 juillet 1857: réponse de Lord Palmerston à M. Berkeley.

C.A. de R.C par Jean Darcy. P. 344

Le percement du canal n'était pour lui (Disraeli) "qu'une entreprise vaine, un projet équivoque et pernicieux, contre lequel devaient être employés tout le pouvoir et toute l'influence de la Grande-Bretagne" (Speech in H. of C. 2 June 1858

C.A. de R.C. P. 345.
par Jean Darcy

Fig. 5 Notes from Jean Darcy, *France et Angleterre: Cent Années de Rivalité Coloniale*

Virginia Woolf also took notes, in Italian, from a book by Dr. Lincoln de Castro, *Nella Terra dei Negus: pagine raccolte in Abissinia* (1915); Leonard Woolf explains that the Negus was the figure who governed as a single emperor (*Empire and Commerce* 140) but this work does not otherwise figure in his book. Virginia Woolf's Italian accenting on the word *difficoltà* is corrected in her own hand.

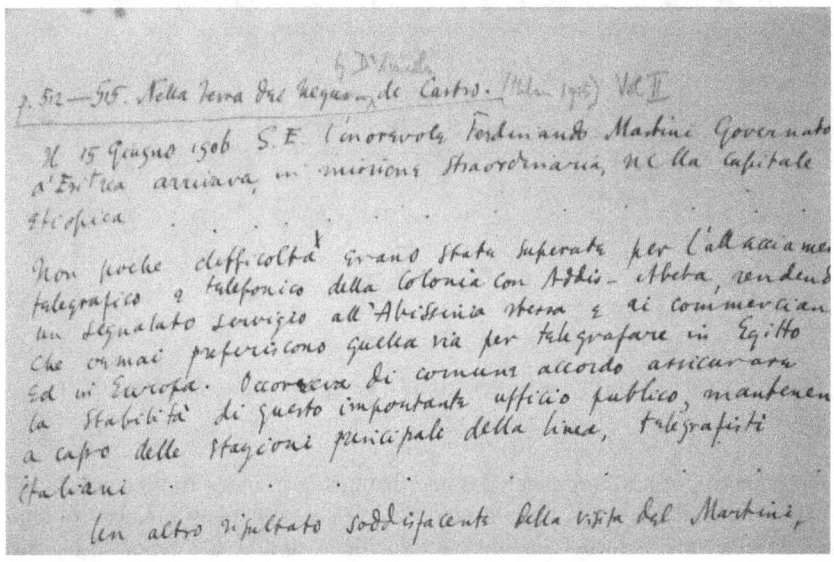

Fig. 6 Notes from Lincoln de Castro, *Nella Terra dei Negus*

She also read *Les Italiens en Erythrée: Quinze Ans de Politique Coloniale* by C. de La Jonquière (1897), and Leonard Woolf has translated one of her extracts and reproduced it in his book: Virginia Woolf has typed out, adding the French accenting by hand, "Cependant le gouvernement français ..." and this appears in the text of *Empire and Commerce* as "It 'was chosen', as a French writer explains, [here LW footnotes Jonquière 42] 'as a stepping-stone on the route to the Far East; from that point of view its position at the exit of the Strait of Bab-el-Mandeb gave it a real strategic importance. At the same time it was possible to hope that it would become a centre of commerce with the Harrar and Shoa, that is to say, with the south of Abyssinia'" (*Empire and Commerce* 152-153).

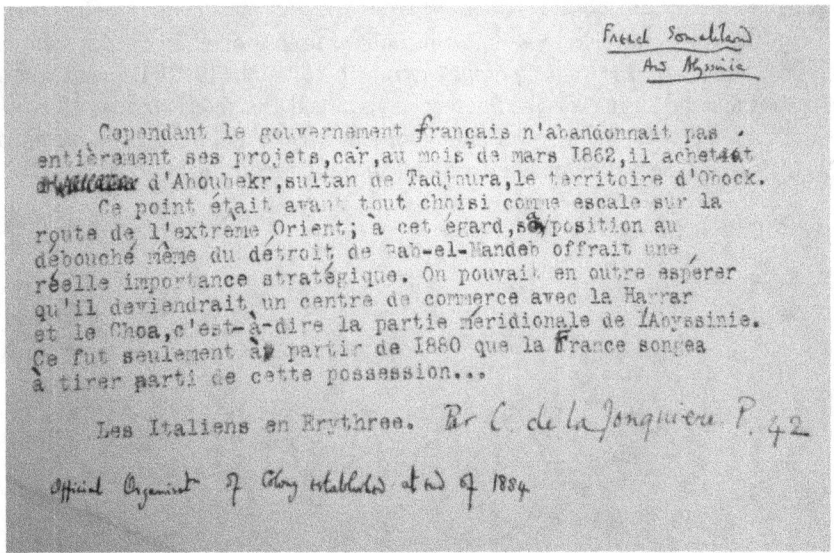

Fig. 7 Virginia Woolf: typed notes from C. de la Jonquière, *Les Italiens en Erythrée*

This run of notecards includes one that has been made by Leonard Woolf; it is distinguishable from Virginia Woolf's notes as he made summaries of arguments rather than simply copying out quotations, and he has typed in his own subject headings at the top. It is from Harry Johnston's *A History of the Colonization of Africa by Alien Races* (1899), which Woolf abbreviates to "C of A"; other works by Johnston, including *The Opening Up of Africa* (1911) and *The Black Man's Part in the War* (1917), are found among Leonard Woolf's books in his own library, held at Washington State University at Pullman.

There are few notes in this collection in which any researcher has made a personal comment, and none by Virginia Woolf. Leonard Woolf, who annotated many of his own books, has added an exclamation mark.

Virginia Woolf made substantial notes on P. L. McDermot's *British East Africa* (1895), many of which she typed and corrected by hand. Leonard Woolf refers to it as "a most important book for the student of economic imperialism. It was written by the Secretary of the British East Africa Company, and is, for that Company and therefore for British economic imperialism on the East Coast, an *apologia pro vita sua*" (*Empire and Commerce* 234).

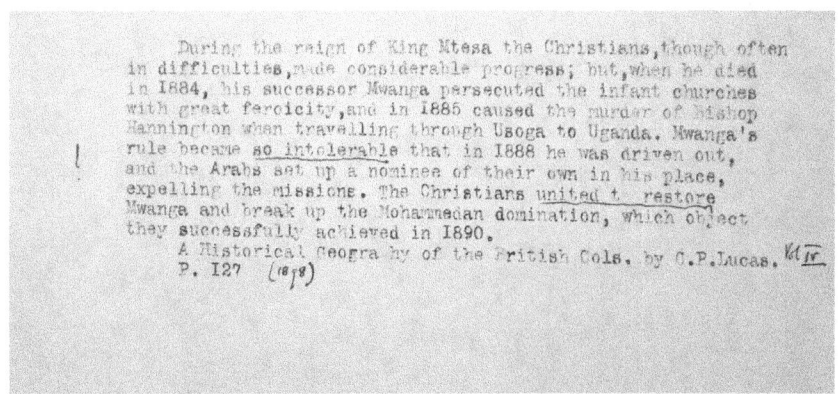

Fig. 8 Leonard Woolf: typed notes from C. P. Lucas, *A Historical Geography of the British Colonies*

For his chapter on "Tunis and Tripoli" Leonard Woolf relied heavily on the memoirs of Francesco Crispi, particularly the third volume, published in 1914. The extensive research notes on this source are all made in Virginia Woolf's hand. At one point the text of *Empire and Commerce* incorporates a long quotation from Crispi's memoir, starting and finishing exactly as Virginia Woolf had copied it out, with the addition of an editorial "he writes." Leonard Woolf refers to "the following remarkable words" of a "distinguished French statesman," a M. Hanotaux, and quotes him as saying:

> Bizerta has the Mediterranean by the throat. At this decisive point Nature herself has dug a lake which offers an area of 15,000 hectares, 1300 of which are sufficiently deep to float the largest vessels. Thus one of the finest ports in the world is situated at one of the world's most important points. It was necessary that we should have that point and that port. (*Empire and Commerce* 117-118)

This quotation appears in Virginia Woolf's notes from Volume 3 of Crispi's memoirs, which include the relevant passage from Hanotaux. She has copied her material exactly as the Hanotaux quotation is given in English translation in Crispi, including two arresting exclamation marks and underlining the dramatic last sentence. These are missing in Leonard Woolf's version of the passage. This would appear to be an example where Virginia Woolf has identified a dramatic passage, for it to be used— but toned down a little— in Leonard Woolf's book.

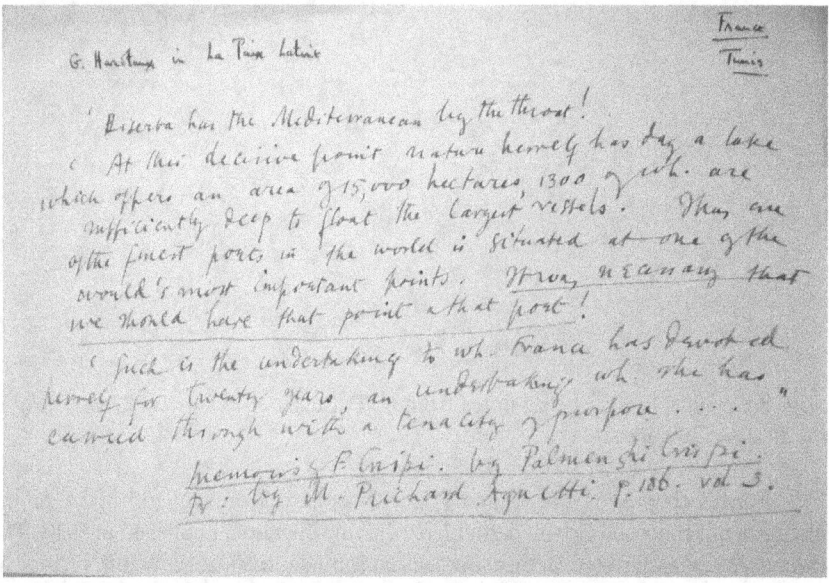

Fig. 9 Virginia Woolf: notes from Francesco Crispi, *Memoirs*

Empire and Commerce in Africa, after considering the Mediterranean coast of Africa, devotes a long section to Abyssinia and the Nile. Leonard Woolf uses the term "Ethiopian Africa" to refer to "the whole block of territory which includes Abyssinia, Eritrea, and the three Somalilands" (British, French and Italian) (*Empire and Commerce* 139). Three of the sources that he used for this section had been read by Virginia Woolf: Augustus Wylde's *Modern Abyssinia*, C. de la Jonquière's *Les Italiens en Erythrée* and Jean Darcy's book on Anglo-French colonial rivalry, usually abbreviated to *Cent Années* or C.A. by Virginia Woolf.

One reference to Wylde's 1901 book illuminates further the modus operandi of the Woolfs on this project. Virginia Woolf has copied out a long quotation beginning with the ringing words "Look at our behaviour to King Johannes from any point of view and it will not show one ray of honesty, and to my mind it is one of our worst bits of business out of the many we have been guilty of in Africa, and no wonder our position diplomatically is such a bad one with the rulers of the country at present." The quotation continues in the same vein:

> England made use of King Johannes as long as he was of any service and then threw him over to the tender mercies of Italy, who went to Massowah

under our auspices with the intention of taking territory that belonged to our ally, and allowed them to destroy and break all the promises England had solemnly made to King Johannes after he had faithfully carried out his part of the agreement. The fact is not known to the British public and I wish it was not true for our credit's sake; but unfortunately it is, and it reads like one of the vilest bits of treachery that has been perpetrated in Africa or in India in the eighteenth century.

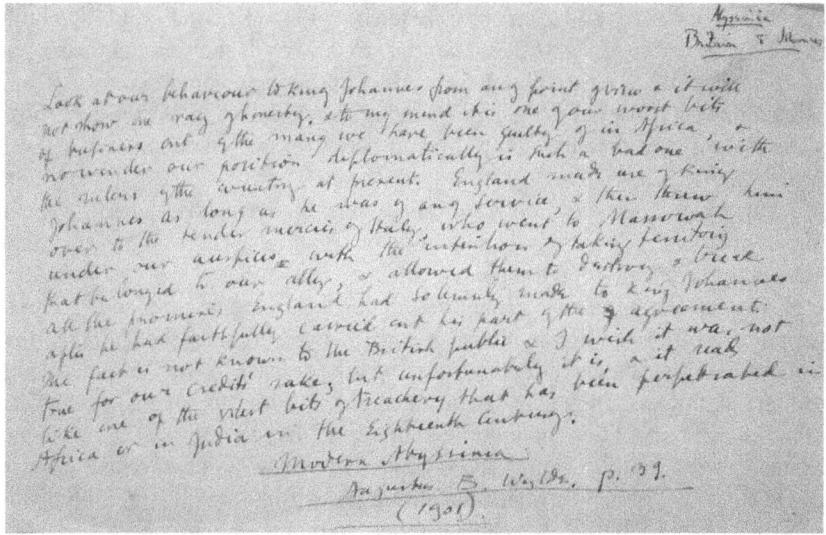

Fig. 10 Notes from Augustus Wylde, *Modern Abyssinia*

Leonard Woolf has picked up this vehement point, but blunted the rhetorical force of the quotation as Virginia Woolf rendered it, by prefacing "Look at our behaviour" with the more neutral sentence that precedes it in Wylde's book ("From the north he ought to have been safe") (*Empire and Commerce* 164). Virginia Woolf searched out the ringing, often accusatory, quotations and later Leonard Woolf revisited the book and folded these passages more neutrally into his argument.

One of the most interesting figures in Leonard Woolf's book is the British imperialist F. D. Lugard. Woolf's uncompromising critique of his actions in the colonization of Uganda and more generally in—to use the words of the title of Lugard's own two-volume work *The Rise of Our East African Empire*— was controversial. Many years later, when she was researching her biography of Lord Lugard in 1955, Marjorie Perham wrote to Leonard Woolf to ask him if he had changed his mind at all in the intervening period. "You must surely see," she wrote, "that Economic Imperialism in the hands of a man like Lugard… has been used for the benefit of people so that the Gold Coast for example is in a far better condition to start life as a nation, than Liberia." Woolf's reply was ambiguous, conceding that "I daresay too I was unfair to Lugard, though not entirely, for I remember how distasteful a good deal of what he said seemed to me at the time and I don't think I can have been altogether wrong about him" (1/L/6).

Leonard Woolf introduces Lugard as an apologist for economic imperialism in his general thesis at the beginning of the book, as well as describing him as a practitioner of it who "added an immense territory to the British Empire." Quoting from *The Rise of Our East African Empire* Leonard Woolf shows us a Lugard who saw the scramble for Africa plainly in terms of "growing commercial rivalry" and claimed that "it is for our advantage"—rather than a duty—to "foster the growth of the trade of this country, and to find an outlet for our manufacturers and our surplus energy" (26-27).

Later in his book, Leonard Woolf summarizes his verdict on Lugard: "Captain Lugard invaded Uganda without any moral or legal right. He went there with the intention of acquiring for a joint-stock company [the Imperial British East Africa Company] a kingdom to which neither he nor the Company had any right. He was prepared from the first to attain his ends by war and bloodshed" (289). Here Leonard Woolf introduces a footnote, on Lugard's defense of war. Virginia Woolf, reading Lugard's voluminously detailed memoirs, in which he sought to defend his actions against his critics and an official investigation, copied out a long passage beginning with the following: "The introduction of law, order, & restraint into a savage country is necessarily accompanied at times by strong measures, involving perhaps war -...- with its attendant suffering, to many who are not the principal offenders." Lugard's attempt to defend himself by making a comparison with Gordon's bloodshed was copied out in full by Virginia Woolf. Leonard Woolf has classified the note as "Necessity of War," and this is how Lugard's point figures in his footnote: "Captain Lugard himself ... explains the necessity of war and bloodshed in such cases" (*Empire and Commerce* 289; Lugard 256).

Leonard Woolf's conclusion about Lugard is patronizing, which may account for its controversial nature: "Captain Lugard acted throughout on the highest principles and from the noblest of motives. But in confused minds, high principles and noble motives are the greatest of public dangers" (293).

Lugard looms large in *Empire and Commerce*, both in terms of his actions and his personal values. Leonard Woolf has gone to the trouble of sorting out his contentious strategy, and discusses his movements in some detail. Virginia Woolf seems to have read his long memoir with an eye to finding quotations that illustrate his imperialist attitudes. She it was who noted the point, which is included in the book (257), that Lugard was upset by French attitudes towards Germans. Leonard Woolf contextualized this by pointing out that Lugard regarded the French rather than the Germans as his main rival in Africa, and then quotes exactly what Virginia Woolf has copied out:

> I object to the mean accusations against the honour of the Germans. This sticks in my throat dreadfully. I may note that a year later, when war broke out, there were almost precisely the same innuendoes, & the Germans were, I believe, appealed to for aid, but my conception of German honour and good faith proved more correct than that of the [French, Catholic] Fathers.

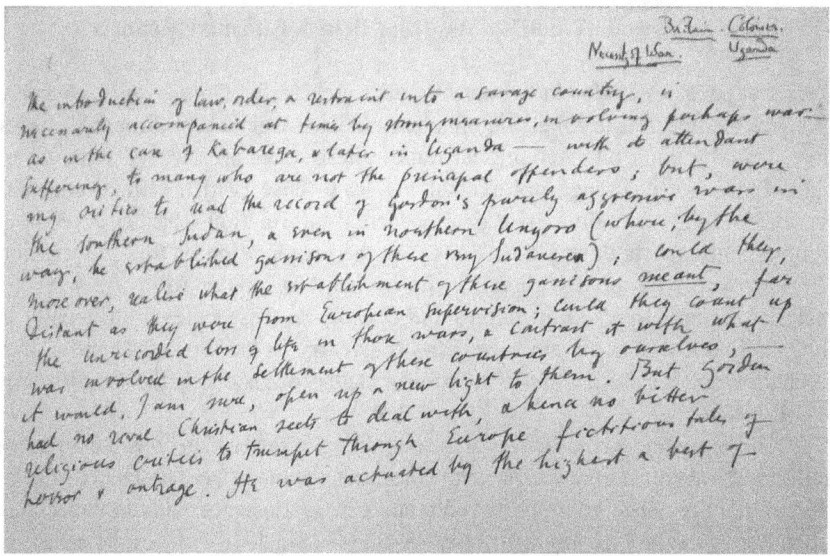

Fig. 11 Notes from Frederick Lugard, *The Rise of Our East African Empire*

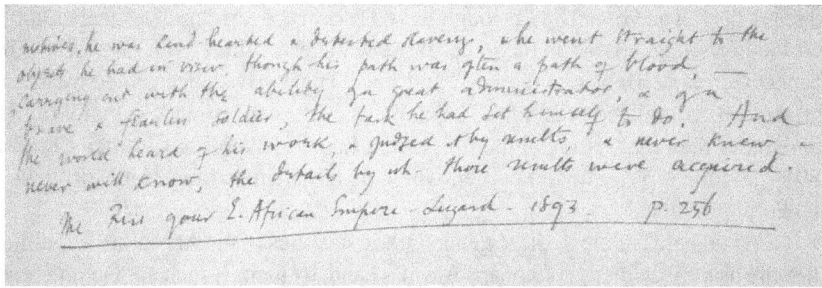

Fig. 12 Notes from Frederick Lugard, *The Rise of Our East African Empire*

These materials on imperialism in Africa provide us with evidence of a Virginia Woolf who was even more incensed by British imperialism than her publicly anti-imperialist husband. They show her familiarity with the rhetoric of imperialism and with its poor historical record. Her research on these materials was extensive, but the amount of background research that she undertook on the global economic context of imperialism in Africa in the 1890s was yet more so. This work involved not reading and making notes from discursive books on the subject, but plowing through factual reports, made by British consular officials around the world, and representing a considerable amount of quantified empirical data.

Virginia Woolf's notes from British Consular Reports

The papers included in Leonard Woolf's archive for *Empire and Commerce in Africa* include a large collection of notes made by Virginia Woolf for the broader purposes of a book on international trade. These notes are largely made up of quotations, mostly though not exclusively from these British official consular reports, and they contain a great deal of factual information—particularly about imports and exports during the 1890s. For the presentation of this information Virginia Woolf frequently copied it out by hand in tabular form. As with the materials eventually used in *Empire and Commerce* these notes are typically in longhand, although some are typed, and they carry in the top right hand corner Leonard Woolf's classification of the subject matter (occasionally this is in Virginia Woolf's hand).

The Argentine Republic was at the beginning of the British consular alphabet and Virginia Woolf started with several note cards she made from an 1893 Consular Report. All her notes are properly referenced, in this instance with an underlined Cons Rep Argentine Republic no 1147 - 1893 (see Fig.13). Many of the cards are made up simply of tables of imports or exports, a typical example being one she has headed "Return of Foreign Trade of the Argentine Republic during the years 1893 - 1891." The years 1883 through to 1891 form the left-hand vertical column and the horizontal spread is made up of percentages of trade with Great Britain, France, Germany, Belgium, the USA and Italy. The card has been ruled by hand, and the cells completed manually. The contents of the card are in Virginia Woolf's hand, other than the writing at the top, where Leonard Woolf has written "1883 - 1891," and the top right hand corner, where he has written "Argentine" followed by "Foreign Trade."

Several cards relate to these general trade statistics of the Argentine Republic. They are usually defined, in Leonard Woolf's hand, by themes such as "Commercial Treaties" or the "Foreign Trade." Other cards cover specific trading issues, and under the headings of 1889–1890, "Frozen meat," Virginia Woolf has copied out, from the 1893 Consular Report, the following prosaic details: "Another large item was 662,000 Kilos of frozen cattle. The frozen sheep export trade has developed immensely, from 12,000 carcasses in 1887 to 20,000 carcasses in 1890. Of exports under this head England took about one-fourth, & Brazil took most of the fallow, fat, preserved tongues, preserved meat, all the frozen cattle, & nearly all the frozen sheep."

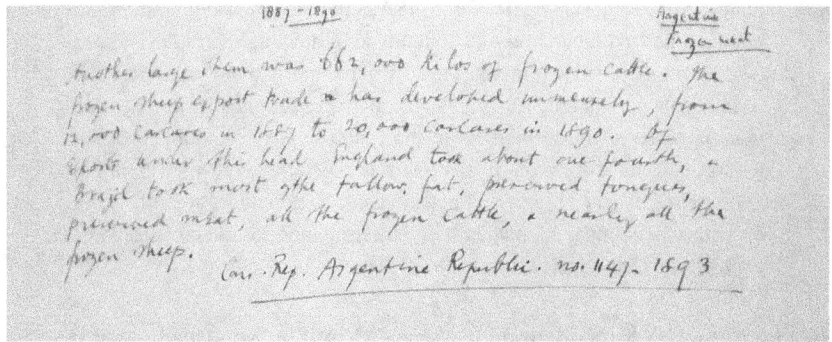

Fig. 13 Virginia Woolf: notes from British Consular Report, Argentine Republic, 1893

The Argentine Republic accounts for 13 pages of these note cards, and is followed by Austria. The 25 sides devoted to Austria are largely made up of discursive quotations in Virginia Woolf's hand, but also include a typed table (which does not appear to be her typing) and one table in her hand. Virginia Woolf has painstakingly reproduced a table of imports to Austria-Hungary, with an introductory quotation: "In order to adequately illustrate the development of the import trade of the Dual Monarchy during the past decade, the following tabular statement might be found useful..." This is taken from the 1896 Consular Report, published from Vienna. Leonard Woolf has headed it as "1895 Austria Foreign Trade."

From the report of the following year (1892, no. 1114) Virginia Woolf has copied out a lengthy summary of the situation with regard to protective tariffs, concluding that:

> a certain stability has been created, 427 items of the tariff having been 'bound', i.e. been fixed for the said period of 12 years. This gives to foreign manufacturers exporting into Austria & merchants here importing foreign goods a certain stability in their transactions, preventing any sudden increase of duty, through wh. a difficulty might at once be raised by the import, & wh. in some cases formerly almost amounted to a prohibition.

Further notes on this issue were taken, following changes in the tariffs imposed over the years. From the 1910 Consular Report Virginia Woolf documents the ongoing political issues around protection and the resumption of specific conflict with Serbia on this front:

> The difficulties placed in the way of the import of cattle from various Balkan States wh. the agrarian parties force the Austro Hungarian Governments to maintain has led these countries to retaliate by levying their highest rates of duty on merchandise in wh. the Austrian exports mainly consist. The result is that commercial rivals are in some degree supplanting the Austrian manufacturers in those markets in the South-East wh. should form the natural field for expansion of Austrian trade. After a short interruption in 1908 the tariff war with Servia began again. Negotiations are still going on with that country, Montenegro & The Argentine for the conclusion of commercial treaties (Report no 4599, 1910).[7]

From the 1908 report from "Bohemia" Virginia Woolf had noted that this tariff war with Serbia had "adversely affected the trade of the Dual Monarchy" and that "it has been estimated the textile exports from Austria-Hungary alone were diminished by 300,000L., & Iron & Ironwares by 100,000L.; the leather trade was also adversely affected, & colonial products wh. Servia formerly imported via Trieste go by another route" (Report from Austria-Hungary (Bohemia) no. 4092, 1908).

Virginia Woolf made out thirty-eight note card entries for the two countries beginning with A (Argentine and Austria-Hungary). The Bs were more complicated, containing one note on Belgium, eleven on Brazil and sixty-five sides of the notes (including seven tables) on Britain.

The British entries fell under headings from Leonard Woolf such as "commercial treaties" or "competition." A report from Turkey, no. 945, dated 1891, shows, according to Virginia Woolf's notes, that "The total trade of Great Britain, exports & imports, nearly equalled in value that of all the other great powers put together, the figures being... ." The figures were Great Britain £14,978,000, France £6,812,000, Austria & Germany £5,524,000, Russia £2,057,000 and Italy £1,113,000, making a total of £15,506,000, all duly copied out in Virginia Woolf's longhand on an unruled note card.

---

[7] Virginia Woolf, when copying from the Reports, uses the spelling "Servia," whereas Leonard Woolf uses the spelling "Serbia." These are alternative transliterations from the Cyrillic script.

EMPIRE AND COMMERCE IN AFRICA

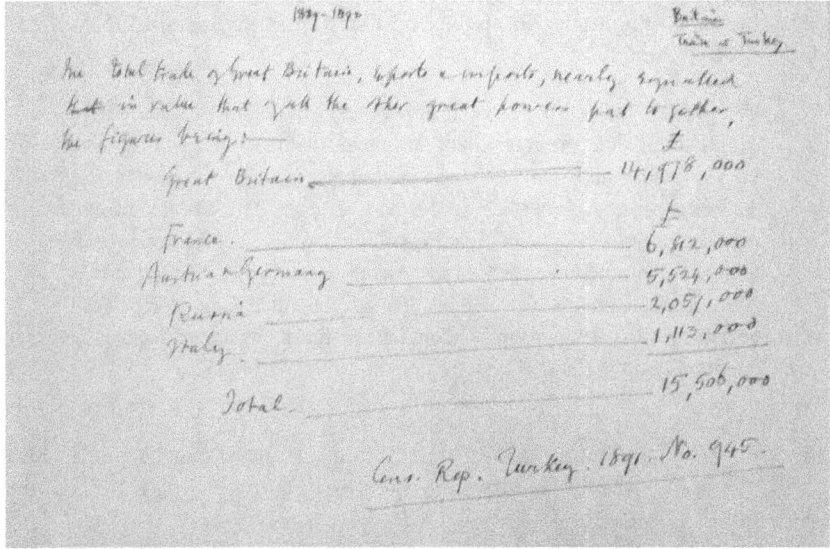

Fig. 14 Notes from British Consular Report, Turkey, 1891

Among the detailed accounts of Britain's trading situation appear some items of more general political interest. Possibly misfiled, as more at home in the notes that were incorporated into *Empire and Commerce in Africa*, are notes on the British East Africa Protectorate. Under Britain here, and subtitled by Leonard Woolf simply "Imperialism," Virginia Woolf has copied out the following passage from G. L. Beer's *The English Speaking Peoples* (1917):

> Imperialism as a political doctrine has often been represented as something tawdry & superficial. In reality it has all the depth & comprehensiveness of a religious faith. Its significance is moral even more than material. It is a mistake to think of it as principally concerned with extension of territory, with 'painting the map red'. There is quite enough painted red already. It is not a question of a couple of hundred thousand square miles more or less. It is a question of preserving the unity of a great race, of enabling it, by maintaining that unity to develop freely on its own lines, & to continue to fulfill its distinctive mission in the world. (171)

At this point in the archive, towards the end of the Bs in a sequence that will end with Zanzibar, the number of note cards that Virginia Woolf had handwritten is 115. On the material transcribed, there are no comments from the scribe, other than the choice of what she was copying. One of the reports documents presented a sharp business opportunity. From the Consular Report for Spain, 1892, no. 1055, Virginia Woolf quoted:

> Last year the Indemnity Marine Insurance co., of London, purchased for 2,000L. or 3,000L, the goodwill of the Lloyd Adaluz, a Spanish Insurance Co. in liquidation. By this purchase the English Co. hopes to monopolise the Marine Insurance business in this part of Spain. This Co. is affiliated with another small English Co., having different offices but the same agent; & here being no competition a most lucrative business is being done. In many cases the premiums which the Spaniards are quite content to pay can be underwritten at Lloyds in London, for one-fourth the amount of the premiums paid in Cadiz (Cons. Rep. Spain. 1892. No. 1055).

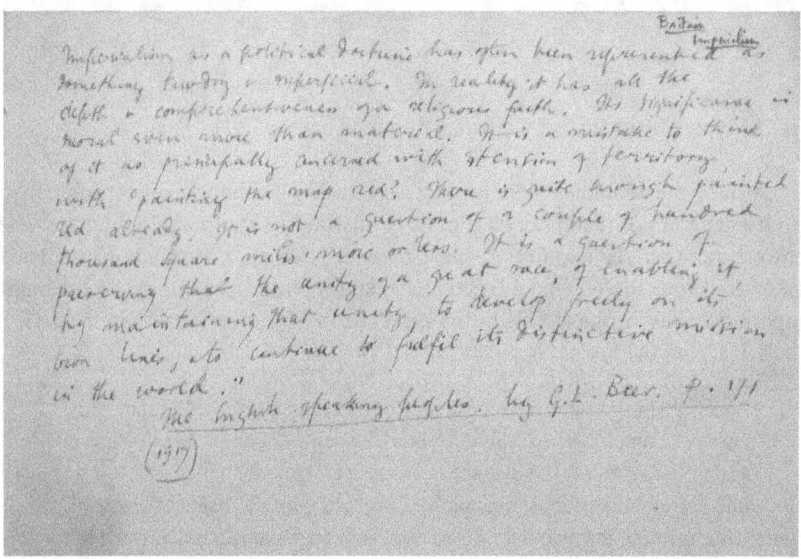

Fig. 15 Quotation from G. L. Beer *The English-speaking Peoples*

The collection runs on with notes on Bulgaria, Chile, China, "Corea," Costa Rica, Cuba, Denmark, Ecuador, Egypt and a large section of ninety-five sides of comments on France. Leonard Woolf has headed an opening page "France Trade of France for past 12 years Consular Report 1889. No 622. Important for French Colonial Policy and Statistics." General statistical information is presented here, as in another hand-drawn table by Virginia Woolf, on the "Value of French Trade with Chief Commercial Nations Exports," itemizing trade with the UK, Belgium,

Germany and the United States. Somewhat amateurishly, she has not left enough space for the far right column of 1898.

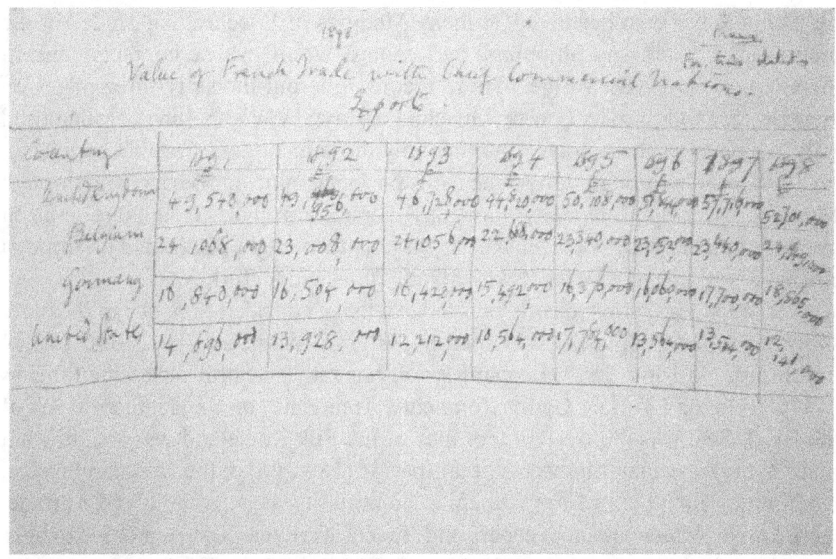

Fig. 16 Table of exports from British Consular Report, France

This table underlines the emphasis that was later to appear in *Empire and Commerce* on the last decade of the nineteenth century.

The research on France incorporates material about French Guinea, New Caledonia and Tahiti. Tahiti's imports, we learn, place the USA food-producing states of California and Oregon in the lead, followed by imports from Britain and its colonies in second place. "France occupies third rank, 12,426L., notwithstanding that her imports pay at Tahiti a duty of 10 to 15 per cent. only, as against that of 30 to 40 per cent. levied on all goods of foreign origin." Cons. Rep. France (Tahiti) No. 1931. 1897. Further quotations in the France section of the research notes point forward to Leonard Woolf's emphasis on the politics and economics of the French colonies in North Africa: much is made of conflicting trade interests as between Tunisia and Algeria and the resultant problem of smuggling: "Algeria has not only to suffer from fictive imports from Tunisia into its markets, but it has equally to support smuggled imports from foreign countries ... principally in groceries, such as sugar." Cons. Rep. France (Algiers).

A second batch of notes runs from Germany to the end of the British consular alphabet. An overview of the notes on Germany shows that though many are in Virginia Woolf's hand, others were made by Alix Sargant-Florence. On the top card of the pile in the image here, she has made a note from a text in German, which is headed in Leonard Woolf's hand "Germany Shipping subventions." Underneath that are the more typical entries made by Virginia Woolf from the Consular Reports, for example her own heading "Germany Methods of Encouraging Trade" or the note headed "Germany Shipping" by Leonard Woolf, whose contents concern the German East Africa Line.[8] These records pile on: the sixty-three pages on Germany are followed by Greece, Guatamala, Hayti [VW's spelling], Holland and Italy, which takes these notes, counting only those in Virginia Woolf's own hand, to 391 sides. On through thirty-nine cards on Japan, nine on Mexico, and through Morocco, Nicaragua, Norway, Paraguay, Persia, Portugal, "Roumania"—all in modest numbers until we reach Russia with its forty-eight pages, and on through Serbia, Siam, Spain, Sweden, Switzerland, Tunis and to Turkey.

At 46 sides, Turkey clearly merited extensive consideration, one of the more shocking reports being the one cited by Virginia Woolf as Cons. Rep. Turkey Trebizond. No 1864. 1897. Leonard Woolf has rather neutrally classified this as "1896 Trebizond Turkey Germ. Competn." Trebizond, on the southern coast of the Black Sea, was the western terminus of the Silk Route and was a significant place in the Armenian Massacres of this period (1894-96) of the Ottoman Empire, when many members of the Armenian community, heavily involved in trade, were killed. Armenian shopkeepers and traders were massacred in order to alter the balance of Muslims and non-Muslims involved in trade. This brutal episode is regarded by some as the precursor to the Armenian Massacres of the First World War period. Virginia Woolf's official source notes that "Commerce in 1896 was almost completely paralysed by the gravity of the political situation," and that "a specific review of the trade of the year wd. scarcely serve any useful purpose." However, the relative decline of British strength against Germany and Austria was a cause for great concern, it seems:

> Suffice it to say that the inhabitants plunged deeper than ever into poverty, sought cheapness, the non-Moslems going to the extent of buying the worst to lose the least, in their apprehension of possible disturbances. Competition under such conditions lost much of its keenness. British goods in particular coped with ill-success against those of Germany & Austria, especially as the latter, though intrinsically inferior, look the same & are in prices lower. Thus, slowly but surely, are we being pushed out of these markets, a fact which should make us consider how to render our position less untenable.

[8] Presumably Alix Sargant-Florence had a better command of German than Virginia Woolf as there are no notes in German from the latter in this collection, despite the fact that we know she passed examinations in German in the Kings College Ladies Department (Kenyon Jones & Snaith, 1-44).

What was she thinking as she copied this out? Virginia Woolf's references to the later Armenian massacres of the First World War in *Mrs. Dalloway* (1925) are controversial. "She cared much more for her roses than for the Armenians. Hunted out of existence, maimed, frozen, the victims of cruelty and injustice (she had heard Richard say so over and over again) – no, she could feel nothing for the Albanians, or was it the Armenians? but she loved her roses (didn't that help the Armenians?)—" (120). Trudi Tate has argued that Woolf is here satirizing and condemning Clarissa Dalloway's "preposterous" childishness and refusal of responsibility (471). However, nearer to the time of taking these notes (which are roughly in the period from late 1917 through 1918), than to the composition of *Mrs. Dalloway,* Virginia Woolf noted in her diary in May 1919 a conversation with Margaret Llewelyn Davies, Lilian Harris and Janet Case as follows: "Indeed this is a melancholy season for them all; but J has more than the usual shadows to depress her. I laughed to myself over the quantities of Armenians. How can one mind whether they number 4,000 or 4,000,000? The feat is beyond me" (*D*1 271).[9]

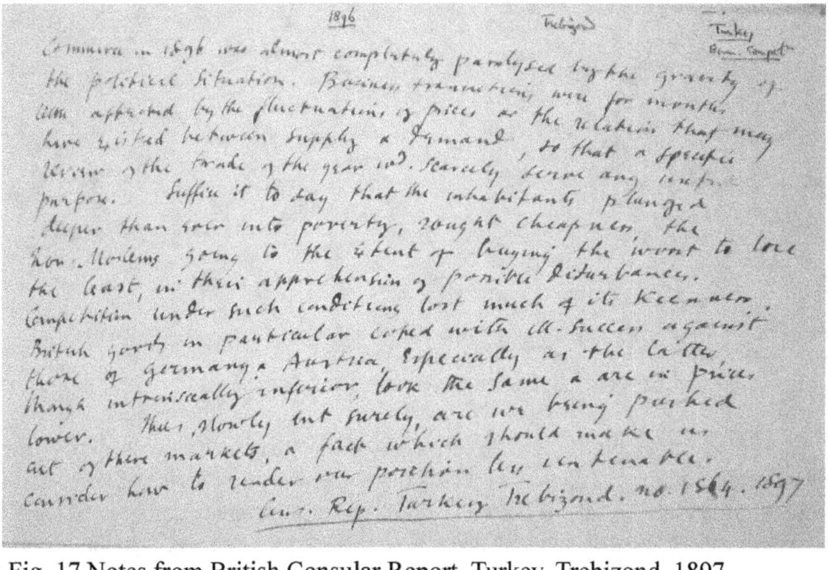

Fig. 17 Notes from British Consular Report, Turkey, Trebizond, 1897

[9] For background on the Armenian massacres see Tanner Akcam, *A Shameful Act: The Armenian Genocide and the Question of Turkish Responsibility* (London: Constable and Robinson, 2007); Vahakn N. Dadrian, *The History of the Armenian Genocide* (Providence: Berghahn Books, 1995); Donald Bloxam, *The Great Game of Genocide* (Oxford: OUP, 2005); Mark Levene, *Genocide in the Age of the Nation State* (New York: Palgrave Macmillan, 1995); Akaby Nassibian, *Britain and the Armenian Question* 1915-1923 (New York: St. Martin's Press, 1984).

The economic position for Britain was looking rather better in another area of Turkish control, this time in the southern Mediterranean. An elaborate table, taken from the (Tripoli) Consular Report of Turkey of 1898 (No 2125), ruled in blue crayon and completed in royal blue ink in Virginia Woolf's hand, shows Britain's share of the imports to Tripoli rising healthily during the period 1887 to 1897. From Turkey to Uruguay and thence to the United States, where several notes are devoted to America's acquisitions of new states, for example Hawaii and "Porto Rico".

Thence finally to Zanzibar, whose imports and exports in a tabular form were faithfully copied out by Virginia Woolf from the 1902 Consular Report.

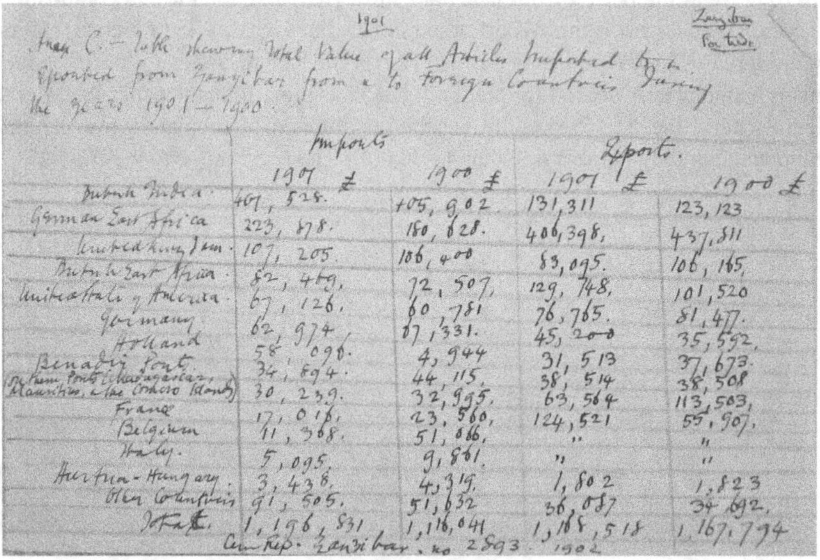

1901

Zanzibar

Table showing Total Value of all Articles Imported to & Exported from Zanzibar from & to Foreign Countries During the years 1901–1900.

	Imports 1901 £	1900 £	Exports 1901 £	1900 £
British India	401,528.	405,902.	131,311	123,123
German East Africa	223,878.	180,828.	406,398,	437,811
United Kingdom	107,205.	106,400	83,095.	106,165,
British East Africa	82,469,	72,507,	129,748,	101,520
United States of America	67,126,	60,781	76,765.	81,477.
Germany	62,974	87,331.	45,200	35,592,
Holland	58,098.	4,944	31,513	37,673.
Benadir Ports	34,894.	44,115,	38,514	38,508
Madagascar, Mauritius, & the Comoro Islands	30,239.	32,995.	63,564	113,503,
France	17,018,	23,560,	124,521	55,907,
Belgium	11,368.	51,886,	"	"
Italy.	5,095.	9,881.	"	"
Austria-Hungary.	3,438.	4,319.	1,802	1,823
Other Countries	91,505.	51,632	36,087	34,692.
Total.	1,196,831	1,116,041	1,188,518	1,167,774

Con. Rep. Zanzibar. No 2893. 1902

Fig. 18 Notes from British Consular Report, Zanzibar, 1902

The country column on the left starts with "British India" and "German East Africa," an emphasis that well concludes this immense series of notes about international trade——by this last entry on Zanzibar there are a total of 666 sides of notes in Virginia Woolf's hand, all taken from the relevant British Consular Reports. Zanzibar provides a fitting end to the series, linking all this broad contextual research on international trade with the more precise, and more political, research that Virginia Woolf undertook for Leonard Woolf's *Empire and Commerce in Africa*.

Virginia Woolf and *Empire and Commerce in Africa*

Virginia Woolf's considerable labors on this research project were not acknowledged at the time, nor subsequently. I take it for granted that she herself did not want her work to be acknowledged—as the research assistance of Alix Sargant-Florence was—in *Empire and Commerce in Africa* as published. A literary reviewer and published novelist would scarcely relish the public image of being her husband's research assistant. However, Leonard Woolf's autobiography, published in 1967, long after her death and at a better moment for candor, glosses over the assistance in saying "I wrote *Empire and Commerce in Africa* in 1918 for the Fabian Society. It is a formidable book of 374 pages and I did a great deal of intensive reading for it" (*Downhill All The Way* 83).

Later in that volume of his autobiography, Leonard Woolf suggested that after writing that book, and his *International Government*, he was treated by the Webbs as "more or less the Fabian and Labour Party 'expert' in international and imperial questions" (219). Victoria Glendinning's recent biography of Leonard Woolf goes over some of the arrangements for the book's research, and tells us that "His research was primary and his material raw. As for *International Government*, for *Empire and Commerce in Africa* Leonard embarked on a crash-course of self-education. ... Facts, uncovered with difficulty, had to be assessed and quantified" (209). She quotes from Leonard Woolf's correspondence with Marjorie Perham about Lugard, contained in the same archive box as these research notes by Virginia Woolf (436). Natania Rosenfeld, in a book on the working relationship of Leonard and Virginia Woolf, does not mention *Empire and Commerce in Africa*, although she states that in general "Virginia pays homage to what she considers Leonard's superior capacity for facts" (114).

We don't know exactly when this research was done. Kathy Phillips, in her *Virginia Woolf against Empire* (1994), relies on an editorial footnote from the first volume of Virginia Woolf's *Diary* to the effect that the work on the consular reports was done in the summer of 1917 (viii). There Virginia Woolf mentions in December 1918 that "L.'s book is almost done; February will see it finished most likely," suggesting that no more research was needed. That suggests that Virginia Woolf's involvement on the research side must have ended at some point during 1918. The *Diary* annotation does not refer to the work that was more directly undertaken for *Empire and Commerce* by Virginia Woolf, in fact the wording of the note suggests that the editorial team was not aware of it: "LW later decided to restrict his study to Africa, and Alix Sargant-Florence helped him with the research" (*D1* 229). Virginia Woolf's note to Leonard about "the notes" (quoted at the top of this paper) is dated October 29th 1917. On that occasion Leonard Woolf was away from home, giving lectures in the north of England and the fact that Virginia Woolf refers to the notes only when he was away suggests, given the volume of work that she put in on them, that this was a topic of everyday conversation for the Woolfs, accompanying them, perhaps, on their visits to the London Library or the 1917 Club.

Among the papers in the archive is a detailed list of how many words Leonard Woolf had written on the book each day, with a running total. A fascinating document, it reveals that on 23 October, 1917, he started with 313 words, writing 2001 by the 26th. By the 4th December he had completed 12,894; in 1918 he wrote steadily, getting up to 30,136 by the end of February and 40, 364 by the 16th March. (On the 12th March Virginia Woolf had commented in her diary that "lately we've written at a terrific pace: L. 40,000 words.") By the end of April he was up to 58,539, reached 100,000 at the beginning of August, and by the end of 1918 he had 148,758 words written. With a final 214 words on the 26 February, 1919, he had reached the total of 166,608 words of *Empire and Commerce*. Leonard Woolf's own diary, from which he assembled the volumes of his published autobiography, records that as well as writing at this pace he was reading as he went along; a typical entry suggests "work morn" with perhaps a library trip in the "aftn" and in the "even" "read a book on Abyssinia" or "read La Jonquiere even" (2/R/1). This reference to La Jonquière, which is one of the books that Virginia Woolf made notes from, confirms the supposition that both of them read the books that he cites in *Empire and Commerce*, albeit the quotations he used were often the ones that she had copied out.

Quentin Bell, in his biography of Virginia Woolf, refers to *Empire and Commerce in Africa* as "a book which Virginia greatly admired" (74). Hermione Lee's more recent biography comments, in discussing Virginia Woolf's attitude to her husband's work, that "her thinking was influenced by his anti-imperialism." Lee refers to a key diary entry in the terms of "she could be wifely, all the same" (339). The entry is for 7 January, 1920, a week before the publication of their books, and Virginia Woolf writes: "Reading Empire & Commerce to my genuine satisfaction, with an impartial delight in the closeness, passion, & logic of it; indeed it's a good thing now & then to read one's husbands work attentively" (*D2* 50). Knowing, as we now do, that she had spent so long contributing research to the book, casts a different light on this "impartial" delight.

Why was she doing it? The most plausible interpretation of this research assistance is that it was considered therapeutic: a useful but mindless task that would enable her to be in a world of books and information without taxing her critical or creative powers. Between 1913 and 1915 Virginia Woolf had by far her worst breakdown, and her own writing time was measured out very carefully. It has been estimated that it took her six years to write *Night and Day*. Julia Briggs, drawing on Leonard Woolf's belief that *Night and Day* had been started as early as 1913, emphasized the context in which it had been begun: "Virginia Woolf slipped into her worst breakdown ever, extending from the summer of 1913 to the autumn of 1915, and bringing her close to death and permanent imprisonment in an institution" (34). Briggs goes on to chart her recovery: by late 1915 she was allowed to resume her writing in short spells, and Briggs quotes Woolf's letter to Lytton Strachey in which she declared "I write one sentence— the clock strikes— Leonard appears with a glass of milk" (48). According to Julia Briggs, Virginia Woolf was "strictly rationed to an hour's work each day" on her novel (51), on which basis she completed the typescript in March 1919 (*D*1 259). It seems possible, indeed likely, that reading and taking factual notes for Leonard in the period from autumn 1917 onwards was construed as a form of work that was not too taxing on her brain, and could be used to fill the time when her own work was deemed too dangerous. The material provided, too, some ground on which she could practice her languages, as we have seen with both French and Italian sources.[10]

The research notes lend themselves to this interpretation, particularly in that she refrained from making summaries of arguments, or commenting on what she was reading, simply copying out passages or tables that had attracted attention. This is very different from the way in which she made notes when she was reading for herself rather than for Leonard's work, as we can see from her own reading notebooks.[11] Her own notes are alive and interactive, full of summaries and summative comments, with quotations bound into her responses to what she was reading. The scholarly apparatus of her own note-taking tends to be fairly light, and many of the publication details and other sources have been provided by Brenda Silver, her later editor. From her reading in 1918 we can take as an example the preface to the *Lyrical Ballads*: "34 Poetry. 'takes its origins from emotion recollected in tranquility'"; also on the romantics, she notes about Colvin's *Life of Keats* "This large book came out a month or two ago. It is an old-fashioned, scholarly work. I suppose irrefutable as far as the facts go…"[12]

It is possible to make a direct comparison between the notes she took as a research assistant and the notes she took for herself, by looking at some reading notes she made in April 1919 very shortly after the period she was doing the work for *Empire and Commerce*. Here, there is some overlap of subject matter, as she was

---

[10] Hermione Lee points out that her learning Italian during this period was a "therapeutic" as well as practical task (359).

[11] Virginia Woolf's reading note books are held at the University of Sussex, the Berg Collection of the New York Public Library, and the Beinecke Library at Yale University; Brenda Silver has published a very useful comprehensive record of them, including quotations, although Woolf's notes themselves are as yet unpublished.

[12] [A Writer's Diary] Holograph Notebook. November 16, 1918 – January 24, 1919, The Henry W. and Albert A. Berg Collection of English and American Literature, The New York Public Library, Astor, Lenox and Tilden Foundations.

reading Defoe's fiction and spent some time on his descriptions of Africa and of slavery in *The Life, Adventures, and Piracies of Captain Singleton*. Her notes are telegraphic: "43 Account of Central Africa – lezards [sic] and lions. The shoes they wore. Wild cats. Civet cats.", and full of reflection: "60 so literal it's hard to read, knowing it fiction – that's the difficulty – imagination won't work." "Probably a much better writer than Stevenson" she notes, before going on to record "143 The Quakers arguments against slavery," "150 William sells the negroes," "191 William the Quaker comes to life." In her plan for the piece she was writing on Defoe, for which she read many of his books, she noted that "he was a man of facts." [13]

The contrast between the pace at which Virginia Woolf was obliged to write *Night and Day* and the speed at which Leonard Woolf was able to write *Empire and Commerce* may lie behind an observation she made in her diary: "The other day L. began his book, & has already done two chapters. He's like one of those mowing machines I used to watch from my window at Asheham; round and round they go, without haste without rest, until finally the little square of corn in the middle is cut, & all is done" (*D1* 76).

Leonard and Virginia Woolf's Working Relationship

These research materials raise some complicated questions about the working relationship of the Woolfs. They are analogous to the materials that Wayne Chapman and Janet Manson discussed some twenty years ago, when they wrote about the paper Leonard Woolf published on "International Relations"— a paper whose draft in the archive is made up of "twenty-one hand-written pages in his wife's longhand" ("Carte and Tierce" 62). That work dates from 1917 and immediately precedes the research notes for *Empire and Commerce in Africa*. Was she simply acting as an amanuensis or secretary? Was it a more jointly-developed work, later to be credited only to Leonard and if so, why? Was her assistance in preparing his non-fiction some kind of pact around the decision that he would stop writing fiction?[14] The valuable work of Chapman and Manson was published in a collection

---

[13] Holograph reading notes. Vol. 3. "The Novels of Defoe," The Henry W. and Albert A. Berg Collection of English and American Literature, The New York Public Library, Astor, Lenox and Tilden Foundations.This is from the same notebook, described by Brenda Silver in *Virginia Woolf's Reading Notebooks* (Princeton: Princeton UP, 1983), p.49.

[14] Suggestion made by Clara Jones. Laura Moss Gottlieb has suggested this division of creative and political pursuits may have inspired resentment, particularly on Leonard's part: "Having given up his strictly literary efforts early in their marriage Leonard may have felt that if his wife was going to be the literary genius, he was entitled to be the sole political commentator" (242).

edited by Mark Hussey, and has since been reprinted,[15] but feminist critics of Woolf have remained relatively silent on the implications of this uncomfortable division of labor between the Woolfs.[16] Chapman and Manson used a fencing metaphor to negotiate the delicate balance between Leonard's and Virginia Woolf's contributions to the paper—*Carte* and *Tierce*, in the title of their article, refers to "attitudes of the wrist in fencing." Chapman and Manson emphasize that Leonard Woolf's position, in this paper as elsewhere, was that international law might need to be enforced, a view not shared by what they call the "hardline idealists" or pacifists—the latter view "tangibly embodied by his wife and half the conference for which they were preparing the paper" ("Carte and Tierce" 63). Chapman and Manson note that "possibly the most interesting impression to arise" from the document "is the way its logic courted her approval" ("Carte and Tierce" 73). They conclude that "Virginia Woolf's authority is inestimable." "How differently," Chapman suggests in a later article, "over the last fifty years scholars might otherwise have judged Virginia Woolf in Leonard Woolf's province!" had her contribution been acknowledged ("L.'s Dame Secretaire" 40).

The research notes for *Empire and Commerce* lend credence to the view that Virginia Woolf was an unequivocal supporter of her husband's very public stance as a leading critic of imperialism. If anything, her notes are more anti-imperialist, more tending towards the damning quotation, than the final book that he published. This sits well alongside the knowledge we have that her critical stance on imperialism in her fiction pre-dates her marriage to Leonard Woolf.[17] Furthermore, as Panthea Reid has convincingly shown, Virginia Stephen had already inherited her father's anti-colonialism, in a specifically African context, by the time of his death in 1904. Reid paints a portrait of Virginia Stephen's father, Leslie Stephen, as an outspoken opponent of colonial violence such as the British attack on Abyssinia in the 1860s. At the time of his final illness in 1903, when his youngest daughter spent a lot of time with him, he was writing lectures that were to be "his final word on colonialism." Reid concludes that "such a sense of history and of the need to reform the colonialist enterprise were thus among Stephen's last legacies to his daughter"

---

[15] *Leonard and Virginia Woolf Working Together and the Hitherto Unpublished Manuscript 'In'l Re'ns,'* ed. and intro. Wayne K. Chapman and Janet M. Manson (London: Cecil Woolf, 1997).
[16] Gina Potts does, however, cite the important work of Chapman and Manson in her essay "Woolf and the War Machine," *The Theme of Peace and War in Virginia Woolf's War Writing: Essays on her Political Philosophy*, ed. Jane Wood (Lewiston: New York: Edwin Mellen Press, 2010):39-59.
[17] See Kathy Phillips, *Virginia Woolf Against Empire* and Andrea Lewis, "The Visual Politics of Empire and Gender in Virginia Woolf's *The Voyage Out*," *Woolf Studies Annual* 1 (1996): 106-119.

(340).[18] Virginia Stephen's background in this regard has been clear since the publication of Quentin Bell's biography in 1972; discussing the life of her paternal great-grandfather Bell wrote that James Stephen "first realized the infamy of slavery when he saw how monstrously a Negro might be treated by the West Indian Courts ... he made himself a restless and consistent friend of the oppressed...he became the trusted ally of Wilberforce, whose sister he married" (3). Her grandfather, another James Stephen, sacrificed his income as a lawyer in order to work in the Colonial office, with a mission to bring about the policy of emancipation: "the protection of the negro was the grand business of his administration" (Bell, 5).

Virginia Woolf's father Leslie Stephen, in a biography of his brother James Fitzjames Stephen, published in 1895, was at pains to emphasize the role their family had played in ending the slave trade. Their father, James Stephen, had family and friends who were all "deeply engaged in the anti-slavery agitation" (*The Life of Sir James Fitzjames Stephen* 46); more than this, he had even drafted the bill himself: "The elaborate Act..., by which previous legislation against the slave trade was finally consolidated and extended was passed in 1824... It was drawn by my father and dictated by him in one day and at one sitting" (*The Life of Sir James Fitzjames Stephen* 46-47). James Stephen was also a key drafter of the legislation that abolished slavery itself, in 1833: the *Oxford Dictionary of National Biography* says of him that "after Stanley, the secretary of state, gave up the task of drafting a bill, it fell to Stephen to do so," adding that "he produced the complex bill, covering twenty-six pages, in forty-eight hours, playing the part of the perfect public servant in helping his minister to implement his policy and making an enormous contribution to its success."[19]

Virginia Stephen was thus the grand-daughter of the civil servant who had drafted the 1824 British legislation regarding the slave trade and the 1833 legislation to abolish slavery. Quentin Bell refers to James Stephen as carrying on "the great family campaign against slavery" (Bell 5). She was, naturally, aware of her family's progressive record in this respect; in 1924 a publication by Leslie Stephen appeared from "Leonard and Virginia Woolf at the Hogarth Press." Stephen's *Some Early Impressions* was introduced by a note, informing the reader that these reminiscences were written by the late Sir Leslie Stephen in 1903 (shortly before he died). Stephen

---

[18] That Virginia Stephen came from a background highly critical of colonialism complicates Susan Hudson Fox's interesting reading of *Night and Day* in which, she argues, "Woolf heaves overboard her inherited subscription to status quo British imperialism" (260).
[19] A. G. L. Shaw, "Stephen, Sir James (1789–1859)," *Oxford Dictionary of National Biography*, ed. H. C. G. Matthew and Brian Harrison (Oxford: OUP, 2004); Online edition, ed. Lawrence Goldman, Jan. 2008, 4 Feb. 2013 http://0-www.oxforddnb.com.catalogue.ulrls.lon.ac.uk/view/article/26374.

characterized his background as a family that "belonged to the second generation of the so-called "Clapham Sect," who were "men who swore by Wilberforce" (*Some Early Impressions* 14).

Virginia Stephen thus brought to her marriage an assured inherited familiarity with liberal critiques of the evils of imperialism; these attitudes were not learned from her husband. There were differences of perspective between her and her husband, which can be clearly seen in their personal papers as well as their published works. If anything, she is the more radical.[20] I have suggested elsewhere that the question of Virginia Woolf's personal political agency is a complex one, characterized by ambivalence.[21] However, on many occasions she made it clear that Leonard Woolf's political work was done on her behalf too. Much later, during the 1930s, she wrote to Ethel Smyth saying, "have just written a firm letter to resign my only office, on the ground that my husband does all that for two— or even one dozen" (*L6* 51). Similarly, she noted in her diary a moment when Leonard was discussing strategies with regard to refugees, saying, "I go in, out of courtesy. He is doing a job for me" (*D5* 205).

Virginia Woolf as Scholar

The research notes Virginia Woolf compiled for her husband throw some light on a greater interest she had in empirical information than is often supposed. Virginia Woolf the research scholar sits somewhat at odds with the view she presented of herself. She is an unreliable witness in this regard. Her own annotated Greek texts (in the Woolf library at Washington State University in Pullman) counter-indicate the image of a writer who is better known for her essay "On Not Knowing Greek." Her reading notebooks also contain examples where she has rendered the Greek in the original and attempted her own translation (Silver 155). Her own books include

---

[20] One of the most interesting is the conversation that took place on 6 January, 1918, which both recorded in their diaries, about the psychological effects of owning capital (a conversation in which Alix Sargant-Florence was a participant). Virginia Woolf records: "L. gave us a great many reasons why we should keep what we have, & do good work for nothing; I still feel, however, that my fire is too large for one person. I'm one of those who are hampered by the psychological hindrance of owning capital. Alix represented some sturdy & hardheaded economy, derived from Strachey's" (*D1* 100-101). Leonard Woolf's account of the conversation is more abrupt: "Alix and Fredegond to supper. Talked about Tolstoiism. Gerald has given up smoking because it's an indulgence. V. said we ought to give up all our capital. I said it was nonsense" (2/R/1). I noted the significance of this discussion my introduction to the 1979 collection of Woolf's essays *Virginia Woolf On Women & Writing* (London: The Women's Press, 1979), pp.16-17.
[21] See "Introduction," *A Room of One's Own/ Three Guineas* ed. Michèle Barrett (London: Penguin, 2000).

Her own books include many works that are ambitious for the age at which we know she read them—Macaulay's substantial volumes of English history, for example. [22] Similarly, Woolf made a great play of being merely self-educated, on which topic people used to exclaim at what a privileged form of self-education she had, given the run of Leslie Stephen's library and reading most ambitiously as a teenager. It transpires, we now know from the work of Anna Snaith and Christine Kenyon Jones, that from the age of fifteen she took courses in English and continental history, beginning and advanced Greek, intermediate Latin and German grammar in the Ladies Department of King's College London during the period 1897-1901. Like most people of her class at the time, she had some knowledge of French and, as we saw in the illustrations, was attempting to learn Italian at the time of this research. She was also involved in translations from Russian.[23]

Woolf's attitude towards "research" was somewhat contradictory: she was amused when readers sought to correct factual errors in her fiction; on the other hand she was adamant that *Three Guineas* rested on "getting up the facts," facts which figure in pseudo-academic footnotes in that text. To Vita Sackville-West she wrote "I took more pains to get up the facts and state them plainly than I ever took with any thing in my life" (*L6* 243), and to Ethel Smyth she said that she had put them at the end of the book rather than at the foot of the page "thinking people might read them, the most meaty part of the book, separately" (*L6* 235). To Smyth she added that "I had a mass more and still have. Yes—very hard work that was."

We already know (not least from the pastiche in *A Room of One's Own*) that Virginia Woolf was familiar with working in the reading room at the British Museum, and that she visited the London Library on a regular basis. The research notes for *Empire and Commerce* show that she had the London School of Economics library at her disposal, and that she was a dab hand at gutting British Consular Reports as well as plowing through weighty tomes such as Lugard, Wylde or McDermot's books. The notes themselves, as I indicated in running through them, demonstrate a pleasure in bibliographic referencing and in footnoting conventions. Virginia Woolf as a researcher and scholar is inimical to the reputation she and at times her estate[24] have cherished of her as a writer of genius, but it is nonetheless

---

[22] Library of Virginia and Leonard Woolf, Washington State University, Pullman, http://ntserver1.wsulibs.wsu.edu/masc/onlinebooks/woolflibrary/woolflibraryonline.htm.

[23] Rebecca Beasley, "On Not Knowing Russian: The Translations of Virginia Woolf and S.S. Kotelianskii."*Modern Language Review* 108 (2013): 1-29.

[24] In the late 1970s, when I was editing *Virginia Woolf: Women and Writing*, Virginia Woolf's literary estate was controlled by the Hogarth Press and, although Quentin and Olivier Bell were very supportive of the project (as the Society of Authors now supports critical scholarship), there was much discussion about how Woolf's non-fictional ideas were to be presented. D J Enright, representing the press, refused to allow the word "theory" to be attached to Virginia Woolf's perspective on literature.

an element that played an important part in her fiction. Katharine Hilbery, in *Night and Day*, is usually referred to as modeled on Vanessa Bell, but perhaps there is something of her author in her "love of facts" (201). As we saw from the reviews of *Empire and Commerce*, "the stern facts, supported by chapter and verse, speak for themselves" and were more illuminating "than any rhetoric would be" [I/L/6].

The subject of imperialism is one that Woolf scholars and critics have recently explored in some depth, often through a post-colonial reading of key texts. To the early influential studies by Jane Marcus and Kathy Phillips have now been added a range of analyses of Woolf's fiction.[25] Attempts have also been made to situate Leonard Woolf's writing in relation to concerns about his work as a colonial administrator and the fiction he wrote drawing on that experience.[26] More general

---

[25] Both Jane Marcus and Kathy Phillips read Virginia Woolf texts to demonstrate an anti-imperialist political agenda. Jane Marcus's "Britannia Rules *The Waves*," first published in 1992 and reprinted in *Hearts of Darkness* (New Brunswick NJ,: Rutgers UP, 2004) was a key influence on these. Kathy Phillips's *Virginia Woolf Against Empire* (1994) sought to show that Virginia Woolf's critical attitude to imperialism, evident in *The Voyage Out*, predated her marriage to Leonard Woolf. Subsequent contributions include David Adams, *Colonial Odysseys: Empire and Epic in the Modernist Novel* (Ithaca: Cornell UP, 2003); Marianne DeKoven, *Rich and Strange: Gender, History, Modernism* (Princeton: Princeton UP, 1991) and June Harwood, "Bloomsbury and the Literature of Empire: Virginia Woolf and Her Voyage Out," *Virginia Woolf Bulletin* 17 (September 2004): 27-34 on *The Voyage Out*; Adam Barrows, "'The Shortcomings of Timetables': Greenwich, Modernism, and the Limits of Modernity," *Modern Fiction Studies* 56.2 (Summer 2010): 262-289; Scott Cohen, "The Empire from the Street: Virginia Woolf, Wembley, and Imperial Monuments," *Modern Fiction Studies* 50.1 (Spring 2004): 85-110; and Nicholas Crawford, "Orientalizing Elizabeth: Empire and Deviancy in *Mrs Dalloway*," *Virginia Woolf Miscellany* 70 (Fall 2006): 20 on *Mrs Dalloway*; Sara Gerend, "Ghosts of Empire in Virginia Woolf's *To The Lighthouse* and Elizabeth Bowen's *The Last September*," *Virginia Woolf: Art, Education and Internationalism*, eds., Diana Royer and Madelyn Detloff, (Clemson: Clemson UP: 1997): 51-56, and Jeanette McVicker "Vast Nests of Chinese Boxes, or getting from Q to R: Critiquing Empire in 'Kew Gardens' and *To the Lighthouse,*" *Virginia Woolf Miscellanies: Proceedings of the First Annual Conference on Virginia Woolf*, eds. Mark Hussey and Vara Neverow-Turk (New York: Pace UP, 1992): 40 – 42; Urmila Seshagiri, "Orienting Virginia Woolf: Race, Aesthetics, and Politics in *To the Lighthouse*," *Modern Fiction Studies* 50.1 (Spring 2004): 58- 85 and James F. Wurtz, "I have had my vision:" Empire and the Aesthetic in Woolf's *To the Lighthouse*," *Woolf Studies Annual* 16 (2010): 95-110 on *To The Lighthouse*; Laura Doyle, "Sublime Barbarians in the Narrative of Empire: or, Longinus at Sea in *The Waves*," *Modern Fiction Studies* 42.2 (Summer: 1996): 323-47; and Christie Purifoy, "Melancholic Patriotism and *The Waves*," *Twentieth Century Literature* 56. 1 (Spring 2010): 25-46 on *The Waves*; and Ann E Harris, "Scraps and Fragments of Empire: The Pageant as Metaphor in Woolf and Walcott," *Virginia Woolf: Texts and Contexts*, eds., Beth Rigel Daugherty and Eileen Barrett (New York: Pace UP, 1996): 210-215 on *Between the Acts*.

[26] See Elleke Boehmer "Immeasurable Strangeness in Imperial Times: Leonard Woolf and W. B. Yeats," in *Modernism and Empire*, eds. Howard J. Booth and Nigel Rigby (Manchester: Manchester U P, 2000); Lilamani Chandra De Silva, "'Imperialist discourse': Critical Limits

considerations of Virginia Woolf and empire can be found in excellent essays by Helen Carr and Anna Snaith.[27]

Leonard Woolf's *Empire and Commerce in Africa* was published on January 14, 1920, the same day as the second printing of Woolf's second novel, *Night and Day*, which was published in London in October 1919. That work has often been seen as somewhat apolitical, although Julia Briggs noted its allusions to Conrad's *Heart of Darkness* (51). Re-reading it now in the light of the research project that accompanied the writing of it is instructive. It is peppered throughout with references to imperial questions, and Fox gives examples of some of the imperial topics aired at teatime conversation at the Hilberys (262). References abound: to Galton on race (*ND* 36) to relatives "from India" (39), to "the plains of India (49), to emigration to the colonies (72), and "living with savages" (72). Mary Datchet finds herself in the Assyrian galleries at the British Museum and "conjured up a scene of herself on a camel's back, in the desert, while Ralph commanded a whole tribe of natives" (83). We are told about Uncle John bringing back his manservant from India, the ladies of Melbury House with their "monkey and the little black dwarf" (116) and Queenie Colquhoun, who "took her coffin out with her to Jamaica" as "you couldn't get coffins in Jamaica" (117). Ralph's sister Joan "suspected the East" and feared to see her brother "toiling through sandy deserts under a tropical sun" (126).

Night and Day gives us a description of a suffrage campaign office, "at the top of one of the large Russell Square houses" that, we are told are now "let out in slices to a number of societies which displayed assorted initials upon doors of ground glass, and kept, each of them, a typewriter which clicked busily all day long" (79). The typewriters, as Mary Datchet goes to her office at the top, were "already at work, disseminating their views upon the protection of native races, or the value of cereals as foodstuffs" (79-80). Woolf's treatment of these diverse political activities, in the words of Katharine Hilbery, is distinctly unimpressed: "On the ground floor you protect natives, on the next you emigrate women and tell people to eat nuts" (88).

These research notes elaborate the evidence about the damage done by economic imperialism, and also reveal a feel for the language in which imperial sentiment was articulated, and both of these clearly contributed to her own writing. They point to a writer who had at her disposal a multitude of facts and critical political opinions, but who sought to incorporate these social materials in a way that subordinated them to literary means of representation. Virginia Woolf's familiarity

---

of Liberalism in Selected Texts of Leonard Woolf and E. M. Forster," Diss. University of North Texas, 1991; Yasmine Gooneratne "Leonard Woolf in Ceylon," *Journal of Commonwealth Literature* 39.3 (September 2004): 1-3.

[27] Carr, Helen. "Virginia Woolf, Empire and Race." *The Cambridge Companion to Virginia*

with the discourse of the economic can be seen in the way, recording an evening with their friend Maynard Keynes, she rattles off an account of his conversation on an aspect of international trade. He was "very fertile" on that occasion, and she gives an easy rendition of Keynes's style of talking about German politics; but her mind is not on the subject at hand, she is thinking about her own literary preoccupation:

> They're doing something very queer with their money. I cant make out what. It may be the Jews are taking away their capital. Let me see, if 2000 Jews were each to take away £2,000 -- Anyhow they cant pay their Lancashire bill. Always the Germans have bought cotton from Egypt, had it spun in Lancashire: its a small bill, only ½ a million, but they cant pay. Yet theyre buying copper all the time. Whats it for? Armaments no doubt. That's one of the classic examples of intn trade – Now Holden has been over & says we wont go in. 20,000 people out of work. But of course there's something behind it. What is the cause of the financial crisis? Theyre doing something foolish – no Treasury control of the soldiers.

Woolf continues "(but I am thinking all the time of what is to end Here & Now. I want a Chorus. a general statement. a song for 4 voices. how am I to get it? I am now almost within sight of the end. racing along: becoming more & more dramatic. And how to make the transition from the colloquial to the lyrical, from the particular to the general?)" (*D4* 235-236). And so it is more generally, perhaps, with these research materials on imperialism in Africa, and the global economic context of the 1890s: they sit in the background, informing her work as a writer of fiction.

Woolf, 2nd ed. ed., Susan Sellers (Cambridge: Cambridge UP, 2010): 197-213; Anna Snaith, *"The Exhibition is in Ruins"*: *Virginia Woolf and Empire* (Southport: Virginia Woolf Society of Great Britain, 2005).

My thanks to the University of Sussex and the Society of Authors as the literary representative of the Estate of Leonard Woolf for permission to quote unpublished material in this article. I am grateful to The Henry W. and Albert A. Berg Collection of English and American Literature, The New York Public Library, Astor, Lenox and Tilden Foundations for permission to quote unpublished material by Virginia Woolf. Thanks also to Nadia Atia and Clara Jones for research and editorial assistance, to Gilly Furse for technical assistance and arrangements for a trip to Pullman WA (home of the Woolfs' library). Thanks to Ellen Ross and Dick Glendon for putting me up during my visit to Woolf's reading notebooks at the Berg Collection in New York. I am grateful to Fiona Courage for giving permission from Sussex, and to Rose Lock at the Sussex University Library Special Collections for her unfailing helpfulness. Thanks also to Brenda Silver. This paper developed from research originally undertaken to speak on Virginia Woolf's "Thoughts on Peace in an Air Raid" at a conference on "Shock and Awe: A Hundred Years of Aerial Bombardment," held in London in 2011 and I am grateful to Paul Gilroy and Les Back for that initial invitation.

Works Cited

Bell, Quentin. *Virginia Woolf: A Biography*. London: Hogarth Press, 1972. Print.

Briggs, Julia. *Virginia Woolf: An Inner Life*. London: Allen Lane, 2005. Print.

Carr, Helen. "Virginia Woolf, Empire and Race." *The Cambridge Companion to Virginia Woolf*. Ed. Susan Sellers. 2nd ed. Cambridge: Cambridge UP, 2010: 197-213. Print.

Chapman, Wayne. "L.'s Dame Secretaire": Alix Strachey, the Hogarth Press and Bloomsbury Pacifism." *Women in the Milieu of Leonard and Virginia Woolf*. Eds. Wayne K. Chapman and Janet M. Mason. New York: Pace UP, 1998. Print.

Chapman, Wayne K. and Manson, Janet M. "Carte and Tierce: Leonard, Virginia Woolf, and War for Peace." *Virginia Woolf and War: Fiction, Reality and Myth*. Ed. Mark Hussey. New York: Syracuse UP, 1991. Print.

——. *Leonard and Virginia Woolf Working Together and the Hitherto Unpublished Manuscript 'In'l Re'ns.'* Ed. and Intro. Wayne K. Chapman and Janet M. Manson. London: Cecil Woolf, 1997. Print.

Crispi, Francesco. *The Memoirs of Francesco Crispi, Volume III*. Trans. Mary Pritchard-Agnetti. London: Hodder and Stoughton, 1912. Print.

Darcy, Jean. *France et Angleterre: Cent Années de Rivalité Coloniale: L'Afrique*. Perrin & Cie: Paris, 1904. Print.

Glendinning, Victoria. *Leonard Woolf*. London: Simon and Schuster, 2006. Print.
Gottlieb, Laura Moss. "The War between the Woolfs." *Virginia Woolf and Bloomsbury: A Centenary Celebration*. Ed. Jane Marcus. Basingstoke: Macmillan, 1987. Print.
Greene, Graham. *Journey Without Maps*. London: Penguin, 1981. Print.
Hochschild, Adam. *King Leopold's Ghost: A Story of Greed, Terror and Heroism in Colonial Africa*. London: Pan, 2000. Print.
Hudson Fox, Susan. "Woolf's Austen/Boston Tea Party: The Revolt Against Literary Empire in *Night and Day*." *Virginia Woolf: Emerging Perspectives*. Eds. Mark Hussey, Vara Neverow and Jane Lilienfield. New York: Pace UP, 1994. 259-665. Print.
Kenyon Jones, Christine and Anna Snaith. "'Tilting at Universities': Woolf at King's College London." *Woolf Studies Annual* 16 (2010): 1-44. Print.
Lee, Hermione. *Virginia Woolf*. London: Chatto and Windus, 1996. Print.
Manson, Janet M. "Margery Perham, the Fabians, and Colonial Policy." *Women in the Milieu of Leonard and Virginia Woolf*. Eds. Wayne K. Chapman and Janet M. Manson. New York: Pace UP, 1998. Print.
McVicker, Jeanette. "Vast Nests of Chinese Boxes, or getting from Q to R: Critiquing Empire in 'Kew Gardens' and *To the Lighthouse*." *Virginia Woolf Miscellanies: Proceedings of the First Annual Conference on Virginia Woolf*. Eds. Mark Hussey and Vara Neverow-Turk. New York: Pace UP, 1992. 40-42. Print.
Phillips, Kathy J. *Virginia Woolf Against Empire*. Knoxville: U of Tennessee P, 1994. Print.
Reid, Panthea. "Virginia Woolf, Leslie Stephen, Julia Margaret Cameron, and the Prince of Abyssinia: An Inquiry into Certain Colonialist Representations." *Biography* 22.3 (Summer 1999): 322-356. Print.
Rosenfeld, Natania. *Outsiders Together: Virginia and Leonard Woolf*. Princeton: Princeton UP, 2000. Print.
Silver, Brenda. *Virginia Woolf's Reading Notebooks*. Princeton: Princeton UP, 1983. Print.
Snaith, Anna. *"The Exhibition is in Ruins": Virginia Woolf and Empire*. Southport: Virginia Woolf Society of Great Britain, 2005. Print.
Stephen, Leslie. *The Life of Sir James Fitzjames Stephen*. London: Smith, Elder & Co., 1895. Print.
——. *Some Early Impressions*. London: Hogarth Press, 1924. Print.
Tate, Trudi. "Mrs Dalloway and the Armenian Question." *Textual Practice* 8:3 (Winter 1994): 467- 486. Print.
Woolf, Leonard. *Downhill All The Way: An Autobiography of the Years 1919-1939*. London: Hogarth Press, 1967. Print.

———. *Empire and Commerce in Africa: A Study of Economic Imperialism*. London: Labour Research Department, 1920. Print.
Woolf, Virginia. *A Passionate Apprentice: The Early Journals 1897-1909*. Ed. Mitchell A. Leaska. New York: Harcourt Brace Jovanovich, 1990. Print.
———. *A Room of One's Own/ Three Guineas*. Ed. Michèle Barrett. London: Penguin, 2000. Print.
———. *The Diary of Virginia Woolf Volume One* 1915-19. Ed. Anne Olivier Bell. London: Hogarth Press, 1977. Print.
———. *The Diary of Virginia Woolf Volume Four* 1931-1935. Ed. Anne Olivier Bell. New York: Harcourt Brace Jovanovich, 1982. Print.
———. *The Diary of Virginia Woolf Volume Five* 1936 -1941. Ed. Anne Olivier Bell. New York: Harcourt Brace Jovanovich, 1984. Print.
———. *Mrs Dalloway*. San Diego: Harvest/Harcourt Brace Jovanovich Inc., 1981. Print.
———. *Night and Day*. New York: Harvest/Harcourt Brace Jovanovich Inc., 1973. Print.
———. *The Letters of Virginia Woolf Volume Two, 1911-1922*. Eds. Nigel Nicolson and Joanne Trautmann. London: Hogarth Press, 1976. Print.
———. *The Letters of Virginia Woolf Volume Six*, 1936-1941. Eds. Nigel Nicolson and Joanne Trautmann. London: Hogarth Press, 1980. Print.
———. *The Waves*. New York: Harvest/Harcourt Brace Jovanovich Inc., 1959. Print.

The Unwitting Anarchism of *Mrs. Dalloway*
John McGuigan

"I'll give it you!" yells Septimus Warren Smith as he leaps to impale himself in one of *Mrs. Dalloway*'s climactic scenes. But to whom exactly is he talking? And what exactly is this "it" he proposes to give? He talks most directly to the approaching Dr. Holmes, the "brute with blood-red nostrils" ever "on him," and by jumping from the window he gives, most immediately, his life. But beyond the literal answers[1] lie others that affect how we read the novel politically, answers that affect how we think of Virginia Woolf politically. The shell-shocked veteran's decision to "throw it all away," as Clarissa Dalloway later describes it, is neither an act of despair on Septimus's part, nor an act of psychosis. It is instead a defiant cry against institutional society, an assertion of free will when faced with the prospect of having none. Septimus attempts to preserve self-governance, to claim the sanctity of the individual and his or her right to determine how to pursue his or her self-interest. What makes the nature of his cry somewhat startling, however, is that by showing this self-determination to be ceaselessly thwarted and corrupted by institutions, and by showing it to be continually renegotiated in the communal web of everyday existence, *Mrs. Dalloway* displays a persistent infusion with the philosophy of nineteenth-century anarchism.

That this anarchism be "unwitting," as this essay claims, seems unlikely in someone who observes herself and society as sharply as Woolf. Though politically astute, Woolf never mentions anarchism or anarchist thinkers in her writing. Lucio Ruotolo has noted that despite her admiration for Tolstoy, anarchism never appears in her writing on him; neither does anarchist philosopher Peter Kropotkin, though her father Leslie Stephen once wrote a public letter in his support (231, 253).[2] But considering the status of "anarchism" in the 1920s may offer some explanation. In the popular imagination, the term by this time was well-wrapped with connotations of random, senseless violence. Anarchism as political practice, as the actions and words of those who labeled themselves "anarchists," had drifted a great deal from its nineteenth-century philosophical roots. Thus what many of Woolf's day considered "anarchism" was, at best, a narrow fringe of anarchist thought. Woolf thought of

---

[1] Of course the phrase itself isn't literal; as Deborah Guth notes, it is a "coarser form of 'I'll just show you'" ("Rituals" 37). But the questions remain: to whom is Septimus talking? What is he trying to prove to them?

[2] In general, Ruotolo is one of the very few critics to work with anarchism and Woolf, but his work doesn't often get beyond its suggestive assertions.

her own political beliefs under various terms, yet the specific perception and valuation of the world promoted in *Mrs. Dalloway* is closely akin to classical anarchism.

When writing *Mrs. Dalloway*, Woolf did not feel her challenging ideas could be properly expressed in the dominant narrative aesthetics of the time—the realist novel. She describes her belief in building new forms from new ideas in her 1928 introduction to the Modern Library edition of the novel. In it she answers critical speculation that the novel's unique aesthetic grew merely from her dissatisfaction with the current styles:

> Dissatisfied the author may have been; but her dissatisfaction was primarily with nature for giving an idea, without providing a house for it to live in. The novelists of the preceding generation had done little—after all why should they?—to help. The novel was the obvious lodging, but the novel it seemed was built on the wrong plan. Thus rebuked, the idea started as the oyster starts or the snail to secrete a house for itself. (*E4* 550)

Though her diary notes indicate that with *Mrs. Dalloway* she wanted to "criticise the social system, & to show it at work, at its most intense" (*D2* 248), Woolf did not explicitly identify the "idea" animating *Mrs. Dalloway* to be anarchism—she does not identify the idea at all—nor do any of the novel's characters explicitly pursue or promote anarchist political activity, though Clarissa, Sally, and Peter all held radical socialist opinions as young adults. But if we cannot find a clear label at the novel's origin, the novel itself—the "house" the idea "secretes"—will suggest the contours of her idea. And strange as it may seem, the idea will be revealed not through political thought, fact, or concept, but by amorphous "feeling." Such, for Woolf, is the foundation of political critique.

Her somewhat obscure 1921 essay "Revolution" suggests an origin for this privileging of feeling. In it, Woolf argues that revolution is indeed an appropriate topic for the novel, but, and here the argument becomes counterintuitive, only if the revolution is long past (*E3* 279). Her reason: the novel privileges feelings over facts. The test of a novel, she proposes, is whether the feelings are accurate, for in a surprising reversal of the objective and subjective, she notes that the so-called "facts" of a revolution will inevitably be the subject of dispute—"they set on to arguing"—while the remembered feeling of those present will be the "fact" with a measure of consistency, "because we feel human beings are too important to be disregarded" (280). Participants argue about who did what, and when, but tend to be uniform in describing the spirit of a time or a historic event. Tracing such unity of "feeling" in *Mrs. Dalloway* points to the anarchist import of the novel, both in terms of its content and its aesthetic nature. As we will see, *Mrs. Dalloway*'s "ideas"—especially (1) the "feelings" privileged by the novel, (2) the analyses of those feelings as they are distorted by the "social system . . . at work," and (3) the relationships offered in the social system's stead—are most accurately seen as anarchist grains of sand around which the modernist pearl of Woolf's aesthetic develops.[3]

Anarchism

Historically, "anarchism" has always been an unwieldy term, in part because the image of crazed, bomb-throwing assassins has stuck to it so well. Even today, "anarchy" in the vernacular serves as shorthand for chaos and senseless violence. The same was true a hundred years ago, as Woolf's Bloomsbury acquaintance Bertrand Russell noted in 1918: "In the popular mind an Anarchist is a person who throws bombs and commits other outrages, either because he is more or less insane, or because he uses the pretence of extreme political opinions as a cloak for criminal proclivities" (49). But the popular image misrepresents anarchism's relationship to destruction, which when proposed—and it was not universally embraced—was not a chance to revel in violence or embrace the inner savage, but instead a chance to "clean the slate" so to speak. Rid of institutions and their corrosive influence, humanity could reorganize itself through the natural development of cooperative, equitable social relations. Anarchism as a political philosophy privileges individual rights and autonomy, but only in the service of communal harmony—relationships among people and groups are characterized by "non domination." Though often mischaracterized as extremely egotistical and prone to violence and sowing chaos, individualism in the anarchist context is emphasized as the best means to promote mutual respect and harmonious relationships, and thus to cultivate the natural human propensity toward "mutual aid."[4]

Three fundamental beliefs characterize anarchism and, when taken together, distinguish it from other political philosophies of the time. First is the priority of individual autonomy and the primacy of individual rights over the rights of groups

---

[3] In concluding his excellent chapter on the novel, Alex Zwerdling, too, evokes the idea of feeling, if the latter is thought of somewhat differently: "Woolf is not only fulfilling her ambition 'to criticise the social system, and to show it at work, at its most intense,' but also contributing indirectly to its replacement by one less hostile to the burden of feeling in every human being. She knew that even the most fundamental institutions and forms of behavior could be altered" (143). For Zwerdling, *Mrs. Dalloway* is a complex analysis of the British "governing class," whose time and stifling regimen of emotional "self-control" was near its end.

[4] Ruotolo notes this propensity in Woolf's later work, finding, "in each case the goal is not chaos but mutuality, the effort to reconstitute social intercourse on more communal grounds" (8).

in which the individual does not freely participate. The final qualification is an important one—anarchism is popularly misunderstood as promoting the *absolute* right of the individual to pursue any desire or whim no matter the consequence, regardless of the individual's rationale or the action's effects. While some anarchist thinkers take individual rights to greater lengths than others (Max Stirner and Benjamin Tucker, most notably), most are very clear that these rights are tempered by social context.[5] The potential effects on collective wellbeing dictate individual behavior and, by extension, shape codes of ethics and morality. In fact, the more one reads of anarchist philosophy, the more one finds it *limits* the range of activities, because paramount is the idea that the individual is entirely responsible for the consequences of her actions. She alone must think through the likely consequences of what she does and determine whether it respects or diminishes the autonomy of others.

Though an individual must self-monitor and direct his actions' effect on the collective, the power is not reversible: the collective cannot force its will on the individual against the individual's will. This belief anchors anarchism's second distinct characteristic, its unyielding critique of institutions. They are criticized as irredeemably corrupting, largely because by definition they impose the will of those who run them on the individuals who live under them, regardless of those individuals' desires, interests, or needs. Mikhail Bakunin, though an influential power in the early International Workingmen's Association with Karl Marx, saw Marx eventually label him a threat and engineer his ouster. Central to their conflict was Bakunin's anarchist belief that institutions were irredeemable. Bakunin attacked Marx and his followers for ignoring what we can think of as the inverted Midas touch of institutions: they corrupt whatever they touch, regardless of the intentions behind their creation or the morality of their actors. For instance, when describing the requisite qualities one must have to join the "international family" of anarchists, Bakunin writes:

> He must understand that the advent of liberty is incompatible with the existence of *States*. He must therefore desire the overthrow of all States and at the same time of all religious, political and social institutions, such as official Churches, standing armies, centralized ministries, bureaucracy, governments, unitary parliaments and State universities and banks, as well as aristocratic and bourgeois monopolies. All this, so that a free human society may arise upon the ruins, no longer organized, as it is today, from high to low and from centre to circumference by means of enforced unity

---

[5] Only Stirner denies the rights and claims of others, and for some scholars that means, categorically, he cannot be considered an anarchist. See Paterson, 126-45.

> high to low and from centre to circumference by means of enforced unity and concentration, but starting with the free individual, the free association and the autonomous commune, from low to high and from circumference to centre, by means of free federation. (88)

This marks an important distinction from all other political philosophies of the time, whether the mainstream capitalism of Britain or the "radical" philosophies of fascism or Communist socialism. In each of those, the State and its attendant institutions are effective means to an end, whether the end be the proper functioning of markets, the strength and purity of the "nation," or the "communism" of a classless society to come. Anarchists argued that no matter the ends of an institution, no matter the quality of person functioning within an institution, the end result will be the same: impersonal institutional will asserts itself at the price of individual autonomy. Institutions, by their very nature, operate according to their own logic, with their own set of priorities, and therefore with their own set of ethics. To the anarchist, the ethics of institutionality can never exist in harmony with an ethics of "mutuality," where free individuals live harmoniously in "free federation" of their own design.

The third defining characteristic of anarchism is the idea that people are fundamentally cooperative social animals. Peter Kropotkin, in particular, makes the case in late nineteenth-century scientific, evolutionary terms. He argues that by focusing on "survival of the fittest" and seeing evolution defined by individual competition and struggle, Herbert Spencer misses half the equation: "in the ethical progress of man, mutual support—not mutual struggle—has had the leading part" (127). Kropotkin claims that looking at animal and human history reveals that those species and societies that prospered were not those based on lone-wolf individualism. Rather, where groups of animals or people recognized their mutual interests and acted in accordance with mutual interests, those species and societies thrived. Critical of Rousseau-inspired primitivism, he argues,

> The savage is not an ideal of virtue, nor is he an ideal of "savagery." But the primitive man has one quality, elaborated and maintained by the very necessities of his hard struggle for life—he identifies his own existence with that of his tribe; and without that quality mankind never would have attained the level it has attained now. (44)

So while laissez-faire capitalism and fascism promoted "mutual struggle" as a means to advance human society, anarchists (with socialists) argued that mutual cooperation was the means to human advancement.[6]

Of ways the ideas of anarchism could reach and influence Woolf's thought, one surprising but likely source is Bertrand Russell. While in prison as a conscientious objector—most anarchists remained pacifists during World War I, regarding it as entirely the purview of the State and the business world—Russell penned *Roads To Freedom* (1918), in which he notes, "Anarchism . . . remains an ideal to which we should wish to approach as nearly as possible, and which, in some distant age, we hope may be reached completely" (209). Though he refuses to describe himself as an anarchist, Russell's book nonetheless strikes the keynotes of anarchism and extends the ideas to other realms of British life. Though Woolf writes very little of Russell, she always refers to him in the familiar, as when she notes in a letter of 23 January, 1916, "Bertie. . . thinks he's going to found new civilizations" (qtd. in Froula xi). [7]

Russell never describes how he'll "found new civilizations"; Anarchist thinkers typically refused to offer prescriptions for reaching their utopian ends—or even to develop significant descriptions of the utopia they envisioned. To put an idea into a form of mass action was to risk institutionalizing it. Perhaps in response to allegations of being naïve daydreamers—the allegation this refusal to plan usually provoked—Russell distances himself from this position early on: "my own opinion—which I may as well indicate at the outset—is that pure Anarchism, though it should be the ideal, to which society should continually approximate, is for the present impossible, and would not survive more than a year or two at most if it were

---

[6] The following simple schematic chart places anarchism in relation to other dominant "radical" political philosophies of the time:

Human Nature → ↓ Nature of Institutions	Cooperative	Competitive
Corrupt and Corrupting	*Anarchism*	*Social Darwinism/ Libertarianism*
Necessary and Adaptable	*Socialism/Marxism*	*Fascism*

For a fuller understanding of anarchism and its major thinkers see Weir 11-41, and Thomas 1-17. For its intersections with American philosophical pragmatism, see Kadlec 9-34.

[7] Critics have begun finding some congruence of thought between Woolf and Russell. See Banfield, Mackin, and Ruotolo, who goes so far as to claim, "the intellectual source of such [anarchist] ideas was no doubt the Bloomsbury circle" (231), though he neither singles out Russell nor describes how this learning happened.

adopted" (12-13).[8] There is a certain sense in which anarchism, even to its admirers, can only exist in the abstract, only as an idea. To bring it into the world as a philosophical proposition or political program is to introduce it to a world so thoroughly determined by social and political institutions that it would become yet another reified revolutionary strain. Yet *Mrs. Dalloway* suggests in many ways that the perspectives of anarchism may find a home in the world of literature.

Septimus

Consider just how profoundly institutions shape every thought and action of shell-shocked veteran Septimus Warren Smith. These include institutions of education (in the Stroud schools, at Miss Pole's lectures), institutions of culture (through which he encounters Shakespeare, romance literature, and the biographies of "great men"), institutions of government (which fix his place in the economic formation and provide war propaganda), institutions of business (which determine the opportunities and limits of a clerk), and, finally, the military. It is significant for the anarchist that each of these influences is somehow unnatural; that is, each is at odds with the natural world around Septimus, his individual human nature, and the natural social orientation of humans. From the anarchist perspective, war—particularly mechanical, scorched-earth trench warfare—may well be the most extreme form of institutional abuse, the ultimate unnatural distortion and "use" of individuals. It "represents the antithesis of mutuality" (Ruotolo 238). Soldiers, families, and entire communities are asked to risk everything to preserve what? To preserve, primarily, the institutions and social structures that make up "England." For "England" is not a quality of the land itself or of the people themselves—they are qualitatively neither distinctively homogenous nor especially distinct from their neighbors. "England" exists, instead, only as an ideal, as a construct. It is an abstraction that permeates the institutions of government and of culture, thereby shaping those institutions at the very same time they provide this idea its only life, its only means of perpetuation and expression.

---

[8] George Bernard Shaw, a leading Fabian, and William Morris also characterize anarchism in this way. Morris's characterizations of the self-declared "anarchists" often sound more like libertarians and the egoists Ayn Rand would celebrate than the mutualists of anarchist philosophy: "I have met with Anarchists who were not at all vague, and who definitely opposed Communism. They had, indeed, this in common with militant Socialism, that they wished to abolish *organized* monopoly; but they supported unorganized monopoly, or the rule of the strongest individual. . . which means the upholding of private property with no association to uphold it, a position impossible and inconceivable" (qtd. in Morris 320-21).

According to *Mrs. Dalloway*'s narrator, "Septimus was one of the first to volunteer. He went to France to save an England which consisted almost entirely of Shakespeare's plays and Miss Isabel Pole in a green dress walking in a square" (86). But rather than ennoble or enable Septimus, as a liberal democracy imagines itself to do, the institutions of England corrupt him. Seduced by the grandeur and romance of *Anthony and Cleopatra*, enchanted by Miss Isabel Pole seen not for who she is but through the lens of romance literature, encouraged by comparisons of his writing to the heroes of the English tradition ("'was he not like Keats?' she asked" [85]), and drawn by the military's promise of English "manliness," Septimus finds these promised goods illusory, mere affects that clash loudly with the grim reality of trench warfare. His disillusion, however, is more profound than disappointment—his whole way of seeing and valuing the world is shattered.

In this new "enlightenment" of shell shock, Septimus reconsiders this disjunction between "civilized" values and inhumane realities. Rereading the literature that once inspired him, he now marvels at "how Shakespeare loathed humanity." Septimus discovers "the message hidden in the beauty of words[,] the secret signal which one generation passes, under disguise, to the next is loathing, hatred, despair. Dante the same. Aeschylus (translated) the same" (88). This treatment of the "great works" of Western culture suggests that "civilization" is not characterized by the enlightenment or progress of humanity, but by "loathing, hatred, despair." The institutions of culture that superficially send high-minded messages of a human nature defined by moral bravery actually reveal the more loathsome qualities of human existence when one gains a perspective outside the ideological machinery. The "idea" Septimus sees under the secretion of English culture is its disdain for the human weakness it envelops and, ironically, helps create.

The curious observation that Aeschylus is translated only highlights the distance between works promoted by culture and the actual people who consume them in a specific spatio-temporal context. All three authors write in a language actually or practically foreign. Dante and Aeschylus in particular are selectively unearthed from the distant past to cobble together a heritage for modern day England that inevitably distorts the work itself, distorts its historical witness to a lost reality, and even distorts the present into which it is redeployed. And it is not just these specific works of culture at fault, but perhaps the structure of culture itself.

Categorically, a culture perpetuated by museums, schools, and businesses cannot help but lead astray because, as anarchists argue, institutionalized culture can only promote an institutional vision of the world. This vision, by its very nature, leaves a substantial gap between itself and the lived experience of the individual, a gap that produces and ensures alienation.

While ideology is normally sufficient to mask and explain away such deficiencies, Septimus loses his connection to the world as institutions facilitate it; in effect, he falls out of its ideological spell. While his new perspective marks him as "insane," it affords Septimus a new vision, a certain wisdom with specifically anarchist undertones.[9] He offers new ideas "hidden in the beauty of words." Sparrows, for instance, expose a popular cultural myth of war by informing him in Greek that "no one kills from hatred" (24).[10] Indeed, combat soldiers are motivated primarily by fear for their individual safety and, much more strongly, the collective good of their comrades. Hatred is a feeling enjoyed not by the soldier, but by people back home caught up in the propaganda and rhetoric of government and media. Septimus similarly re-conceives the relationship of people to each other and the world around them. The "supreme secret" is, "first that trees are alive; next there is no crime; next love, universal love" (67). In noting that trees "are alive," Septimus recognizes the interconnectedness of life and suggests a primitivist longing for a more "natural" state of living. This fantasy was unique to anarchists among political radicals at this time, though fascists often mobilized a rhetoric of a vigorous, vital nature corrupted by the "softness" of modern life and liberal thought. For anarchists, however, humanity's primitive past was a time before institutions, a time when the needs of the tribe depended on, and thus privileged, the unique contributions of individuals, each of whom had a life-or-death stake in the tribe's success. Any overlap with fascism is eliminated by the third message, that of "universal love." In his reflections on morality, Kropotkin noted, "man is appealed to, to be guided in his acts, not merely by love, which is always personal, or at the best tribal, but by the perception of his oneness with each human being" (126). This universal love would also distinguish Septimus's message from that of Social Darwinists and libertarians who, like fascists, saw "competition" as humanity's natural state, necessary for strengthening the species or culture.

Septimus's radical ideas are part of what mark him "insane," and such a condition puts him in the jurisdiction of the institutions condemned with greater ferocity than any other in *Mrs. Dalloway*: the medical establishment. Dr. Holmes tells Rezia time and again there is nothing whatsoever wrong with Septimus—a little cricket and attention to "real things" will snap him out of his "little funk." Holmes spends his time, instead, trying to charm Rezia, going so far as to invite her to tea. Dr. William Bradshaw—whom Rezia, Clarissa, Peter, and Sally *instinctively* dislike—is at least medically more competent; he recognizes the muddled work

---

[9] This may be an ironic instance of the "change blindness" Harker finds throughout Woolf. Characters generally fail to recognize changes in the world around them, though here Septimus sees clearly while everyone else remains "blind" to how the world has changed.
[10] "Greek" from "birds" is not random, if perhaps a bit obscure. See Barber, Kolocotroni, and Harker.

of Holmes and the severity of Septimus's disconnection from normalcy. But his solution is wholly off the mark. His prescription of separation and isolation is one learned, spread, and even enforced by institutions—in response to Rezia's resistance he tells her, "there was no alternative. It was a question of law" (96-7). Law represents the mechanism by which institutions can ultimately exert their "will" over individuals, particularly those individuals who are unmoved by institutional demands and requirements.

As the novel shows, however, it is not isolation but *communication* that leads to health, for Septimus only finds happiness again in his simple relationship with Rezia and in the knowledge that "she is with him." A perfect understanding—what Kropotkin calls "the perception of [our] oneness with each human being" (126)—develops again between them in the moments before Septimus's death, and in this miniature anarchist community they realize their individual best interests lie in their well-being as a couple.[11] From the safety of this relationship Septimus sees Rezia transformed, significantly, into Mother Nature herself:

> She was a flowering tree; and through her branches looked out the face
> of a lawgiver, who had reached a sanctuary where she feared no one . . .
> . Yet judges [Holmes and Bradshaw] were; who mixed the vision and the
> sideboard; saw nothing clear, yet ruled, yet inflicted. "Must" they said.
> Over them she triumphed. (148)

This passage holds natural human compassion as an ideal which those working through institutions cannot reach when they "mixed the vision and the sideboard." The sideboard inevitably distorts the vision. It is the connection between people, sanctioned by the natural "lawgiver," that lies smothered by the ideas and laws of unnatural institutions, ideas and laws that must be "ruled" and "inflicted." Institutions follow laws—whether literal or conceptual—rather than the immediate reality of human life or the immediate necessity of a human situation. And they have the power to enforce rules, however poor the fit. "What right has Bradshaw to say 'must' to me?" Septimus finally demands in anger (147). Only an institutional right, the anarchist answers, an institutional right that exercised even in the name of health and happiness cannot help but pervert the very same.

---

[11] Kaley Joyes sees this in gendered terms, arguing, "the Smiths' shared happiness about the hat demonstrates the potential benefits of destabilizing gender roles, as Woolf shows individual happiness to be contingent on a balance between relationship with others and individual wholeness" (76). This essay suggests, however, that gender is just one of the many means by which institutions unsettle the anarchist balance she describes.

In proposing communication as a new direction for mental health, Septimus establishes the foundation of anarchist utopia, the *feeling* of human connection upon which one could build community: "communication is health, communication is happiness, communication—" (93). Against the Holmeses who dismiss patients in order to flirt with wives, against the Bradshaws who finalize opinions in exactly three minutes and end every session at forty-five, Septimus proposes communication. The mutual understanding it facilitates would clearly have saved Septimus. Communication—both with others and with "nature"—is the means by which people come to understand not only themselves as individuals but also their connections with those around them. Communication offers a means to human happiness and political freedom because it is personal in a way that exposes institutional constraints and privileges personal relationships. When not distorted by institutional influences, communication strengthens both the individual and the communal. The health of one becomes the health of the other. The happiness of one facilitates the happiness of the other.

But Septimus will not be communicated with and will not be saved. His end, like his beginning, is figured in the products of institutional culture. Upon realizing he has only one means of escape, Septimus reflects, "There remained only the window, the tiresome, the troublesome, and rather melodramatic business of opening the window and throwing himself out. It was their idea of tragedy, not his or Rezia's (for she was with him). Holmes and Bradshaw like that sort of thing" (149). Lying among the reasons Septimus regrets this method of dying is the fact that it will follow the plots of melodrama and tragedy. He intends his death to be neither, but recognizes that limited by their institutionally-mediated understanding of the world, Holmes and Bradshaw will categorize the event as a conventional "tragedy." When the narrator notes, "why the devil he did it, Dr. Holmes could not conceive" (150), one of the ironies is that Holmes does not recognize the very convention-driven plot trajectory he himself has imposed on Septimus's existence—unless, of course, part of the convention itself is that such melodramatic suicides are "inexplicable." Thus, when we consider to whom Septimus addresses his cry, "I'll give it you!" it is not just to Holmes, but to the whole institutional apparatus that has led him, almost inevitably, to his choice—jumping with his personal sovereignty intact or existing on institutional terms largely incongruent with human nature. He recognizes that the "it" he gives is merely his physical body. The defining essence of his "life" he takes with him, and thus he plunges with the right of self-determination, plunges "holding his treasure," as Clarissa will later describe it (184).

Clarissa

That Clarissa seems to understand Septimus's commitment to self-sovereignty raises poignant questions about her own philosophy, politics, and mode of living. As such, Woolf's use of Clarissa may go beyond the presentation of female consciousness and critique of male domination for which the novel is renowned. The full complexity of Clarissa's values and perceptions—and of Woolf's presentation of her—emerge more clearly when considered in the terms of anarchism. For example, Woolf scholars often note the multiple parallels and connections between Septimus and Clarissa—and indeed Woolf's diaries reveal this intention—but to celebrate the androgyny of consciousness the pairing suggests often requires emphasizing Clarissa's empathy and minimizing the less savory elements of her reaction to his suicide. Anarchism provides a context equally suitable to both.

Clarissa *does* understand Septimus' situation with telepathic ease, nailing even his poetic sensibility: "There were the poets and thinkers. Suppose he had had that passion, and had gone to Sir William Bradshaw, a great doctor yet to her obscurely evil, without sex or lust, extremely polite to women, but capable of some indescribable outrage—forcing your soul, that was it" (184). Considered in anarchist terms, Clarissa reveals both the rhetoric and the mechanisms through which institutional will is exerted over the individual. Despite the label of praise that social, medical, and cultural institutions attach to Bradshaw—"a great doctor"—Clarissa instinctively recognizes a deep-seated evil in him. That her natural perceptions are those of an anarchist becomes further evident when we compare the conventional terms of praise with the defects she observes. He is "extremely polite to women," and while in the terms of her cultural and social milieu this may have been admirable, Clarissa imagines it not to be generous and kind, but rather condescending and patronizing. Woolf emphasizes this with "extremely," which implies a forced, strained quality to both the action and the praise it elicits. What Bradshaw seems to lack is natural feeling, as she indicates by his lack of "sex or lust" and his habit of "forcing the soul." An anarchist outrage, "forcing the soul" of another is possible only when one considers action and exercises power strictly on selfish terms, *without* regard to the other or to the larger communal context. In her sympathetic recognition of Bradshaw's selfish mistreatment of Septimus, Clarissa emerges as an admirable fellow human being from a number of ideological perspectives, including the anarchist's.

But on the other hand, harder to celebrate are Clarissa's admissions that "she did not pity him, with all this [her party] going on," and her joy that "he made her feel the beauty; made her feel the fun" (186). We might wonder, initially, how she can find "fun" and "beauty" in his suffering. Though it may seem inconsistent with her empathy, the specific way she understands his choice of suicide reveals an anarchistic logic empathetic in its own way. Clarissa's initial reflections on "why he had done it" move beyond the idea that Septimus lost everything:

> She had once thrown a shilling into the Serpentine, never anything more. But he had flung it away . . . . A thing there was that mattered; a thing, wreathed about with chatter, defaced, obscured in her own life, let drop every day in corruption, lies, chatter. This he had preserved. Death was defiance. Death was an attempt to communicate. (184)

The text fails to state directly what exactly this "thing . . . that mattered" is, but having concluded that it is self-sovereignty which Septimus feels he preserves, one could argue Clarissa values this same self-sovereignty in her reflection on his death. In this sense, the right of self-determination is the thing that matters most—it is a thing "obscured" in day-to-day living, forgotten and ignored except at those moments it is endangered. And often we endanger it without much consideration. The "chatter," the lip service we give to individual autonomy with labels like "liberty," "freedom," "democracy," does not automatically promote such self-determination. Instead, with the clumsy inaccuracy of the institutions that promote such words, the false labels "obscure," "deface," and even "corrupt" what anarchists consider the primary human right. As Bakunin writes, "There is only one dogma, one law, one moral basis for men, and that is liberty. To respect your neighbour's liberty *is duty*; to love, help and serve him, *virtue*" (65). While one can agree with critics like Joyes, who argue "Septimus's suicide becomes part of [Woolf's] critique of post-war Britain's rigid power dynamics" (77), anarchism shows it to be a very specific critique of institutionalized power. Clarissa recognizes that Septimus preserved this sense of liberty by jumping, and she calls it a "treasure" in the very next paragraph.

And reflecting further on the "thing . . . that mattered" in her own life, Clarissa comes to recognize the interconnected nature of communal life—a reality even in cosmopolitan London, though perhaps obscured by social formations and cultural "wisdom" about urban life. In so doing, Clarissa admits her own failure in "duty" and "virtue" (as Bakunin describes them), her own culpability in driving Septimus to his impossible choice:

> Somehow it was her disaster—her disgrace. It was her punishment to see sink and disappear here a man, there a woman, in this profound darkness, and she forced to stand here in her evening dress. She had schemed; she had pilfered. She was never wholly admirable. She had wanted success. (185)

With this in mind, Clarissa's seemingly insensitive comments come into sharper focus. "Pity" would indeed be the wrong reaction to Septimus's death—the condescension it implies would violate the anarchist belief in our natural equality; it would fail to respect his liberty. Further, pity would "obscure" (and thus "corrupt" and "deface") the truth and the reality motivating his suicide. His conscious choice, his "defiance" of institutional claims on his sovereignty, would remain unexamined and thus be rendered inexplicable—the very narrative trajectory Septimus fears. Clarissa understands this; "she felt somehow very like him" (186). With a touch of unwitting anarchism, Clarissa feels that given the failure of the community to communicate and understand Septimus's individual needs—and she condemns herself as one of the status-driven ignorant—he made the right choice, the only choice, to preserve his self-sovereignty. This is why "she felt glad that he had done it; thrown it away." His death offers her a position from which she recognizes the degrees to which she, too, is "forced" to behave as she does, to "stand here in her evening dress," as well as the extent to which she makes herself a willing participant ("She had schemed. . . . She had wanted success").[12]

In recognizing a certain wisdom in Septimus's choice, Clarissa also recognizes the privilege of her own situation, where the protections of class position and a respected and respectful marriage with Richard largely insulate her from the "musts" that drive Septimus to the window. When feeling attacked, "she could crouch like a bird and gradually revive" (185) under the protection afforded by Richard. It is *this* awareness that helps her to "feel the beauty . . . feel the fun" in her own life. Circumstance has allowed Clarissa to preserve "that something that mattered" at the same time it forced Septimus to a life or death decision. Clarissa believes that "death was an attempt to communicate" (184), and when we find she can again see the beauty and the fun in her own life, we understand she has gotten the message.

Relationships

This is not to suggest the novel promotes marriage and class status as solutions to individual suffering, but instead that Clarissa understands mutual respect and material security as the foundations of liberty. Finding Clarissa, and Woolf's presentation of her, infused with a degree of anarchism does impact received notions of their respective feminism, however, and the most peculiar manifestation of this is in the issue of marriage, where criticism remains vital and evolving. For

---

[12] Guth has offered some of the most severe readings of Clarissa's relationship to Septimus, arguing that she neither understands the reality of his suffering nor undergoes any true transformation herself. See "Fiction as Self-Evasion" and "Rituals of Self-Deception." But while Guth offers a necessary corrective to overly celebratory readings of Clarissa, the passages quoted above—noting Septimus's temperament, refusing to pity him, admitting her complicity—display some of the empathy, honesty, and depth of understanding Guth precludes.

example, Jesse Wolfe's work on marriage in *Mrs. Dalloway* follows numerous scholars in noting its genuinely revolutionary and provocative treatment of gender identity and human sexuality. But whereas Eileen Barrett concludes, "the novel's scathing depictions of heterosexuality in marriage demonstrate Woolf's lesbian-feminist critique of this institution" (147), Wolfe finds this critique equivocated by the characters' pragmatic acceptance of conventional marriages. An anarchist reading pushes this claim even further: it is not marriage as a relationship the novel critiques so much as its frequent institutional perversions. For while Clarissa indeed marries in keeping with the expectations of her class, she also seems surprisingly satisfied with her pragmatic decision. She can "feel the beauty" and "feel the fun" after all—a contentment explicable perhaps only from an anarchist perspective. Even more surprising than her contentment is the fact that she attributes it to Richard: "It was due to Richard; she had never been so happy" (185).[13] The once radical Sally, too, marries a conventional businessman and brags of five sons. While Christine Froula describes Sally-as-Lady Rosseter as a "trophy" of "Conversion" (124), what this apparent contradiction between their feminism and their marriages suggests is less a conventional view of marriage on Woolf's part than the valuing of certain types of relationships, types that I would argue are consistent with anarchist privileging of mutually beneficial agreements reached between freely choosing individuals. Is it not autonomy that Clarissa finds in her marriage to Richard, that Sally finds with her businessman? This self-determination, however, is not absolute, nor is it without cost—Woolf is not an unwitting libertarian, after all. The price Clarissa and Sally have paid for their sovereignty seems to be romantic passion, yet if one considers the relationships in the novel dominated by passion one could reasonably conclude the novel does not consider it much of a price.

Anarchist activists tended to oppose marriage; when seen as a static institution ensconcing male privilege, it is seriously flawed. Emma Goldman went so far as to declare: "the institution of marriage makes a parasite of woman, an absolute dependent. It incapacitates her for life's struggle, annihilates her social consciousness, paralyzes her imagination, and then imposes its gracious protection, which is in reality a snare, a travesty on the human character" (235). *Mrs. Dalloway* reveals the dangerous results of such male domination all too clearly in the character of Lady Bradshaw, victim of "conversion, fastidious Goddess, [who] loves blood better than brick, and feasts most subtly on the human

---

[13] Problematic as biographical parallels can be, Woolf periodically records such happiness, generally connecting it to the private world she and Leonard create for themselves. She notes in 1925, after suffering together through a particularly miserable social weekend, "L. and I were too too happy, as they say; if it were now to die etc. Nobody shall say of me that I have not known perfect happiness" (*D*3 8-9).

will" (100). Lady Bradshaw, through the many institutional apparati that encourage a wife's submission to husband, "had gone under. It was nothing you could put your finger on; there had been no scene, no snap; only the slow sinking, waterlogged, of her will into his" (100). The repeated use of "will" is significant in these passages, for it suggests that the self-determination so primary to anarchism is the primary sacrifice in a marriage of the unequal, where legal, religious, and social institutions enable "conversion" of the wife's will to the husband's. Woolf highlights the unnatural quality of this state in the novel's description of Lady Bradshaw: "once, long ago, she had caught salmon freely: now, quick to minister to the craving which lit her husband's eye so oilily for dominion, for power, she cramped, squeezed, pared, pruned, drew back, peeped through" (101). The list of uncomfortable contortions point to the unnatural perversion of human nature the Bradshaws' marriage has generated, particularly when contrasted with her previous self-sufficient love of sport and the outdoors. His partner's spiritual death is completely lost on Dr. Bradshaw, who cites to patients as evidence that "life was good" the decidedly unnatural product of his conversion: "Lady Bradshaw in ostrich feathers hung over the mantelpiece" (101). What the relatively happy marriages of Clarissa and Sally Seton might suggest, then, is that the institution of marriage has become disconnected from the human relationship upon which it was founded. As the anarchist would predict, institutionalization facilitates exploitation and distortion in what should be a reciprocal relationship.[14]

Mrs. Dalloway identifies another danger in marriage, one found only by moving beyond feminist critiques of the institution to anarchist critiques of domination. The danger is that of romanticization—of fantasies of passion so intense and fantastical as to be largely disconnected from the realities of everyday life with a partner. This type of unequal "marriage" is promoted by institutional culture, and Woolf exposes it through Peter's "failures." Peter fails time and again in marriage because he approaches it through the lens of romance novels. Thinking of Daisy's photo sent from India, he muses, "And the dark, adorably pretty girl on the verandah exclaimed (he could hear her). Of course, of course she would give him everything! she cried (she had no sense of discretion) everything he wanted! she cried, running to meet him, whoever might be looking" (157). Such a melodramatic surrender of the "pretty girl" might well serve as the climax of a novel, but in Peter's "real" world it creates a conflict. For while he consistently figures his relationships with Daisy (and even Clarissa) in the terms of romance literature, he also recognizes on another level that adoration and mad passion are not in fact what he really wants

---

[14] Rosenfeld argues Woolf views marriage both as a largely positive metaphorical possibility and as a frequently grim reality of domination (3); see especially Chapter 1.

He seeks a seemingly impossible situation with Daisy where he can "just haunt and hover. . . swoop and taste, be alone, in short, sufficient to himself; and yet nobody of course was more dependent upon others . . . it had been his undoing" (158). Approached through literature, marriage seems unfit to provide Peter the emotional support he needs. (Elsewhere he describes "his undoing" as his "susceptibility to tears.") Peter wants and needs exactly the paradoxical combination of autonomy and support found in Clarissa and Richard's marriage. Companionship is had without smothering, comfort without adoration. In Peter we find the failure of conventional marriage—as conceived by institutions of culture—to provide either.

But unnatural distortion in a relationship is not unique to marriage. Relationships where one is smothered—even in the name of "love"—are highly problematic in the anarchist terms of the novel. And here *Mrs. Dalloway* moves even further beyond feminist critique of marriage to address human relationships more broadly. Fear of individual dissolution drives Clarissa's dislike of Doris Kilman; reflecting on the intensity of Kilman's bond with Elizabeth, Clarissa roundly condemns "love and religion" because they "destroy . . . the privacy of the soul" (126-27). Religion and love—at least the obsessive, romance-driven variations that require submission and subservience—restrict human nature through categorical descriptions and categorizations. They codify and enforce a limited number of acceptable channels for the expression of nebulous, expansive, indescribable human emotions. Though her "narrow bed" is a source of emotional sorrow for Clarissa, it is also a retreat and "welcome escape" that maintains the "privacy" of her soul. Thus a marriage where each individual is granted a degree of independence and agency, yet a share in the safety and comfort offered by the union, seems like the sort of free-will association that anarchism promoted:

> And there is a dignity in people; a solitude; even between husband and wife a gulf; and that one must respect, thought Clarissa, watching him open the door; for one would not part with it oneself, or take it, against his will, from one's husband, without losing one's independence, one's self-respect—something, after all, priceless. (120) [15]

The language of this passage is particularly well-suited to the anarchist conception of social relationships; "dignity," "will," "independence," and "self-respect" are the

---

[15] Russell makes a strikingly similar point in *Roads to Freedom*: "Marriage should be a free, spontaneous meeting of mutual instinct, filled with happiness not unmixed with a feeling akin to awe: it should involve that degree of respect of each for the other that makes even the most trifling interference with liberty an utter impossibility, and a common life enforced by one against the will of the other an unthinkable thing of deep horror" (204).

"priceless" things that "one must respect" even in the most seemingly intimate of unions.

Understanding the anarchist objection to obsessively passionate relationships could also clarify the novel's equivocal treatment of lesbianism. As Barrett notes, "Clarissa rejects the idea that same-sex love is a crime against nature, yet she projects onto Doris all the negative, distorted stereotypes of lesbians." For Barrett this indicates that Woolf has been overpowered by the cultural formulations of homophobia and has reproduced them: "By echoing the imagery of Clarissa's fantasies in her descriptions of Doris's and other characters' lesbian desires, Woolf also illustrates the power of the sexologists to pervert the erotic language of romantic friendship into the language of homophobia and self-hatred" (148). While it could well be that Woolf is showing the conflicted attitudes she feels as a feminist in a hetero-normative patriarchal culture, from an anarchist perspective one could also argue that Clarissa rejects Kilman's lesbian desire not because it is lesbian but because it is domineering—the same reason she herself rejected Peter's heterosexual desire. It is a form of "conversion," which in Kilman's case is the double conversion of "love and religion" crushing "the privacy of the soul." Elizabeth's own reaction reinforces this interpretation, for the relationship appears to end when Elizabeth feels a need to escape. She runs from Kilman (appropriately enough at the Army and Navy Stores) and "was delighted to be free" (135). She feels her freedom even more intensely by imagining herself "a pirate"—lawless—riding aimlessly atop a double-decker bus "like the figure-head of a ship" (135, 136). The novel expresses Elizabeth's anarchist need for self-determination, not her need for a conventional relationship; domination is critiqued in *Mrs. Dalloway* even within a subculture itself suppressed.[16] The travesty may be more easily seen in the mainstream, but constricting the privacy of the soul remains unacceptable wherever it occurs.

Politics

Recent work on Woolf's politics often assumes Woolf's thoughts on larger political issues to be outgrowths of her feminism.[17] But what if we reverse the terms, considering these wider political concerns to be the grounding of her feminism, rather

---

[16] Similarly, Tuzyline Jita Allan finds "soul death" in Clarissa and attributes it to the death of her lesbian desire mandated by middle class patriarchy (109). Clarissa's equivocal attitude toward marriage challenges this reading, as do the characters' desires considered more broadly. To limit Clarissa's desire to the "lesbian" denies the polymorphous nature of desire the novel offers at every turn—Clarissa is passionate toward Sally, Peter, and Richard; Septimus is passionate toward both his wife and his commanding officer.

[17] See Jane Goldman (9) and Black (7), among others.

than its offspring? The reality is surely a complex interaction between the two, but this interaction would place her in the tradition of Mary Wollstonecraft and Emma Goldman, whose feminism was grounded in anarchist political ideals, explicitly in the latter.[18] Though beyond the scope of this paper, the history of feminism and the history of anarchism are inextricably entwined at so many points in the nineteenth and early twentieth century. By foregrounding the broader political thought, however, this essay humbly hopes to move Woolf more squarely into the broader political debates of her day, where her perspicuity and intellectual force surely demand she be.

Melba Cuddy-Keane has moved in this direction, characterizing Woolf's politics as "democratic highbrow." Woolf, she argues, seeks thoughtful, independent intellectuals everywhere. As "an advocate for both democratic inclusiveness and intellectual education" (1), Woolf demands high levels of intellectual curiosity and reading skill—for which she is often characterized as an elitist[19]—but tempers that call by demanding that everyone have the opportunity to pursue this self-improvement. Key to understanding this political attitude is distinguishing between "the mass" as undifferentiated and unthinking, and "the masses" as that great number of people born of lesser circumstance with limited access to education, culture, and knowledge. Woolf reveals an anarchist tint where Cuddy-Keane notes her preference for the masses over the mass. Such a distinction clarifies, too, the seemingly ambiguous attitude towards forms of collectivism critics like Michael Tratner describe in Woolf.[20]

The three primary consciousnesses of *Mrs. Dalloway* are linked quite clearly, offering a miniature version of the masses. Clarissa understands Septimus and Peter

---

[18] Nearly any Emma Goldman essay reveals this condition. For example, "Woman Suffrage" takes it as a given that women have the same right to vote as men, but then argues that the mental suffrage of both men and women is a far more crucial step towards social justice for women.

[19] See Hussey on Bloomsbury's enduring reputation of elitism, a reputation mobilized to great effect by Margaret Thatcher in the 1970s and '80s. See also Zwerdling (87-88).

[20] In proposing collectivism's triumph over individualism in the twentieth-century, Tratner minimizes the persistence of individualist concerns, which can be found even in the rhetoric of Lenin and Trotsky. But most importantly, anarchism championed the maintenance of individualism within the collective context. Tratner's discussion of "guild socialism" makes many of these propositions without linking it to anarchism. He describes both "the collectivist social system that the Woolfs hoped would replace individualism" and "Woolf's visions of societies operating without any central sovereignty" (237, 243), which, taken together, sound like anarchism's vision of a collectivism that fosters individual liberty. See also Mackin, who describes, "Woolf's reluctance to surrender the private, despite her drive toward a Russellian generality. Thus what I believe she's trying to envision is a way to achieve Russell's public world without sacrificing the private one—to lose the 'I' without losing the self" (121).

nearly telepathically, as Peter does her. Unique phrases re-appear word for word in all three minds. But the fact that Woolf mobilizes varied positions of gender, sexuality, and class draws attention, in anarchist terms, to the similar ways their consciousnesses are shaped; it emphasizes the fundamental connectedness of the human condition. Indeed for Jane Goldman this unity of disparate perceptions is the "Woolfian moment" that grounds Woolf's progressive political thought.[21] But if we consider the differences between kindred spirits of Clarissa, Septimus, and Peter (who shares Clarissa's status and Septimus's gender), class emerges as the decisive arbiter of fate. While status affords Clarissa the space to survive, Septimus is crushed by state machinery. And the telling difference between them is not gender, for Peter survives as well. A specifically feminist indictment of patriarchy would presumably show women to be the most victimized, so Woolf's decision to kill Septimus may suggest a more universal nature of the problem and a more broader-reaching culprit for her indictment.

If we are to argue that the novel is infused with philosophy of nineteenth-century anarchism, that it shapes the perceptions and values of the text and many of its characters, it might seem peculiar that three central characters—Clarissa, Sally, and Peter—are failed revolutionaries. Each has settled into the comforts of an upper middle-class lifestyle. Peter was "sent down" at Oxford because he was a Socialist, yet he reflects on this day that for as much as he hates King, Empire, and so on, there is something comforting in it: "the show was really rather tolerable" (55). At Bourton, Sally and Clarissa once planned to change the world: "they meant to found a society to abolish private property" (33). This cannot help but evoke Pierre-Joseph Proudhon's rallying cry, "Property is theft!"—and its deployment is perfectly appropriate because, as David Weir notes, the slogan is typically misunderstood in exactly this manner (23). Sally and Clarissa read Shelley and the "Communist" William Morris, who argued "for a *public conscience* as a rule of action: and by all means let us have the least possible exercise of authority" (qtd in Morris 316). They are careful to wrap presents in plain brown wrappers. Yet by the day of the party, both are material successes with no indication of giving it up. Zwerdling claims that simply through age and class comfort they've come to adopt the "governing class spirit" (136), so how can such characters be Woolf's vehicles for an anarchist critique of 1920s England?

Woolf once wrote, "though it would be far easier to write history . . . that method of telling the truth seems to me so elementary, and so clumsy, that I prefer, where truth is important, to write fiction" (qtd. in Dalgarno 135). Isolating the "truth"

---

[21] Melissa Bagley reads it quite differently, finding "common understanding" among characters evidence of just how ubiquitous male figuration of the feminine in natural and naturalized terms really is (39).

of *Mrs. Dalloway*—the idea that animates it—requires returning to the distinction between a philosophy's ideals and their distortion in the practice of politics. Revealing the transitory nature of characters' political commitments supports the anarchist argument that putting a revolutionary program into institutional practice will inevitably corrupt it. Any attempt at political policy, no matter the end, creates a story, an artificial unity, a false logic across disparate fragments of material existence and the isolation of human consciousnesses. The transformation of exploitative social arrangements will not happen on the backs of plain brown wrapping paper, which merely tells another story. It will not come with slogans, red flags, or books of philosophy mailed to the Himalayas. It will come instead with a transformation of consciousness itself, with a change in the way people see themselves, the world around them, and the function of institutions within it. The whole "idea" has to change, and as Woolf sensed at *Mrs. Dalloway*'s inception, the novel had been limited in the stories it could tell; it was no longer the right "house" for an anarchist change in ideology. In the end, though Clarissa has clearly abandoned her seemingly anarchist goal of abolishing private property, she has come to recognize the fates of all individuals as inextricably linked and to move somewhat closer to embodying the ideals that informed such utopian fantasies: as the novel closes, she has exceeded all institutional labels and categories. She simply "is."

The author wishes to thank his colleagues at the Center for 21st Century Studies at the University of Wisconsin-Milwaukee for their helpful reading of this essay when he began it there all those years ago.

Works Cited

Allan, Tuzyline Jita. "The Death of Sex and the Soul in *Mrs. Dalloway* and Nella Larsen's *Passing*." *Virginia Woolf: Lesbian Readings*. Ed. Eileen Barrett & Patricia Cramer. New York: New York UP, 1997. 95-115. Print.

Bagley, Melissa. "Nature and the Nation in *Mrs. Dalloway*." *Woolf Studies Annual* 14 (2008): 35-45. Print.

Bakunin, Michael. *Michael Bakunin: Selected Writings*. Ed. Arthur Lehning. Tr. Steven Cox and Olive Stephens. London: Jonathan Cape, 1973. Print.

Banfield, Ann. *The Phantom Table: Woolf, Fry, Russell and the Epistemology of Modernism*. Cambridge: Cambridge UP, 2000. Print.

Barber, Stephen M. "States of Emergency, States of Freedom: Woolf, History, and the Novel." *Novel* 42.2 (Summer 2009): 196-206. Print.

Barrett, Eileen. "Unmasking Lesbian Passion: The Inverted World of *Mrs. Dalloway*." *Virginia Woolf: Lesbian Readings*. Ed. Eileen Barrett & Patricia Cramer. New York: New York UP, 1997. 146-64. Print.

Black, Naomi. *Virginia Woolf as Feminist*. Ithaca, NY: Cornell UP, 2004. Print.

Cuddy-Keane, Melba. *Virginia Woolf, the Intellectual, and the Public Sphere*. New York: Cambridge UP, 2003. Print.

Dalgarno, Emily. "A British War and Peace? Virginia Woolf Reads Tolstoy." *Modern Fiction Studies* 50.1 (2004): 129-150. Print.

Froula, Christine. *Virginia Woolf and the Bloomsbury Avant-Garde: War, Civilization, Modernity*. New York: Columbia UP, 2005. Print.

Goldman, Emma. *Anarchism and Other Essays*. 1917. New York: Dover, 1969. Print.

Goldman, Jane. *The Feminist Aesthetics of Virginia Woolf: Modernism, Post-Impressionism, and the Politics of the Visual*. New York: Cambridge UP, 1998. Print.

Guth, Deborah. "Rituals of Self-Deception: Clarissa Dalloway's Final Moment of Vision." *Twentieth Century Literature* 36.1 (Spring 1990): 35-42. JSTOR. PDF file.

——. "'What a Lark! What a Plunge!': Fiction as Self-Evasion in *Mrs. Dalloway*." *The Modern Language Review* 84.1 (1989): 18-25. JSTOR. PDF file.

Harker, James. "Misperceiving Virginia Woolf." *Journal of Modern Literature* 34.2 (2011): 1-21. Print.

Hussey, Mark. "Mrs. Thatcher and Mrs. Woolf." *Modern Fiction Studies* 50.1 (2004): 8-30. Print.

Joyes, Kaley. "Failed Witnessing in Virginia Woolf's *Mrs. Dalloway*." *Woolf Studies Annual* 14 (2008): 69-89. Print.

Kadlec, David. *Mosaic Modernism: Anarchism, Pragmatism, Culture*. Baltimore: Johns Hopkins UP, 2000. Print.

Kolocotroni, Vassiliki. "Still Life: Modernism's Turn to Greece." *Journal of Modern Literature* 35.2 (Winter 2012): 1-24. Print.

Kropotkin, Peter. *Kropotkin: Selections from his Writings*. Ed. Herbert Read. London: Freedom Press, 1948. Print.

Mackin, Timothy. "Woolf, Russell, and Photographic Vision." *Journal of Modern Literature* 33.3 (2010): 112-30. Print.

Morris, May. *William Morris: Artist, Writer, Socialist; Volume the Second: Morris as a Socialist*. New York: Russell & Russell, 1966. Print.

Paterson, R.W.K. *The Nihistic Egoist Max Stirner*. New York: Oxford UP, 1971. Print.

Rosenfeld, Natania. *Outsiders Together: Virginia and Leonard Woolf*. Princeton, NJ: Princeton UP, 2000. Print.

Ruotolo, Lucio. *The Interrupted Moment: A View of Virginia Woolf's Novels.* Stanford: Stanford UP, 1986. Print.
Russell, Bertrand. *Roads to Freedom: Socialism, Anarchism and Syndicalism.* 1918. London: George Allen and Unwin, 1948. Print.
Thomas, Paul. *Karl Marx and the Anarchists.* London: Routledge & Kegan Paul, 1980. Print.
Tratner, Michael. *Modernism and Mass Politics: Joyce, Woolf, Eliot, Yeats.* Stanford: Stanford UP, 1995. Print.
Weir, David. *Anarchy & Culture.* Amherst: U of Massachusetts P, 1997. Print.
Wolfe, Jesse. "The Sane Woman in the Attic: Sexuality and Self-Authorship in *Mrs. Dalloway.*" *Modern Fiction Studies* 51.1 (2005): 34-59. Print.
Woolf, Virginia. *The Essays of Virginia Woolf,* 4 vols. Ed. Andrew McNeillie. New York: Harcourt Brace Jovanovich, 1986, 1987, 1988, 1994. Print.
——. *Mrs. Dalloway.* 1925. New York: Harcourt Brace, 1990. Print.
——. *The Diary of Virginia Woolf,* 5 vols. Ed. Anne Olivier Bell. London: Hogarth Press, 1977-1984. Print.
Zwerdling, Alex. *Virginia Woolf and the Real World.* Berkeley: U of California P, 1986. Print.

"Little Accidents": Virginia Woolf and the Failures of Form in "The Moment: Summer's Night"

Jamie Horrocks

"What are the elements of which the universe is composed," asks Leslie Stephen in his 1876 *History of English Thought*, "and how are they woven into a continuous whole?" (45). Stephen's question—a question about the possibility of perceiving unity in a fractured world—arises from his discussion of Hume and the crisis of thought Hume's work generated among eighteenth-century philosophers (Banfield 246). It leads to other questions: "Why do I conceive the world as something different from a series of sensations?" and then "Why do I regard the world thus constituted as regulated by certain invariable relations?" (Stephen 45). These questions of composition, sensation, and relation, written almost a decade before the birth of Stephen's youngest daughter, would be taken up in nearly identical terms by that daughter in a narrative essay published after her death, the title piece of *The Moment and Other Essays* called "The Moment: Summer's Night."[1] Echoing her father (perhaps intentionally?), Virginia Woolf poses in the opening paragraphs of this "essay-turned-fiction" a question that reverses his telescopic concern and focuses instead on the quotidian minutiae that held such interest for Woolf: "Yet what composed the present moment?" (9).[2]

This inquiry into the composition of the moment that unfolds in "Summer's Night" leads Woolf, like Stephen, to questions of "sensations" and "relations," but it does so in the context of aesthetics—specifically, the formalist aesthetics that arose from Roger Fry and Clive Bell's theorization of Post-Impressionist art. Much has been written in recent years about Woolf's relationship with Bloomsbury aesthetic theory, the best of which has provided a record of Woolf's initially reluctant movement toward and eventually (in the words of Christopher Reed)

---

[1] Published in 1947, "Summer's Night" has eluded the attempts of scholars to date it. The editors of *Modernism* place it "c.1927" (Kolocotroni, et al. 392). Guiguet (294) and Goldman (*Feminist* 2) suggest "c.1929." Hussey, however, pushes this date back to 1938 with the belief that the essay is "related to the composition of *Between the Acts*" (164). I find Guiguet's comparison of "Summer's Night" with several of Woolf's diary entries quite compelling, especially as this would align the piece chronologically with the conclusions Reed has drawn regarding Woolf's engagement with formalist aesthetics.

[2] Lee describes the cross-generic nature of Woolf essays like "Summer's Night," which makes them difficult to categorize ("Essays" 95). I call "Summer's Night" a narrative essay but do so recognizing, as Lee does, that "everywhere you look" in Woolf's non-fiction, "there is cross-fertilisation, overlap and the dissolving of divisions. Essays turn into fictions, fictions into essays" (95).

"through formalism."[3] In the first decades of the twentieth century and especially during the years when Roger Fry was organizing the first and second Post-Impressionist exhibitions, Woolf had little interest in the visual arts and the formalist doctrine that had, at the time, correspondingly scant interest in the literary. Despite (or, as Diane Gillespie has suggested, because of) her sister Vanessa Bell's active participation in London's artistic scene, Woolf kept herself aloof from visual art, claiming to regard literature as "the only spiritual and humane career" (*L2* 382).[4] Painting, on the other hand, Woolf felt "tend[ed] to dumbness," and artists were "rather brutes" (qtd. in Morrell 204), an "abominable race" (*L2* 15) for whom the adjective "literary" was something of a derogatory slur (Reed, "Through" 22).

As Woolf's relationship with Fry evolved throughout the nineteen-teens and -twenties, however, Woolf began to revise her conception of what formalism could offer her as a writer even as Fry began to revise his assessment of literature as an impure aesthetic medium. Woolf's 1920s novels attest to her engagement with formalism and its central aesthetic concept—"significant form"—which both Fry and Clive Bell came to agree could be articulated in "a pure or nearly pure art of words" as well as in painting (Fry qtd. in Dowling 17).[5] But as Reed has aptly demonstrated, Woolf's commitment to formalism, strongest in the 1920s, waned in her later work as she became equally committed to exploring extra-aesthetic political, sexual, and social issues in her writing ("Through" 37-38).

Though banished from the opening pages in favor of a strictly formalist landscape, these issues ultimately press their way into "Summer's Night," a piece that has not been given the critical attention it merits within conversations about Woolf's literary aesthetics. Their impact on the "sensations" and "relations" that Woolf makes central to the microcosm enclosed within this narrative essay significantly alters the composition of "the present moment" as well as the composition of the essay itself. For "Summer's Night" is a composition, in the pictorial sense of the word, a carefully structured aesthetic arrangement of color, line, and texture that attempts to capture the equally artistic composition of one characteristically Woolfian "moment of being." The importance of the essay, however, lies not in the aesthetic dexterity with which it has been crafted. Rather, it lies in its demonstration of a fairly decisive end, the culmination of Woolf's aesthetic experiments with formalism. The reasons Woolf offers as to why formalism fails to provide her

---

[3] In addition to Reed's "Through Formalism," see his "Forming Formalism," as well as work by Leighton, McNeillie, Prettejohn, Dowling, Uhlmann, and Gillespie (*Sisters*'). Falkenheim's older text also provides an excellent overview of Fry's formalism.

[4] Gillespie offers a compelling account of the manner in which sibling rivalry, as well as shared interests and collaboration, shaped Woolf's work and opinions; see *Sisters*' 104-61.

[5] Consider, for example, Woolf's desire to dedicate the highly formalist *To the Lighthouse* to Fry, who she claimed had "kept [her] on the right path, so far as writing goes, more than anyone" (*L2* 385).

with a complete aesthetic—reasons illustrated in "Summer's Night" by a striking pair of "little accidents"—reveal something else as well: the failure of literary form to reconcile "aesthetic rapture" with what Woolf calls the structural "buttresses" necessary for supporting this rapture. With its own partial collapse incumbent upon the failures of form, "Summer's Night" offers readers a compelling argument for a revision of literary form itself, a reinvention of narrative as a hybrid thing capable of serving the beautiful as well as addressing the political and ethical exigencies that remained a concern for Woolf throughout her literary career. The essay is thus, as Hermione Lee has argued regarding Woolf's non-fiction generally, a crucial piece in the "great complex web" of Woolf's multi-generic literary endeavors ("Essays" 93).

As the editors of *Modernism* point out, "Summer's Night" is "much cited" but little discussed (Kolocotroni, et al. 392), despite its intriguing intertextuality with many of Woolf's other works (it calls to mind short prose pieces like "Blue and Green" and "Kew Gardens," as well as longer fiction like *To The Lighthouse*, *The Waves*, and *Between the Acts*). One of the earliest references to the essay, made by Morris Beja in 1964, establishes "Summer's Night" as an example of that key Woolfian "technical device": the moment of being (138). Beja attunes the reader to the "mystical quality" of such moments and associates them with similar revelatory moments in Woolf's own life (137). More recently, Ann-Marie Priest uses the same mystical elements to offer a brief reading of "Summer's Night" through the lens of neuroscience. Priest characterizes the essay's representation of transcendent consciousness as a surprisingly accurate depiction of right-brain perception, which eschews order and sequence in favor of a luminous simultaneity of time, self, and the world (300). This luminousness, rather esoteric in Priest's account of the essay, is brought back into the realm of the material by Hermione Lee who, in a 1984 essay, notes that Woolf's moments of being, like the one captured in "Summer's Night," are often rendered in concrete metaphors for illumination: mirrors, glass, and other reflectors ("Burning"19). Such symbols of sight and insight make epiphanic experience visible for Woolf's readers.

The materialization of these moments is the focus of the longest critical examination of "Summer's Night," a 1975 article by Jean Guiguet. In this piece, Guiguet suggests that the transformation of the abstract into the concrete that Woolf narrativizes in "Summer's Night" defines all of Woolf's essayistic ventures. Guiguet points out that in this essay, "all the components of the moment, from the most superficial or peripheral to the deepest and most central are rendered in concrete terms" (296). But while Guiguet gives ample attention to the portions of portions of "Summer's Night" that emphasize "weight, perdurability, rootedness" (297), Jane Goldman—who also discusses the essay in the introduction to *The Feminist Aesthetics of Virginia Woolf*—contends that too little attention has been given by any examiner of "Summer's Night" to the political valences of such materialization. She alone locates the Woolfian moment of being in the "real world" (1) and recognizes "Summer's Night" as foregrounding one of several transcendent moments throughout Woolf's oeuvre in which a specifically material intervention takes place (5). In these moments, Goldman argues, we see Woolf attempting not just to present life but to alter it (8-9). Accounts of Woolf's moments of being that examine the aesthetics of the moment, Goldman claims, tend to neglect this aspect of real-world intervention, privileging the ecstatic or the mystical at the expense of the political (9).

In "Summer's Night," however, the moment of being that Goldman rightly identifies as constituting a material intervention fraught with political import at the same time encompasses a significant aesthetic intervention. One cannot consider the essay in either/or terms, for here Woolf's engagement with aesthetics is simultaneously an engagement with the political. This is why I will begin where "Summer's Night" begins, with the unapologetically aesthetic description of a table: "The night was falling so that the table in the garden among the trees grew whiter and whiter; and the people round it more indistinct" (9).

An appropriate opening line, this description captures the strangely discomposing feeling of Woolf's composition. The characters in the essay, "four separate bodies" (10), remain "indistinct" throughout. None are named, and readers have no way of ascertaining which of the characters speaks any or all of the essay's three lines of dialogue. Instead, "Summer's Night" proceeds as a literary experiment much like "Kew Gardens," with only the thinnest of plots: four companions sit in a garden, watch the deepening dusk, and then return indoors. Action is subservient to image, although who is recording the images that comprise the essay remains unclear. The narrator alternately uses second- and first-person pronouns, sometimes including him/herself in the scenes as if he/she were one of the four people sitting around the table, and sometimes projecting his/her observations outward, toward the reader. The effect is unsettling, ambivalent. Narration mirrors the paradoxically intangible solidity that characterizes images throughout the opening paragraphs of the essay.

The table that appears in the first sentence of "Summer's Night" possesses this paradoxical quality, thus calling to mind another enigmatic table in Woolf's work. In *To the Lighthouse*, Andrew Ramsay uses the same object in his verbal verbal illustration of Mr. Ramsay's work on the "nature of reality": "think of a kitchen table," he tells Lily Briscoe, "when you're not there" (23).[6] Like Andrew's

---

[6] This scene plays an important role in Banfield's work on Woolf and the Bloomsbury philosophical tradition, to which I am much indebted; see Banfield 37. The fading table in "Summer's Night" also reminds readers of those very real tables in Woolf's work—the dinner table in *To the Lighthouse*, the "narrow table" (155) around which characters in *The Waves* remember their dead friend, Percival—that suggest brief, tenuous moments of human connectivity.

hypothetical table, the table in "Summer's Night" introduces an epistemology, one based on the visual apprehension of physical forms.[7] Achieving visibility, or rather, capturing in physical, material images an entity—"the present moment"—that resists pictorialization is the primary task Woolf undertakes in her attempt to anatomize the summer evening.

To render an account of this moment, then, Woolf must present the temporal in terms of the spatial, making textually visible a unit of time. She describes the collapse of non-visible time into physical space with a pair of similes that follows her description of the table in the garden: "If you are young, the future lies upon the present, like a piece of glass, making it tremble and quiver. If you are old, the past lies upon the present, like a thick glass, making it waver, distorting it" (9).[8] Like a transparent pane of glass, Woolf suggests, time is perceived in terms of its effects; one sees more or less darkly, more or less distinctly, depending on one's age and experience. The image of the glass set upon either the past or the future, turning time into a kind of narrative window through which one's sight is altered, indicates Woolf's reliance in this essay upon visuality as both an epistemology, the means of knowing what the moment is made of, and an aesthetic, the means of translating this knowledge into literature.

The importance of the visual, and of material embodiment in general, becomes still more apparent in Woolf's initial answer to her own rhetorical question: "Yet what composed the present moment? [. . .] To begin with: it is largely composed of visual and of sense impressions" (9). The "impressions" that follow launch us into a landscape sketched out according to principles that we immediately recognize as central to the aesthetic formalism promoted by Fry and Bell in the inter-war period (Reed, *Roger* 306-07). Consider Woolf's depiction of two objects, both described in the opening paragraphs of "Summer's Night," which Woolf finds integral to the moment's composition. The first is "An owl, blunt, obsolete looking, heavy, weighted, [which] crossed the fading sky with a black spot between its claws" (9). The description is visually potent yet oddly puzzling: how might an owl be "obsolete looking"? What exactly distinguishes a "blunt" owl from a non-blunt (a sharp?) one? The second object, a garden chair, is similarly defamiliarized in the course of Woolf's description, for as soon as Woolf conjures it, it begins to take on decidedly

---

[7] I differ here considerably from Urano, who claims that "Summer's Night" is "not really concerned with the visual" (6). While Urano argues that in the Woolfian moment of being, vision (especially mental perception) is "diminished or relativized" (5), I find both physical and intellectual acts of perception to be central to the aesthetic structure and content of this essay.

[8] Lee mentions this passage in "Summer's Night" briefly in her essay "A Burning Glass," in which she offers an insightful reading of glass images in Woolf's literature as metaphors for "the mind in its moments of creative intensity" (16).

un-chair-like qualities. She writes, "But this moment is also composed of a sense that the legs of the chair are sinking through the centre of the earth, passing through the rich garden earth; they sink, weighted down" (9). The chair is both vaporous and at the same time remarkably dense, materially present yet somehow made capable of dissolving into the soil by its own weightiness.[9] This growing heaviness is accompanied by an erasure of color—"the sense of the light sinking back into darkness seems to be gently putting out with a damp sponge the colour in one's own eyes" (9)—and what is left "in the colorless dark," to quote Ann Banfield's description of this effect when it occurs in a similar passage in *Mrs. Dalloway*, "are the slumbering forms of things" (259).[10]

In both of these descriptions, Woolf is indeed rendering "impressions," "visual impressions" (an owl, a chair) that remain corporeal but nevertheless slip into another realm of "sense," of feeling, emotion, or psychology. In the mind's eye, the appearance of owl or chair alters according to the "sense impression" (bluntness, weightiness) that its physical form evokes, until visual form and emotional/psychological form merge, becoming a new aesthetic entity, "significant form." The idea of significant form, which Clive Bell first postulated in 1912 but explains at greater length in his 1914 treatise *Art*, is closely aligned with the formalist theories that Fry developed in the early twentieth century. During this time, Fry advocated an aesthetic which, in contrast to the mimetic representationalism of what he called "narrative" art, privileged the basic elements of formal design: "rhythm of line, mass, proportion, light and shade, colour, and perspective" (Reed, "Through" 22). Post-Impressionists like Henri Matisse and, especially, Paul Cézanne foregrounded such formal features in their art by rejecting traditional representation in favor of flattened blocks of color, altered physical proportions, and heavy outlines. For this reason, Post-Impressionist art, which calls attention to shape and emphasizes a plastic materiality, typified formalist excellence for Fry and Bell.[11] When criticized for promoting a style that struck some observers as "ahistorical and anti-content"

---

[9] In Drewery's estimation, this makes the chair itself analogous to the moment of being, as the moment is both solid (having a sense of unity) and fleeting (105). Lee also notes the paradoxical nature of Woolf's moments, as both "in and out of time" ("Burning" 17).

[10] In her analysis of *Mrs. Dalloway*, Banfield quotes a passage that resonates with "Summer's Night": "But though [the outline of houses and towers] are gone, the night is full of them; robbed of colour, blank of windows, they exist more ponderously" (24).

[11] Cézanne was the Post-Impressionist that Fry and Bell praised above all others for his ability to represent significant form; see, for example, Fry's 1927 *Cézanne* or his justification of the artist in *Vision and Design* (156-57). Bell also proclaimed Cézanne's greatness in his 1922 collection of essays, *Since Cézanne*. Fry's adoration for Cézanne was fervent enough that it occasionally became the subject of Woolf's satire, as when she wrote: "Roger very nearly lost his senses [upon seeing Maynard Keynes's Cézanne]. I've never seen such a sight of intoxication[.] He was like a bee on a sunflower" (qtd. in Gillespie 49).

in its most extreme instances of abstract design (Dowling 12), Bell argued that form alone had the potential to express something profound and moving, something that "lies behind the appearance of all things—that which gives to all things their individual significance, the thing in itself, the ultimate reality" (Bell 69-70). This "ultimate reality"—significant form—was "shared by all objects that provoke our aesthetic emotions," according to Bell (8). In such objects, "lines and colours" and "forms and relations of forms" combined in a particular way to "stir our aesthetic emotions. These relations and combinations of lines and colours, these aesthetically moving forms, I call 'Significant Form'" (8).

To discover the significant form latent within an object and to capture it on canvas, artists must to do more than simply record the colors and shapes they see. Registering the external world of forms is only the first step, the initial foray into aesthetic creation. According to Fry and Bell, it is here that the Impressionist artists who preceded the Post-Impressionists stopped short. Rather than attempting to draw out the "relations and combinations of lines and colours" that characterized significant form, Impressionists offered "sense-data" itself, visually accurate but without the kind of aesthetic processing that would organize this data into a formally unified pattern or design. As Banfield explains, "Impressionism is pure empiricism; Post-Impressionism transforms its data as scientific theory does" (274). Impressionism might present objects as they exist in the visible world, but Post-Impressionism attempted to "reach the unseen world of persisting objects, of enduring forms" (274) and thence to "construct forms which are equivalent images for, rather than scientific representations of, the things—or figures—seen" (Roe 183).

Woolf clearly understood the Post-Impressionist project. In her 1930 essay "Street Haunting," she wrote that while the eye can "brea[k] off little lumps of emerald and coral," it cannot "compose these trophies" and so offers "beauty pure and uncomposed" (CE 157). Like Fry and Bell, Woolf, too, felt that the creation of significant form required not just the accurate translation of visual impressions into words but the composition of these visual or sense impressions into a unified pattern. It was the ordering of them into a design that revealed the "relations and combinations" that made them aesthetically moving: "when we speak of form we mean that certain emotions have been placed in the right relations to each other; then that the novelist is able to dispose these emotions and make them tell" ("On Re-Reading" 129). [12]

---

[12] For more on Woolf's conception of literary form, especially her use of words as formal structuring devices, see Leighton's excellent "Just a Word." Briggs similarly examines Woolf's development of formal design in fiction, claiming that after the nineteen-teens, Woolf "began consciously [. . .] to think of form as an essential element in fiction—and one that might have a visual or spatial, even a 'plastic' dimension" (100).

Transforming ordinary objects into significant forms lies at the heart of Woolf's compositional efforts in "Summer's Night." Woolf's representation of temporality in spatial, visual terms (what Sue Roe calls a "vision of simultaneity" [179]) and her defamiliarizing treatment of objects that appear as images and then dissolve into emotions or feelings speaks to her awareness of the early formalist theories of Fry and Bell. It also suggests that she is quite consciously shaping the moment she isolates in "Summer's Night" according to a formalist aesthetic. In the essay, Woolf first notes the concrete, physical things that compose her narrative landscape—an owl, as we have seen, or the four people who have gathered in the garden—and then reduces them to the most basic formal elements of visual design: a "blunt" form with a "black spot" beneath it, or a "knot of consciousness: a nucleus" that appears as just another dark spot on the literary canvas (10). A chair stops being merely a chair and becomes an atomized "sense" of strangely ponderous permeability, a form that exists primarily to evoke an aesthetic emotion that is brought from beneath or behind the materiality of the chair itself.

The reduction of characters and objects to significant forms that elicit aesthetic emotions or, as Fry's friend Charles Mauron called them, "psychological volumes" (Dowling 16), creates for Woolf the compositional design that Fry and Bell praised in Post-Impressionist art.[13] Thus, after her description of the chair sinking into the ground as night falls, Woolf writes in "Summer's Night" that such "changes, unseen in the day, coming in succession seem to make an order evident" (9). This carefully composed "order," endowing the evening with the sense of unity that Beja describes as characteristic of Woolfian "moments of being" (116), is impersonal and disinterested, as formalist principles determined art should be.[14] As human beings disappear into "knots" and animals into "spots," the moment seems to recede from human influence, becoming as untouchable as if it were taking place under the thick pane of glass Woolf mentions earlier. "Nothing," Woolf writes, "can interfere with the order" that materializes, and so "we have nothing to do but accept, and watch" (9-10). Such passivity, compared by Woolf to that of "spectators" of a "pageant" (9), accentuates the general quiet of the evening. The sounds the narrator hears—the

---

[13] Dowling provides a helpful description of Mauron's influence on Bloomsbury formalism, both visual and literary (see 16-19). Additionally, see Banfield on the manner in which Mauron's "volumes" functioned as a literary equivalent of formalist notions of design and plastic color (319-20).

[14] See Fry's "Preface" to the *Catalogue* of the Second Post-Impressionist Exhibition on the "disinterestedly passionate state of mind" that comprised the formalist ideal (*Vision and Design* 159), and Goldman on Fry (*Modernism* 47).

murmuring of trees, the humming of "an aeroplane" (9)—register only from a distance, and when one of the four characters speaks, his or her words "explode like a scent" rather than a sound (10).[15] Quiet and composed, the moment communicates only color, shape, and form. As Woolf has sketched it here, it is the literary equivalent of a Cézanne.

That this Cézannesque moment is constructed almost entirely outside the realm of narrative convention (a marked difference from Woolf's 1920s novels, which experiment with formalist principles in similar ways) means that the aesthetic experience of form, rather than plot or character, becomes the driving principle in "Summer's Night." As Woolf once said of her sister's Post-Impressionist paintings, in the opening pages of "Summer's Night," "no stories are told" (Foreword 171), and no narrative action takes place. Instead, Woolf stacks image upon image, form upon form. "Pure concepts [are] transmuted into a physical substance," Guiguet writes in his analysis of the essay (296), but as compositional elements, these physical substances exist primarily as aesthetic "impressions." The materiality or corporeality that the present moment comes to possess transforms the temporal event of the summer evening into something like a still-life, frozen in time and hanging on a gallery wall. We observe it as we would observe a painting, our interest in the piece coming not from a curiosity about the human figures that populate the moment and what they might do or say next but from the heightened aesthetic emotion that "Summer's Night" generates independent of narrative. Bell called this intense formalist emotion "aesthetic rapture," a spiritually-tinged feeling of "extraordinary exaltation" that derived from the contemplation of significant form (*Art* 68). He asserted that, "For those who can feel the significance of form, art can never be less than a religion," a mystical faith that endows worshipers with "that emotional confidence, that assurance of absolute good, which makes of life a momentous and harmonious whole" (*Art* 291-92).

One finds, in Woolf's essay, a gradual sharpening of aesthetic intensity as the author moves readers in this direction, toward "rapturous" contemplation of the beautiful forms that emerge from and exist within the moment. As the sun sets, the characters begin to converse. We hear only one fragment of the conversation: "He'll do well with his hay" (10). The banality of this line seems an indication of the essential unimportance of the content of this conversation. Much more significant is the aesthetic shape that the conversation takes. Like other elements in the

[15] Woolf particularly associated silence with painting and painters, as in her 1930 foreword to an exhibition catalog of her sister's paintings when she writes of the pieces, "No stories are told; no insinuations are made. The hill side is bare; the group of women is silent" (Foreword 171) and of Bell, "Mrs. Bell says nothing. Mrs. Bell is as silent as the grave. Her pictures do not betray her. Their reticence is inviolable" (Foreword 172). See also Gillespie on the "sublime silent fish-world" that Woolf claimed was inhabited by visual artists (74).

the essay, it, too, is reduced to forms laden with aesthetic emotion. Woolf describes the speakers' words as "seeds," and as these seeds fly from the mouths of speakers, they become "extraordinary arrow[s]" that "suffuse the whole dome of the mind" with "incense, flavour" (10). Pouring from an "ambiguous envelope" of lips, these words expand to fill the garden with pungent emotion: "desire," "laughter," "malice," and "amusement" (10). Woolf's prose begins to rise in pitch and tone as "all this"—an increasingly escalating concentration of feeling—"shoots through the moment" (10). Readers find themselves drawn upward as well, encircled in the arms of Woolf's first-person pronouns. "With our wings spread," writes Woolf, "we too fly, take wing, with the owl, over the earth and survey the quietude of what sleeps, folded, slumbering" (10). We experience a kind of rarefied supervision as, like the owl, we are lifted above the world of forms by the sheer beauty of the forms themselves. From far above, hedges and parcels of land become "hidden compartments of different colours" that are "all swept into one colour by the brush of the wing" (10). "Could we not fly," Woolf asks, "with broad wings and with softness [. . .] and so visit in splendour, augustly, peaks; and there lie exposed, bare, on the spine, high up, to the cold light of the moon rising, and when the moon rises, single, solitary, behold her, one, eminent over us? Ah, yes, if we could fly, fly, fly. . ." (10-11).

And then the vision stops. Our aesthetic transcendence is brought to an abrupt, mid-sentence halt. As they so often do in Woolf's works, these ellipses signal an important authorial intervention. Rather than continuing in rapturous flight with the owl, soaring toward some formalist climax of aesthetic experience, our ascent is interrupted by the first of two "little accidents" (11). It is an incident constructed with such strange absurdity and having such exaggerated repercussion that it forces one to reconsider Woolf's apparently forthright espousal of the formalist aesthetic that directs the essay to this point. The disturbance that checks our progress is, oddly enough, a sneeze—a jarring, body-contorting sneeze—described by Woolf with a disconcertingly violent simile: "Here the body is gripped; and shaken; and the throat stiffens; and the nostrils tingle; and like a rat shaken by a terrier one sneezes" (11). Startling in its animal brutality, this image of a rat trapped in the jaws of a dog and being swung back and forth until senseless conjures a feeling of unease that contradicts the pastoral serenity and aesthetic detachment that have characterized the essay thus far. In one instant, readers are brought sharply and summarily from the airy heights of aesthetic rapture back into the realm of savage mortality. Moreover, Woolf's failure to attribute the sneeze to any one of the four "bodies" in "Summer's Night" compounds the oddity of the interruption. The objective, impersonal "one" who sneezes might be the reader, the narrator, or Woolf herself. Yet whether it comes from inside or outside the text, the sneeze has enormous textual consequence: "the whole universe" inscribed within the essay "is shaken" by the cataclysm (11). "Mountains, snows, meadows; moon"—all are thrown "higgledy, piggledy, upside down, little splinters flying" (11). Woolf's composition, so dexterously painted with formalist perfection and so orderly in its design, is suddenly pitched into chaos, without warning and without moderation, by a *sneeze*.

Both satirical and subversive, this "little accident" precipitates a monumental change in the manner in which Woolf perceives and represents the moment. To begin, issuing from the forms and shapes that have been upended by the sneeze, a woman emerges. In contrast to the earlier "nucleus" of multiple beings that have melted into one "knot," this woman's embodied appearance suggests the first inklings of individual personhood, described by Woolf in all of its greatness ("somebody of importance") and insignificance ("not the least venerable to other human beings") (11). The unnamed woman is conspicuously not defined as a "shape" or a "knot" or a "body." In fact, Woolf offers no physical description of her at all, making this woman the first entity in the essay to be represented in non-formalist terms. Her character is instead revealed by what she does, and her actions command particular attention, appearing, as they do, in a text that has until now postulated passivity as the primary method of engaging with the moment. First and foremost, this woman actively sees; Woolf calls her "the observant, the discriminating" (11). Her gaze penetrates the abstractions of form and color that comprise her environment, preventing her from being distracted or misled. Attentive and perceptive, she "isolates cases from the mists of hugeness, sees what is there all the more definitely" with the result that she is "skeptical withal," "cannot believe in miracles," and "refuses to be bamboozled" (11).

Something—perhaps her perception, perhaps her agential power—enables the woman to resist reduction to significant form or aesthetic emotion. We begin to take a human, psychological interest in her, and this interest is heightened when the woman, rather than allowing the moment to compose her, begins to alter the composition of the moment. Her emergence from the aesthetic collapse of the sneeze, Woolf writes, is the reason "why the moment becomes harder, is intensified, diminished, begins to be stained by some expressed personal juice" (11-12). Elsewhere in Woolf's writing, the "stain" of the personal is something to be avoided. In *A Room of One's Own*, Woolf explains that "one must strain off what was personal and accidental in all these impressions and so reach the pure fluid, the essential oil of truth" (25). It's no surprise, then, to find that this "juice" deconstructs the impersonal formal order that organizes earlier portions of the essay. The result of this, as Guiguet has noted, is that "Summer's Night" begins to break down textually; "in the four sentences covering eighteen lines [after the sneeze] there are no less than twenty-eight segments separated by semi-colons" (300). The essay's scant narrative follows suit, fragmented by the appearance, alongside the woman, of "self-assertion" (which "steals" into the moment), of desire ("the desire to be loved"), and finally of a second "little accident" that completes the aesthetic rupture begun by the sneeze (11-12).

This second "accident," violent in a way that parallels the shaken rat, reverberates through the second half of "Summer's Night" with even greater consequence than the sneeze. The "accident" appears unexpectedly and without preamble, flashing in the eyes of readers and then disappearing just as quickly as it appears:

> Then a light is struck; in it appears a sunburnt face, lean, blue-eyed, and the arrow flies as the match goes out:
> "He beats her every Saturday; from boredom, I should say; not drink; there's nothing else to do."
> The moment runs like quicksilver on a sloping board into the cottage parlour; there are the tea things on the table; the hard windsor chairs; tea caddies on the shelf for ornament; the medal under a glass shade; vegetable steam curling from the pot; two children crawling on the floor; and Liz comes in and John catches her a blow on the side of the head as she slopes past him, dirty, with her hair loose and one hairpin sticking out about to fall. And she moans in a chronic animal way; and the children look up and then make a whistling noise to imitate the engine which they trail across the flags; and John sits himself down with a thump at the table and carves a hunk of bread and munches because there is nothing to be done. A steam rises from his cabbage patch. Let us do something then, something to end this horrible moment, this plausible glistening moment that reflects in its smooth sides this intolerable kitchen, this squalor; this woman moaning; and the rattle of the toy on the flags, and the man munching. Let us smash it by breaking a match. There—snap. (12)

Even more strikingly than in the previous "accident," one notes the noisy human element that forces its way into the text here, asserting itself in blatant contradiction to the silence, the impersonality, and the disinterestedness of earlier portions of "Summer's Night." If before the pair of accidents, Woolf's essay had resembled a Cézanne in its composition, it now seems to be espousing a distinctly different aesthetic. The scene revealed by the flare of the match is too naturalistic, too emotionally-fraught, to be interpreted as an arrangement in color or form. Instead, it calls to mind Fry's description of the German-born British painter Walter Sickert, whom Fry criticized in 1911 for his "odd refusal to have any dealings with the material of romance, a persistent devotion to the banal and trivial situations of ordinary life, at times even an attraction for what is squalid" ("Mr. Walter" 143).

Fry's early twentieth-century disapproval of Sickert is not surprising. As Woolf noted in her 1934 essay on the artist, Sickert's work was intentionally unlike other Post-Impressionist painters praised by the Bloomsbury art theorists when they were formulating the formalist principles that become, according to Reed, the "foundation of modernism" (*Roger* 306). Perhaps because of Fry's initial disparagement of him, Woolf felt a kinship with Sickert.[16] Following his own description of himself in a letter, Woolf called Sickert "a literary painter" ("Walter" 243), in whose works one could read "any number of stories and three-volume novels" (238). By "literary," Woolf seems to mean not "narrative" in the sense that nineteenth-century British paintings exemplified that quality, but in the sense of not having receded entirely into the autotelic world of purely formalist aesthetics. "Human nature," Woolf writes, "is never exiled from [Sickert's] canvas—there is always a woman with a parasol in the foreground, or a man selling cabbages" (240). This makes Sickert something of a "hybrid," in Woolf's assessment: some artists "bore deeper and deeper into the stuff of their own art; others are always making raids into the lands of others. Sickert it may be is among the hybrids, the raiders" (243). A Post-Impressionist who raids the literary realm in search of what formalism does not or cannot provide, Sickert offers Woolf an important alternative to the Cézannesque aesthetic style that exemplified formalism in its most perfect state—the aesthetic style that Woolf employs before the "little accidents" that disrupt "Summer's Night."

Alongside her formalist exploration of "visual and sense impressions," then, Woolf begins to shape a different portrait, one that allows—indeed, is incumbent upon—what Woolf calls "human nature" in Sickert. Like the unnamed woman who appears amid the rubble of the sneeze and who might, in fact, be the striker of the match that illuminates this second "little accident," Woolf's characters Liz and John assert a psychological presence that the earlier "knot" of bodies in the garden do not. They are fully human, made so by the introduction into "Summer's Night" of certain elements of narrative convention. What was almost wholly descriptive prose before the "accidents" has become fiction. For example, it should not escape the reader's notice that Liz and John enjoy the distinction of being the only named characters in "Summer's Night." Their "cottage parlour" provides a setting so conventional it is almost a novelistic cliché. John's entrance and abuse creates a recognizable, if abbreviated, plot. And while the objects in the scene ("windsor chairs," "tea caddies," toy "engine") share the solid materiality of objects mentioned earlier in

---

[16] It should be noted that in the course of what Reed calls Fry's "post-war reassessment of formalism," Fry came to acknowledge Sickert's contributions to British modern art: "it would be absurd to reject the extraordinary beauty of Sickert's drawing," Fry wrote, even if it failed to provide as much pleasure as "the pleasure derived from the suggestion to the mind of plastic form" (qtd. in Reed, *Roger* 308).

the essay, one would be hard pressed to find in them any hint of the significant form that would justify aesthetic contemplation. They exist instead as the narrative tools with which Woolf attaches human feeling (sprung from a recognition of the commonplace-ness of these items) to character, setting, and plot. In fact, Woolf actively prevents us from considering these objects in aesthetic terms by pronouncing them patently un-aesthetic: ugly, dirty, and cheap. Of course, even the ugliness, the "squalor" of the "intolerable kitchen," humanizes Liz, John, and the children.

The scene further separates itself from the formalist principles that characterize the first half of the essay by its means of engagement with the reader. Rather than launching readers toward aesthetic rapture, inviting us to spread our wings and "fly, fly, fly" as Woolf's earlier descriptions had done, this "accident" elicits a different kind of readerly response.[17] In the miserable circumstances and the grimy desperation of the family—desperation that Woolf makes viscerally apparent in vegetable steam, loose hair, and children crawling on the floor—we feel the incursion of the political that Goldman remarks (*Feminist* 9). Issues of poverty, social class, and above all gender make an appeal to readers that has nothing to do with aesthetics and everything to do with the social and material conditions that shape rather un-beautiful lives. More compelling still, the violence perpetrated against Liz in full sight of the children asserts an undeniable ethical claim on the reader. Our shock at witnessing the blow, and at hearing "boredom" announced as the habitual motivation for it, triggers both surprise and anger on Liz's behalf, emotions that stretch far beyond the milieu of formalist aesthetics. John's assault provokes a desire on the part of the reader to, as the narrator says, "do something [. . .] to end this horrible moment." This desire crosses yet another aesthetic boundary by rousing the kind of social interestedness that Woolf inveighs against in "Mr. Bennett and Mrs. Brown."[18] It also marks a repudiation of the passivity ("We have nothing to do but accept, and watch") that previously characterized the moment.

Thankfully and to our relief, the narrator feels the ethical compulsion of Liz's situation as strongly as the reader and intervenes, breaking the match and so returning us to the garden where "Summer's Night" began. With the narrator's "There—snap," however, something in the essay snaps as well. Things become

---

[17] Lee suggests that a consideration of our responses is particularly appropriate for Woolf's non-fiction prose, as this was a primary concern for Woolf. Her essays, Lee claims, prove Woolf a "pioneer of reader-response theory" (89) who was "above all interested in how a book works on the reader's feelings" (98).

[18] One of the criticisms Woolf levels against what she calls "Edwardian" books in this 1924 essay is that "In order to complete them it seems necessary to do something—to join a society, or, more desperately, to write a cheque" (12). In this earlier essay, she makes clear her aversion to this kind of literature, notwithstanding the plea she voices in "Summer's Night."

"higgledy, piggledy" once again. Night falls: "the owl flutes off its watery bubble. But the sun is deep below the earth" (12). Whereas the fading light had earlier "ma[d]e an order evident" (9), a pattern of shapes and colors composed with evident deliberation, now "no order is perceptible; there is no sequence" (12). As blackness envelops the garden and the countryside beyond, we lose the visual acuity so crucial to the essay's earlier aesthetic. There are "cries to the left and to the right," Woolf writes, but "nothing can be seen" (12). Nothing can be known, this statement seems to imply. Our loss of vision, understanding, and sense of order spells the final disintegration of the essay's formalist aesthetic. Formalism itself has fallen short. It has failed to prevent the so-called "accidents" that shake it to its foundation. But more importantly, the disruption these "accidents" cause allows us to realize that what John, Liz, and their dingy kitchen contribute to the composition of the moment cannot be expressed in terms of form alone. Comprehending their experience as integral to the experience of this time and this place requires the addition of something more.

Though reached in the midst of domestic violence and narrative collapse, this realization comes as a revelation, the central revelation communicated in "Summer's Night." For readers familiar with Woolf's work, its centrality is immediately apparent, for framed by the striking of a match, the episode recalls other instances wherein Woolf indicates significant moments of revelation by invoking this motif. In *Mrs. Dalloway*, for example, Clarissa's recollection of Sally's kiss impresses itself on her memory as "an illumination; a match burning in a crocus; an inner meaning almost expressed" (34). A fleeting instant of homosexual intimacy that profoundly affects Clarissa's sense of self, the lit match marks a defining moment of intense clarity, an experience of self-awareness and self-understanding that is not surpassed elsewhere in her youth. Similarly, in *To the Lighthouse*, Lily's struggle to complete her painting leaves her with the realization that while "The great revelation had never come. The great revelation perhaps never did come," there remain "little daily miracles, illuminations, matches struck unexpectedly in the dark" (161). Ironically, coming to this conclusion enables Lily to have her "great revelation," her moment of vision, and so to complete her painting. And in *A Room of One's Own*, Woolf describes the mistaken efforts of female authors to imitate the literary cadences of their male counterparts as "like a person striking a match that will not light" (80). In this case, as in the previous two instances, a lit match indicates intellectual and psychological enlightenment, a moment wherein one sees (or writes) clearly and intensely and is changed as a result.

The match struck in "Summer's Night" initially seems to suggest just the opposite. The scene that comes into view in the flickering light is angry and violent, marred by subjugation rather than enlightenment. The vision the match illuminates seems one best forgotten, best consigned to the darkness that overtakes it when the match is smashed and the scene is aborted. Everything about this scene feels wrong, from the ethical outrage that John's actions inspire, to the textual crisis the incident provokes, to Woolf's transformation of her readers into voyeurs made to peer into a lighted window that we have no business peering into. But our discomfort only reiterates Woolf's literary intent, making formalism's failure register on a personal as well as an intellectual level. What this scene reveals is shocking, literally and aesthetically, but its revelation is no less illuminating for its shock. In fact, if one recalls Woolf's assertion in "A Sketch of the Past" that a "shock-receiving capacity" made her capable of receiving literary insight (72), one might argue that what the vignette discloses about a formalist literary aesthetic is illuminating precisely because of the shock with which it is conveyed.[19]

The shocking discovery that Woolf makes in the light of the match can be stated quite simply: formalism fails because its exclusions undermine its aesthetic viability. The network of human relations that lends this second "little accident" its emotional potency—Liz's suffering at the hands of her husband, and the unexplored but inevitable ramifications her ongoing victimization will have for her children—must be reduced to color, form, and rhythm of line in order for the scene to be rendered faithfully in accordance with a formalist aesthetic. As we see earlier with the owl and the chair, this artistic reduction represents a unique type of embodiment. Art, explains Laura Doyle in her examination of *To the Lighthouse*, even as it "redefines bodies . . . as abstractions, . . . also redefines thought as embodied" (65). But as Woolf suggests with the folding of "Summer's Night" at this point, attempting to redefine Liz and John as aesthetic abstractions would make a costly sacrifice. It would forfeit Liz and John—literally embodied figures with "bodily emotions" (Doyle 42) that, in turn, invoke emotional responses in the reader—for the colors and shapes that constitute significant form. As interested as Woolf is in questions of aesthetics, in "Summer's Night," this interest does not preclude the concern with politics and ethics, especially feminist politics and ethics, that Woolf embeds in the bodies of Liz and John. As Jessica Berman points

---

[19] Parkes examines the role "shock" plays in the writing of Woolf, complicating her reclamation as "one of modernism's preeminent writers of trauma" by asserting that one might productively think of the "Woolfian moment as the product of collaboration between two different types of shock—one conscious, material, historical, the other unconscious, traumatic, timeless" (147). Banfield also notes the importance of jarring, disconcerting moments in Woolf's fiction and prose. For Woolf, Banfield writes, "reality . . . is a shock, arresting the observer," as we are arrested by this scene in "Summer's Night" (340). While some shocks "may reveal order," others "fail to yield a pattern" (340), resulting instead in the "peculiar horror and physical collapse" that this essay narrativizes (Woolf qtd. in Banfield 340-41).

out, these "human" issues, which strict formalism divorced from the realm of art, remain intertwined with artistic embodiment in Woolf's work. Not only in "Summer's Night" but especially there, we find that aesthetics cannot exist for its own sake, however rapturous that existence might be. Often, claims Berman, Woolf employs aesthetics as a means of achieving an end that she regards as related to the claims of art, as when Woolf uses aesthetics to create "an ethical realm [. . .] between the potentially universal and the personal" (159). For Woolf, moments of sympathy—like the moment summoned up by the light of the match when we are asked to consider Liz not as an aesthetic object but as an individual subject—are "not only mediated by, but occur within, the process of aesthetic reflection" (Berman 170).

Without the political and ethical concerns introduced into "Summer's Night" by the second "accident," then, the formalism Woolf employs in the first half of the essay remains compositionally beautiful but fundamentally incomplete, lacking what she described to her sister as "buttressing." In a letter to Vanessa Bell written in 1927, Woolf recounts the dilemma of reconciling aesthetics with the equally exigent demands of non-aesthetic issues, a problem that asserts itself in Vanessa's Post-Impressionist art as well as in Woolf's own writing. Describing Vanessa and herself as mutually "mistresses of our medium as never before," Woolf concedes that they are "both therefore confronted with entirely new problems of structure" (*L*3 341). Addressing these problems requires finding an aesthetic capable of upholding significant form: "All your pictures are built up of flying phrases," Woolf writes, reminding us of the "flying phrases" that appear in "Summer's Night" immediately before the first "accident." "I daresay your problem will now be to buttress up this lyricism with solidity" (341). She goes on to tell her sister, "I should like you to paint a large, large picture; where everything would be brought perfectly firmly together, yet all half flying off the canvas in rapture" (341).

"Summer's Night" might well have been composed to attempt just this, a literary picture that flies "off the canvas" in formalist "rapture" but at the same time is "brought firmly together" by the structural support of those concerns that make up the whole of "human nature." If this is the case, however, it is important to note that the essay is not entirely successful in its attempt. Formalism falls short in "Summer's Night," but the essay itself also fails in part, falling into disarray rather than being strengthened and unified by Woolf's introduction of non-aesthetic "buttressing" material. Both "little accidents" are called "accidents" for good reason: they dis-compose rather than fortify the composition of the moment. This conveys a second insight, worthy of (but not granted) a match of its own: Woolf's recognition of the need for (and the difficulty of fashioning) a hybrid literary aesthetic capable of preserving the intense emotion generated by significant form without sacrificing the volubility of the personal and the political.[20] If successful, such a piece of literature would be able to reconcile aesthetic "rapture" with those subjects that Woolf, again speaking in the context of her sister's Post-Impressionist painting, regarded as detrimentally "held at bay" within a formalist aesthetic: "mortality," "psychology," "the loquacities and trivialities of daily life," and "morality" (Foreword 172-73).[21]

"Summer's Night" is not the only place where Woolf explores the possibility of a new literary aesthetic, of course, but within the essay, this idea comes to be embodied by Liz. The character around whom Woolf's aesthetic discussion coalesces, Liz is thus a pivotal figure. She plays both a narrative and a figurative role in the essay, checking the privileging of formal design with her decidedly unaesthetic circumstances and calling to mind, as she does so, Woolf's descriptions of fiction itself. In Woolf's 1927 "The Art of Fiction," an essay that explores many of the same questions posed in "Summer's Night," Woolf prefaces a discussion of E. M. Forster's novels with the observation, "That fiction is a lady, and a lady who has somehow got herself into trouble, is a thought that must often have struck her admirers" (106). Fiction is not merely in trouble, however; she is actually complicit in her own abuse. Woolf suggests as much a few years earlier in "Modern Fiction," where she writes, "And if we can imagine the art of fiction come alive and standing in our midst, she would undoubtedly bid us break her and bully her" (110).

When this allegorical being is given a name and a kitchen full of tea caddies as she is in "Summer's Night," the metaphor Woolf draws here becomes more than a little unsettling. Moreover, it strikes one as odd, especially in light of the indignation Woolf solicits from readers in the Liz and John episode, to find Woolf adopting the self-justifying rhetoric of the abuser who believes his victim to be "asking for it." This oddity remains inexplicable until one asks why it is that fiction must be beaten and bullied, why Liz apparently must be dealt a blow to the head that leaves her moaning. Woolf goes some way toward an explanation in "The Narrow Bridge of Art." In this 1927 essay, she argues that the literary distinction

---

[20] The editors of *Modernism* acknowledge but leave unexplored the generic hybrid that "Summer's Night" attempts to be. They write that the essay represents, "an experimental merging of fact, polemic, and fiction" (Kolocotroni, et al. 392).

[21] About the same time that Woolf was writing this to Vanessa Bell, Fry was coming to a similar conclusion. Reed recounts Fry's efforts "during the period between the wars" to revise the formalist aesthetic that he made famous (*Roger* 310). In his 1920s and '30s writing, Reed asserts, Fry begins to blur the "formal and moral categories across the boundary that Fry earlier delineated with the labels 'art' and 'life'" (310).

between aesthetics (which Woolf aligns with poetic writing) and the "common purpose[s] of life" (typically aligned with prose fiction) must be collapsed to create a new kind of literature capable of expressing both "exaltation" and "ordinariness" (223, 224). While it will certainly "differ from [fiction] as we know it now" (224), this new literature will provide readers and writers with a text wherein everything appears "in the right relation to each other," as Woolf had written earlier ("On Re-Reading" 129). "It will resemble poetry," Woolf writes, "in this that it will give not only or mainly people's relations to each other and their activities together, [. . .] but it will give the relation of the mind to general ideas and its soliloquy in solitude" ("Narrow" 225). Most importantly, once literature has been broken down and re-shaped into something new, its form will be reconciled with the extra-aesthetic content that resists reduction to shape and design, preventing writers from "attempting what they cannot achieve," namely, "forcing the form they use to contain a meaning which is strange to it" (218).

To accomplish this, Woolf, like Walter Sickert, must become a raider. As we see her do in "Summer's Night," she must invade the realm of visual aesthetics, not to remain encamped there, as the essay initially suggests she might, but to take from formalism the principles that would aid her in "bend[ing]," "model[ing]," or "invent[ing]" a new literary aesthetic ("On Re-Reading" 129). Once obtained, these principles—the aesthetic doctrines that posit significant form in color, shape, and design—must themselves be remodeled so as to resist narrative collapse when buttressed by the un-aesthetic elements of "human nature." This type of raiding becomes apparent in the concluding paragraphs of "Summer's Night." After the narrator smashes the match that illuminates the second "accident" and thereby pitches the essay into an orderless darkness, Woolf writes:

> Then comes the terror, the exultation; the power . . . to be swept away to become a rider on the random wind; the tossing wind; the trampling and neighing wind; the horse with the blown-back mane; the tumbling, the foraging; he who gallops for ever, nowhither travelling, indifferent; to be part of the eyeless dark, to be rippling and streaming, to feel the glory run molten up the spine, down the limbs, making the eyes glow, burning, bright, and penetrate the buffeting waves of the wind. (12-13)

Like the match, this equestrian figure is a familiar motif in Woolf's work. Diane Gillespie, noting Woolf's frequent conflation of raiding, riding, and writing, explains that "Woolf's image of the raider with its visual associations of gallops on horseback into and out of alien territory relates in a curious way to an equestrian image she varies constantly in her diaries when she tries to describe both her life and her creative process" (1).

A description, then, of the raiding writer or of writing itself—the process or the product—this passage reminds us of a previous moment of imagined rapture, when the essay's formalist musings swept us upward on the wings of a "blunt" shape hovering above a "black spot" (9). We feel the same sense of exultant freedom, the same enormity of possibility. Then we lay "exposed, bare, on the spine" of the earth (11); now we have become part of the "splendour," so that the "glory" of it "run[s] molten up the spine" that is our spine, and "down the limbs" that are our limbs. In that earlier moment of aesthetic flight, however, the transcendent vision emerged from the "visual and sense impressions" that seemed to compose the moment. Here, it springs from the "accident" that crumbles the beautiful composition and so confirms formalism's failure. The image of the horse and rider, full of breathless energy and galloping fearlessly into the "eyeless dark," suggests the limitless potential of the new literary aesthetic that might arise from that failure. But the fact that formalism alone does, ultimately, fall short cannot be contested.

The aesthetic alternative that Woolf portrays as the difference between the owl, whose brilliant flight is checked by a sneeze, and the raiding horse with the "blown-back mane" is reiterated in the final scene of "Summer's Night." When the "knot" of figures that began the essay in the garden decides that it is "Time to go in" (13), its dispersal pulls readers away from Liz, John, matches, and riders and back into the strictly formalist moment that Woolf's "little accidents" had foreclosed. As in the opening paragraphs of the essay, we find ourselves once again wandering among lines and shapes, tables and chairs. "One shape heaves and surges and rises," Woolf writes, and as the figures enter a door, "the square draws its lines round us, and here is a chair, a table, glasses, knives, and thus we are boxed and housed, and will soon require a draught of soda-water and to find something to read in bed" (13). The essay concludes with this last appeal to the solid objects and weighty forms that had previously offered readers a glimpse of significant form. And yet now, instead of injecting us with aesthetic emotion, these shapes leave us feeling "boxed and housed," as though we were nothing more than objects in a mechanized suburbia. The dead-endedness of formalism hits hard when we realize that in returning to a formalist aesthetic, we have traded molten glory for soda-water.

In "Summer's Night," the "rider on the random wind" represents a kind of promised land, something unattained in the essay but clearly envisioned. Bloomsbury formalism offers Woolf a great deal, a rapturous aesthetic capable of rendering the ineffable in physical, material terms and so giving the "present moment" the corporeality of a piece of Post-Impressionist art. But such a composition—silent, disinterested, wholly aesthetic—allows no place for John or Liz, no place for the woman who emerges from Woolf's first "little accident" and the human concerns these characters denote. In order, then, for the political, psychological, and ethical exigencies that formalism would hold at bay to be recognized as part of the moment's composition, literature itself must be made into something new, a hybrid form prosaic enough to encompass kitchens and failed relationships but poetic enough to preserve aesthetic artistry. This is the contribution "Summer's Night" makes to the aesthetic evolution that Woolf undergoes throughout her literary career. It is a record of the "little accidents" that move Woolf toward a literature that allows her to render both the "sensations" and the "relations" that comprise all the present moments of our lives on one aesthetically unified canvas.

Works Cited

Banfield, Ann. *The Phantom Table: Woolf, Fry, Russell, and Epistemology of Modernism*. Cambridge: Cambridge UP, 2000. Print.
Beja, Morris. "Matches Struck in the Dark: Virginia Woolf's Moments of Vision." *Critical Quarterly* 6.2 (1964): 137-52. Print.
Bell, Clive. *Art*. New York: Frederick A. Stokes, 1914. Print.
——. *Since Cézanne*. New York: Harcourt, 1922. Print.
Berman, Jessica. "Ethical Folds: Ethics, Aesthetics, Woolf." *Modern Fiction Studies* 50.1 (2004): 151-72. Print.
Briggs, Julia. *Reading Woolf*. Edinburgh: Edinburgh UP, 2004. Print.
Broughton, Panthea Reid. "The Blasphemy of Art: Fry's Aesthetics and Woolf's Non-'Literary' Stories." *The Multiple Muses of Virginia Woolf*. Ed. Diane F. Gillespie. Columbia: U of Missouri P, 1993. 36-57. Print.
Dowling, David. *Bloomsbury Aesthetics and the Novels of Forster and Woolf*. New York: St. Martin's, 1985. Print.
Doyle, Laura. "'These Emotions of the Body': Intercorporeal Narrative in *To the Lighthouse*." *Twentieth Century Literature* 40.1 (Spring 1994): 42-71. Print.
Drewery, Claire. *Modernist Short Fiction by Women: Dorothy Richardson, May Sinclair, and Virginia Woolf*. Burlington: Ashgate, 2011. Print.
Falkenheim, Jacqueline V. *Roger Fry and the Beginnings of Formalist Art Criticism*. Ann Arbor: UMI, 1980. Print.
Fry, Roger. *Cézanne, A Study of His Development*. New York: Macmillan, 1927. Print.
——. "Mr. Walter Sickert's Pictures at the Stafford Gallery." 1911. *A Roger Fry Reader*. Ed. Christopher Reed. Chicago: Chicago UP, 1996. 141-43. Print.
——. *Vision and Design*. London: Chatto and Windus, 1920. Print.
Gillespie, Diane Filby. *The Sisters' Arts: The Writing and Painting of Virginia Woolf and Vanessa Bell*. Syracuse: Syracuse UP, 1988. Print.

Goldman, Jane. *The Feminist Aesthetics of Virginia Woolf: Modernism, Post-Impressionism, and the Politics of the Visual.* Cambridge: Cambridge UP, 1998. Print.

———. *Modernism, 1910-1945: Image to Apocalypse.* New York: Palgrave, 2004. Print.

Guiguet, Jean. "A Novelist's Essay: 'The Moment: Summer's Night' by Virginia Woolf." *Der Englische Essay: Analysen.* Ed. Horst Weber. Darmstadt, Germany: Wissenschaftliche Buchgesellschaft, 1975. 291-303. Print.

Hussey, Mark. *Virginia Woolf A-Z.* Oxford: Oxford UP, 1995. Print.

Kolocotroni, Vassiliki, Jane Goldman, and Olga Taxidou, eds. *Modernism: An Anthology of Sources and Documents.* Chicago: U of Chicago P, 1998. Print.

Lee, Hermione. "A Burning Glass: Reflection in Virginia Woolf." *Virginia Woolf: A Centenary Perspective.* Ed. Eric Warner. London: Macmillan, 1984. 12-27. Print.

———. "Virginia Woolf's Essays." *The Cambridge Companion to Virginia Woolf.* 2nd ed. Ed. Sue Roe and Susan Sellers. Cambridge: Cambridge UP, 2010. 89-106. Print.

Leighton, Angela. *On Form: Poetry, Aestheticism, and the Legacy of a Word.* Oxford: Oxford UP, 2007. Print.

McNeillie, Andrew. "Bloomsbury." *The Cambridge Companion to Virginia Woolf.* 2nd ed. Ed. Sue Roe and Susan Sellers. Cambridge: Cambridge UP, 2010. 1-28. Print.

Morrell, Ottoline. *Ottoline: The Early Memoirs of Lady Ottoline Morrell.* Ed. Robert Gathorne-Hardy. London: Faber and Faber, 1963. Print.

Parkes, Adam. *A Sense of Shock: The Impact of Impressionism on Modern British and Irish Writing.* Oxford: Oxford UP, 2011. Print.

Prettejohn, Elizabeth. "Out of the Nineteenth Century: Roger Fry's Early Art Criticism, 1900-1906." *Art Made Modern: Roger Fry's Vision of Art.* Ed. Christopher Green. London: Merrell Holberton, 1999. 31-44. Print.

Priest, Ann-Marie. "Virginia Woolf's Brain: Mysticism, Literature, and Neuroscience." *Dalhousie Review* 89.3 (Autumn 2009): 298-305. Print.

Reed, Christopher. "Forming Formalism: The Post-Impressionist Exhibitions." *A Roger Fry Reader.* Ed. Reed. Chicago: U of Chicago P, 1996. 48-60. Print.

———, ed. *A Roger Fry Reader.* Chicago: U of Chicago P, 1996.

———. "Through Formalism: Feminism and Virginia Woolf's Relation to Bloomsbury Aesthetics." *Twentieth-Century Literature* 38.1 (1992): 20-43. Print.

Roe, Sue. "The Impact of Post-Impressionism." *The Cambridge Companion to Virginia Woolf.* Ed. Sue Roe and Susan Sellers. Cambridge: Cambridge UP, 2000. 164-90. Print

Stephen, Leslie. *History of English Thought in the Eighteenth Century.* Vol. 1. 2nd ed. London: Smith, Elder, and Co., 1881. Print.

Uhlmann, Anthony. "Virginia Woolf and Bloomsbury Aesthetics." *The Edinburgh Companion to Virginia Woolf and the Arts.* Ed. Maggie Humm. Edinburgh: Edinburgh UP, 2010. 58-73. Print.

Urano, Kaoru. "Virginia Woolf's Refutation of Ocularcentrism: The Eyelessness in the Moment of Being." *Journal of the Ochanomizu University English Society* 1 (2010): 5-15. Print.

Woolf, Virginia. "The Art of Fiction." 1927. *The Moment and Other Essays.* London: Hogarth, 1947. 106-12. Print.

——. Foreword. *Recent Paintings by Vanessa Bell.* 1930. *The Bloomsbury Group: A Collection of Memoirs, Commentary, and Criticism.* Ed. S. P. Rosenbaum. Toronto: U of Toronto P, 1975. 169-73. Print.

——. *The Letters of Virginia Woolf.* Ed. Nigel Nicolson. 6 vols. New York: Harcourt, 1975-77. Print.

——. "Modern Fiction." 1925. *Collected Essays.* Vol. 2. London: Hogarth, 1966. 103-110. Print.

——. "The Moment: Summer's Night." *The Moment and Other Essays.* Ed. Leonard Woolf. London: Hogarth, 1947. 9-13. Print.

——. *Mr. Bennett and Mrs. Brown.* London: Hogarth, 1924. Print.

——. *Mrs. Dalloway.* 1925. New York: Harcourt, 1981. Print.

——. "The Narrow Bridge of Art." 1927. *Collected Essays.* Vol. 2. London: Hogarth, 1966. 218-29. Print.

——. "On Re-Reading Novels." 1922. *Collected Essays.* Vol. 2. London: Hogarth, 1966. 122-30. Print.

——. *A Room of One's Own.* 1929. New York: Harcourt, 1981. Print.

——. "A Sketch of the Past." 1939. *Moments of Being.* Ed. Jeanne Schulkind. New York: Harcourt, 1985. 64-159. Print.

——. "Street Haunting." 1930. *Collected Essays.* Vol. 4. New York: Harcourt, 1967. 155-66. Print.

——. *To the Lighthouse.* 1927. New York: Harcourt, 1981. Print.

——. "Walter Sickert: A Conversation." 1934. *Collected Essays.* Vol. 2. London: Hogarth, 1966. 233-44. Print.

——. *The Waves.* 1931. New York: Harcourt, 2006. Print.

Wedding Rituals: Julia Strachey, Virginia Woolf, and Viola Tree[1]

Diane F. Gillespie

I. Introduction: "a . . . remarkable acidulated story" –V. Woolf

Although weddings transform people's identities, human tendencies to thwart perfection often mar these rites of passage, the past remains ever-present, and the unpredictable realities of married life lie ahead. The Hogarth Press, itself one result of Leonard and Virginia Woolf's own wedding, became over the years increasingly heterogeneous in its interests and more likely to blur boundaries between so-called "highbrow" modernist and "middlebrow" writing.[2] Between 1928 and 1937, for instance, the Press published three very different books by women writers, all of whom undermined or revised one important aspect of the traditional marriage plot—the culmination of courtship and fulfillment of desire in an idealized wedding. The book that caught my eye was a 1932 first edition of Julia Strachey's satirical novella called *Cheerful Weather for the Wedding*.[3] Strachey's focus on a wedding day called to mind a more familiar 1928 precedent, the verbal *tour de force* that is the wedding scene in Virginia Woolf's *Orlando: A Biography*. Although Woolf constantly interrogates the ambiguities of both unmarried and married states throughout her fiction, *Orlando* contains the only on-stage wedding ceremony Woolf published during her lifetime.[4] Then, in 1937, actress and writer Viola Tree bookended Julia

---

[1] My thanks to Jean Rose of Random House Group and Nancy Fulford for access to the Hogarth Press papers in Special Collections at the University of Reading Library; to Trevor Bond and Jeff Kuure of Manuscripts, Archives, and Special Collections at Washington State University (WSU) for the Grant dust jacket image; to the E. J. Pratt Library, Victoria University, University of Toronto, for the Duncan Grant sketch image; to the Random House Group, Ltd. for permission to reproduce the dust jacket; to the Artists Rights Society (ARS), New York / DACS, London for permission to reproduce the sketch; and to two anonymous reviewers whose helpful suggestions stimulated some final revisions.

[2] See Southworth, *Leonard*, for a sense of the wide range of social issues the Press interrogated in its publications, especially Sullivan on middlebrow women writers. Gordon notes that the Press "performed an impressive balancing act, oscillating between the poles of commercial and noncommercial, democratic and elitist" (vii). See also Gillespie ("Please").

[3] The novella, with original dust jacket, is still among the Woolfs' books at Washington State University Libraries.

[4] "Lappin and Lapinova" does begin with a short paragraph describing a married couple leaving in a car after a wedding ceremony. Woolf's story was published by Harper's Bazaar in 1939 and reprinted in *A Haunted House* and *Other Short Stories*, published posthumously by the Hogarth Press in 1944. Dick provides the history of this late story (CSF 309-10). As Gilbert points out, Orlando is "the first Woolf novel in which a meditation on the configura-

Strachey's *Cheerful Weather for the Wedding* with examples, opinions, and often amusing, common-sense advice about weddings in Chapter V of another Hogarth publication, this one an unusual hybrid of autobiography and advice called *Can I Help You? Your Manners—Menus—Amusements—Friends—Charades—Make-Ups—Travel—Calling—Children—Love Affairs*.[5] Julia Strachey's novella, indeed each of these distinctive treatments of weddings, takes on new resonance in the context of the other two. Together, they accept the wedding ritual and, at the same time, criticize it in ways that suggest the need for change.

To Clive Bell, Virginia Woolf described Julia Strachey's manuscript as "a very cute, clever, indeed rather remarkable acidulated story" (*L5* 27). To Carrington, who had painted her friend and Lytton Strachey's niece in 1928,[6] Woolf wrote early in March 1932 that the manuscript was "astonishingly good . . . extraordinarily complete and sharp and individual" (*L5* 29). Hoping to distract Carrington from her grief after Lytton's death, Virginia tempted her with "scenes that want illustrations," possibly "woodcuts in the text" to ensure the book's success (*L5* 29). Sadly, her effort failed to prevent Carrington's suicide.[7] With no other illustrators in line for the job,[8] Duncan Grant, Julia Strachey's cousin, agreed to design a jacket [Figure 1][9]. Although Grant thought it "poorly lettered," in need of Vanessa Bell's color sense, and somewhat "vulgar," Frances Partridge thought it "entirely appropriate" (Spalding, *Duncan* 317), and James Beechey calls it one of Grant's "most fluent" (19). The eye-catching cover focuses, as Strachey does, on the bride. On the back is a floral bouquet with a bright rose-colored bow. On the front,

---

tions of the family as it is structured around the stereotypical heterosexual couple does not . . . dominate the plot" (212).

[5] See Gillespie ("Please") for Virginia Woolf's defense of both the author and two books she published with the Hogarth Press. The earlier book was *Castles in the Air: A Story of My Singing Days* (1926).

[6] For a discussion of the complexities of this friendship and Carrington's portrayal of Julia Strachey, see Gerzina, 259-60.

[7] Lee thinks that although Woolf "chose words of great beauty," her desire that Carrington should be for them a continuation of "the best part" of Lytton's life might have helped to persuade Carrington that she was the "less significant" one (Lee 618). Carrington, who did get as far as a quick sketch for Strachey's cover (Bradshaw, 80), previously had provided four woodcuts to illustrate the Woolfs' first Hogarth Press book, their own *Two Stories* in 1917 (*L2* 162) as well as a woodcut for the cover of Leonard's *Stories of the East* (1921).

[8] In April 1932 correspondence with the Hogarth Press (University of Reading), Julia suggested one illustrator, dismissed another, and said she could do nothing good enough herself. The Press (John Lehmann) rejected any possibility of color illustrations as well as a patterned paper cover before Duncan Grant came into the picture (July 11, 1932; University of Reading).

[9] Less prolific with dust jacket designs than Vanessa Bell, Grant did "relatively few in the inter-war years" (Spalding *Duncan* 317). Later, he did illustrate a Hogarth Press novel by another Strachey, Dorothy Bussy, who wrote *Olivia* by "Olivia" (1949).

title and author frame a white-gowned and veiled bride with downcast eyes. The background is bright rose, as are the bride's lips and necklace, and the dots and lines forming her hair and outlining her veil are blue. A blurb on the inside flap markets the author as the late Lytton Strachey's niece. It is Julia's text, however—what Leonard Woolf calls "the immaterial inside of a book"—that evokes a mixture of absurdity and despair in the face of social expectations (*Downhill* 80).[10]

Dust jacket illustrated by Duncan Grant taken from *Cheerful Weather for the Wedding* by Julia Strachey, published by The Hogarth Press. Courtesy of Manuscripts, Archives and Special Collections, Washington State University. Used by permission of The Random House Group Limited.

What attracted Woolf, as fiction reader for the Press, to Strachey's story? Rather like Julia's bride Dolly Thatcham, young Virginia Stephen had thought she and her sister seemed fated to wed. When Vanessa, whom Virginia recalled as both "reluctant and yielding," said, "'Of course, I can see that we shall all marry,'" Virginia felt "a horrible necessity" that would "descend . . . just as we had achieved

---

[10] The dust jacket flap says "Miss Strachey, who is a niece of the late Lytton Strachey, has written a first novel which is not only extremely entertaining, but shows remarkable insight and sense of character. It is the story of the wedding of Dolly Thatcham to the Hon. Owen Bingham in a village by the sea. The guests assemble in Mrs. Thatcham's house: it is March, and a howling gale blows all day." The same blurb appears in the Hogarth Press Autumn List (1932). A number of early reviews assume that Julia Strachey inherited her satirical eye from her uncle.

freedom and happiness'" (*MOB* 192). Unlike their Victorian predecessors, especially those of the lower and middle-classes, who thought civil ceremonies suitable only for pregnant brides and eloping couples trying to preserve some degree of respectability (Wolfe 20), Bloomsbury often chose them to avoid religious rituals and assumptions. Their circle also practiced complex cohabiting, extramarital, and/ or same-sex relationships. Yet, although they "were no less reverent toward love than their ancestors, different though their morality was" (Wolfe 191), weddings as seemingly obligatory entrees to traditional adult gender roles remained a concern. Modern varieties of late Victorian "New Women" were wary of marriage as an all-consuming profession, an inescapable prison, or the equivalent of prostituting themselves for financial security without love or sexual fulfillment (Wolfe 8). Ann Ardis describes how several "new women" writers created alternatives by imagining "worlds quite different from the bourgeois patriarchy in which unmarried women" were respected rather than "deemed odd and superfluous 'side character[s] in modern life'" (3).[11]

II. "Nessa's curse on marriage" –V. Woolf

Changes between, and controversies about, Victorian and early twentieth-century marriage are widely represented in fiction and drama by both men and women, as well as closely examined in scholarship on the subject. As Jane Eldridge Miller notes, changes in property, custody, and divorce laws,[12] as well as information about contraception, smaller families, greater "sophistication . . . about sex and marriage," new professions for women, and coverage of controversies about the "marriage problem" in Edwardian period books, newspapers, and advice columns all challenged marriage as "an unproblematic ideal" (40, 45). Miller's interest is "the convergence of feminism and realism in the 1890s" to produce "a new kind of realism," a precursor to further challenges to "narrative forms and prose styles" we call "modernism" (8, 199). More recently, Jesse Wolfe focuses on Bloomsbury and its contemporaries and the ways their "ambivalent contributions . . . share a resistance to simple resolutions" as they reflect in both subject and style, "controversies regarding modern intimacy—marriage and divorce, roles and opportunities for the sexes, attitudes toward same-sex desire in particular and erotic life in general" (24). Wolfe, like most writers on the marriage problem and the new woman, however,

---

[11] In 1909 Cicely Hamilton, for instance, defined "a woman as a potentially inquiring, independent being whose value is not dependent upon her marital status, . . . for whom sex is only one of many possible parts of life," and who, if she does not marry," must have opportunities to support herself (Gillespie, "Introduction" 34-35).

[12] For the controversies about divorce and divorce laws as reflected in actual cases and in Edwardian novels, see Harris.

equates "marriages" and "weddings." True, the latter brief events only precipitate more prolonged relationships, but weddings too carry the weight of a couple's past as well as augur their future and reflect evolving cultural values. Julia Strachey's *Cheerful Weather for the Wedding* and, before and after it, Virginia Woolf's wedding scene in *Orlando* and Viola Tree's wedding chapter in *Can I Help You?* all highlight the ritual itself as significant.

Ronald L. Grimes, professor of religion and culture, carefully does distinguish between *marriage*, a "legal and spiritual state," and a *wedding*, the evolving cultural rite that creates it (*Deeply* 156). North America and Europe lack "nationwide rites of initiation" into womanhood or manhood, Grimes says, and therefore weddings remain central rites of passage, events we consciously "*enact*" and remember rather than ones, like our births and deaths, we merely "*undergo*" (*Deeply* 152, 5-6). Scholars have described wedding rituals as perpetuators of "lineages" or creators of family alliances; as exchanges or reassignments of "community wealth"; or as ways to fulfill duties to "family, nation, or tradition" (Grimes, *Deeply* 162).[13] In the western world, however, Grimes thinks wedding rituals are mostly about "sanctifying romantic love" in ways "emotionally and ceremonially beautiful" (*Deeply* 162). He notes, however, that romantic traditions encounter resistance, and idealized rituals inevitably confront human realities (*Deeply* 177).[14] Because rituals are "impure" or hybrid genres (*Ritual* 192)—"transformative" as well as "performative," involving as they do both language and gesture—participants, on display, risk embarrassment. They may feel nervous, oppressed, or threatened; they may find the ritual contrived, even amusing (Grimes, *Deeply* 7-9, 11, 158; Bell 40).

In other words, like other rituals, Grimes says, weddings teeter on the brink of "ritual infelicity" or "ritual failure." Although a wedding rite makes a relationship legal, it may "fail to generate a festive air" (Grimes, *Ritual* 193, 201).[15] Other than inclement weather, costume malfunctions, contentious or unruly participants, or disapproving observers, however, are worse possibilities. Among them, Grimes notes, a wedding can "misfire" if the person performing the ceremony is not authorized to do so, or it can be "abused," if one of the participants says "'I do' while secretly resolving" to breach the vow and thus eventually make the ceremony ineffectual.

---

[13] Bell's book presents, in greater detail than Grimes's, theories from all the disciplines that contribute to the complexities and controversies of ritual studies. For those new to the field, Grimes's books are more accessible.

[14] Bell prefers the term *ritualization* to suggest practices that "require the external consent of participants" to social control "while simultaneously tolerating a fair degree of internal resistance" (221).

[15] At the same time, Grimes rightly asks "by what criteria do participants judge rites? (*Ritual* 193).

The ceremony can be "ill-timed," happening "too soon or too late" in a couple's relationship, or it can gloss over any number of serious "contradictions or major problems" (Grimes, *Ritual* 194 200-1).[16] Weddings, moreover, are increasingly dominated by a "wedding industry" determined to deny such infelicities. Instead, Grimes adds, wedding ceremonies often are the products of "fantasy, fed on the fat of media images[,] . . . advertising," and "conspicuous consumption." Weddings, instead, should help to establish a realistic "common ground" that will enable two ever-changing individuals with different backgrounds and personalities, whether straight or— increasingly in today's Western world—gay, to flourish together (*Deeply* 153-5, 210-11, 214).

A case in point is the wedding of Julia Strachey (1901-1979) to sculptor Stephen ("Tommy") Tomlin (1901-1937) in July of 1927. Julia was part of the "Cambridge-Bloomsbury network" (Willis 207) and of a younger generation that aroused Virginia Woolf's curiosity and often criticism. She called Julia a "gifted wastrel" (*D2* 324) and, "teasingly but to my face," Julia herself wrote, "'the black sheep of the family'" (Partridge, *Julia* 33). Daughter of Lytton Strachey's elder brother Oliver, Julia was born in India but lived with friends and relatives in England[17] after her parents' divorce. Charming, perceptive, and creative, she disliked "the practical side of life," was chronically late for appointments, and ultimately was unable to support herself by forays into careers like commercial art and modeling (Partridge, *Julia* 104-107). Mostly she defined herself as abandoned by her family.[18] Her "'one real occupation'" was to live out a fantasy of belonging—in her words, "'to find a loved one and get married'" (Partridge, *Julia* 105). When she accepted Tomlin, it was not because she genuinely loved him, Frances Partridge says, but because she was "*desperately* lonely" (*Julia* 107).

The Woolfs attended the Strachey/Tomlin wedding, held to please Justice Tomlin, Tommy's father, in St. Pancras Church. Virginia described it to Vanessa Bell, not as festive, but as "prosaic . . ., though the service always fills my eyes with tears. Also the grotesqueness is so great. The Strachey women were of inconceivable drabness," she continued, and Tommy's father the Judge, dressed "like a shop walker . . . got locked into his pew," and barely got out "to sign the register."

---

[16] Drawing on the work of other scholars, Grimes lists in the ninth chapter of *Ritual Criticism* a number of possible ritual failures or infelicities, not all of which apply to weddings.

[17] Those who felt most responsible for Julia were Alys Pearsall Smith ("Aunty Loo"), wife of Bertrand Russell whom Julia met through Ray Costelloe who became her stepmother. A long-time friend was Frances Marshall (Partridge) who edited *Julia* (1983).

[18] Ruby Mayer, Julia's mother, had "four more children by different men" (Blain 1036) and her father began a relationship with Ray Costelloe. Oliver Strachey took no responsibility for Julia and ultimately disinherited her (Partridge, *Julia* 268). In 1940, Julia published "Fragment of a Diary," a story in which she uses a male character to mirror her own sense of desolation.

Behind them, Angus Davidson, enamored of Tommy, sat "glowering" (*L*3 401-2, Spalding, *Duncan* 253).[19] Virginia, who could see "no physical charm" in the groom, "that little woodpecker man," voiced further reservations by shifting the emphasis to the bride and teasing Vanessa: "I handed on your curse, just before the ceremony—Nessa's curse on marriage, it is called; and has been known to strike a Bride dead on the altar steps" (*L*3 401).[20] Virginia referred to a letter Vanessa had sent in 1918 to Barbara Hiles, "said to have arrived the morning" she was to wed Nick Bagenal (Spalding, *Vanessa* 168). Given Barbara's unrealistic plan to divide her year between husband and lover, Saxon Sydney-Turner, "'to have a child by each, and no-one to have any jealousy or cause for complaint,'" Vanessa had advised her not to marry (Spalding, *Vanessa* 168). Barbara's fantasy of married life recreated for Vanessa some of the tensions in her own. Wed to Clive Bell, father of their two sons but none too faithful himself, Vanessa gravitated towards painters and was in love first with Roger Fry, then more seriously and long-term, with Duncan Grant with whom she had a daughter, Angelica. In spite of her anxieties over Grant's male lovers, both he and Fry helped to affirm, in the face of demands of motherhood and domesticity, Vanessa's self-image as a painter. In Julia's case the domesticity of marriage initially provided a sense of purpose and belonging. "Tomlin's bouts of manic depression" and distant manner, however, along with his threats of suicide soon left her lonely again and vainly in search of consolation in a series of love affairs (Spalding, *Duncan* 253; Partridge, *Julia* 107, 120-21, 124, 127). By 1934, slowly and painfully, the marriage had broken down.[21]

In the background of Julia Strachey's wedding and expectations of marriage, therefore, were Vanessa's and, by then, Virginia's. When Clive Bell proposed, Vanessa wrote him of her desire, above all, to paint (Spalding, *Vanessa* 54, cf. 58). Five years later, Virginia sent Leonard Woolf her own doubts, not only her fears that she was unstable, unresponsive to his desire, and unable to ignore his Jewish background, but also her determination not to think of marriage as a "profession" (*L*1 496). Vanessa did accept Clive, and Virginia, with some difficulty, accepted the loss of her sister. At least their 1907 civil ceremony was, Virginia noted, "successful,—very quick and simple" (*L*1 279).[22]

---

[19] Yet "they dined with us afterwards," Virginia Woolf says of the newly married couple (*L*3 401). Later, in 1931, she recorded her dislike of sitting for Tomlin's well known bust of her (e.g. *L*4 360, *L*5 378).

[20] When Frances Partridge quotes this passage, she leaves out the "Nessa's curse" sentence (*Julia* 108).

[21] Tomlin died suddenly in 1937 at age 36. Julia later met (1939) and eventually married (1952) a younger artist and critic, Lawrence Gowing (1918-1991). Gowing didn't provide Julia with the "'family life' she so constantly longed for" either (Partridge, *Julia* 223), and this thirty-year relationship also ended in divorce.

[22] It seems portentous that no picture seems to exist of Vanessa and Clive taken at the time of their wedding.

Likewise, in June of 1912, Virginia accepted Leonard Woolf and wrote to several friends announcing her engagement. Lytton Strachey, who had encouraged Leonard's suit after having proposed to Virginia himself in 1909, a prospect from which they both soon recoiled, received only a brief "Ha! Ha!" (*L*1 501).[23] In part for the entertainment of her correspondents, Virginia even enjoyed the idea of ritual infelicities. In a letter to Violet Dickinson, she caricatured some of those likely to attend and to Duncan Grant made light of conflicts with Leonard's "poor old Mother Wolf" (sic) (*L*1 507-8).[24] Decades later, Leonard recalled that, although civil weddings exact no promises "according to God's holy ordinance,'" he and Virginia "could see [. . .] tombstones" through the window reminding them "of the words 'till death us do part'." Into this juxtaposition of marriage and death, Leonard injects "comic relief . . . characteristic of the Stephens" by mentioning how Vanessa "interrupted the Registrar" to ask about changing her son's name (*Beginning* 69-70).[25] Hermione Lee sums up the day as stormy; the registrar, "'half blind;'" the wedding party "ill-assorted" (317; cf. King 198-9).

Some years later, in 1921, Duncan Grant echoed Vanessa Bell's "curse" for a different reason in a letter to David Garnett on the brink of his wedding to Ray Marshall. "A legal marriage is at once a reality in the eyes of the world of the most odious sort (in my opinion)," Grant wrote, "and it is impossible . . . to escape the pyramid that the world builds up every day round yr. personal relationship" (Spalding, *Vanessa* 190). Although it is certainly true that the Woolfs' wedding and marriage have been the subjects of much public scrutiny and speculation both during their lives and after their deaths, they defied curiosity and any odds against them enough to forge what was largely an affectionate and productive relationship.

III. *Orlando*—"ritual felicity"

Three months after the Strachey/Tomlin wedding, Virginia Woolf began her mock biography of Vita Sackville-West, published by the Hogarth Press as *Orlando:*

---

[23] See the Lytton Strachey/ Leonard Woolf correspondence in *Letters of Leonard Woolf* 147-50.

[24] Virginia Woolf says the "rows" were over "not being asked to the wedding" (*L*1 508). Also, however, the Woolfs held the wedding on Saturday August 10th which was "the Sabbath, the one day of the week Mrs Woolf would not attend a civil ceremony" (King 198).

[25] Some biographers are more critical of Vanessa than Leonard is. Reid speculates that having to move the wedding date from the 12th to the 10th so the painters could attend an exhibition in Cologne, irritated Leonard and, along with Vanessa's interruption of the ceremony, agitated Virginia. Still the Bells provided a reception after the wedding (136). Dunn thinks that Vanessa's "vagueness" was a bid to reclaim "her share of the emotional spotlight . . . in her sister's life" (184).

A Biography in October of 1928.²⁶ In her parodic Preface, Woolf thanks "*Mr. and Mrs. Stephen Tomlin*" (viii) whose wedding must have reminded her of ritual elements she needed for Orlando's.²⁷ Having met Vita in 1922, Virginia had not witnessed her 1913 wedding to Harold Nicolson in the chapel at Knole, the lavish reception for hundreds afterwards, or the huge display of wedding gifts. Among them was emerald and diamond jewelry, showered upon Vita by her delighted mother, Lady Sackville, who ultimately was "too unwell to attend the ceremony" (Glendinning 61-3). On that occasion, as photographs show, Vita donned an elegant dress of "natural-colored silk encrusted with gold" (Glendinning 62, photo between 106-7). It was the kind popularized by Queen Victoria's own elaborate ivory gown and veil, worn for her marriage to Albert in 1840 and designed to display less purity than social status, wealth, power, and (with yards of English lace) patriotism (Oakes 2, Grimes, *Deeply* 155-56).

Woolf's Orlando alludes to this influential wedding by observing a statue, where one "of Queen Victoria now stands," heaped with "ill-assorted objects" including "bridal veils" and "excrescences" like "wedding cakes" (*O* 232). Orlando also makes a "discovery, whether," she says, "Queen Victoria's or another's, that each man and each woman has another allotted to it . . . till death them do part" (*O* 245). Fortunately Shelmerdine, Orlando's "allotted," is, like her, both manly and womanly (*O* 252) and, like her, wants to retain an independent life. Virginia Woolf uses *Orlando*, her generic hybrid of fiction and biography, not only to subvert "familiar romance novel characteristics" but to use them, with playful modifications, to grant her main character all she desires (Gillespie, "Virginia" 123). In what Nigel Nicolson calls "her most elaborate love letter" to Vita (*L3* xxii), Virginia gives her "husband, child, literary success," and Knole, the estate "entailed away from her in real life" (Gillespie, "Virginia" 123-24).²⁸ She also grants Vita an imaginary wedding more appropriate to the Nicolsons' untraditional and often volatile life as both married couple and parents. It was a relationship, as Vita suggested, based largely on "'friendly sincerity'" (Glendinning 61), in which each could be intimate with others, as well as pursue their separate careers.

In Woolf's revision, courtship is short and engagement quick, but both are sufficient for Orlando and Shelmerdine to communicate, often by transcending ordinary words, all they need to know of mutual pasts and predilections. The wind

---

²⁶ *Orlando* is one of only four of Woolf's books—along with *Flush, Reviewing*, and *A Letter to a Young Poet*—without a cover by Vanessa Bell.

²⁷ Southworth describes Tomlin and Strachey as part of "fringe" or "new" Bloomsbury whose names Woolf disperses throughout her list ("Virginia" 89). Strachey also is among Hogarth "authors-yet-to-be" on the list ("Virginia," 92).

²⁸ So deft was Woolf's subversion of the traditional romance novel plot that she received a fan letter from popular novelist Berta Ruck (See Gillespie, "Virginia").

calling Shelmerdine back to sea is what sends the couple running spontaneously to the chapel. The narrator mentions no planning, no procession, no lavish wedding gown, and no aristocratic audience or expensive gifts. "Bells were rung. People were summoned," and lights haphazardly were lit, but passive grammatical constructions remove anyone in charge (*O* 261). Mr. Dupper does emerge, "catching at the ends of his white tie and asking where was the prayer book." One "thrust" into his hands, he locates the right page and instructs the couple to "kneel down" (*O* 261). They do. Light and shadow alternate. Woolf's prose is breathless, and rhythmic repetition of "and" and "now" creates dramatic immediacy. Reiterated words and sounds obscure the service: growling organ music vacillates between "loud and faint," "innumerable doors" bang, and an unidentified "sound [is] like brass pots beating." Servants sing and pray, a thunderclap obliterates the word "Obey," and the wedding ring, so annoyingly important when Orlando is without one, is reduced to a "golden flash" (*O* 261-2). The ceremony is a windswept swirl of sound and motion. Anticipating the upsets and reversals of Mikhail Bakhtin's "carnivalesque,"[29] Woolf, in the midst of this unseemly melee, liberates Orlando from the traditional aristocratic chapel ritual by suspending class and gender dichotomies and inequalities.

There is neither reception nor honeymoon, and the wedding is not the culmination of the story. As Rachel Blau Duplessis observes, "heterosexual romance and marriage are set aside precisely in being achieved" (63). Shelmerdine returns to his life sailing "round Cape Horn in the teeth of a gale" (*O* 252, 262). Orlando, less transformed into a traditional wife than liberated and made legitimate by the wedding ring and rite—as the "spirit of the age" demands—is able again to write. It is possible, she concludes, to be both married and true to herself (*O* 264-66). This is a version of the balancing act to which Vanessa, Virginia, and Vita all aspired. Inevitable difficulties notwithstanding, Virginia had already written, not to Vanessa, but to Vita, "In all London, you and I alone like being married" (*L3* 221). These exceptions prove how problematic marriage as a rule really is.[30]

DuPlessis notes that Woolf, in the course of her fiction, moves from the individual protagonists of the marriage plot to "a communal protagonist . . . . a large family, a group of friends, an audience, . . . members of all ages and sexual persuasions" (48). Orlando's on-stage wedding seems a reversal until we remember that

---

[29] See, for example, Bakhtin's chapter on "Popular-Festive Forms and Images in Rabelais." Woolf gives us no carnivalesque thrashings in Orlando's wedding scene, but the repetitive sounds suggest the drumming supposed to inject eroticism into the wedding ritual. In the Woolfs' library (WSU), are *The Works of Francis Rabelais*. 4 vols. Trans. by Jacob Le Duchat (London: T. Evans, 1784).

[30] As Briggs writes, Vita and Virginia accepted marriage "in their daily lives," yet saw it as "a potential threat to women's autonomy, as well as a source of perplexity" (205).

this protagonist *is* a whole community—of "seventy-six different times all ticking in the mind at once" and "say two thousand and fifty-two people" representing past and present, youth and adult, male and female "built up, one on top of another, as plates are piled on a waiter's hand" (*O* 308). In a workable marriage of two such multiplicities, some facets will mesh companionably but others will remain comfortably independent.

IV. *Cheerful Weather for the Wedding*—"ritual failure"

If Vanessa Bell's "curse on marriage" grew from experience, so Julia Strachey wrote her novella during one of the Tomlins' trial separations (Partridge, *Julia* 113). She chose to publish it neither as "Julia Tomlin" nor disguised by a pseudonym, but under her maiden name.[31] Julia Strachey, with her love of similes and metaphors, vivid characterization, and dramatic dialogue,[32] counter-balances the poetically condensed, revisionary wedding ceremony Woolf creates in *Orlando*. Using twenty-three-year-old Dolly Thatcham's ritualized wedding day,[33] Strachey, one of the "middlebrow" women writers published by the Hogarth Press, undermines the traditional customs not with poetic obscuring and leveling, but with satiric exposure of unpleasant private realities glossed over by traditional public proceedings.

Strachey's title is ironic. The "really savage" March wind in her novella does not animate the ritual as in *Orlando*, but rather enervates it by casting a chill over the wedding participants and their customary activities (*Cheerful* 12, 20-21, 26). A bridesmaid, for instance, imagines "'standing [coatless] in that draughty church!'" with her "'sopping-wet bouquet of flowers!,'" and concludes that "'these quaint old customs are no joke'" (*Cheerful* 19). Yet, certain that human customs take precedence over nature, the bride's dithering mother, the "middle-class widow," Mrs. Thatcham (*Cheerful* 5), dubs the weather "cheerful" and bumbles ahead, oblivious to the discomfort of others gathered in her country house. She is based, according to Frances Partridge, on Stephen Tomlin's mother (Preface vi).[34]

---

[31] A letter (May 25, 1932) from the Press to Edward Garnett indicates Julia's preference for her maiden name on the cover. All the Press correspondence, however, is to "Mrs. Julia Tomlin" or "Julia," and that is also the way she signs her name. Since "Strachey" links Julia to her well known uncle, perhaps marketing also was a factor.

[32] In 1936 Julia Strachey submitted an almost-completed play to the Hogarth Press, but they rejected it. Leonard "very nicely said . . . that he and Virginia had a 'blind spot about that particular genre of writing'" (Partridge, *Julia* 150).

[33] Lee mentions that *Cheerful Weather for the Wedding* "had learnt from Virginia Woolf" (368). We have, for instance, the single day, important event, and past love (*Mrs. Dalloway*), musings of a working woman (*To the Lighthouse*), and Dolly's empty room (*Jacob's Room*).

[34] Partridge notes that "Julia had nothing at all in common with her future parents-in-law,"

Unlike Orlando the poet and more like Julia Strachey herself, Dolly has no real sense of vocation. Something of a "new woman," she has run with a modern set of people, acquired unconventional opinions, and on her wedding day is exhibiting such irreverent behavior that her awkward and self-conscious younger sister Kitty calls her values "BEASTLY" (*Cheerful* 57). Yet Dolly is about to conform to the career of the wealthy Hon. Owen Bigham, introduced as "eight years older . . . , in the Diplomatic Service," and soon to take his bride to South America (*Cheerful* 5). Like Clarissa's choice of Richard Dalloway over Peter Walsh in Woolf's *Mrs. Dalloway*, Owen Bigham seems the conventional choice over Dolly's former beau, Joseph Patten. At odds with Dolly's traditional mother and naïve younger sister, Joseph is studying, as one of the cousins mocks, to be an "'Anthro-pop-ologist!'" (*Cheerful* 29), a fact that calls attention to the wedding as a cultural rite, an evolving construction rather than a hardened reality. Liking to upset uncritical people, he starts to describe Minoan Island puberty rituals to Kitty.[35] Mrs. Thatcham quickly intervenes to draw attention back to the potentially less disturbing Western rite by showing off a wedding gift from someone amusingly named Miss Dodo Potts-Griffith. Joseph counters by dismissing the badly hand-decorated lampshade as "'a most skillfully contrived expression, and gratification, of the herd instinct . . . and, as such, a really most appropriate gift for a wedding'" (*Cheerful* 34-5).[36] He also bluntly counters Kitty's statement that Englishmen "in love lacked poetry" in contrast to Continental men who unashamedly wooed women with poetry and ukuleles. Such male behavior Joseph calls "'un-English. My own aim,'" he says, "'is still the clean-limbed, dirty-minded, thorough English gentleman.'" When Kitty challenges Dolly, "'Is Cousin Bob dirty-minded?' (She alluded to the Canon.) 'Was Dad dirty-minded?'" a disillusioned Dolly only murmurs "'Terribly. Terribly'" (*Cheerful* 58-9).

If Orlando's wedding ritual is a series of exhilarating accidents, Dolly's wedding day is a comedy of bad manners and a succession of ominous blunders. Owen, whose face was usually "flushed, simple, [and] affectionate," now looks as if "there was something miserably guilty and anxious . . . behind his rigid features" (*Cheerful* 40, 42). He arrives where the groom shouldn't be before the ceremony to collect the ring from the bride who shouldn't have it. Similarly Dolly, exhausted from sorting a dead aunt's effects with no help from her ineffectual mother, is upstairs

---

and when she met them, "she tripped on the threshold of their stately London drawing-room, and shot in over the parquet floor face downwards, as though tobogganing" (*Julia* 108).

[35] The Minoans were a bronze-age culture on the Greek island of Crete (3000-1100 BCE).

[36] Although others were studying group or crowd psychology, Wilfred Trotter's *Instincts of the Herd in Peace and War* (1914) made popular the term "herd behavior." A 1916 printing is among the Woolfs' books (WSU).

getting ready. Drinking straight out of a bottle of Jamaica rum while donning her traditional wedding costume, she wears "a reproachful, stupefied expression" (*Cheerful* 48). She puts on her make-up, Strachey writes, like "a performing elephant . . . ,—languidly, clumsily, as though her arms were made of iron" (*Cheerful* 49). She has dirtied her white satin shoes, looks "at the long wedding-veil stretching away forever, and at the women, too, so busy around her," and knows "that something remarkable and upsetting in her life was steadily going forward . . . as if she were reading about it . . . instead of . . . living through it" (*Cheerful* 52).

Both Dolly, the hiccoughing and tearful bride-to-be caught in an archaic marriage plot, and Joseph, her unsettled not-groom, keep mentally reviewing their unresolved relationship of the previous summer. Joseph had looked lovingly at Dolly, but never spoke the word. If he said it now, both wonder what they would do, but neither knows. When Joseph finally catches up with Dolly, she is late, tipsy, and "staring insanely," having knocked an open ink bottle onto her white satin dress. Joseph helps disguise the spot "big as a tea-pot," and she rushes belatedly to the nearby church (*Cheerful* 74-5). Unable to face the ceremony, Joseph listens to the organ from the house as it signals the bride's procession to the altar (*Cheerful* 79). Instead of the service, he overhears a village woman setting out food and mumbling a version of Vanessa's curse: "'in my opinion, marriage is a totally mistaken idea. . . . My husband has been dead seven years. Thanks be for that then. And never no more nothink of anythink of that again for me!'" (*Cheerful* 81).

The wedding party returns from the church, and Duncan Grant's original cover sketch, this time showing the bride's be-ringed left hand splayed at her throat rather than the less emotional final version with a round brooch, captures the agitation of the now married Dolly [Figure 2]. Appropriate is an ill-omened joke that emphasizes her feelings of entrapment. It is told by a small boy who has borne Dolly's train: "'What is the difference between a honey-comb and a honey-moon?'" he asks. "'A honey-comb has one million cells, and a honey-moon has one'" (*Cheerful* 84-85).[37] When Joseph finally gets Dolly alone, she is dressed to leave. Too late they try to sort out their miscommunications. Joseph remains so agitated that Dolly embraces him just as Owen emerges to forbid her taking to South America a live tortoise we know Joseph once gave her. The couple departs, their "lack of high spirits" disguised by the "cutting, furiously buffeting wind" (*Cheerful* 100). Left behind, Joseph's odd coup de grace for Mrs. Thatcham is news, insultingly delivered and utterly unbelievable to her, that she is the grandmother of twins to whom Dolly had given birth and left Albania when she was there the previous autumn

---

[37] Strachey draws an amusing but sympathetic portrait of little Jimmy Dakin, one of several characters beyond the scope of this essay.

Duncan Grant, Sketch for the cover of *Cheerful Weather for the Wedding* (1932). Courtesy of the E. J. Pratt Library, Victoria University, University of Toronto. ©2013 Artists Rights Society (ARS), New York / DACS, London..

(*Cheerful* 111-12). The reader gets no confirmation or additional information, but Dolly's soiled wedding shoes, ink-stained white dress, and marriage to Owen accrue the symbolic weight of hidden past, present desperation, and uncertain future. Still unable to untangle his past with Dolly from a marriage incomprehensible to both of them, Joseph concludes that what he thought was love was just "some depressing kind of swindle after all" (*Cheerful* 116).

Although sales were steady and better than expected for an author's first book,[38] Leonard Woolf was unhappy with early reviews that were perfunctory or missed the point (Willis 207). He enlisted the help of David Garnett who reviewed the book as "really new and first-rate" (320) with "something of the realism of the stage" (480).[39] Still, Strachey's grimly amusing satire of ritual misfires and its appeal to what she calls "the 'heart'" (Victorian for 'subconscious') as well as the head" (Partridge, *Julia* 123) have helped it to survive as what Willis calls "a minor classic" (206-7). Persephone Books, in the latest reprint blurb (2009),[40] includes it among books "neither too literary nor too commercial" and thus "guaranteed to be readable." If readers enjoy even the pitfalls inherent in the wedding ritual, one wonders why, as C. F. Carter notes in an early anthology, renditions of weddings were relatively scarce in pre-1900 fiction, poetry, and painting (v).[41] With the advent of the cinema, however, weddings have found their medium. "Since 1890," as Grimes pointed out already in 2006, "there have been over 350 films containing

[38] Leonard Woolf to Julia Tomlin (Oct. 31, 1932) University of Reading.
[39] Viking got the American edition, although there were inquiries from several other presses as well as from presses in other countries. The 1933 American reviews (Reading has two pages of excerpts) were positive. In 1947 Leonard signed the rights over to Strachey (April 14 and 19, 1947; University of Reading). Penguin reissued the novella in 1978 in a volume with Strachey's later novel, *The Man on the Pier* (1951). Today, *Cheerful Weather for the Wedding* is dubbed a "feminist" satire (Young 184), one that reveals Virginia Woolf's "tastes in contemporary women's fiction" (Lee 606). Sullivan places Strachey's novella among those of middlebrow women writers (59). Willis, who uses Grant's cover, along with Garnett's early reviews, as examples of "the Cambridge-Bloomsbury network advancing "the work of one of its own" (207), calls the novella a "brisk little book" (206). Holland's dissertation places Julia Strachey's work, along with Dorothy Bussy's, in "dialogue with modernity." A number of contemporary websites and blogs review the book.
[40] The pagination in the 2009 reprint is the same as in the first edition.
[41] Strachey's novella includes the first and the last of Carter's division of wedding representations into dramatic, romantic, sentimental, and humorous (vi). Her narrative does not conform to Carter's assertion that most wedding fiction ends with lovers having reached "an 'understanding'" (vi). Virginia Woolf was familiar with much of the literature Carter excerpts.

the words 'wedding' or 'bride' in the title" (*Ritual* 48)—and many more since. One of the latest is Cheerful Weather for the Wedding itself, adapted in the UK late in 2011 for the screen.[42]

V. *Can I Help You?*—ritual practicality

Five years later, the Hogarth Press offered another woman's perspective on weddings in chapter V of Viola Tree's hybrid of advice and personal experience called *Can I Help You?* (1937). Unlike *Cheerful Weather for the Wedding* and *Orlando: A Biography*, Tree's book is no longer in print. It is still amusing reading, however, and the common-sense advice is not as out-of-date as one might expect seventy-five years later. Was Tree familiar with Dolly Thatcham's violations of wedding protocol and behavior in Julia Strachey's novella? She doesn't mention it, but both writers are aware of the live-performance aspect of the wedding ritual, with its costumed role-playing and its potential mishaps. Seventeen years older than Strachey, Tree could draw on her theatrical experience, the bohemian as well as society weddings she had witnessed, and her own large church wedding in 1912 to drama critic Alan Parsons.[43] Unspoken may also be advice for a younger generation of women like her daughter Virginia Parsons who illustrated *Can I Help You?*[44] Tree, whose own experiences cause her to identify with brides, uses her etiquette-book genre to present a more detailed run-through of wedding preparations, ceremony, and aftermath than either Woolf's or Strachey's fictional narratives provides. Resistant as all three women are to aspects of a ritual they on some basic level accept, Tree is the one able to voice her criticisms and opinions most candidly and directly.

Tree invents "a love match" (*Can* 116) between a veiled Margaret Vayle and a groom with the magical name H. R. Aladdin (a Canadian studying at Oxford). Tree uses her brief dramatic narrative to cover examples of invitations for large and small weddings, financial responsibilities, and appropriate clothing. Unlike Dolly Thatcham, who clutches her rum bottle and sends her flustered mother away,

---

[42] Directed in the UK by Donald Rice, adapted by Rice and Mary Henely MaGill, and produced by Teun Hilte at Goldcrest Films, the movie stars Felicity Jones as Dolly Thatcham, Elizabeth McGovern as Mrs. Thatcham, MacKenzie Crook as David Dakin, and Luke Treadaway as Joseph Patten. IFC Films has US rights.

[43] Viola Tree (1884-1938) was one of three daughters of the famous actor-manager Sir Herbert Beerbohm Tree (1853-1917) and actress Helen Maud Tree (1858-1937). Viola was educated at the Academy of Art and the Royal College of Music. In 1920, she contributed to Max Beerbohm's edition of her father's memoirs. For eight years, she wrote an advice column called "Can I Help You?" upon which her book is based, for the *Sunday Dispatch*. She also managed theatres, directed and wrote plays, and published on various topics in newspapers and in *Vogue*. She had several minor film roles in the 1920s and 1930s.

[44] Virginia Parsons did not illustrate the wedding chapter. Her long, worrisome relationship with David Tennant finally resulted in his divorce from actress Hermione Baddeley. Parsons

Margaret's mother hands her milk to drink before she leaves for the church. Tree recreates what the bride is thinking and feeling and, as Woolf does in *Orlando*, mentions Queen Victoria's influence. Driving past the Albert Memorial, Margaret, who considers herself "a modern" woman, still hopes her marriage will endure like Queen Victoria's (*Can* 118). At the church, Margaret, milk notwithstanding, frets about gloves, veil, and bridesmaids. "Pull yourself together," says Tree who clearly is directing this production; "if you cannot think of Mr. Aladdin" silhouetted at the far end of the aisle, "think of your father on your left . . . The organ peals, the choir go first . . . . Now think of your future" with that "nice scholarly man. . . . Don't walk too slowly, but not too quickly . . . . look at [your groom but], not furtively" (*Can* 118-19). After the service, for which Tree substitutes Edmund Spenser's idealized "Epithalamion," the couple signs the marriage certificate and walks back down the aisle. Tree, criticizing and explaining the "winged victory expression" she wore at her own wedding, directs the bride—"the observed of all observers—to look "cheerful and natural" instead and then, as carriages leave, "radiant" (*Can* 121).

Tree critically examines more parts of the ritual. Her opinion on wedding photographs, for instance, agrees with Julia Strachey's description of the obligatory photograph session, held outside in the cold wind, and leaving "the whole party look[ing] more dead than alive" (*Cheerful* 90). Tree italicizes, "*it would be merciful if this ceremony could be postponed for another time, or never performed at all*" given how "spiritless and detached" everyone looks (*Can* 123). As for the wedding feast, Tree prefers a sit-down dinner to what Strachey describes as the disorganized wedding tea in Mrs. Thatcham's drawing room. The standard wedding cake, what Orlando dismisses as an "excrescence" on an elaborate Victorian statue (*O* 232) and even Mrs. Thatcham ignores in favor of scones, Tree criticizes as usually a hired concoction, only partially edible, that "generally resembles a white sarcophagus with a Georgian temple on the top of it, on which rest wax lilies and deformed doves" (*Can* 125).

Tree has a lot more to say about clothing and customs. For a bridal gown she accepts white satin, like Dolly Thatcham's, as "incomparable" (*Can* 127). As for the bridal veil, Tree is less critical than Orlando who reduces it to one of a statue's conglomerate of "ill-assorted objects" (*O* 232) or Dolly who views her long one as a burden and a portent. Tree simply advises against any veil that, too submissively perhaps, "hide[s] the bride's face" (*Can* 127).[45] Although we know that Dolly's

---

and Tennant married, but quietly, shortly after Viola Tree's sudden death in 1938, the year following the one in which *Can I Help You?* appeared.

[45] In *Three Guineas* Woolf says that "the Victorian, Edwardian and much of the Fifth Georgian conception of chastity was based, to go no further back, upon the words of St. Paul," particularly "his famous" but complex personal opinion "on the matter of veils" that symbolize women's subjection (*TG* 166-67 n. 38).

attendants wear yellow, we don't know if they would please Tree who dislikes bridesmaids "looking like waxworks of Mary Queen of Scots, or like female beefeaters, or bedraggled Botticellis" in their impractical, one-wearing-only costumes (*Can* 129). She also advises the groom and best man against donning "detestable" spats (*Can* 131-32). Instructing the groomsman in his duties, she gives amusing examples of a variety of wedding toasts and speeches—"*irresponsible . . . from the groomsman, . . . more serious . . . from the bridegroom*" (*Can* 136). Yet, whatever the potential imperfections of these ritual occasions, Tree stresses the need "to be sweet to all. *Tempers are stripped to the last sticking-point at weddings*—fatigue, excitement and the anti-climax of its being over, all help to make your nerves ragged" (*Can* 125). In this much-performed play, every scene, every role demands acting, if not feeling, calm. In spite of her often amusing criticisms, Tree, who is describing a "love match" (*Can* 116), accepts the wedding ritual but, at the same time, gives advice that is both practical and critical of excesses. Reviewers of the book as a whole dub her as helpful, wise, witty, kind, and amusing.[46]

VI. Conclusion: "the ceremony / has not yet been found" –Philip Booth

Not long after Woolf's exhilarating, topsy-turvy treatment of Orlando's wedding, Strachey's amusing and despairing satire, and Tree's candid commonsense opinions about wedding protocol, the Hogarth Press published *Three Guineas* (1938). Why did Virginia Woolf exclude photos of "dazzling" and symbolic wedding rituals from among the hierarchical costumes and processions she criticized (*TG* 19)?[47] In *Can I Help You?* Tree does acknowledge the bride and bridegroom who think "that publicity and fine clothes are all vanity, and that the only important thing is to get the blessing of the Church or State and be off" (*Can* 128), a description that comes closer to the civil weddings of Virginia and Vanessa Stephen. They are not the kinds of people who need Tree's detailed advice. Virginia Woolf's reason for excluding elaborate versions of these rituals from *Three Guineas*, therefore, is not personal culpability.

Neither can Woolf fault the patriarchy exclusively for wedding vanities. True, the masculine clerical establishment was responsible historically for moving weddings from private homes to churches. There Catholic clergy oversaw publicly announced and witnessed vows that turned weddings into religious sacraments or, with the Protestant Reformation, "ritually simpler" occasions with longer sermons designed for "moral exhortation and edification" (Grimes, *Deeply* 202-204). Not traditionally religious herself, Woolf was no doubt aware that, for believers, weddings were religious occasions. Tree herself anticipated "criticism" for advising

---

[46] The Hogarth Press papers at the University of Reading contain quotes from reviewers on a draft order form.

people who choose church weddings "how to behave on so sacred an occasion," but adds that although the "deeply religious" may be able to act natural, everyone else is self-conscious and needs her verbal rehearsals (*Can* 121). Woolf also knew that women like Queen Victoria, Lady Sackville, Mrs. Thatcham (based on Mrs. Tomlin), and Tree's invented Mrs. Vayle, collaborated in, and perpetuated elaborate wedding rituals. Whether consciously or unconsciously, they wished to display wealth and power, social status or aspiration. At the very least, they enjoyed proudly exhibiting feminine beauty and husband acquisition.

Woolf notes in *Three Guineas* the hypocrisy of men who criticize women's "love of dress" while approving their own regalia as "Admirals, Generals, Heralds, Life Guards, Peers, Beefeaters, etc." (*TG* 150 n. 16). Should Woolf therefore criticize not only men, but also women when the satin shoe fits? Not necessarily. Woolf's main concern in *Three Guineas* is that the "daughters of educated men" (*TG* 4), as they begin to have more educational and professional opportunities and join the costumed and ritualized processions of the hierarchical public world, should decide "on what terms," with what degrees of acceptance and resistance, they should do so (*TG* 62). Woolf would have these women try to retain values learned in obscurity as they leave the private home and, in the process, help to transform the public realms they enter.

Unlike women newly admitted to the professions, however, traditional brides are not "traipsing along somewhere in the rear" of masculine ritual processions that represent their public positions and rankings (*TG* 69). Brides are stars of wedding dramas, ironically front and center in a public ritual by which they enter a traditionally private but increasingly contested gender role. As Tree says, brides are "the observed of all observers" (*Can* 123), elegantly dressed and processing with their own and their families' values on display. Although Woolf does say in *Three Guineas* that it would be absurd for women to advertise "motherhood by a tuft of horsehair on the left shoulder" (*TG* 20-21), she gives at least a partial pass to the ring acquired at the wedding ceremony to advertise marital status. *Orlando* is in part a defense and justification of wearing a wedding band, as Woolf herself does, as a compromise with "the spirit of the age" (265).[48] If pressed on the subject of wedding rituals in relation to values learned in obscurity, then, Woolf would have had to continue discursively what she had begun imaginatively in *Orlando*. There the whirlwind wedding reflects beginnings of mid-twentieth-century changes in the traditional ritual. A bride may be accompanied to the altar, for example, but no longer is she given away, and the word "obey," dictating the bride's relationship to her husband, evolves into more symmetrical promises (Grimes, *Deeply* 205).

[47] See Koppen for a recent discussion of Woolf's "ridicule of ceremony" (25) and "ceremonial dress and uniforms of all kinds" (29) and Briggs for Woolf's inclusion of heralds among the *Three Guineas* photos but exclusion of the ultimate patriarch, the King. As Woolf wrote

Orlando: A Biography, along with Julia Strachey's *Cheerful Weather for the Wedding* and Viola Tree's *Can I Help You?* comprise a trio of sometimes contradictory revisions, warnings, and common-sense advice on weddings from the perspectives of women of the 1920s and 1930s. Ever-evolving wedding rituals still have a long way to go, Grimes says, to bridge the idealized, commercialized, emotional, and "temporary 'world' of the ceremony and the 'real'," troubled, social "world outside it" (*Deeply* 213). Add to the usual tensions the desire for a rite of passage that crosses racial and religious divides or unites same-sex couples in marriage (Grimes, *Deeply* 213). All rituals, as Woolf realized, ultimately are microcosmic of a continuum of functional and dysfunctional relations among selves and others—not just within couples, but within families, communities, nations, and even the windswept natural world. As Philip Booth cautions in "Saying It," "Daily, as we are daily / Wed, we say the world is a wedding for which / as we are constantly finding, the ceremony / has not yet been found" (244-5).

---

the book, rumors about Edward VIII escalated until they culminated in his abdication and marriage to Mrs. Simpson (Briggs 325; *D5* 40-44).

[48] In photographs where her left hand is visible, Woolf wears a wedding band. "Professions for Women" describes her own negotiations with the "spirit of the age" (*E6* 480).

Works Cited

Ardis, Ann. *New Women, New Novels: Feminism and Early Modernism*. New Brunswick, NJ: Rutgers UP, 1990. Print.

Bakhtin, Mikhail. *Rabelais and His World*. Trans. Helene Iswolsky. Cambridge, MA: MIT Press, 1968. Print.

Beechey, James. "Introduction." *The Bloomsbury Artists: Prints and Book Design*. Aldershot, Hants: Scholar Press, 1999. 9-24. Print.

Bell, Catherine. *Ritual Theory, Ritual Practice*. New York: Oxford UP, 1992. Print.

Blain, Virginia, Patricia Clements, and Isobel Grundy, eds. *The Feminist Companion to Literature in English: Women Writers from the Middle Ages to the Present*. New Haven and London: Yale UP, 1990. Print.

Booth, Philip. *Relations: Selected Poems 1950-1985*. New York: Viking, 1986. Print.

Bradshaw, Tony. "Catalogue." *The Bloomsbury Artists: Prints and Book Design*. Aldershot, Hants: Scholar Press, 1999. Print.

Briggs, Julia. *Virginia Woolf: An Inner Life*. San Diego: Harcourt, 2005. Print.

Carter, C. F., ed. *The Wedding Day in Literature and Art: A Collection of the Best Descriptions of Weddings from the Works of the World's Leading Novelists and Poets, richly illustrated with Reproductions of Famous Paintings of*

Incidents of the Nuptial Day (1900). Detroit: Singing Tree Press, Book Tower, 1969. Print.

Dunn, Jane. *A Very Close Conspiracy: Vanessa Bell and Virginia Woolf*. Boston: Little, Brown and Co., 1990. Print.

DuPlessis, Rachel Blau. *Writing Beyond the Ending: Narrative Strategies of Twentieth-Century Women Writers*. Bloomington: Indiana UP, 1985. Print.

Garnett, David. Review of *Cheerful Weather for the Wedding*. *Saturday Review of Literature* 9.425 (February 11 1933): 320. Print.

———. Review of *Cheerful Weather for the Wedding*. *Spectator* 149: 638 (November 4 1932): 480. Print.

Gerzina, Gretchen. *Carrington: A Life*. New York and London: W. W. Norton and Company, 1989. Print.

Gilbert, Sandra. "*Orlando*: Introduction." *Introductions to the Major Works*. Ed. Julia Briggs. London: Virago, 1994: 187-217. Print.

Gillespie, Diane F. "Virginia Woolf and the Curious Case of Berta Ruck." *Woolf Studies Annual* 10 (2004):109-138. Print.

———. "'Please Help Me!' Virginia Woolf, Viola Tree, and the Hogarth Press." *Contradictory Woolf: Selected Papers from the Twenty-first Annual Conference on Virginia Woolf*, Ed. Derek Ryan and Stella Bolaki. Clemson, SC, Clemson U Digital P, 2012: 173-80. Print.

——— and Doryjane Birrer, eds. "Introduction." *Diana of Dobson's: A Romantic Comedy in Four Acts* by Cicely Hamilton. Peterborough, Ontario, Canada: Broadview Press, 2003. 13-60. Print.

Glendinning, Victoria. *Vita: The Life of V. Sackville-West*. New York: Alfred A. Knopf, 1983. Print.

Gordon, Elizabeth Wilson. Woolfs'-head Publishing: *The Highlights and New Lights of the Hogarth Press*. Edmonton, Alberta: U of Alberta Libraries, 2009. Print.

Grimes, Ronald L. *Deeply Into the Bone: Re-Inventing Rites of Passage*. Berkeley: U of California P, 2000. Print.

———. *Rite Out of Place: Ritual, Media, and the Arts*. Oxford: Oxford UP, 2006. Print.

———. *Ritual Criticism: Case Studies in Its Practice, Essays on Its Theory*. Columbia SC: U of S Carolina P, 1990. Print.

Harris, Janice Hubbard. *Edwardian Stories of Divorce*. New Brunswick, NJ: Rutgers UP, 1996. Print.

Holland, Kathryn. *Dorothy Bussy and Julia Strachey: Dialogues in Modernity*. Diss. University of Oxford (St. Anne's College), 2008.

King, James. *Virginia Woolf*. London: Penguin, 1995. Print.

Koppen, R. S. *Virginia Woolf, Fashion and Literary Modernity*. Edinburgh: Edinburgh UP, 2009. Print.

Lee, Hermione. *Virginia Woolf*. New York: Alfred A. Knopf, 1997. Print.

Miller, Jane Eldridge. *Rebel Women: Feminism, Modernism, and the Edwardian Novel*. London: Virago Press, 1994. Print.

Oakes, Leimomi. "Queen Victoria's wedding dress: the one that started it all." Web. 1/7/2012.http://thedreamstress.com/2011/04/queen-victorias-wedding-dress-the-one-that-started-it-all/. 1-13.

Partridge, Frances. *Julia: A Portrait by Herself & Frances Partridge*. London: Victor Gollancz, 1983. Print.

——. "Preface." *Cheerful Weather for the Wedding* by Julia Strachey. London: Persephone Books, 2009. Print.

Reid, Panthea. *Art and Affection: A Life of Virginia Woolf*. New York: Oxford UP, 1996. Print.

Southworth, Helen, ed. *Leonard and Virginia Woolf: The Hogarth Press and the Networks of Modernism*. Edinburgh: Edinburgh UP, 2010. Print.

——. "Virginia Woolf's *Orlando* Preface, the Modernist Writer, and Networks of Cultural, Financial and Social Capital." *Woolf Studies Annual* 18 (1912): 75-107. Print.

Spalding, Frances. *Duncan Grant: A Biography*. London: Chatto and Windus, 1997. Print.

——. *Vanessa Bell*. London: Weidenfeld and Nicolson, 1983. Print.

Strachey, Julia. *Cheerful Weather for the Wedding* (Hogarth 1932). London: Persephone Books, 2007. Print.

——. "Fragment of a Diary." *Folios of New Writing*. London: Hogarth Press, 1940: 98-114.

Sullivan, Melissa. "The Middlebrows of the Hogarth Press: Rose Macaulay, E. M. Delafield and Cultural Hierarchies in Interwar Britain." *Leonard & Virginia Woolf: The Hogarth Press and the Networks of Modernism*. Ed. Helen Southworth. Edinburgh: Edinburgh UP, 2010. 52-73. Print.

Tree, Viola. *Can I Help You? Your Manners—Menus—Amusements—Friends—Charades—Make-Ups—Travel—Calling—Children—Love Affairs*. London: Hogarth Press, 1937. Print.

Wolfe, Jesse. *Bloomsbury, Modernism, and the Reinvention of Intimacy*. Cambridge: Cambridge UP, 2011. Print.

Woolf, Leonard. *Beginning Again: An Autobiography of the Years 1911 to 1918*. New York: Harcourt Brace Jovanovich, 1963. Print.

——. *Downhill All the Way: An Autobiography of the Years 1919 to 1939*. New York: Harcourt Brace Jovanovich, 1967. Print.

——. *Letters of Leonard Woolf*. Ed. Frederic Spotts. San Diego: Harcourt Brace Jovanovich, 1989. Print.

Woolf, Virginia. *The Complete Shorter Fiction of Virginia Woolf*. 2nd ed.. Ed. Susan Dick. San Diego: Harcourt Brace Jovanovich, 1989. Print.

——. *The Diaries of Virginia Woolf*. Ed. Anne Olivier Bell. 5 vols. New York: Harcourt Brace Jovanovich, 1977-1984. Print.

——. *The Essays of Virginia Woolf*. 6 vols. Vol. 6 1933-41 and Additional Essays 1906-1924. Ed. Stuart N. Clarke. London: Hogarth Press, 2011. Print.

——. *The Letters of Virginia Woolf*. 6 vols. Ed. Nigel Nicolson and Joanne Trautmann. New York and London: Harcourt Brace Jovanovich, 1975-80. Print.

——. *Moments of Being*. 2nd ed. Ed. Jeanne Schulkind. San Diego: Harcourt, Brace Jovanovich, 1985. Print.

——. *Orlando: A Biography*. 1928. New York: Harcourt Brace Jovanovich, 1956. Print.

——. *Three Guineas*. 1938. New York: Harcourt, Brace and World, 1966. Print.

Young, John K. "'Murdering an Aunt or Two': Textual Practice and Narrative Form in Virginia Woolf's Metropolitan Market." *Virginia Woolf and the Literary Marketplace*. Ed. Jeanne Dubino. NY: Palgrave Macmillan, 2010. 181-95. Print.

Variations on *Mrs. Dalloway*: Rachel Cusk's *Arlington Park*

Monica Latham

Rachel Cusk's contemplations on motherhood, which brought about so much controversy in the media after the publication of *A Life's Work: On Becoming a Mother* (2001), have also nourished her fiction; *Arlington Park* (2006) is a case in point. The novel follows the lives of five young women (Christine Lanham, Juliet Randall, Maisie Carrington, Solly Kerr-Leigh, and Amanda Clapp) in a well-off suburb over the course of one rainy day: most of them are stay-at-home mothers struggling to overcome routine, which creates utmost frustration, acrimony, and deep interrogations. The lives of the middle-class housewives echo one another during the day and finally intersect in the evening, at a dinner party hosted by the Lanhams. Despite the obvious differences from Virginia Woolf's *Mrs. Dalloway*— differences of chronotope, of the characters' ages, social and domestic preoccupations and of representation of women's lives almost a century apart— sophisticated critics and common readers alike have noted the resemblance to Woolf's novel;[1] they have pointed out the style and texture of Cusk's writing, which is strongly reminiscent of Woolf's own prose. The contemporary author uses "Dallowayisms" (Chatman 274), that is to say features and templates of her predecessor's circadian novel, and transposes them to the present-day novel to dissect domestic middle-class suburban life in Britain. Just like *Mrs. Dalloway*, Cusk's observational novel drifts through time and consciousness. Her novel is made up of an accumulation of little "patches of life" (*Arlington Park* 220) and the narrative switches between various characters who lead Woolfian lives, microscopically observed by the narrator who renders their obsessive self-analyses and questionings. Cusk's novel focuses on the overwhelming awareness of the moment and the passage of time with its layers and thickness. It deals with what goes unsaid under the surface: fleeting moods, thoughts and unspoken communication. Like Woolf, Cusk offers the reader a multitude of aural and visual perceptions— the sensory impressionism chiselling out inner turmoil— and has a cult for the object and for the powerful, arresting triviality of the non-event. The contemporary author shares with her predecessor the art of

---

[1] More than any of her other novels, Virginia Woolf's *Mrs. Dalloway* has inspired numerous contemporary writers and has generated a large number of mimetic or transformative literary products. See Monica Latham, "Mrs. Woolf, Our Twenty-First-Century Contemporary," *A Contemporary Woolf*, eds. Claire Davison-Pégon and Anne-Marie Di Biasio-Smith (Montpellier: Presses Universitaires de la Méditerranée, forthcoming 2012) and "Virginia Woolf's *Mrs Dalloway*: Genesis and Palimpsests."

scrutinizing material details using the same sharp eye with which she explores the characters' minds. Besides, Cusk's epiphany bears resemblance to the Woolfian "moment of being," the various refrains and repetitions give her prose a musical quality, and her characters constantly attempt to give a definition of the texture of life and reality.

In this essay I would like to capture the Woolfian aura of *Arlington Park* and more particularly examine the overt resonances with *Mrs. Dalloway*, as well as raise questions about Cusk's neo-modernism. Indeed, Cusk's narrative, stylistic and thematic features seem to position her novel at the confluence of two traditions: firstly, her writing stems from modernism and prolongs modernist techniques, especially the Woolfian legacy; Cusk can thus be said to be a neo-modernist writer. I am here using the term neo-modernism, which implies a continuation and updating of the Woolfian modernist heritage, as Cusk clearly renegotiates and enhances modernist literary legacies[2]. Secondly, her work belongs to the current "literary fiction" genre: it is an elitist, lyrical, "writerly" type of fiction born with modernist aesthetics.

In *Arlington Park* Rachel Cusk dissects the social and the domestic, following the interactions among the five young women and concentrating on their experiences or hidden pains. The female characters all have certain facets and features of Clarissa Dalloway and constitute twenty-first-century variations of the Woolfian character. As in Woolf's *Mrs. Dalloway* in which the points of view of different characters alternate, intersect and take over from one another, in *Arlington Park* the characters' lives echo one another as they take turns to narrate the story, giving a 360-degree panorama of domestic life in the suburb. These interconnecting stories mirror Woolf's initial project of composing *Mrs. Dalloway*, namely to create completely separated chapters which would contain some kind of fusing links and which would converge upon the party at the end.[3]

Cusk adopts *Mrs. Dalloway*'s temporal framework. As Stephen Connor has noted, the use of the single day temporal structure is "less and more at once: less than the world in its concentration and condensation [...] and yet containing more than

---

[2] My contention is that Cusk does not propel Woolf's legacy into postmodernism: the relationships between Woolfian and Cuskian texts are not those of playful intertextuality, parody or pastiche (for definitions of these notions, see Julia Kristeva, Gérard Genette, Frederic Jameson, Linda Hutcheon, and Simon Dentith). For a discussion on Woolf's postmodernist (contemporary authors whose writing is imitative, [Michael Cunningham or Robin Lippincott, for instance]) and neo-modernist (writers whose prose offers more intricate narrative, thematic or stylistic resonances to *Mrs. Dalloway* [Ian McEwan or Rachel Cusk, for example]) literary heirs, see Monica Latham, "Mrs. Woolf, Our Twenty-First-Century Contemporary."

[3] The original project noted in a manuscript notebook on 6 October 1922 was to write a book to be called either *The Party* or *At Home*, which was to consist of six or seven chapters converging on the final event—Mrs. Dalloway's party.

the world of accumulation of allusion and interconnection" (Connor 68). The narration is punctuated by the clock and extended by the psychological time of the characters, who navigate in their pasts and presents. The characters face their resurfacing memories and explore their own consciousnesses while confronting the present in their kitchens, shops, and changing rooms. The day thus unfolds through the women's shifting perspectives. The day-in-the-life format compresses the time scale but at the same time opens up to encompass all the other days, which allows Cusk to pierce through several temporary layers and probe into contemporary womanhood. Thus, this particular day enables the author to dive into her characters' pasts, to varying degrees.

The universality of this day in the women's lives and its repetition reveals their existences. The content of the day overflows the strict temporal mold and branches out into events and thoughts that go beyond the strict narrowness of one specific day. In *Mrs. Dalloway*, the past keeps surging and "dissolves" in the present throughout the day; present moments are pregnant with fragments of memories from Clarissa's youth at Bourton when she plunged into life and experienced a sensation of freedom, metaphorically expressed by her bursting open the French windows. In *Arlington Park*, what the narrative voice implies about Amanda's momentous day could be applied to all the characters: "[…] this day of her life in which all the other days seemed to be coming together and showing themselves at last" (77). But instead of conferring a sense of opening, in *Arlington Park* the day becomes the rigid cast of the women characters' lives as they feel inexorably trapped by time. Their only freedom in this domestic routine is that of taking refuge in thoughts: they reflect on their lives, interpret events or incidents and try to find meaning in them. The ordinary events in the lives of these ordinary women unfold as the ordinary day progresses toward a party and the arrival of guests. This "ordinariness" is oppressive, as illustrated by Amanda's vision of her humdrum life:

> Her life had been an ordinary life: her parents and grandparents were ordinary, they had said and done ordinary things together. They had all lived together ordinarily, in their ordinary home. They had gone to sleep and got up again and eaten their meals and done their work in an ordinary way. If there was a wrong, then it was an ordinary kind of wrong. (74)

The women in *Arlington Park* compose the portrait of specific well-off suburbanites whose lives echo each others': although materially privileged, they are exhausted and frustrated and are weighed down by husbands and families. They are "[…] portrayed as solitary islands of thought, feeling and self-reflection, who fastidiously brush themselves down after each agoraphobic venture into the community" (Schoene 160). They form together "broken mosaics" of "atomized subjectivities" (Schoene 155) and borrow the Woolfian "rising and falling" mood pattern to express the vision of their own lives.

Christine Lanham, who somehow holds the framework of the novel together, is preparing for a dinner party on the same day she learns her grandmother has died in a nursing home. A Mrs. Dalloway or a Mrs. Ramsay for our suburban age, she is a dinner hostess who gathers together some of her Arlington Park neighbors. She drifts through her day, shopping, preparing for her dinner party that night and ruminating on her life. Her dinner reunites other suburban couples and provides its climax in the form of a drunken epiphanic outburst: "'You've got to love life,' she said blearily. 'You've got to love just— being alive'" (238). Like Clarissa Dalloway, behind her social mask, there are "faults, jealousies, vanities, suspicions" (*MD* 32). Christine appears to be optimistic and cheerful, but this is gradually revealed to be little more than a protective façade. The result of living with her husband, Joe, is that she is constantly thinking with "the front of her brain" (214), progressively abandoning her primal, instinctive, deeper, sensual, emotive "body."

Juliet Randal, "aged thirty-six, mother of two, a teacher at Arlington High School for Girls" (8), is often assailed by waves of uplifting and disheartening moods: momentarily happy, high-spirited sensations ("[…] Juliet was overpowered by a new realisation, the realisation that life was meant to be wonderful" [13]) are followed by anti-climactic moods ("Life did not seem to be meant to be as wonderful as it had done earlier. Wherever she looked she saw the sheen coming off it" [15]). For a moment, she is blinded by the luster of life conferred by the prosperous suburb and her social position, but the domineering mood of dissatisfaction and emptiness is nevertheless prevalent. She is stifled by "the solid, bourgeois, profitable ordinariness of life," and laments the fact that she has buried her own ambitions beneath the demands of her husband and children, gradually becoming overwhelmed by bitterness: "she was full of the deposits of wasted days" (36). A mere container of wasted, silted time, Juliet dreams of a less confining place which would allow her to "open out all the petals packed inside her" (32). The part-time English teacher, who reflects on her womanhood, concludes that all men, including her husband, Benedict, end up wiping out women's identities and ambitions. Juliet is angry at all men, like Sally Seton in *Mrs. Dalloway*, who thinks men ("the Hughes and the Dalloways and all the other 'perfect gentlemen'") would "stifle [Clarissa's] soul" (64). Juliet could have been professionally successful but she has wound up in Arlington Park with Benedict, her well-meaning liberal husband, and their two young children. "All men are murderers, Juliet thought. All of them. They murder women. They take a woman, and little by little they murder her" (18). The slow and painless metaphorical death is due to a gradual and almost imperceptible confinement to a narrow, limited and unfulfilling professional and domestic life. This repeated image is a lament on the loss of self at the core of marriage and motherhood. The ordinariness of her life inexorably leads to death. However, she feels endowed with a lofty mission, as the hidden feminist aim of her book club is to open young girls' eyes and shield them "from the bullet of an ordinary life" (28).

Maisie Carrington, thirty-eight, is also experiencing an "unstable level of dissatisfaction" which causes several angry outbursts at the expense of her own children and of a woman in a car park. She is clearly frustrated with parenthood and like Juliet, she feels "imprisoned for life" (173), especially in her kitchen: "It was here that Maisie felt most divorced from her own motives, saw her husband and children most as the strangers they occasionally were" (174). After having convinced her solicitor husband, Dom, to move out of the "churn of London," out of the "thick vortex of multitudinous screaming wants" (192) to a lesser job, she then discovered that "she could not endure the life they were making for themselves" in an "atmosphere of sordid confinement, like an old shoe" (172). Maisie has the feeling that the "wind" of her dissatisfaction, "this variable force of discontent," inevitably and inescapably blows in only one direction, sending her "to what was fixed and narrow" (183). Inertia and a sort of claustrophobia seem to characterize not only her family life, but the lives of all the Arlington Park women.

Solly Kerr-Leigh believes marriage should be a state of hyphenation, like her last name, not a matter of absorption or defeat, like the pronunciation of this very name, "Curly." Now pregnant for the fourth time, Solly suddenly feels overblown, whilst her husband seems, on the contrary, to be blooming into a "lean, vertical masculinity" (113). Perhaps the most outwardly frustrated of all the women, Solly is sure that a part of her is irretrievably lost; this is the reason why she is trying to find her vanished femininity in the other female tenants who occupy her spare room and their feminine possessions that she inspects in their absences. By diving into the consciousness of the diverse female characters and by following their thoughts and moods, Cusk is engaged in "a painstaking, often unrelenting exploration of the contemporary female psyche" (Schoene 161).

All these Clarissa Dalloway-like characters share the space of the suburb. This area gives clues about its inhabitants, just as her portion of London and her house reveals something about Clarissa, not only her social status but mostly her private, intimate life. In *Arlington Park*, it is mainly the kitchen, perfect symbol of domesticity, which reveals the housewives the most. The house is a confined space, prison for the wives and the mothers, who most of the time remain tethered to the kitchen: ("The kitchen was like a person with whom she had tried to get on and failed: barely tried, so impatient was she to settle into her enmity with it" [175]); this is probably why Amanda knocked down walls and designed a kitchen of excessive size to give her the luring sensation of freedom ("you could fit a jumbo jet in here" [64]), but instead realizes she has created emptiness: "They had knocked through until they had created not space but emptiness" (64). The women are confined in the desirable yet bleak suburb, stuck in a domestic rut, trapped in the ordinariness of their lives, in their marriages and motherhoods: "We're all such good *wives* and good *mothers*, and there we are feeding our families these healthy meals and taking our children to piano lessons and making our houses all perfect [...]" (97).

The loneliness, isolation and emptiness of these women's lives reflect Clarissa's feeling of being "invisible; unseen; unknown" (*MD* 9). The suburban women in their thirties, who are mainly stay-at-home mothers, reflect on their oppressing "domestic slavery" (*Arlington Park* 128) and the servitude of motherhood. The women are all mired in marital dissatisfaction and stranded in their narrow lifestyles. Maisie, for instance "saw herself as imprisoned for life— violent feelings poured from her in a righteous torrent, feelings that came as though from some geological past, like lava" (173). The only physical escape for them is the bleak shopping mall trying clothes which reveal their ungraceful and unaesthetic bodies distended by repeated pregnancies and age: the "spare tire," "the great wobbling band of fat around [their] middle"; "flabby tummies" and "flabby tits" (91) are opposed to the enviable "untouched masculinity" (121) of the male body. Like Clarissa who feels "suddenly shriveled, aged, breastless" (*MD* 26), Cusk's women also experience the "crisis of the flesh" (*Arlington Park* 121).

In the spare room where "the weight of her family seemed to move away from her" (113), Solly experiences soothing moments. It is a room of her own to feel free, to expand, to forget the envied "vertical masculinity" (113) of her husband. The spare room recalls Clarissa's bare room, which encapsulates her sense of "an emptiness about the heart of life" (*MD* 26). She is like a "nun withdrawing, or a child exploring a tower" (26). In *Mrs. Dalloway*, Clarisssa thinks extensively of the lack of intimacy and dissatisfaction of marital life— her "virginity" (27) being expressed symbolically through her stretched sheet and narrow bed— but finds meaning in life during crucial epiphanies, like Cusk's solitary creatures who are haunted by despairing loneliness, intimations of mortality and disheartening lamentations, but who are also occasionally uplifted by small, significant epiphanies.

Cusk borrows Woolf's technique of digging out invisible caves behind her characters,[4] and weaves the interior lives of the characters into their external worlds: beneath the surface respectability of the external world of the leafy suburb, the richness of the interior lives lies like a volcanic outburst of frustration, fury and despair. While permanently confronted with the reality of domesticity, the *Arlington Park* characters inhabit their inner worlds where they express their pains, true feelings and harshly comment on their exterior lives. The reader follows the movement in

---

[4] "I dig out beautiful caves behind my characters: I think that gives them exactly what I want; humanity, humour; depth. The idea is that the caves shall connect and each comes to daylight at the present moment" (*D2* 263).

and out of their minds, and the pulses of their inner worlds while the narrator documents all the insanity, fears, petty jealousies, resentments and love that battle there. Their meandering trains of thoughts are carefully recorded and alternate with conversations that anchor the social being in the present time. The characters are constantly pulled out from their musings by the interaction with their children, husbands, neighbors and friends: "[Amanda] looked out of the window at the garden, as though expecting to see her grandmother there, with her face at the glass. Then the doorbell rang" (62).

The unfolding of the characters' ordinary day is interrupted by splinters of the past that erupt in the present: Cusk borrows Woolf's method of fragmenting the past and "telling [it] in instalments, as [she] need[s] it" (*D2* 272), distilling it throughout the unfolding of the day. The elasticity of the present moment enables the author to incorporate past memories and significant episodes. The flexible time stretches, compresses and expands "as though the whole compressed day had suddenly been uncorked and allowed to come loudly exploding out" (*Arlington Park* 169).

Cusk proves to be a minute observer of human thought, of the way individuals perceive themselves and their positions in the world around them. Her typically Woolfian narrator focuses on moments of the characters' everyday lives, on their memories and movements of the mind, on their deep meditations on trivial things, on microscopic facts, objects and minor events which trigger significant insights. By doing so, the narrative moves away from the surface, migrating inwards and exploring that private space. Cusk's writing continues Woolf's preoccupation with mental processes transcribed into a fluid narrative.

The contemporary author examines consciousness with the same intensity as she probes situations and surrounding objects, penetrating their essence. She has an acute Woolfian eye for minute details. The most mundane objects and moments are investigated scrupulously, and painted with luxurious precision.[5] Cusk celebrates the cult of the small but envelops it in a thick yet fluid prose. Examples of such small, vivid points capture the women's gazes and illuminate their lives; these miniatures feature a luxuriance of delicate, minute pictorial details:

> Then she [Solly] noticed, in the far corner of the garden beneath the tree, a little clump of primroses. She walked slowly across the grass and stood over them. They were so delicate, so pretty— she towered over them like some dumb, shaggy creature that had just issued from its cave, examining the beautiful intricacy of life. Their petals were beaded with rain. She looked at them, dimly remembering the line of a song. (122)

---

[5] See Max Duperray, *Le Banal dans le roman britannique contemporain* and Mahmoud Sami-Ali, *Le Banal*.

> One day she [Betty] came downstairs wearing a pair of black silk trousers with pink roses embroidered on them, little flat embroidered shoes and a little pink jacket with silk-covered buttons; and Solly didn't know why, but the sight of these things made her eyes fill with tears. They reminded her of something, of childhood, of things that were small and perfect and mysteriously beautiful. (114)

This kind of Woolfian poetic and visual prose requires the reader to linger over it with a magnifying glass in order to fully appreciate its precise, meticulous and carefully wrought consistency. The descriptions function like small embroideries which, put together, form the special fabric and texture of the Cuskian text. What some critics[6] deemed to be an over-weaved narrative burdened with microscopic, apparently insignificant details of the external world, the minutiae of humdrum everyday life and the intricate working of the mind, constitutes in fact the very essence of Cusk's prose, in the same vein as her modernist predecessor.

Cusk's compulsive observation derives from the Woolfian minuteness of recording trivial events: just like Woolf, she records "the atoms as they fall upon the mind in the order in which they fall" and traces "the pattern, however disconnected and incoherent in appearance, which each sight or incident scores upon the consciousness" (Woolf, "Modern Fiction" *E4* 161). Cusk scrutinizes her characters' lives, following their movements in time and space closely, as well as the flow of their thoughts. Patterns of ordinary lives on an ordinary day are examined; the "trivial," the "evanescent," the minute fascinations of the mundane are recorded "with the sharpness of steel" (*E4* 160).

Present time, which seems endless to the mothers of small children, is compartmentalized, evolving around the infants, their needs and school timetables. School time gives a dull rhythm to the mothers' domestic lives. Time is heavy, like the "leaden circles" which "dissolved in the air" in *Mrs. Dalloway* (4, 41, 80, 158); "people burdened by time" (*Arlington Park* 41) is a recurrent motif in *Arlington Park*. Not only does time have a destructive impact on the physical beings (all women reflecting on the decay of their bodies), but it also leaves indelible marks on their selves. Just like their families, time is a leaden burden: "Instead [Juliet] was heavy, full of lead. She sank like a stone through the onrush of time." Amanda has a short moment of freedom while her children are at school: "she had a feeling of rapid ascent, as though the members of her household were sandbags she was heaving

---

[6]"There are some great moments," Lucy Ellmann wrote, "but [Cusk] tends to over-egg the pudding with metaphor, simile, and melodramatic hyperbole when all she's describing is a set of materially advantaged women getting through the day."

one by one out of the basket of a hot-air balloon" (40), but overall, time is like a "boulder she had to single-handedly lift and move laboriously out of her path" (41).

Time is depicted through metaphor as a mechanism implying an inescapable trap: "women were as though snared in the mechanism," "caught between the blank river and the churning wheels. Trapped as they were, every movement caused them pain" (148); "time set everything whirring and churning and grinding again and you felt the agony of the turning wheels" (150). Time is an all-pervasive means of control over the women; clock time is associated with restrictions and regulations. It is related to physical coercion, just like in *Mrs. Dalloway*: "Shredding and slicing, dividing and subdividing, the clocks of Harley Street nibbled at the June day, counselled submission, upheld authority, and pointed out in chorus the supreme advantages of a sense of proportion [...]" (*MD* 87); Clarissa "fear[s] time itself, and read[s] on Lady Bruton's face, as if it had been a dial cut in impassive stone, the dwindling of life" (*MD* 26); and the "great booming voice" (*MD* 42) of Big Ben is the "voice of authority" (*MD* 12). Clock time announces the dwindling of time and ultimately of life.

According to Virginia Woolf, "moments of non-being" are moments that the individuals are not consciously aware of even as they experience them. When the women in *Arlington Park* perform routine tasks such as walking, taking the children to and from school, shopping, preparing meals, without thinking about these actions, this part of their lives is "not lived consciously," but instead is embedded in "a kind of nondescript cotton wool" (Woolf, "A Sketch of the Past" *MOB* 70). Their cotton wool lives are made of a long and painful chain of numerous unextraordinary "leaden" moments of non-being.[7]

However, the oppressive, engulfing, long and slow time offers the female characters numerous evocative brief moments, Woolfian "moments of being."[8] They are

---

[7] On a discussion of how the "cotton wool" of habit and routine is central to Woolf's modernism, see Liesl M. Olson, "Virginia Woolf's 'cotton wool of daily life'"; see also Georges Perec's definiton of "infra-ordinary" as the most insignificant and imperceptible banal events that happen and recur every day: "the banal, the quotidian, the obvious, the common, the ordinary, the infra-ordinary, the background noise, the habitual" (Perec 11-12). One lives these moments without questioning them or tracking them down from the dross in which they remain mired. Cusk actually gives the banal a "tongue" to let it speak about the suburban housewives.

[8] "Moments of being" are moments in which an individual experiences a sense of reality, in contrast to the states of "non-being" that dominate most of an individual's conscious life, in which they are separated from reality by a protective covering. Such "moments of being" could be the result of instances of shock, discovery or revelation.

flashes of awareness that reveal the hidden pattern behind the cotton wool of their daily life. These moments are paradoxically both fleeting and enduring. For Woolf a moment of being is a moment when individuals are fully conscious of their experience, a moment when they are not only aware of themselves but catch a glimpse of their connection to a larger pattern hidden behind the opaque surface of daily life. Unlike moments of non-being, when individuals live and act without awareness, performing acts as if asleep, the moment of being opens up a hidden reality. As Clarissa and Septimus experience exquisite moments of awareness and intense moments of vision, Cuskian characters also experience moments of being in the middle of their trivial daily acts. The significance of the modernist author's moments of being is explained by Michael Cunningham,[9] and could be also applied to Cusk's characters: "what's important in a life, what remains at its end, is less likely to be its supposed climaxes than its unexpected moments of awareness, often arising out of unremarkable experience, so deeply personal they can rarely be explained" (Cunningham xx). Like Woolf, Cusk manages her small moments "beautifully" (Cunningham xx) and endows them with resonant significance.

Indeed, in the bleak atmosphere of the suburb and in the women's routine there are ordinary miracles, moments of self-awareness that lighten the day of the characters. It is their inner selves that experience epiphanies, not the women as social beings. Some thoughts, objects and dreams have the power to "alter the colour" of their minds (159) and the perception of ordinary life: "These moments came and they were beautiful, fragile pauses, like bubbles, in which Amanda experienced a feeling of summation, almost of symbolism" (56). The characters, who are like "a bee with honey, laden with the moment" (*MD* 42) live these intense, fragile, fleeting, solitary, private moments and at the same time analyze them, dissecting their beauty and significance. Cusk multiplies epiphanies and instances of experiencing these moments as she portrays Clarissa Dalloway-like characters: each of them has access to their own such intense moments.

For instance, Juliet's moments of being allow her to glimpse beauty beyond the veil of anger which wraps her suburban existence: "All she needed was the chance of her Friday afternoons, to step aside for a moment, to take a single step away and look out, look up. Then she saw beauty: she saw the world not filtered through her veil of anger, but as it was" (167). One of her epiphanies is situated in between reality and vision and reveals essential things about the truth and beauty of life:

---

[9]Cunningham's own homage to Woolf's *Mrs. Dalloway* in his highly acclaimed novel *The Hours* has been amply discussed by numerous scholars. See, for instance, Tory Young, *Michael Cunningham's The Hours: A Reader's Guide*; Birgit Spengler, "Michael Cunningham Rewriting Virginia Woolf: Pragmatist vs Modernist Aesthetics"; Seymour Chatman, "*Mrs. Dalloway*'s Progeny: *The Hours* as Second-degree Narrative."

> Then Juliet saw, rising from the dark folds, rising from the trees, a pair of swans. They were flying side by side, throats outstretched, beneath the descending night. Their bodies were a pale, unearthly white; together they flew in a kind of ecstasy, lifting themselves from the shadows with their slow, labouring wings. Juliet watched them. She watched their glimmering forms fly through the dark. Side by side they flew, beautiful and alive, exulting. (168)

Although their torpors stem from different experiences— in Juliet's case it results from lassitude and dissatisfaction at home and has domestic repercussions, while in Septimus's case it is induced by his war trauma and has political implications— both Juliet and Septimus experience similar intense moments of vision. As he sits on a park bench, he is transfixed by the rising and falling movement of the trees and the display of the colorful vision before his eyes:

> Happily Rezia put her hand with a tremendous weight upon his knee so that he was weighted down, transfixed, or the excitement of the elm trees rising and falling, rising and falling with all their leaves alight and the colour thinning and thickening from blue to the green of a hollow wave, like plumes on horses' heads, feathers on ladies', so proudly they rose and fell, so superbly would have sent him mad. (*MD* 22)

Septimus feels a strong connection between himself and the natural world. The fact that he suffers from shell shock makes him more receptive to the facts of the natural world that most people fail to see:

> They beckoned; leaves were alive; trees were alive. And the leaves being connected by millions of fibres with his own body, there on the seat, fanned it up and down; when the branch stretched he, too, made the statement. The sparrows fluttering, rising, and falling in jagged fountains were part of the pattern. (*MD* 22)

Such visions of pure beauty and revelation spark momentary fireworks that illuminate these characters' days and awaken them from their torpor. They give them a temporary impression of freedom and evasion from the normality, "proportion" (*MD* 84) and routine in which they are trapped. A different sense of perspective and of proportion is thus found by characters during their illuminating moments: towards the end of *Arlington Park*, Christine, for instance, experiences "a sense of perspective, of the reach of the universe, of its strange but necessary dimensions. It was this sense of order," she concludes, "that allowed life in Arlington Park to be what it was" (222). Maisie's still moments are also like secondary states that suspend her from running time and disconnect her from domestic chores. These interruptions can expand and overflow over several days and allow her to reflect on her "existence" or "essence" while outside, "the cotton wool" of life goes on uninterrupted.

The introspective characters ponder the reality/unreality and solidity/ephemerality of the moment; the smallest and most insignificant, imperceptible life moments are invested with a heightened and acutely perceived awareness. Like Clarissa who "plunge[s] into the very heart of the moment, tranfixe[s] it" (*MD* 31), all the female characters in *Arlington Park* experience such moments. The moment of being is for Cuskian characters the shining instant devoid of its temporal husk. It is intense, short and oxymoronic, being at once beautiful and tragic.

The small, typically Woolfian epiphanies[10] are nevertheless profound and saturated moments since the characters probe, examine and ponder the smallest particles of their being. As a result, the moment of being gives renewed impulse to the subject. Woolf's aim and design in *Mrs. Dalloway*— which also seems to be Cusk's intention in her novels— was to saturate the moment with thoughts and sensations, and eliminate from the unfolding of time ("from lunch to dinner") the superfluous fillers (what is "false, unreal, merely conventional" [*D3* 209]). The poetic conciseness of the moment, its condensation and intensity and the capturing of its minimalist essence constitutes Woolf's heritage that Cusk fruitfully draws upon, prolongs and renews.

Epiphanies allow characters to build threads of connections between themselves and the surrounding world. The pattern behind "the cotton wool of daily life," or the opaque woolly curtain of everyday existence, unexpectedly becomes clearly visible and comprehensible and the characters can finally experience the intensity of life. Cusk, just like Woolf, uses an evocative, rich poetic language to express the deep meaning of her characters' moments of being. Thus, these inner, private moments can be read as brief poems which resurface behind the trivia of everyday life.

Pictorial language is amply used to color the rich introspective lives of the characters but is also more conventionally put to use to paint outside landscapes and create natural, impressionistic tableaux which function like Woolfian interludes in *Arlington Park*. These interludes trace the progress of the sun throughout the day, verbally rendering the changes wrought by light. Cusk, as a skillful poet and

---

[10] Woolf uses different metaphors in her novels to describe these moments: "little daily miracles, illuminations, matches struck unexpectedly in the dark" (*TTL* 218); "an illumination; a match burning in a crocus; an inner meaning almost expressed" (*MD* 27). See Jensen 112-125.

painter of the passage of time, borrows Woolf's varied palette of colors,[11] lights and shadows, and like her predecessor, she imparts an impressionistic quality to her prose when, for example, she creates vignettes of different "times of the day", reminiscent of the interludes in *The Waves* and specific scenes in *Mrs. Dalloway* (118; 158) where the wind plays with the clouds, veiling and unveiling the sun, which in turn sends shafts of light and darkness to the earth in order to provide the visual background to Septimus's hallucinations. In Cusk's novel the passage of time is also rendered in terms of movement of clouds, wind, and change in ambient colors, which envelop and paint the suburb. The profusion of similes and syntactic repetitions give the impression that the cloud-like waves advance, invade the cityscape, change the skyscape and adjust the intensity of light:

> The clouds came from the west: clouds like dark cathedrals, clouds like machines, clouds like black blossoms flowering in the arid starlit sky. They came over the English countryside, sunk in its muddled sleep. They came over the low, populous hills where scatterings of light throbbed in the darkness. At midnight they reached the sky, valiantly glittering in its shallow provincial basin. Unseen, they grew like a second city overhead, thickening, expanding, throwing up their savage monuments, their towers, their monstrous, unpeopled palaces of cloud. (1)

This type of pictorial prose has a dynamic visual quality: one can see shapes and feel textures as well as picture the movement and metamorphosis of the dark clouds. The lush and abundant prose grows out of repeated comparisons that depict the variety of shapes and metamorphosis of these shapes. The Cuskian scene is highly reminiscent of the devouring darkness invading and spreading all over the Ramsays' house, dissolving all colors and shapes in Woolf's *To the Lighthouse* (171).

Stylistically, Cusk's technique consists of proceeding by short linguistic units, strokes and touches: "The rain fell on Arlington Park, fell on its empty avenues and its well-pruned hedges, on its schools and its churches, on its trees and its gardens. It fell on its Victorian terraces with their darkened windows, on its rows of bay-fronted houses, on its Georgian properties behind their gates, on its maze of tidy streets where the little two-storey houses were painted pretty colours. It fell

---

[11] Woolf asserts that "All great writers are great colourists, just as they are musicians into the bargain; they always contrive to make their scenes glow and darken and change to the eye" ("Walter Sickert" 23). By following Clive Bell's and Roger Fry's guidelines, Woolf infused literature with a painterly vision; she did not merely write, but created images out of words.

joyously over the dark, deserted sward of the park, over its neat paths and bushes" (5). Haunting anaphoric descriptions composed of binary and tertiary segments extend a first paratactic statement, like an avalanche of descriptive clauses stemming from a short, declarative observation: "It beat down, washing the pavements, sluicing along the drains, drumming on the bonnets of the parked cars" (5). The atmosphere of the suburb is flooded by incessant, monotonous rain, rendered linguistically in repetitions and refrains, which confers on the rain an overwhelming power: everything is drenched and crushed by the rain, just like the women characters are crushed by the monotony of their everyday lives.

The juxtaposition of nominal sentences with their ceaseless articulations resembles a cinematic technique of recording which focuses on a multitude of events at the same time, creating simultaneousness and continuity. These intense and exhausting descriptions seem to go from the core to the periphery of events, incidents or still lives painted in circular strokes. The narrator's close and intent scrutiny of every detail, some essential and symbolic, others merely adorning and cumulative, participating in the thickness of the prose, offers the reader a typical Woolfian experience of reading.

Cusk's chapters are interspersed with short observations on the quality and texture of light, her equivalent of Big Ben chiming and announcing the time. "The sky was grey. The light was ebbing from it, ebbing, standing back to let the darkness come" (160); "The library was filling with purple light" (165); "It was just past five o'clock: the sky was violet and black, bruised, swimming with clouds. A last faint gauze of light hung over everywhere" (167); "At six o'clock, when the last bruised light of afternoon had ebbed away and blackness stood at the window, Dom Carrington opened his front door" (169).

Cusk's pictorial skill is given full rein in the descriptions of nature in which she lingers on details and penetrates their essence. The author proves to be an expert painter of light expressed in a lyric prose. This specific prose corresponds to a Woolfian sensory approach to create an outside mood that reverberates with the characters' inner turmoil. With an eye for detail and an ear attuned to noises and voices, to their imperceptible movements, nuances and tones, Cusk composes the atmosphere of a place. The rhythm and fluidity of her style come from detectable combinations of Dalloway-esque elements, repetitions, refrains, up and down, rising and falling wave-like movements. For both Woolf and Cusk, plot is secondary to rhythm and language, which is richly metaphorical, dense and complex.[12] Both authors

---

[12] When compared to Woolf in the way she uses language as a craft in itself, Cusk gladly acknowledges the similarity but she also states her originality and complexity that stem from her own experience, which is being wrought in her prose. See the interview by Miranda Purves in *Elle*.

perpetuate the cult of the small, and envelope it in a thick yet fluid prose. The penetrating observations on both outside natural sceneries and private domestic lives are expressed with the same intensity in lyrical passages which describe both the continuous movement of the exterior world and characters' fluid streams of interior life.

Rachel Cusk's prose is thus a perfect example of current neo-modernist literary fiction in the wake of Virginia Woolf; Cusk's style undoubtedly bears the imprint of her predecessor's literary legacy. In *Arlington Park* Cusk clearly borrows and updates familiar Dalloway-isms: the narrative switches between the various mothers, and thickens page after page from the accumulation of little points of life; like Woolf, Cusk describes fleeting moods, focuses extensively on what remains unsaid and astutely recreates women's inner lives as they collide with society's expectations; finally, like her predecessor, Cusk is a microscopic observer of human thought and of the way individuals perceive themselves and their positions in the world around them.

Moreover, besides the technical aspect of the prose, aesthetic questions are raised in Cusk's fiction where she provides typical Woolfian interrogations on the essential definition of "life," "truth" or "reality." Through her characters, the contemporary author offers her own answer to the Woolfian question "what is life?" Like Woolf (who expressed her aesthetic belief in many essays, especially in "Modern Fiction," and provided her own definition of "life," "truth" or "reality"), by writing stories of everyday life, Cusk asserts her artistic credo. Her aim is to "make things life-like" and for this, she advocates a place for stories set in the present (not fantasy dealing with big historical events or serious subjects) which stage little dramas of private lives. Her novels celebrate ordinary, domestic experiences:

---

[13] Here is Woolf's metaphoric definition: "Life is not a series of gig lamps symmetrically arranged; life is a luminous halo, a semi-transparent envelope surrounding us from the beginning of consciousness to the end" ("Modern Fiction", *E*4 160).

[14] Cusk discusses the readers' taste for "important subjects" and provides an explanation for it: "that way, representations of private life can be camouflaged." See Cusk's essay on book clubs, "The Outsider," which can be considered her manifesto on contemporary British fiction. In 2005, she joined a women-only book club whose members met monthly. She found that these readers divided books into two types: heavy-going and not heavy-going. Although they constantly insisted on reading sophisticated, serious literature, like Chekhov's short stories, they persistently disliked it, being unable to grasp it. Cusk therefore broke out in impatience one day: "Oh, for heaven's sake, I said. What do you want? Lies? More books about time-travel, or some past that never existed, or people who grow wings and fly around the place? Or happy endings, or characters the like of which you'll never meet in your life, or books about things that never actually happen to people?"

"ordinary experience of sorrow, of doubt, of morality, of time." (Cusk, "The Outsider"). Cusk argues that other contemporary writers, for whom the domestic backdrop is toned down, and who aspire to a greater aim, are afraid of being relegated to the "ribald category" of "lad and chick-lit" if they deal with "the unadorned matter of life in a modern household, on a modern street," that is to say to the quotidian with its small-scale events which are mere accessories to something bigger and more important: for them, the quotidian is "subjugated, or furbished up like a painted backdrop for the reader to glimpse on occasion." Thus, Cusk writes against the grain of current fiction, just like Woolf did in her own time when she tried to capture "the trivial, the evanescent, the insignificant" ("Modern Fiction" *E*4 160).

Cusk has been criticized by readers looking for literary grandeur and a bigger scope in her novels; however, this is exactly what makes the force and specificity of her prose: there certainly is grandeur in the minute, piercing observations on domestic life expressed in lyrical passages and the painterly attention given to inner lives and outside atmospheric interludes. The lack of narrative thrust and character development constitute the very same objections Arnold Bennett formulated about Virginia Woolf's innovative fiction at the beginning of the twentieth century.[15] However, these are precisely the stylistic ingredients Cusk deliberately and successfully has chosen in order to "make things life-like."

As Woolf's literary heir, Cusk attaches grand themes to the most trivial incidents. She offers her readers deep meditations on microscopic facts, objects and events that trigger significant moments; her novels celebrate female domestic "trivia" and follow her predecessor's example, who, in *A Room of One's Own*, contended that women had written a kind of fiction which had its own nature, based on the very experience of being a woman. Functioning at the heart of the family, Woolf observed, women's training inevitably included the observation of character and the analysis of emotion. These are faculties women acquired unconsciously in the course of daily activities and they are more easily put to use in a novel than elsewhere in fiction. However, she wryly argued that this subject was thought less important as material for fiction than male subjects such as waging war or playing football.[16]

---

[15] See Woolf's essay "Mr Bennett and Mrs Brown" (*E*3 384-389) written as a response to Bennett's attacks.

[16] "Speaking crudely, football and sport are 'important'; the worship of fashion, the buying of clothes 'trivial'. And these values are inevitably transferred from life to fiction. This is an important book, the critic assumes, because it deals with war. This is an insignificant book because it deals with the feelings of women in a drawing-room. A scene in a battle-field is more important than a scene in a shop— everywhere and much more subtly the difference of value persists (*AROO* 74). See also Cusk's article "Shakespeare's Daughters" in which she argues that the same masculine system of values prevails.

Cusk's *Arlington Park* originates in modernist fiction and continues the tradition of lyrical fiction started by Woolf and her "spiritual" contemporaries. Cusk is a current practitioner of literary fiction[17] for which modernist authors have definitely paved the way with innovative techniques such as the representation of consciousness and the celebration of interiority at the expense of the external;[18] the minuteness of the characters' private lives; the little miracles of the ordinary life; the fragmentation, open-endedness, and impressionism of the narration; the "obsessive subjectivism" (Lukács 480) which obscures the material and social reality; and the attention given to style and the texture of writing. Literary fiction uses an elevated, poetic, or idiosyncratic prose style and defies the readers' plot expectations. Such novels are appreciated for their style and elegance. They are densely written books and their authors use language in a fresh way.[19] The reader savors the language and this slows down the reading; they indulge in overtly poetic, lush, lyrical prose, downplay the importance of plot, and follow the meanderings of the stream of consciousness. Things may happen on the surface, but what is really important are the characters' inner thoughts, desires, and motivations. The plot points all relate to the inner mind, and the climaxes and nadirs are almost hidden in quiet moments and small-but-powerful revelations. Authors who practice this fiction alternate points of view among the characters and the endings of their novels are often inconclusive as they deliberately choose not to tie up loose ends. These literary novels (like most modernist novels) "appeal first to the mind rather than to the heart or emotions"; they are "complex, literate, multilayered novels that wrestle with universal dilemmas" (Saricks 178).

Modernism, as Malcolm Bradbury defines it, relies upon the metaphoric: "the distortion of the familiar surface of observed reality" and the "disposition of artistic contents according to the logic of metaphor, form, or symbol" (84). This definition could very well be applied to Cusk's neo-modernist literary fiction, which does not follow a strict linear story or psychological progress and is dominantly metaphoric.[20] Like *Mrs. Dalloway*, *Arlington Park* is a "writerly" text[21] in which the

---

[17] See Joyce G. Saricks's discussion on the characteristics of literary fiction. Saricks 177-178.
[18] "In Woolf's case the exterior events have actually lost their hegemony, they serve to release and interpret inner events" (Auerbach 475).
[19] "Authors and readers pay attention to words and how they are woven together with elegant, often poetic language" (Saricks 178).
[20] See David Lodge's distinction between metaphoric and metonymic modes of discourse in *Modes of Modern Writing*.
[21] In *S/Z* Barthes distinguishes between two types of texts: "readerly" (lisible) and "writerly" (scriptible). The readerly text is a conventional text which does not disturb the reader's expectations. The writerly text is more challenging and involves the reader in its production. It incorporates "multiple voices" and "different wavelengths" that are liable to "dissolve" into one another and "shifts from one point of view to another without warning" (Barthes 174).

author borrows the Woolfian approach of sensory impressionism that depicts the characters' innermost unrest and psychological depth. The novel is character centered, not plot oriented, and style, language and imagery largely prevail over content. Indeed, what happens is not as important as how it is written; the form and medium of the words are prevalent. Like Woolf, Cusk stakes everything on her ability to make art out of the details of ordinary life, applying to the most mundane objects and moments an attentiveness that brings ordinariness to a state of magnetism.

Works Cited

Auerbach, Erich. *Mimesis: the Representation of Reality in Western Literature.* Trans. Willard R. Trask. Princeton: Princeton UP, 1968. Print.
Barthes, Roland. *S/Z*. Trans. R. Miller. Oxford: Blackwell, 1990. Print.
Bradbury, Malcolm. *Possibilities: Essays on the State of the Novel.* Oxford: OUP, 1973. Print.
Chatman, Seymour. "*Mrs. Dalloway*'s Progeny: *The Hours* as Second-degree Narrative." *A Companion to Narrative Theory*. Eds. James Phelan and Peter J. Rabinowitz. Oxford: Blackwell, 2005. 269-282. Print.
Connor, Steven. "Postmodernism and Literature." *The Cambridge Companion to Postmodernism*. Ed. Steven Connor. Cambridge: Cambridge UP, 2004. 62-81. Print.
Cunningham, Michael. Introduction to *The Voyage Out*, by Virginia Woolf. New York: Modern Library, 2000. v-xliv. Print.
Cusk, Rachel. *Arlington Park*. London: Faber & Faber, 2006. Print.
———. "The Outsider." *The Observer*, Sunday 20 August 2005. Web. March 2011.
———. "Shakespeare's Daughters." *The Guardian*, Saturday 12 December 2009. Web. March 2011.
Dentith, Simon. *Parody*. London: Routledge: 2000. Print.
Duperray, Max, ed. *Le Banal dans le roman britannique contemporain*. Paris: L'Harmattan, 1997. Print.
Ellmann, Lucy. "Suburban Squall." *The New York Times*, 28 January 2007. Web. March 2011.
Genette, Gérard. *Palimpsestes*. Paris: Le Seuil, 1982. Print.
Hutcheon, Linda. *A Theory of Parody: The Teachings of Twentieth-Century Art Forms*. New York: Methuen, 1985. Print.
Jameson, Fredric. *Postmodernism, or, The Cultural Logic of Late Capitalism*. Durham, NC: Duke UP. 1991 Print.

Jensen, Meg. "Tradition and Revelation: Moments of Being in Virginia Woolf's Major Novels." *The Cambridge Companion to the Modernist Novel*. Ed. Morag Shiach. Cambridge: Cambridge UP, 2007. 112-125. Print.

Latham, Monica. "Virginia Woolf's *Mrs Dalloway*: Genesis and Palimpsests." *Rewriting / Reprising: Plural Intertextualities*. Ed. Georges Letissier. Newcastle: Cambridge Scholars Publishing, 2009. 50-64. Print.

Kristeva, Julia. *Desire in Language: A Semiotic Approach to Literature and Art*. New York: Columbia UP, 1980. Print.

Lodge, David. *Modes of Modern Writing: Metaphor, Metonymy, and the Typology of Modern Literature*. Ithaca, NY: Cornell UP, 1977. Print.

Lukács, Georg. "The Ideology of Modernism." *Twentieth Century Literary Criticism*. Ed. David Lodge. London: Longman, 1972. 474-488. Print.

Olson, Liesl M. "Virginia Woolf's 'cotton wool of daily life'." *Journal of Modern Literature* 26.2 (Winter 2002-2003): 42-65. Print.

Perec, Georges. *L'infra-ordinaire*. Paris: Seuil, 1995. Print.

Purves, Miranda. "Rachel Cusk's *A Life's Work: On Becoming a Mother*." *Elle*, 14 April 2010. Web. March 2011.

Sami-Ali, Mahmoud. *Le Banal*. Paris: Gallimard, 1980. Print.

Saricks, G. Joyce. (2001) "Literary Fiction." *The Readers' Advisory Guide to Genre Fiction*. Chicago and London: American Library Association, 2009. 177-195. Print.

Schoene, Berthold. *The Cosmopolitan Novel*. Edinburgh: Edinburgh UP, 2010. Print.

Spengler, Birgit. "Michael Cunningham Rewriting Virginia Woolf: Pragmatist vs Modernist Aesthetics." *Woolf Studies Annual* 10 (2004): 51-80. Print.

Woolf, Virginia. *The Diary of Virginia Woolf*. Ed. Anne Olivier Bell. 5 vols. London: Hogarth, 1979-1985. Print.

——. *The Essays of Virginia Woolf*. Ed. Andrew McNeillie. 4 vols. London: Hogarth, 1989-1994. Print.

——. *Mrs. Dalloway*. Oxford: Oxford World's Classics, 2008. Print.

——. *A Room of One's Own*. 1929. London: Penguin, 1945. Print.

——. "A Sketch of the Past". *Moments of Being*. Ed. Jeanne Schulkind. 2nd ed. New York: Harcourt, 1985. 64-159. Print.

——. *To the Lighthouse*. Oxford: Oxford World's Classics, 2008. Print.

——. *Walter Sickert: A Conversation*. Ed. Richard Shone. London: The Bloomsbury Workshop, 1992. Print.

Young, Tori. *Michael Cunningham's* The Hours: *A Reader's Guide*. New York: Continuum, 2003. Print

Guide to Library Special Collections

This guide updates the information in volume 18.

Name of Collection: The Beinecke Rare Book and Manuscript Library

Contact: Kevin Repp, Curator of Modern Books and Manuscripts
Nancy Kuhl, Curator of American Literature

Address: Yale University Library
P.O. Box 208240
New Haven, CT 06520-8240

URL: http://beinecke.library.yale.edu/

Hours: Mon.–Thu. 9 AM–7 PM
Fri. 9 AM–5 PM

Access Requirements: Registration required at first visit.

Holdings Relevant To Woolf: General Collection includes autograph manuscript of "Notes on Oliver Goldsmith." Comments on Edward Gibbon, William Beckford Collection. Letters from Virginia Woolf in the Bryher Papers, the Louise Morgan and Otto Theis Papers, and the Rebecca West Papers. Related material: 41 letters from Vita Sackville-West to Violet Trefusis; files relating to Robert Manson Myers's *From Beowulf to Virginia Woolf* in the Edmond Pauker Papers.

Yale Collection of American Literature includes typewritten manuscripts of "The Art of Walter Sickert," "Augustine Birrell," "Aurora Leigh," "How Should One Read a Book?" "Letter to a Young Poet," "The Novels of Turgenev," "Street Haunting." Dial/Scofield Thayer Papers: manuscripts of "The Lives of the Obscure," "Miss Ormerod," and "Mrs. Dalloway in Bond Street." Letters from Virginia Woolf in the William Rose Benet Papers, the Benet Family Correspondence, the Henry Seidel Canby Papers, the Seward Collins Papers, the Dial/Scofield Thayer Papers, and the *Yale Review* archive. Material relating to translations of Woolf in the Thornton Wilder papers. Related material: Clive Bell, "Virginia Woolf" (Dial/Scofield Thayer Papers); 43 letters from Leonard Woolf to Helen McAfee (*Yale Review*); 11 letters from Leonard Woolf to Gertrude Stein.

Name of Collection: The Henry W. and Albert A. Berg Collection of English and American Literature

Contact: Isaac Gewirtz, Curator

Address: New York Public Library, Room 320
Fifth Avenue & 42nd Street
New York, NY 10018

Telephone: 212-930-0802
Fax: 212-930-0079
Email: isaacgewirtz@nypl.org

Hours: Tue.–Wed. 11 AM–6:45 PM
Thu.–Sat. 10 AM–6 PM
Closed Sun., Mon. and legal holidays

Access Requirements: After acquiring Library card in room 315, check outerwear and *all* containers (briefcases, computer cases, handbags, folders, etc.) in Ground Floor cloakroom, and proceed to the Berg Collection. Traceable and photo identification required. Undergraduates working on honors theses need letter from faculty advisor.

Restrictions: Virginia Woolf's bound MSS are now made available on microfilm and CD. URL for Berg finding aid: http://www.nypl.org/research/manuscripts/berg/brgwoolf.xml. N.B. All the *Berg's Woolf MSS*

GUIDE TO LIBRARY SPECIAL COLLECTIONS 217

are on microfilm and 90 percent of them on CD published by Research Publications and available at many research libraries.

Holdings Relevant To Woolf: Manuscripts/typescripts of all of the novels except *Orlando*, including: *Between the Acts, Flush, Jacob's Room, Mrs. Dalloway* (notes and fragments), *Night and Day, To the Lighthouse, The Voyage Out, The Waves, The Years*; 12 notebooks of articles, essays, fiction and reviews, 1924–1940; 36 volumes of diaries; 26 volumes of reading notes; correspondence with Vanessa Bell, Ethel Smyth, Vita Sackville-West and others. Su Hua Ling Chen's Bloomsbury correspondence.

Recent Acquisitions: Proof copy of *A Room of One's Own* (July 1929); ALS Vanessa Bell to Vita Sackville-West, April 29, 1941 [in Marler, *Selected Letters* 478-80]; Frank Dean, *Strike While the Iron's Hot: Frank Dean's Life as a Blacksmith and Farrier in Rodmell*, ed. Susan Rowland (S. Rowland, 1994) [includes map, accounts of search for VW's body and of her funeral]; Vita Sackville-West. *Marian Stranways*, authograph manuscript, [1913].

Name of Collection: The British Library Manuscript Collections

Contact: Manuscripts Enquiries

Address: 96 Euston Road
London NW1 2DB
England

Telephone: 0207-412-7513
Fax: 0207-412-7745
Email: mss@bl.uk

Hours: Mon. 10 AM–5 PM;Tue.–Sat.: 9:30 AM–5 PM

Access Requirements: British Library Reader Pass (signed I.D. required and usually proof of post-graduate academic status, or other demonstrable need to use the collections—see www.bl.uk). In addition, access to most literary autograph material only available with letter of recommendation.

Restrictions: Paper Copies, Microfilms, and Photography of selected items available upon receipt of written authorization for photo duplication from the copyright holder.

Holdings Relevant to Woolf: Diaries 1930–1931 (microfilm); Mrs. Dalloway and other writings (1923–1925) three volumes; letter from Leonard Woolf to H. G. Wells (1941); two letters from Virginia Woolf and three letters from Leonard Woolf to John Lehmann (1941); letter written on behalf of Leonard Woolf to S. S. Koteliansky (1946); notebook in Italian kept by Virginia Woolf; notebook of Virginia Stephen (1906–1909); A sketch of the past revised ts (1940); letters from Virginia Woolf in the correspondence files of Lytton and James Strachey; letter from Virginia Woolf to Mildred Massingberd; letter from Virginia Woolf to Harriet Shaw Weaver (1918); letters from Virginia Woolf to S. S. Koteliansky (1923–1927); letter from Virginia Woolf to Frances Cornford (1929); letter from Virginia Woolf to Ernest Rhys (1930); correspondence of Virginia Woolf in the Society of Authors archive (1934–1937); letter and postcard from Virginia Woolf to Bernard Shaw (1940); three letters (suicide notes) from Virginia Woolf (1941); two letters from Virginia Woolf and three from Leonard Woolf to John Lehmann (1941). "Hyde Park Gate News" 1891–1892, 1895 (add. MSS 70725, 70726). Letters of Virginia and Leonard Woolf to Lady Aberconway, 1927–1941.

Letter from Virginia Woolf to Frances Cornford. Letters from Virginia Woolf to Macmillan Co. 1903, 1908. Collection of RPs ("reserved photo copies"– copies of manuscripts exported, some subject to restrictions).

Name of Collection: Harry Ransom Humanities Research Center

Contact: Research Librarian

Address: The University of Texas at Austin
P.O. Box 7219
Austin, TX 78713-7219

Telephone: 512-471-9119
Fax: 512-471-2899
Email: reference@hrc.utexas.edu

Hours: Mon.–Fri. 9 AM–5 PM
Sat. 9 AM–NOON
Closed holidays; intersession Saturdays; one week each in late May and late August.

Access Requirements: Completed manuscript reader's application; current photo identification.

Holdings Relevant To Woolf: The manuscript collection includes the typed manuscript with autograph revisions of *Kew Gardens*, and the typed manuscript and autograph revisions of "Thoughts on Peace in an Air Raid." The Center holds 571 of Woolf's letters, including correspondence to Elizabeth Bowen, Lady Ottoline Morrell, Mary Hutchinson, William Plomer, Hugh Walpole and others. Further mss. relating to Virginia Woolf include letters to her from T. S. Eliot and reviews of her work. A substantial collection of the first British and American editions of Woolf's published works, as well as 130 volumes from Leonard and Virginia Woolf's library and a collection of books published by the Hogarth Press, is also housed.

An art collection holds a landscape painting of Virginia's garden and a series of Cockney cartoons in a sketch book, signed "V.W." The center also has extensive holdings of materials related to Leonard Woolf, Ottoline Morrell, Mary Hutchinson, Lytton Strachey, Dora Carrington, E. M. Forster, Clive Bell, Roger Fry, Vanessa Bell, Bertrand Russell, Elizabeth Bowen, William Plomer, Stephen Spender and Hugh Walpole.

Name of Collection: King's College Archive Centre

Contact: Patricia McGuire, Archivist
King's College

Address: Cambridge CB2 1ST

Telephone: 01223-331444
Fax: 01223-331891
Email: archivist@kings.cam.ac.uk

Hours: Mon.–Thu. 9:30 AM–12:30 PM and 1:30 PM–5:15 PM. *Closed during public holidays and the College's annual periods of closure.*

Access Requirements: Proof of ID, letter of introduction, appointment in advance.

Holdings Relevant To Woolf: Woolf MSS and letters: Minute book, written up by Clive Bell, of the meetings of a play-reading society, with cast lists and comments on performances by CB. Dec. 1907–Jan. 1909, Oct. 1914–Feb. 1915. Players included variously Clive and Vanessa Bell, Roger and Margery Fry, Duncan Grant, Walter Lamb, Molly MacCarthy, Adrian and Virginia Stephen, Saxon Sydney-Turner. *Freshwater, A Comedy*—photocopy of editorial typescript prepared from the MSS at Sussex University and Monk's House; photocopy of covering letter from the publisher to "Robert Silvers," Jan. 29, 1976. Papers relating to the Virginia Woolf Centenary Conference held at Fitzwilliam College, Cambridge, Sept. 20-22, 1982. TS with corrections of "Nurse Lugton's Curtain." Typed transcript of R. Fry's memoir of his schooldays. Correspondence with Clive Bell, Julian Bell, Vanessa Bell, Richard Braithwaite, Rupert Brooke, Mrs. Brooke, Katharine Cox, Julian Fry, Roger Fry, John Davy Hayward, J. M. Keynes, Lydia Keynes, Rosamond Lehmann, Charles Mauron, Raymond Mortimer, Frances and Ralph Partridge, G. H. W. Rylands, J. T. Sheppard, W. J. H. Sprott, Thoby Stephen, Madge Vaughan. Woolf-related archival collections held: Charleston Papers; Rupert Brooke Papers; E. M. Forster Papers; Roger Fry Papers; J. M. Keynes Papers; Frances Partridge Papers; George Humphrey Wolferstan ('Dadie') Rylands Papers; J. T. Sheppard Papers; W. J. H. Sprott Papers. Various works of art by Vanessa Bell, Duncan Grant, and Roger Fry, held in various locations around King's College. Access via Second Bursar's secretary.

Name of Collection: The Lilly Library

Contact: Breon Mitchell, Director
Cherry Williams, Curator of Manuscripts

Address: The Lilly Library, Indiana University
1200 East Seventh Street
Bloomington, IN 47405-5500

Telephone: 812-855-2452
Fax: 812-855-3143
Email: liblilly@indiana.edu, mitchell@indiana.edu
chedwill@indiana.edu

Hours:	Mon.–Fri. 9 AM–6 PM; Sat. 9 AM–1 PM; *Closed Sundays and Major Holidays*
Access Requirements:	Valid photo-identification; brief registration procedure.
Restrictions:	Closed stacks; material use confined to reading room; wheelchair-accessible reading room and exhibitions (but no wheelchair-accessible restroom).
Holdings Relevant To Woolf:	Corrected page proofs for the American edition of *Mrs. Dalloway*; letters to Woolf from Desmond and Mary (Molly) MacCarthy; 77 letters (published in *Letters*) from Woolf to correspondents including Donald Clifford Brace, Robert Gathorne-Hardy, Barbara (Strachey) Halpern, Richard Arthur Warren Hughes, Desmond MacCarthy and Molly MacCarthy; "Preliminary Scheme for the formation of a Partnership between Mr Leonard Sidney Woolf and Mr John Lehmann to take over The Hogarth Press" (includes contract signed by Lehmann, Leonard Woolf, and Virginia Woolf and receipt for Lehmann's payment to Virginia Woolf to purchase Virginia Woolf's share in the Hogarth Press); photographs of Virginia Woolf, Leonard Woolf, Lytton Strachey, Strachey family, Roger Fry, and Vanessa Bell (Hannah Whitall Smith mss.); (Richard) Kennedy mss. (four hand-colored lithographs of Virginia Woolf: artist's proofs for RK's portfolio, VIRGINIA WOOLF: "AS I KNEW HER"; Sackville-West, V. mss. (10,529 items: includes the correspondence of Vita Sackville-West, and Harold Nicolson); MacCarthy mss. (ca. 10,000 items: papers of Desmond and Molly MacCarthy); correspondence between LW and Mary Gaither regarding publication of *A Checklist of the Hogarth Press* (1976, repr. 1986); Todd Avery, *Close and Affectionate Friends: Desmond and Molly MacCarthy and the Bloomsbury Group* (The Lilly Library / Indiana University Libraries, 1999).

GUIDE TO LIBRARY SPECIAL COLLECTIONS

Name of Collection: Culture & Literature, Special Collections, University of Maryland, College Park, Libraries

Contact: Ann Hudak, Culture & Literature, Special Collections Librarian

Address: University of Maryland Libraries
College Park, MD 20742

Telephone: 310-405-9213
Fax: 301-314-2709
Email: ahudak@umd.edu

Hours: Dates and hours of operation subject to change. Contact Ann Hudak or Jason Speck before planning a research visit.

Access Requirements: Photo ID.

Holdings Relevant To Woolf: Papers of Hope Mirrlees contain five autograph letters and postcards (1919–1928) from Virginia Woolf to Mirrlees. Also in the collection are 113 letters from T. S. Eliot to Mirrlees, and three letters from Lady Ottoline Morrell to Mirrlees. A finding aid is available at http://hdl.handle.net/1903.1/1536.

Name of Collection: Monks House Papers/Leonard Woolf Papers/Charleston Papers/Nicolson Papers

Special Collections is moving to The Keep

It is hoped that we will move into the new building over Summer 2013 with a view to opening late Autumn 2013. This means that we are unable to guarantee access to the collections after the end of May 2013.
Please contact us if you have any queries.

http://www.eastsussex.gov.uk/leisureandtourism/localandfamilyhistory/esro/thekeep/default.htm

Contact: Fiona Courage, Special Collections Manager

Address: University of Sussex Library
Brighton
Sussex BN1 9QL
England

Telephone: 01273-678157
Fax: 01273-678441
Email: Library.Specialcoll@sussex.ac.uk
URL: www.sussex.ac.uk/library/speccoll

Access Requirements: By appointment. Identification to be presented on arrival. Application for access (including contact details of referee) to be completed on arrival.

Restrictions: Photocopying strictly controlled.

Holdings Relevant To Woolf: The University of Sussex holds two large archives relating to Leonard and Virginia Woolf: The Monks House Papers, primarily correspondence and MSS of Virginia Woolf, including the three scrapbooks relating to *Three Guineas*; and The Leonard Woolf Papers, primarily correspondence and other papers of Leonard Woolf. (Monks House Papers are available on microfilm in many research libraries.) The Charleston Papers consist in the main of letters written to or by Clive and Vanessa Bell and Duncan Grant which had accumulated in their home; the library houses Quentin Bell's photocopied set; letters from Roger Fry, Maynard Keynes, Lytton Stachey, Virginia Woolf, Vita Sackville-West, E. M. Forster, T. S. Eliot, Frances Partridge and others. The Maria Jackson letters comprise some 900 letters from Maria Jackson to Julia and Leslie Stephen. The Nicolson Papers complement these three Sussex archives relating to the Bloomsbury Group, and consist of Nigel Nicolson's correspondence relating to his editorial work as principal editor of the six-volume *Letters of Virginia Woolf*, published between 1975 and 1980.

The Bell Papers. A. O. Bell's correspondence relating to her editorial work on Virginia Woolf's diaries, a parallel collection to the Nicolson Papers. Collection level description may be accessed at www.archiveshub.ac.uk

Name of Collection: The Morgan Library & Museum

Contact: Reading Room

Address: 225 Madison Ave.
New York, NY 10016

Telephone: 212-590-0315
Email: readingroom@themorgan.org
URL: www.themorgan.org

Access Requirements: Admission to the Reading Room is by application and by appointment. See http//www.themorgan.org/research/reading.asp for application form.

Holdings Relevant To Woolf: Virginia Woolf. Autograph manuscript notebook, 1931 Sept. 24. 1 item (52 p.) ; 265 x 208 mm. Contains drafts of "A Letter to a Young Poet," a brief letter to the press entitled "The Villa Jones" [ff. 3–5] and a monologue by a working-class woman [ff. 44–46]. MA 3333. Purchased on the Fellows Fund with the special assistance of Anne S. Dayton, Enid A. Haupt, Mrs. James H. Ripley, Mr. and Mrs. August H. Schilling, and John S. Thacher,1979.

Virginia Woolf. Autograph letters signed (2) and typed letter signed, dated London [etc.], to E. McKnight Kauffer, 1931 Apr. 4–23, and undated.

3 items (4 p.). Concerning a drawing of her and a bibliography of her works. MA 1679. Purchased in 1959.

Vanessa Bell. 84 autograph letters, 3 typed letters, 7 postcards, and 3 telegrams. Most, but not all, are written by Vanessa Bell to John Maynard Keynes. Concerning Duncan Grant, Roger Fry, Clive Bell, the Bell children, Leonard and Virginia Woolf, Lytton Strachey, John Maynard and Lydia Lopokova Keynes, David Garnett, Ottoline Morrell, and others. MA 3448. Items in this collection are described in 97 individual records (MA 3448.1-97). Purchased on the Fellows Fund, special gift of the Gramercy Park Foundation (Mrs. Michael Tucker), 1980.

Name of Collection: University Museums and Special Collections Service

Contact: University Archivist

Address: University of Reading
Redlands Road
Berkshire RG1 5EX
England

Telephone: 0118-378-8660
Fax: 0118-378-5632
Email: specialcollections@reading.ac.uk

Access Requirements: Appointment needed to consult material. Permission required to consult or copy material in the Hogarth Press and Chatto & Windus collections from Random House, 20 Vauxhall Bridge Road, London SW1V 2SA, UK. (Jean Rose, Library Mgr. JRose@Randomhouse.co.uk)

GUIDE TO LIBRARY SPECIAL COLLECTIONS 227

Holdings Relevant To Woolf: Hogarth Press (MS2750): editorial and production correspondence relating to publications of the Press including Woolf's own titles. Production ledgers 1920s–1950s. Correspondence between Leonard Woolf and Stanley Unwin about progress with his collected edition of the works of Freud. Order books – e.g. lists of booksellers, book clubs and how many books they have ordered for a particular title. Newscuttings – press clippings of advertisements for Hogarth Press books including Virginia Woolf publications.

Chatto & Windus (MS2444): small number of letters 1915–1925; 1929–1931. Various letters and notes by Leonard Woolf; outgoing letters to Leonard Woolf: 22 November 1927 (Letter Book 119); outgoing letters to Virginia Woolf: 29 January 1936 (Letter Book 171), 22 December 1931 (Letter Book 135), 31 December 1931 (Letter Book 135), 15 December 1920 (Letter Book 100), 20 December 1920 (Letter Book 100).

George Bell & Sons (MS1640): 5 letters from Leonard Woolf 1930–1966.

Routledge (MS1489): Reader's report by Leonard Woolf on George Padmore's "Britannia rules the blacks" (1935); "How Britain rules Africa." 1 letter from Leonard Woolf (June 1941) from Miscellaneous publishing correspondence 1941-1942 Wi-Wy RKP 174/15. Draft introduction by Leonard Woolf to *Letters on India* by Mulk Raj (1942) and 1 letter to Leonard Woolf from Mulk Raj Anand 1942-1943 RKP 178/3. Correspondence concerning the publication of *The War for Peace* by Leonard Woolf, 1939-1940 RKP 160/5. 1 letter from Virginia Woolf declining an invitation from Routledge to write a biography of Margaret Bondfield, 25 May 1940 RKP 160/5.

Megroz (MS1979/68): 2 letters from Leonard Woolf, 1926.

Allen & Unwin (MS3282): Correspondence with Leonard Woolf c.1914-1918 (re. his book *International Government*), 1923-1924; 1939-1940; 1943; 1946; 1950-1951; 1953; 1965 (concerning ill-founded rumors about the Hogarth Press); 1967 (concerning a reprint of *Empire and Commerce in Africa*).

Jonathan Cape (MS 2446): All correspondence from file JC A43. Correspondence between Jonathan Cape and Virginia Woolf and Cape and A.C. Gissing concerning Virginia Woolf's introduction to George Gissing's *Ionian Sea* to which A.C. Gissing objects. 1 postcard (1935), 1 letter (1933), 2 letters (1932) from Virginia Woolf. 1 letter (1932) from Virginia Woolf declining to write an introduction to Jane Austen's *Northanger Abbey*. 4 letters (1931) from Virginia Woolf declining to write an introduction to one of Miss Thackeray's books.

Letters from Vanessa Bell: 1 letter from Bell CW 152/2;1 letter from Bell CW 171/10; 2 letters from Bell CW 578/1; 1 letter from Bell CW 59/9; 1 letter from Bell (1936) CW 61/10. Artwork by Vanessa Bell for various Virginia Woolf titles

Artwork by Angelica Garnett, Philippa Bramson and others for various books.

Name of Collection: Frances Hooper Collection of Virginia Woolf Books and ManuscriptsElizabeth Power Richardson Bloomsbury Iconography Collection.

Contact: Karen V. Kukil, Associate Curator of Special Collections

GUIDE TO LIBRARY SPECIAL COLLECTIONS 229

Address:	Mortimer Rare Book Room
	William Allan Neilson Library
	Smith College
	Northampton, MA 01063
Telephone:	413-585-2906
Fax:	413-585-4486
Email:	kkukil@email.smith.edu
URL:	www.smith.edu/libraries/libs/rarebook
Hours:	Mon.–Fri. 9 AM–5 PM
Access Requirements:	Appointment to be made with the Curator.
Holdings Relevant To Woolf:	The Hooper Collection emphasizes Woolf as an essayist but also includes many Hogarth Press first editions, limited editions of Woolf's works, and translations. The collection includes page proofs of *Orlando*, *To the Lighthouse,* and T*he Common Reader,* corrected by Woolf for the first American editions, a proof copy of *The Waves* that Woolf inscribed to Hugh Walpole, and the proof copies of *The Years* and of *Flush*. The Collection also has one of the deluxe editions of *Orlando* that was printed on green paper. Other items include twenty-two pages of reading notes from 1926, three pages of notes on D. H. Lawrence's *Sons and Lovers*, thirty-three pages of notes for *Roger Fry*, a six-page ms. "As to criticism," a five-page ms. of "The Searchlight," and a fourteen-page ms. of "The Patron and The Crocus." The Hooper Collection also owns 140 letters between Woolf and Lytton Strachey as well as other correspondence, including a 13 February [1921] letter to Katherine Mansfield and ten letters to Mela and Robert Spira.

The Richardson Collection is a working collection of books and materials used by Richardson in preparing her *Bloomsbury Iconography*. It includes

Leslie Stephen's photograph album, ninety-eight original exhibition catalogs dating back to 1929, clippings and photcopies of such items as reviews of early Woolf works, and Bloomsbury material from British *Vogue* of the 1920s. The Collection also has three preliminary pencil drawings by Vanessa Bell for *Flush*.

The Mortimer Rare Book Room also owns Woolf's 1916 Italian ms. notebook and her corrected typescripts of "Reviewing" and "The Searchlight." In addition, there is a 1923 photograph of Woolf at Garsington. Original cover designs for Hogarth Press publications include *The Common Reader, On Being Ill,* and *Duncan Grant*. The Mortimer Rare Book Room also has a Sylvia Plath collection that includes eight of Woolf's books from Plath's library, several of which are underlined and annotated, as well as Plath's notes from her undergraduate English 211 class at Smith (1951–1952) in which she studied *To the Lighthouse*. The collection also includes Woolf's 26 February 1939 letter to Vita Sackville-West, a 1931 bronze bust of Virginia Woolf by Stephen Tomlin, a 1923 Hogarth Press edition of T.S. Eliot's *The Waste Land*, a 1919 Hogarth Press edition of *Paris* by Hope Mirrlees and first editions of Vita Sackville-West publications. Online exhibitions are available on the Mortimer Rare Book Room's web site.

Name of Collection: Woolf/Hogarth Press/Bloomsbury

Contact: Robert C. Brandeis

Address: Victoria University Library
71 Queens Park Crescent E.
Toronto M5S 1K7
Ontario Canada

Email: victoria.library@utoronto.ca

URL:	http://library.vicu.utoronto.ca/special/bloomsbury.htm
Hours:	Mon.–Fri. 9 AM–5 PM
Access Requirements:	Prior notification; identification.
Restrictions:	Limited photocopying.
Holdings Relevant To Woolf:	This collection, the most comprehensive of its kind with nearly 5,000 items, contains all the work of Virginia and Leonard Woolf in various editions, issues, variants and translations; all the books hand-printed by Leonard and Virginia Woolf at the Hogarth Press, including many variant issues and bindings, association copies and page proofs; a nearly comprehensive collection of Hogarth Press machine printed books to 1946 (the year Leonard Woolf and the Press joined Chatto & Windus) including presentation copies, signed limited editions, page proofs, variants as well as substantial amounts of ephemera, such as the *Catalogue of Publications to 1939* with annotations by Leonard Woolf. The collection is also very strong in Bloomsbury Art and Artists, especially the decorative arts, including important examples of Omega Workshops publications and exhibition catalogues. Materials include the catalogue of the second post-impressionist exhibition, 1912; catalogues relating to Vanessa Bell and Duncan Grant exhibitions; bronze medal of Virginia Woolf by Marta Firlet; oil on canvas portrait of Amaryllis Garnett by Vanessa Bell (c.1958); Portrait sketch of Leonard Woolf by Vanessa Bell; Duncan Grant and Vanessa Bell designed Clarice Cliff dinner plates; original Vanessa Bell and Duncan Grant sketches and designs for dust jackets, novels, and other special projects; bronze busts of Lytton Strachey and Virginia Woolf by Stephen Tomlin (1901–1937); as well as the Marcel Gimond bust of Vanessa Bell

and the Tomlin bust of Henrietta Bingham. Original correspondence and mss material includes that by Vanessa Bell; Leonard Woolf; Ritchie family re: Anne Thackeray Ritchie/Stephen family; Duncan Grant; Quentin Bell; S. P. Rosenbaum mss. Letters from E. M. Forster, Bertrand Russell, James Strachey, Raymond Mortimer, David Garnett, Nigel Nicolson and others in the Bloomsbury Circle; as well as biographers, scholars and bibliographers such as Joanne Trautmann, Carolyn Heilbrun, J. Howard Woolmer, Leon Edel, Leila Luedeking, P. N. Furbank, Noel Annan and others.

Name of Collection: Library of Leonard and Virginia Woolf (Washington S U)

Contact: Trevor James Bond
Special Collections Librarian

Address: Washington State University Libraries
Pullman, WA 99164-5610

Email: tjbond@wsu.edu

URL: www.wsulibs.wsu.edu/holland/masc/masc.htm

Hours: Mon.–Fri. 8:30 AM–5 PM

Access Requirements: Letter stating nature of research preferred; student or other identification.

Restrictions: Materials must be used in the MASC area under supervision. Photocopying or photographing is permitted only when it will not harm the materials and is permitted by copyright.

Holdings Relevant To Woolf: WSU has the Woolfs' basic working library including many works which belonged to Woolf's father, Sir Leslie Stephen, and other family members. Over 800 titles came from their Sussex home, Monks House, including some works bought at auction soon after Leonard Woolf died in 1969. Later additions include: 1,875 titles from his house in Victoria Square, London; 400 titles from his nephew Cecil Woolf; and over 60 titles from Quentin and Anne Olivier Bell. WSU has been actively collecting: all works in all editions by Virginia Woolf; all titles by Leonard Woolf; works published by the Woolfs at the Hogarth Press through 1946; books by their friends and associates, especially those by Bloomsbury authors and about Bloomsbury artists; relevant correspondence and original works of art. Original artwork by Vanessa Bell; scattered letters by Vanessa Bell, E. M. Forster, Roger Fry, Leslie Stephen, Lytton Strachey, and Leonard Woolf. Original artwork by Richard Kennedy for illustrations in his book *A Boy at the Hogarth Press*; scattered letters by Roger Fry, Leslie Stephen, Ethel Smyth, and Leonard Woolf. Virginia Woolf's initialed copy of *Cornishiana*; Leonard Woolf's annotated copy of *An Anatomy of Poetry* by A. William-Ellis; Leslie Stephen's copy of *Lapsus Calami and Other Verses*, inscribed by James Kenneth Stephen. Several letters from Virginia Woolf, including two written in 1939 to Ronald Heffer, and a letter to Edward McKnight Kauffer. New in the Hogarth Press Collection are a copy of E. M. Forster's *Anonymity, an Enquiry*, bound in cream paper boards, and what Woolmer calls the third label state of Forster's *The Story of the Siren*.

Name of Collection: Yale Center for British Art

Contact: Elisabeth Fairman, Senior Curator of Rare Books and Manuscripts

Address: 1080 Chapel Street
P.O. Box 208280
New Haven, CT 06520-8280

Telephone: 203-432-2814
Fax: 203-432-9613
E-mail: elisabeth.fairman@yale.edu

Hours: Tue.-Fri. 10 AM-4:30 PM

Access Requirements: Permission needed in order to reproduce.

Holdings Relevant To Woolf: Rare Books & Mss Department: 94 letters from Vanessa Bell and Duncan Grant to Sir Kenneth Clark; Prints & Drawings Department: 4 drawings by Vanessa Bell; 4 drawings by Duncan Grant; 6 drawings by Wyndham Lewis; 1 drawing by Frederick Etchells; Paintings Department: 1 painting by Vanessa Bell, 4 paintings by Duncan Grant (including portrait of Vanessa Bell); 3 paintings by Roger Fry.

Recent Acquisitions: 6 letters from Lytton Strachey (to Clive Bell, Siegfried Sassoon, et al.).

Reviews

Civil Antisemitism, Modernism, and British Culture, 1902-1939. Lara Trubowitz (New York: Palgrave Macmillan, 2012) ix +269pp.

Lara Trubowitz's *Civil Antisemitism, Modernism, and British Culture, 1902-1939* is an important and difficult book. It is important because it offers an alternative method for evaluating the role of antisemitism in twentieth-century modernism and Woolf studies; it is difficult because it entails detailed close readings of rhetorical strategies that reveal modernism's "civil" antisemitism.

Though at first glance an oxymoron, "civil antisemitism" refers to the social and political pressures of the public sphere in which overt bigotry is seen as objectionable. Trubowitz argues that "Antisemitism becomes a 'style' of speech or writing, best understood and criticized in rhetorical and narrative terms, an elaborate or even tortuous compromise between rival traditions of hatred and politesse" (1). Rather than focus on the use of stereotype or explicit antisemitic expressions, the rhetorical analysis in this study allows us to look below the surface of denotative language and to trace the history of antisemitic sentiment from the beginning of the century through WWII. Most studies of modernist antisemitism begin in the late thirties and forties when antisemitism is most obvious, without considering the history and evolution of the discourse itself. For Trubowitz, " 'the Jew' becomes a prime modernist figure in the mode of 'civil antisemitism' . . . on the level of style or technique itself, a repertoire of methods of indirection, occultation, and dissimulation, all highly fruitful for the experimentation of modernist writing" (2).

Civil Antisemitism is loosely divided into two sections: the first half examines the political constructions of civil antisemitism, as argument, in parliamentary deliberations over immigration legislation, protofascist media, newspapers, and best-selling conspiracy novels. The second half of the book moves to literary modernism of the late 1930s, specifically the work of Djuna Barnes, Virginia Woolf, and Wyndham Lewis. Trubowitz chooses this triad because "it is in the nature of their modernist projects to engage acrobatically with everyday speech imagery," to "thrill in deliberate rhetorical hyperbole, heteroglossic play of voices, fragmentation of popular speech and polemic, and condensation of both popular and literary forms" (21).

The first chapter, "Acting Like an Alien: The Rhetoricized Jew in British Immigration Law, 1902-1914," is a fascinating analysis of the debates over alien (Jewish) immigration. Trubowitz establishes her method of reading through a rhetorical analysis of Major William Evans-Gordon's *The Alien Immigrant*. She illustrates the slippages of language that contribute to the "rhetoricized Jew." The language used by Evans-Gordon—as well as a range of other contemporaries involved in the immigration debate—turns on itself; it both makes the claim of tolerance toward Jewish immigrants, while at the same time using that tolerance to deny Jews entry into Britain. This embodies the very notion of "civil antisemitism" that Trubowitz argues for.

Chapter Two, "Philosemitic Fascists and the Conspiracy Novel," picks up in 1930. Though the narrative of the book could be reinforced with some kind of reference to the intervening years of 1915-1929, the chapter itself is an interesting discussion of the minor and less studied genre of the conspiracy novel. Trubowitz looks at two vehemently anti-Jewish interwar writers, Robert Hart and Nesta Weber, as well as the protofascist newspaper *Jewry Ueber Alles*, to illustrate the "production of 'publicly acceptable' antisemitism and . . . the particular ways in which the self-regulation of antisemitism operates within protofascist discourse" (53). She gives a detailed analysis of the rhetorical strategies that define the paradox of "beneficent antisemitism" and quotes long sections from these texts, often at the risk of the clarity of her own prose. Still, one might forgive this since she is working with texts that are not easily accessible to her readers. The chapter as a whole, however, does not serve as a strong segue to the chapters that follow, and when we come to the third chapter, "In Search of 'the Jew' in Djuna Barnes's *Nightwood*," the transition seems a rough jump.

The strength of the third chapter, about Barnes, is not dependent on this weak connection to what precedes it, and the analysis of the Jew in *Nightwood* provides us with a new strategy for understanding representations of Jews and Jewishness that are not explicitly stated in the text. Trubowitz demonstrates that *Nightwood*'s shape and style are "intricately linked to [the Jewish] Felix or , more precisely,to the Jew that Felix and his father Guido represent" (72). This is a challenging thesis, especially since Felix and his Jewishness disappear early in the novel. Still, Trubowitz argues that "absence itself is one of the crucial 'Jewish' attributes that Barnes uses to construct both the figurative systems . . . and her distinctive narrative style" (73). She ultimately argues that the "civility of the antisemitic stereotype," which was adumbrated in the previous chapters, reaches a kind of "apotheosis" in *Nightwood* and is "virtually equivalent to the indirectness of modernist narration" (83); Barnes transforms "the wandering of the Jew into a wandering structure and style" (84).

Following this chapter is the first of two interludes. "Interlude I" begins by tracing the origins of etiquette manuals from the end of the eighteenth century through the nineteenth. It then moves to a discussion of ethnography as a post-etiquette discourse, arguing that "Jewish ethnography [of the early twentieth century] inherits the fundamental concerns of the etiquette book" and "effectively functions as a new kind of manual, offering lessons about the nature of 'civility' and 'savagery' to Britain's gentile population without having to directly examine British deportment as such" (109). Though the point of view is provocative, one wonders why Trubowitz didn't synthesize these ideas with those of the introduction where she could have developed and connected them more precisely to the primary works she discusses. This would have helped to strengthen the larger structural weaknesses of this book.

The chapter following "Interlude I" concerns Virginia Woolf and brings with it a thoughtful and thought-provoking approach to our understanding of Woolf's relationship to Jews and Jewishness. Titled "Concealing Leonard's Nose: Virginia Woolf, Antisemitism, and 'The Duchess and the Jeweller,'" the chapter convincingly illustrates that "antisemitism is not simply an attitude toward Jews, but rather a technique" (115). With a detailed close reading of "The Duchess and the Jeweller," Trubowitz traces the remains of antisemitic stereotypes in the story. Woolf was famously asked by her agent to remove the most offensive stereotypes, but the removal of the stereotypes, according to Trubowitz, set into motion a more "figural and latent [antisemitism], a form of rhetoric that may appear to express, if not a wholly philosemitic attitude toward Jews, then at least Woolf's aesthetic and cultural engagement with Anglo-Jewish history and with ostensibly Jewish characteristics" (118). Antisemitism for Woolf is "*material* to be shaped and reshaped" (118). As readers, we must "reconstruct Jewishness as Woolf herself constructed it, reading specifically for a Jewishness that, in its most provocative forms, can appear not to be Jewish at all, [and is] the same type of complex rhetorical indirection or misdirection" we observed in previous chapters. This is in many ways the best chapter of the book as it illustrates a method to analyze the less explicit use of Jews and Jewishness in Woolf's work.

What follows is "Interlude II: Civil Antisemitism and the Jewish Refugee Crisis of the 1930s," which very much suffers from the same weaknesses as "Interlude I." This interlude is designed to prepare us for a reading of Wyndham Lewis. Although, like Ezra Pound, Lewis is recognized as one of modernism's most blatant anti-Semites, Trubowitz reads his novels and prose work for the rhetorical style she has defined. She carefully moves through *The Apes of God, Hitler, Left Wings Over Europe, The Hitler Cult, and The Jews, Are They Human?* to demonstrate the "artfulness of antisemitism" in Lewis's work. The readings are quite successful in that they reveal Lewis's antisemitism as even more lethal than originally thought—through the use of "civil" rhetoric, he manages to objectify and manipulate the Jew for his own aesthetic and political purposes.

The conclusion of *Civil Antisemitism* comes in an analysis of the English Defense League, an organization established in 2009 and which added a Jewish

Division in 2010. Trubowitz uses this opportunity to argue for the use of rhetorical antisemitism during the present day: the EDL claims it is "tolerant of Jews, Jews cause intolerance, therefore, the EDL is not antisemitic, and it is rather the Jews themselves who are the primary antisemites or racists" (189). An important and insightful conclusion, it does remind the reader of the historical gaps and leaps made in *Civil Antisemitism*; it ignores about six decades in between Wyndham Lewis's novel and the EDL.

Civil Antisemitism, Modernism, and British Culture, 1902-1939 is an ambitious study that attempts to trace a rhetorical method of indirection from the beginning of the twentieth century to the first decade of the twenty-first. The historical span is probably what hurts the book the most—the attempt to cover so much forces Trubowitz to leave out decades of history. There are jarring juxtapositions between most of the chapters, leaving questions about the consistent evolution of "civil antisemitism" as a style through the century. However, the book contains some crucial insights into our study of antisemitism and modernism. *Civil Antisemitism* moves us away from the discussion of Jewish stereotype to a method that reveals a hidden and complicated rhetoric regarding Jews, and it opens up a new realm of investigation for those interested in Woolf and Jews. It is a worthy book because its methodology serves as a model for further investigations into the impact of Jews and Jewishness on Woolf and her modernist contemporaries.

—Beth C. Rosenberg, *University of Nevada, Las Vegas*

A Russian Jew of Bloomsbury: The Life and Times of Samuel Koteliansky. Galya Diment (Montreal and Kingston: McGill-Queen's UP, 2011) xii + 438 pp

Translator of over thirty books from Russian to English (including seven for the Hogarth Press), nurturer of literary talent for the nearly fifty years he lived in London, and passionate friend or staunch enemy of many Bloomsbury artists and writers, Samuel Solomonovich Koteliansky (1880-1955) has long seemed a silent center of British modernist history. While he rendered into English the voice of, among others, Chekhov, Dostoevsky, and Tolstoy, Koteliansky withheld his own voice from print. When entreated by Stephen Spender in 1952 to write his memoirs, Koteliansky demurred, explaining that he was not "a real writer" (328). His afterlife has been limited: he has made cameos in others' memoirs, informed scholarship on the Hogarth Press, and haunted his friends' biographies with the stern face that stares out of photographs. Galya Diment's handsome biography delivers the voice of the man as well as the complexity of his life. Complementing its engaging narrative are abundant photographs, useful appendices, and a well-organized index.

That his voice has been little known until now might have satisfied Koteliansky. "Kot," as he was known to his English-speaking friends and as Diment calls him, lived ascetically and scorned pursuit of renown. He chose to be cremated and refused a tombstone (298). Yet that his voice has been recovered might have pleased him, too. Frieda Lawrence, one of Kot's arch-enemies, wrote, "he always *pretends* he is a humble person, but in his heart he thinks he is very great" (68). Whichever his response might have been, he could hardly have asked for a more rigorous and thoughtful scholar to write his biography. Diment is a Nabokovian who has also published on Virginia Woolf, Lytton Strachey, and Bloomsbury's reception of Tolstoy. Dual expertise in Russian literature and British modernism allows Diment to write with confidence and clarity on Kot's Russian Jewish background and on the British literary world in which, as an adult, he found a home. Her writing depends on research far-flung and intensive: Diment pursued Kot's letters in public and private archives from Israel to New Zealand; interviewed Kot's family and the descendents of his close friends; visited his small hometown in the Ukraine; and studied the research materials of George Zytaruk, the editor of Dorothy Brett and D. H. Lawrence's letters to Kot. This book, almost ten years in the making, is a triumph of both archival research and friendly collaboration between biographer and living sources.

What does Kot's voice sound like? It is firm and pithy, betraying its owner's frank and emotional personality (as well as his non-native language skills). "If you only knew what sometimes means the desire to be, to talk, to commune with one, who understands, and how painful sometimes is loneliness," he writes to Mark Gertler (93). To Sarton, he writes of Virginia Woolf, "[when] V. is at peace, her face is lit up with great beauty" (141). Kot's voice gains command from formality and existential claims. To John Middleton Murry, he writes, "Here is my notion of truth...: truth *felt, seen* by great men, chiefly by writers, is truth, and such truth is always reticent and shy" (153). This voice reveals unsuspected pleasure in the senses. Kot recalls that Russian cherries "used to be twice the size and fifty times as good" as English ones (113), and he mourns Mansfield, "It is her being . . . the aroma of her being, that I love" (121). Another surprise is playfulness, as when Kot rhapsodizes for a paragraph about which side he prefers of a two-tone quilt given by Ottoline Morrell (224) and when he addresses Sarton as "Maylume," a blend of "May" and "luminous" (248). This playfulness tempers the many aching reports about what Kot called his "black moods." With the plaintiveness of a child, he writes, "But, Ottoline, what can I do to get out of this utter darkness and despair? The means that good men and women naturally possess to overcome such trial, seem to be barred to me" (242). He insists, "I am a shuddering, pitiable creature" (228).

While Kot's letters reveal his full voice, Diment's thoroughly documented narrative reveals his complicated life. Born into a wealthy Hasidic family in Ostropol, Kot receives both a Jewish and a secular education and endures six years of police surveillance for subversive political activity. A blood libel against the Jews of Kiev in Spring 1911 spurs Kot's move to London, which is meant to be temporary. But Kot never leaves England. On his arrival, he finds a job at the Russian Law Bureau. An acquaintance there introduces him to D. H. Lawrence, who in turn introduces him to Mansfield, Murry, Gertler, and Beatrice and Gordon Campbell. In 1915, in collaboration with Murry, Kot translates his first book from Russian to English. He initiates friendships with H. G. Wells and the Woolfs: the couple study Russian with him and, between 1919 and 1923, publish his translations. The chapter on Kot's collaboration with the Hogarth Press adds to the fine recent scholarship of Rebecca Beasley, Stuart N. Clarke and Laura Marcus, Claire Davison-Pégon, and Roberta Rubenstein. Diment concedes the clumsiness of Kot's "word-for-word translation" (183), even when it was smoothed over by the Woolfs or others. Kot himself wrote that he did "not mind very much if the English is not excellent. The translation literally is correct, and that is all I care for" (126). Surely Kot's readers cared for more, though they were glad he made foreign literature accessible.

The early 1920s are Kot's most productive time professionally but a painful time personally: his father and one of his two sisters die of typhoid, his brother-in-law is killed by the Bolsheviks, and Mansfield dies of tuberculosis. In 1923, he and the Woolfs part ways because of his imperiousness and their impatience. In 1924, he feuds with Murry over their co-founded magazine *The Adelphi*. The rest of Kot's life is patterned by personal tragedy. In 1925, his nephew dies in an accident, and in 1926 he experiences the first of several debilitating depressions. The deaths of his mother, Lawrence, and Gertler pain him deeply, and he suffers through years of horrific news about Jews in Eastern Europe. A probable sufferer of Post-Traumatic Stress Disorder brought on by repeated family tragedies (168), Kot once attempts suicide.

For all this, however, the book does not feel bleak. This is partly because Kot's pain usually stems from devotion and loyalty. His methods of care are at times unorthodox: he seeks to help Lawrence by both typing manuscripts and scheming a separation from Frieda, to nourish Mansfield by both sending gifts and encouraging Gertler to win her away from Murry. And his standards for friendship are unusually high: swift and uncompromising in judgment, he abruptly ends relations when he feels slighted. But when he does not inspire insult, he inspires faithfulness. A lifelong bachelor, Kot was emotionally and at times physically sustained by the attention of close friends who occupied familial roles. He regarded Gertler as a younger brother or perhaps son (259) and James Stephens as a twin (267). In the midst of a deep depression, he wrote to Morrell that he "needed a mother or a wife" to help him "manage" (228). His need was met by Juliette Huxley, Dilys Powell, and Marjorie Wells, all of whom watched over him for decades as if he were their son or platonic husband. Kot shrouded his sexuality. Diment suggests that Kot's attraction to Mansfield and Sarton, which could be construed as physical, was purely paternal (67; 247-48), and she speculates that Kot's affection for Lawrence was indeed erotic (68-75). Whether familial or romantic, pursued with admirable or dubious means, Kot's love of friends is impressive and affecting.

Another reason the book does not dispirit is that Diment allows Kot to illuminate the cultural world around him. She proves Kot's influence on the reading and writing of his friends, in particular Lawrence. Kot served as a model for Benjamin Cooley, the title character of *Kangaroo* (1923), and brought to Lawrence's attention the writings of Vasily Rozanov, whose views on sex and religion confirmed and encouraged Lawrence's own, even finding their way into *Lady Chatterley's Lover* (1928). To illustrate Kot's concerns, Diment offers many compelling excursions on Russian history and literature. And to clarify British antisemitism, she studies Kot's reception as a Russian Jew. Arriving in England at the height of the British fondness for Russian ballet and literature, Kot fascinated as a messenger from an exotic land. But Lawrence and others derided Kot's Jewishness in person and in letters to him, evidently expecting him not to mind. Yet, he was proud of his Jewish heritage, though unobservant. He taught his Gentile friends Hebrew songs and urged them to see *The Dybbuk*, a play set in a Hasidic shtetl and written by a fellow Russian Jew, S. An-sky. Among his Jewish friends, such as Gertler, Sidney Waterlow, and Leonard Woolf, he found comfort. Long after collaborating with the Hogarth Press, Kot twice sought Leonard out: when in 1940 he was overwrought by the news of Jews in Germany and when, in 1955, he was dying.

Enriching this study of Kot's life is attention to mental illness. Diment sensitively discusses Kot's breakdowns and his few possible manic periods (149, 249), reinforcing what Woolf scholars have long known, that medical and lay attitudes towards mental illness at the time were rarely helpful and often pernicious. To cure Kot's depression, one doctor extracts almost all of Kot's teeth, while another recommends heart surgery. Electroshock therapy does mitigate the misery, but it also erases Kot's short-term memory of the unique visit of his Canadian niece, Polly. Friends tell a depressed Kot simply to cheer up, and when Polly herself suffers a mental breakdown, Kot tells her the same, adding that she should deny to the doctors that there is any family history of the disease. On Virginia Woolf's suicide, Kot wrote to Sarton, "Virginia's death is a great blow to me. She was one of the finest human beings, apart altogether from her uniqueness as a writer. And she, among other English men and women, is a victim of the war as made by the Germans. This is not an exaggeration, but a sober fact" (266).

In 1947, around a year after learning of the massacres of Jews in the Ukraine and of the concentration camps, Kot cut his throat. His physical wounds healed quickly, though his psychic ache endured. Kot nearly joined Woolf as a victim of the war and of the inadequate understanding and treatment of depression.

One aspect of Kot's character that especially disturbs is his unscrupulousness. Just as Kot plotted to separate his friends from their spouses, he operated professionally with occasional ethical lapses. Kot chooses to translate living Russian authors because their copyright under the Bolsheviks is not recognized by the West, and so he cheats these authors out of their due payment (127). At times he takes full credit for a translation on which he had help (170). And he tricks the Cresset Press and J. M. Dent into committing themselves to more Dorothy Richardson books than they had intended to issue (236-37).

Clearly, we meet in this book a Koteliansky less mysterious and more flawed than we had known. No longer a mute portrait that rouses curiosity and reverence, Kot lives now as a man with a voice who stirs sympathy and frustration. Kot once wrote to his niece, "You must always remember that I am difficult, perhaps strange" (284). The reader of Diment's biography will always remember Kot as difficult, but perhaps not strange. Kot's loyalty, suffering, and sometimes questionable judgment make up nothing more strange than a human being.

—Emily Kopley, *Stanford University*

Works Cited

Beasley, Rebecca. "On Not Knowing Russian: The Translations of Virginia Woolf and S. S. Kotelianskii." *Modern Language Review* 108.1 (Jan. 2013): 1-29.

Davison-Pégon, Claire. "Samuel Solomonovich Koteliansky and British Modernism." *Translation and Literature* 20.3 (Nov. 2011): 334-347.

Marcus, Laura. Introduction. *Translations from the Russian by Virginia Woolf and S. S. Koteliansky.* Ed. Stuart N. Clarke. Southport, UK: Virginia Woolf Society of Great Britain, 2006.

Rubinstein, Roberta. *Virginia Woolf and the Russian Point of View*. New York: Palgrave, 2009.

Zytaruk, George. "Dorothy Brett's Letters to S. S. Koteliansky." *D. H. Lawrence Review* 7 (1974): 240-74.

———. Ed. *The Quest for Rananim: D. H. Lawrence's Letters to S. S. Koteliansky, 1914 to 1930*. Montreal and London: McGill-Queen's U P, 1970.

Virginia Woolf and the Migrations of Language. Emily Dalgarno (Cambridge: Cambridge UP, 2012) ix + 215pp.

For Virginia Woolf, the means and ends of translation changed significantly throughout her career. What began as a pragmatic and, as she would claim, amateur reading practice—employed by a reader simply wishing to access the work of Leo Tolstoy, Marcel Proust, and others—evolved into a critical practice that transformed her work with the English language. In *Virginia Woolf and the Migrations of Language*, Emily Dalgarno argues that Woolf came to understand translation as an opportunity to challenge and revise the dominant language such that it might better accommodate diverse voices and perspectives. This revision, as Dalgarno explains, accords with Woolf's career-long desire to rethink the English language at the level of the sentence "in order better to meet the requirements of women writers" (1). Dalgarno reads scenes of translation in Woolf's fiction alongside her private reading notebooks in order to uncover how the writer's translation practices informed her composition. Pointing to Woolf's sustained fascination with Greek, French, and Russian, Dalgarno acknowledges but ultimately disputes Woolf's claims to amateurism. These self-critical attitudes, Dalgarno explains, emerged in tandem with Woolf's sense of herself as both "an outsider and a critic of institutionalized learning" (2). Such a strategically adopted outsider's lens would prove valuable to theorizing the role of the translator as a mediator between cultures and nations.

Woolf was "clearly someone for whom foreign languages redrew the map of the world" (2)—almost literally, it seems, as translation would in fact become central to Woolf's understanding of national identity in the 1930s. In exploring how translation allowed Woolf to participate in debates about nation and nationalism, Dalgarno contributes to scholarship on Woolf and colonial discourse by Laura Doyle, Mark Wollaeger, Urmila Seshagiri, and Jed Esty. From the outset of her argument, Dalgarno considers Woolf's writings alongside theories of translation, lucidly introducing the writings of Walter Benjamin, Paul de Man, Jacques Derrida, and Lawrence Venuti. When read alongside Woolf's fiction and non-fiction, according to Dalgarno, these theories "reveal the scope of her attempts to redesign the sentence and to recreate the dominant language" (1). By forging new connections between Woolf studies and translation studies, Dalgarno's project contributes richly to both. Absent from this exchange, however, is scholarship on translation and modernism, perhaps because many such studies have focused on classical literature, with translation cast as a temporal leap between ancients and moderns. Dalgarno usefully varies this pattern by considering Woolf's negotiations with Sophocles as well as contemporaries Proust and Tolstoy.

Beginning with the essay "On Not Knowing Greek," Dalgarno contextualizes Woolf's words by tracing a longstanding cultural debate about the social role of translation. Familiar with mandates for legible translations that presume the reader's reliance on the translator's expertise, Woolf was also drawn to translations that "magnify foreignness" in order to approximate the experience of reading in a different language. According to Dalgarno, Woolf ultimately "shaped for herself a position more like that of an explorer than a university professor." Even as she advocates for the common reader, she also "domesticates translation" by way of intertextual references to the British literary canon (23).

Woolf not only read and composed translations, but also published them. The Hogarth Press translations of Russian literature, as Dalgarno explains, appealed to the already growing British readership for Dostoyevsky and Tolstoy. At the same time, these translations helped transform what had been a small, insular press into an operation with a discernible "stake in international modernism" (6). In her third chapter, Dalgarno attributes some of Woolf's narrative experiments—notably, the plot of *Mrs. Dalloway*—to her fascination with the "double plot[s]" of Tolstoy's *War and Peace* and *Anna Karenina*. In examining holograph drafts of *The Years*, Dalgarno shows that "Woolf gradually revised the novel to align the events of the family with the history of the nation," an experiment that closely resembles what Tolstoy had termed the "Essay-Novel" (80-81). Woolf's project of translation thus "creates the possibility of dialogue" between families and nations, a mediation that becomes particularly urgent in wartime (89, 85).

Translation, for Woolf, was paradoxically an opportunity to engage the untranslatable. A persistent thread connecting Dalgarno's chapters is Woolf's recurrent concern with experiences, as she herself phrased it, "on the far side of language." In translating Proust, for instance, Woolf increasingly explored the suggestive ambiguity that results when a text resists a one-to-one correspondence between words. Woolf shared with Proust a concern for "the unseen world that lies behind the seen"—a world that, as Dalgarno explains in Chapter Four, sometimes includes those "sexual preferences and behaviors that the narrator is forbidden to avow" (97). This unseen world would become a central concern in *Orlando*. With the trials of Radclyffe Hall's *The Well of Loneliness* (1928) in recent memory, Woolf used the untranslatable as a site to acknowledge but also "shield" homosexuality, a topic too fraught to be "named in ordinary public discourse" (11, 122). In so doing, Woolf stresses the mediating duties of the reader, who must be, Dalgarno contends, "capable of reading *Orlando* as a narrative in which the visible signs of lesbianism are contingent and ambiguous" (123).

Woolf envisioned a common reader who could flexibly and strategically inhabit the role of outsider. Her personal identification as an outsider and amateur becomes crucial here because, as Dalgarno explains, "translation comes to mark the position of the outsider who, excluded from the traditions of university teaching, reads a foreign text without institutional support" (147). To explore the political subtleties of this exclusion, Dalgarno turns to *The Years* in Chapter Five. Here, *Antigone* becomes a pivotal text, exposing a telling contrast between the reading practices of the university-educated Edward Pargiter, and his unschooled cousin Sara. Choosing not to translate particular lines of *Antigone* into English, Woolf de-emphasizes the text "as a finished product," instead underscoring the responsibilities of the common reader (146).

Of particular concern for Dalgarno are those institutional boundaries policing female participation in public discourse. In examining *Three Guineas*, Dalgarno demonstrates how Woolf's reading of *Antigone* poses new questions about the stakes of female literacy because "the feminine subject could not speak the public language as it currently existed" (65). In addressing this impasse, Woolf introduces Antigone's unintelligible cry of mourning as an example that "exceeds the limits of language and becomes untranslatable" (60). Dalgarno stresses the historical specificity of this conflict, connecting Woolf's 1930s reading of *Antigone* to emerging trends in German scholarship in which classical texts became opportunities to dispute Fascist rhetoric. When language becomes a site of restriction and policing, Dalgarno explains, "the subject seizes upon the untranslatable as a signal to bring her history to light" (68). By contesting such terms as "freedom" and "feminist," Woolf uses translation to "challenge old vocabularies and replace them with new" (49). Translation, in other words, gives rise to semantic confrontations that prove productive for the female subject.

Woolf's concern for female literacy is closely tied to her mandates for social transformation through language—a position that, as Dalgarno claims, "makes her work compelling to writers who are struggling against their colonization" (10). One such writer was Assia Djebar, an Algerian novelist and translator. In a gesture that broadens the book's chronological and geographical scope, Dalgarno considers Djebar's identifications with Berber, Arabic, and French— "each of which to some extent both requires and evades translation" (15). Like Woolf, Djebar struggles with the ethics of translation and resists the pressure "to translate the private rituals of mourning into a dominant language" (175). Even as Djebar understands this challenge as unique to Maghrebian culture, Dalgarno finds precedence for this resistance in Woolf's work—an inheritance that informed Djebar's "agonizing decision to represent her mother tongue and its culture in the language of the colonial occupier" (187). In closing with this chapter, Dalgarno reaffirms Woolf's commitment to reshaping public discourses for female voices, positioning Djebar's work as evidence of Woolf's enduring relevance to translation studies.

—Emily James, *University of St. Thomas*

Virginia Woolf: The Patterns of Ordinary Experience. Lorraine Sim (Farnham: Ashgate, 2010) viii + 220 pp.

Such is the pace of academic publishing, and indeed reviewing (*mea culpa*), that when a book identifies its contribution to a neglected field, by the time the book comes to be reviewed, said field often no longer looks quite so neglected— if, that is, the book is correct in identifying it as ripe for further investigation. This is very much the case for *Virginia Woolf: The Patterns of Ordinary Experience*. Lorraine Sim observes in her introduction that "The ordinary and everyday in modernism remain relatively unexplored topics" (3), but since the book's publication this situation has shifted. Indeed, the topic of the 2013 Modernist Studies Association conference is to be "Everydayness and the Event"; much exploring of the ordinary and the everyday in modernism is now underway. Thus Sim's book makes an important contribution both to Woolf studies, and to our developing understanding of the fertile relationship between the everyday as critical and theoretical tool, and modernist studies more generally.

Sim is not the first to address the everyday in Woolf's work, but this is the first monograph on the subject concentrating entirely on Woolf. The terms of her title alert us to Sim's approach to the everyday, helpfully carving out a position in relation to what can be an unmanageably vague concept. Sim insists on the particular appropriateness of the term "ordinary" in relation to Woolf, as a term Woolf herself uses more frequently than "everyday." Sim also prefers it because, she argues, it signals Woolf's "keen interest in things" (2), as well as lacking the "degree of repetition and, potentially, monotony" which is implied in the "everyday." She makes the distinction thus: "illness, celebrations and falling in love are a part of ordinary experience and life but are not typically a part of everybody's everyday life" (2). But despite setting up an apparent distance from the regular temporal aspect of the everyday, Sim also prefers "ordinary" precisely because it is etymologically linked to the "pattern" which Woolf, and Woolf's work, recognizes.

The other notable aspect of Sim's approach to the everyday is that, rather than Michel de Certeau and Henri Lefebvre, or even Georg Simmel and Walter Benjamin, her primary theoretical reference-points are the eighteenth-, nineteenth-

and early twentieth-century philosophers with whom Woolf was familiar, such as David Hume, G. E. Moore, and Bertrand Russell. This not only makes for good historically grounded literary criticism, but also provides a welcome enlargement of the more usual critical context for everyday life studies (Ben Highmore does something similar in the "Everyday Aesthetics" chapter of his recent book *Ordinary Lives*). So, for example, Sim aligns Woolf with Hume in their shared valuing of habit and custom, but argues that they differ from each other in a number of significant ways, perhaps most importantly insofar as Woolf views the sublime as, not separate from, but part of, common life.

Sim foregrounds relatively neglected texts, focusing on diary entries, memoir, short stories and essays, as well as the novels. This is of a piece with Sim's conceptual framework and powerfully demonstrates the richness of Woolf's engagements with the ordinary across her oeuvre. Sim pays close attention to, for example, "Blue and Green," "On Being Ill" and *The Voyage Out*, "Evening over Sussex" and a related diary entry, as well as texts which might be more obviously central to a discussion of Woolf and the ordinary such as the memoir "A Sketch of the Past," and the essay "Mr Bennett and Mrs Brown."

In the first section of the book, "Quotidian Things," Sim explores the object in a number of short stories. So, for example, in the first chapter, Sim moves on from the relatively familiar observation that, in *To the Lighthouse*, Mr. Ramsay's thought aligns with the British empiricist philosophy of the period, to show how Woolf implicitly challenges this approach in short stories such as "The Mark on the Wall" and, of course, "Solid Objects." Sim's careful attention to the formal qualities of each— such as the proliferation of questions in "The Mark on the Wall"— gives further weight to the general point that these texts challenge the "standard" conception of reality represented by Mr. Ramsay (and his kitchen table), offering everyday objects as subject to significant uncertainty and thus generating, not anxiety, but "excitement at the mystery and strangeness of the world" (47). In this section Sim draws upon contemporary aesthetic theory to good effect, most notably Roger Fry's concept of "significant form" which plays an important part in supporting her argument that for Woolf, form does not ossify into universality or disinterestedness, but is instead in a dialectical relationship with subjective emotional states, as well as specific political and historical contexts.

Having focused in the first section of the book on objects, Sim then goes on to address "ordinary experience"— being ill, motoring, and "moments of being" in each chapter respectively. The first two experiences are of course both easier to define, and less specific to Woolf's work, than the third, and helpfully exemplify what Sim means by the "ordinary." The chapter on moments of being separates these experiences, as they appear in Woolf, into positive and negative; drawing on Woolf's indebtedness to Wordsworth, Sim insists on the groundedness of these moments in material experience. The significance of being ill to Woolf's own ordinary experience hardly needs emphasizing, nor does its capacity to engage the sublime (we think of Woolf's auditory hallucination of birds singing in Greek), and in the second chapter in this section Sim provides an attentive reading of how Woolf represents illness. Sim argues that "illness as a mode of experience can facilitate self-knowledge," and shows instances of where this appears to be the case in "On Being Ill" and *The Voyage Out*. It also makes some important points about the political implications of being ill— of being excluded from healthy society and thus necessarily exempt from its more aggressive institutional activities, such as war. The chapter on motoring— or technologies of travel more generally— draws our attention to the trajectory of Woolf's thought on this subject: initially feeling negative about cars, Woolf develops, alongside her own experience of motoring, an appreciation of the sensations of speed, lightness and freedom it offers. Sim provides a very enjoyable reading of the four selves present in the "Evening over Sussex," "each of which approaches the problem of too much beauty in a different way" (131), and observes that the essay culminates in "a final act of imaginative synthesis," but one "conditional upon the body's safety and comfort" (133), as befits Woolf's alertness to the aesthetics and politics of the material. While the readings in these two chapters are rich and persuasive, both would have benefited from some more explicit explanations of some key assertions: how, precisely, does the ecstasy expressed in "Evening over Sussex" "rewrite the beautiful-sublime dichotomy," or does illness facilitate self-knowledge, as Sim asserts?

The third section of the book contributes to the rich seam of current work on Woolf and ethics. Here, Sim continues her project of recovering the idea of form or pattern in Woolf from the negative associations it was given in some earlier criticism. Or, in a less loaded, more specific way, Sim insists on the value in the "pattern" lying behind the "cotton wool of everyday life" which, in other versions of modernist aesthetics, is the insignificant background to moments of being, epiphanies, and suchlike. This idea finds important expression in the trajectory Sim traces in Woolf's novels from *The Voyage Out* to *The Years*, arguing that "the nature of Woolf's pattern has shifted from an emphasis on logical or rational order to aesthetic form" (167). This chapter is the book's most compelling reminder of Woolf's attachment to the concept of pattern and her responsibility to express it— her "gift," as Sim reminds us (173)— and also demonstrates Sim's facility in meta-level analyses of texts, as well as in the close reading in which much of this book consists.

The final chapter offers a delineation of Woolf's "ethics of the ordinary," returning to some of the figures discussed in earlier chapters, including Hume and Moore, but also turning to more recent theoretical contexts: feminist ethics, and the ethical philosophy of Emmanuel Levinas. There is now a large body of work on Woolf and Levinas; while acknowledging this positive relationship, Sim draws our attention to the difference between the two insofar as Woolf's ethics insists on embodied experience, while Levinas's model of the encounter with the other "transcends the particular" and "does not depend on particular psychological dispositions or properties inherent in the I or the other" (189). "Mr Bennett and Mrs Brown" exemplifies Woolf's position in this regard; Sim draws on some of the novels to show how, in Woolf, "the visible patterns that people create through habits, gestures and behaviour are repeatedly linked to moral character and the process of moral judgment" (195). Sim's careful, even-handed and meticulous book certainly enriches our understanding of Woolf, but also offers a nuanced and novel model of literary criticism in the field of everyday life studies.

—Bryony Randall, *Glasgow University*

The Waves. Virginia Woolf. Ed. Michael Herbert and Susan Sellers, with research by Ian Blyth. *The Cambridge Edition of the Works of Virginia Woolf* (Cambridge: Cambridge UP, 2011) cxvii + 456 pp.

Virginia Woolf never really repeated herself, never wrote a book that was just like any other of her books. But even within that context, *The Waves* stands alone—perhaps not her very greatest achievement but surely her most *distinctive* one, and that of course is saying a great deal indeed. As if one needed corroboration or evidence, examining the process of Woolf's art through all the materials compiled and presented in this edition of her most complex novel brings home what a careful as well as triumphant accomplishment it is. But one also realizes all the more how allusive and intricate—how resistant to casual reading, how "difficult"—it is.

Difficult of course for her as well: "If ever a book drained me, this one does," she wrote in her diary in March 1930 (*D3* 295); "never have I screwed my brain so tight over a book" (*D4* 8)—this in early February 1931, less than a month after observing that "Few books have interested me more to write than The Waves" (*D4* 4), no doubt at least in part because she wondered "if The Waves is my first work in my own style!" (*D4* 53).

As readers, in any case, we have our own difficulties (as well as intense pleasures), and scholars and critics can help us—as can (and must) editors. Editors of course have to assist us in determining in the first instance precisely *what* we are to read when we read *The Waves*, and, in the second instance, what some of it simply *refers* to. Before long it will be a century since the novel was published, and without some assistance many of its references and allusions are lost on even learned readers.

We have been fortunate in the last couple of decades that dedicated editors have provided us with much better texts, and extremely helpful annotations, for the novels of Virginia Woolf. (In the interest of full disclosure, I must mention that I have myself edited *Mrs. Dalloway* in a different series of editions from the present one. [1]) Each edition may be considered, at a stretch, like the red carnation Bernard observes within *The Waves*: "—a whole flower to which every eye brings its own contribution" (100).[2] Inevitably, then, as Jane Goldman and Susan Sellers observe in their "General Editors' Preface" to the *Cambridge Edition of the Works of Virginia Woolf*, "we would be foolish to ignore the fact that the act of editing is always and already bound up with reading precisely as an interpretative act" (xv). My own procedure here will take its cue from Bernard, who urges us to pretend that we can be "plain and logical . . . so that when one matter is despatched . . . we go on, in an orderly manner, to the next" (201).

My first observation is that for the common reader (to coin a phrase), the appearance of the pages of the novel itself within the Cambridge edition will probably be a bit off-putting. At the foot of every page we see for example "EN" (for "Explanatory Notes"), or "TA" (for "Textual Apparatus"), or "TN" (for "Textual Notes"), each followed by a series of numbers, often a dozen or so in total, referring to the line numbers glossed at the end of the volume.

Ah, but the text itself is exemplary. Both the present Cambridge edition and the earlier Shakespeare Head edition have chosen as the copy text for *The Waves* the first British edition. Actually, that has been the general policy of all the volumes in the Cambridge series, a decision with which I have problems.[3] However, it was certainly the correct one in the present instance, for the British edition clearly had more substantive revisions from the uncorrected proofs than the American edition. No marked proofs have survived.

Near the start of their lengthy Introduction to this edition, Ian Blyth, Michael Herbert, and Susan Sellers present an extremely detailed and helpful "Composition History" (itself twenty-three pages, supplemented later by a sixteen-page "Chronology of the Composition of *The Waves*"). The "History" especially

---

[1] Virginia Woolf, *Mrs. Dalloway*, ed. Morris Beja (*Shakespeare Head Press Edition of Virginia Woolf*). Oxford: Basil Blackwell, 1996. And my name appears in the "Acknowledgements" in Virginia Woolf, *The Waves*, ed. James M. Haule and Philip H. Smith, Jr. (*Shakespeare Head Press Edition of Virginia Woolf*). Oxford: Basil Blackwell, 1993.
[2] All quotations from *The Waves* are from the edition under review.
[3] For my edition of *Mrs. Dalloway* I chose as the copy text the extant corrected proofs from which the American first edition was prepared; Susan Dick made the same decision for the Shakespeare Head Press edition of *To the Lighthouse*.

is illuminating, as in its account of how Woolf reached that key word for the monologues, "said" (from "Susan thought" or "Rhoda thought" to the evocative yet marvelously mysterious "said Susan" and "said Rhoda"), and in its summary of the evolution of the nature of Rhoda's death from her imagining herself drowning to Bernard's report that she was a suicide.

The editors' "Publication History," at ten pages, is similarly thorough, and tells of the dramatic loss of the typescript to the novel; Woolf sat down "in despair" to begin a re-write, when she "gave a sweep of my hand; looked up; there was the carbon copy before me" (lx; see *L4* 362-63).

We then have an account of the "Early Critical Reception," through, that is, to 1941; it is the policy of the Cambridge Edition to end such an account with Woolf's death.

In the appendices, the sections "Textual Apparatus" and "Textual Notes" are also extremely thorough and detailed. But they could be clearer. The editors have no separate list of emendations; one has to read through all the entries under "Textual Notes" to see when an emendation has occurred. It is within that long list, for example, that the editors explain that they have chosen the unhyphenated version "mastheads" and give their reasons for that decision (425, for p. 13, l. 8 of the novel). They say there that they have "adopted" the unhyphenated form; elsewhere they use the term "rectified" (as in a passage in which the "omission of closing quotation marks" in the first British edition "has been rectified" [431]). Consistency of terminology, or better a separate list of emendations, would have been clearer. The emendations themselves are sensible and rationally applied. Sometimes, of course, they have entailed a judgment call, as when the first British edition had "when woman carried red pitchers to the Nile" while the American edition had "women," which they choose for this edition (429, for p. 51, l. 9).[4]

The section "Textual Apparatus" "normally records all extant states of the text from proof and includes every edition published in Woolf's lifetime" (xix). The resulting list is impressively, even astoundingly, detailed. Readers nevertheless wishing to make their own comparisons have not only the various editions to consult, but also J. W. Graham's edition of the holographs.[5]

The detailed comprehensiveness that most readers of a scholarly edition will most notice and pay attention to will be that of the "Explanatory Notes." And extraordinarily exhaustive these notes are, for better or worse. The general editors

---

[4] In this instance the editors of the Shakespeare Head edition, which does have a separate appendix of "Emendations," prefaced by a rationale for their choices, made the emendation "a woman" (42).

[5] Virginia Woolf, *The Waves: The Two Holograph Drafts*. Transcribed and edited by J. W. Graham. London: The Hogarth Press, 1976

for the Cambridge editions state their "aim to be more thorough than in any previous edition, with regard to historical, factual, cultural and literary allusions" (xv), while the editors here state that they "have striven in our Explanatory Notes to walk the fine line between information and interpretation" (lxxxvi); no one will be shocked that they have not always fully succeeded.

Given how painstaking and full the notes are, it perhaps sounds churlish to observe that sometimes they seem to go too far—that the novel is, well, *over*-annotated. Many of the notes seem more impressive than necessary or helpful. The very first note (to "*The sun had not yet risen . . .*") begins with Genesis, and goes on to possible allusions to works by Caroline Emilia Stephen, Shelley, Katherine Mansfield, and Tennyson, none of them truly convincing. A few lines later, the word "couched" (in "*as if the arm of a woman couched beneath the horizon*" [3]) is glossed as "'Laid or lying down; lying hidden or concealed; covert' (OED)" (241). When Neville observes that "The Train slows and lengthens, as we approach London" (55), we are told by the editors that "This imagery corresponds to the 'exaggerated relativistic effects' described by Einstein" (296; a similar comparison has been made to a passage in one of Jinny's soliloquies, 289).

When the name Shakespeare first appears in the novel (36), a reader of this edition of *The Waves* will probably not need the lengthy note we are given (280-281); similarly, such a reader will not require all the information we get about Edinburgh when it is first mentioned (53, note on 294). Or sometimes one may wonder if the emphasis is right. When Bernard begins his final monologue by remarking that "I met you once, I think, on board a ship going to Africa" (191), we get a note about Desmond MacCarthy's dislike for Africa, and about a Dr. Norman Leys who spent some time in Africa (375), when we wonder surely not about Africa but about who the person is that Bernard is addressing, or whether we are certain that he is in fact addressing anyone, whether he is actually speaking to some particular person who actually hears him.

Every proper name is combed through, even those for minor figures referred to only once. For the major figure of Bernard, the editors mention what seem like every Bernard whom Woolf ever knew or heard of, including Bernard Henry Holland, Bernard Berenson, Bernard Darwin, and Bernard Shaw—and even St. Bernard (242-244). For Neville, they feel compelled to mention Neville Chamberlain, although they acknowledge that he did not become Prime Minister until 1937 and "was still a relatively minor political figure when VW was composing *W*" (246). For Louis, they of course mention many of the echoes of the works of T. S. Eliot (as well as that he was "born in St. Louis") and then also bring in Louis Conard, Louis XIV, Robert Louis Stevenson, and the character Louis Vechantor in Frank Swinnerton's *Shops and Houses*, as well as the French poet Pierre Louÿs (247).

Yet sometimes the unexpected annotation turns out to be welcome and illuminating. One might not have thought it necessary to provide a note for the word "Negro," but their gloss on it puts the usage in a helpful historical context (256). And the editors' intimate knowledge of the full range of Virginia Woolf's writings frequently pays off, as in their brief but telling note about the name Florrie (259). Similarly, their command of Woolf's biography proves extremely valuable, as in their note on Mrs. Moffat (325).

Missed opportunities are rare. But when Louis reflects that "these attempts to say, 'I am this, I am that' . . . are false," and then on the same page Neville refers to "these false sayings, 'I am this; I am that'" (108), we could be reminded that Clarissa Dalloway says to herself that "she would not say of Peter, she would not say of herself, I am this, I am that" (9).

Yet for a reader not gifted with total recall and an absolute command of the entire novel, an especially welcome aspect of the Explanatory Notes are the many cross-references from one passage in *The Waves* to another, in particular when the editors point to parallels in phrasing between two or more characters, or between an interlude and a monologue.

There are also many instances of allusions to, or echoes of, other writers of Woolf's own time, including Joyce; the notes, for example, show an interesting echo in Louis's "cracked looking-glass" (135) of Stephen Dedalus's in the first chapter of *Ulysses* (348). But even more evocative and fascinating are the frequent echoes of Woolf's other writings, her essays and fiction. When Neville reflects on how, "like a volley of shot, a tree falls" (159), the editors quote an interesting passage from the essay "Reading" and two from the novel *Jacob's Room* (359-360); but when they quote a relevant passage from the latter for Bernard's "to sum up," we surely do not also need their definition of the phrase, "i.e., to summarise, recapitulate" (375).

But I hope it is clear that I gladly accept what I feel may be some unneeded notes for all the enlightening ones provided here, and certainly I am grateful for the care, intelligence, and scholarship that have produced this edition. As the editors express it at the end of their Introduction, they "labour under no delusion that they have established 'the' text; but they are confident in presenting a transparent and informative edition of one of the most innovatory, allusive and poetic novels of the twentieth century" (lxxxvii). Of any century.

—Morris Beja, *The Ohio State University*

Between the Acts. Virginia Woolf. Ed. Mark Hussey. The Cambridge Edition of the Works of Virginia Woolf (Cambridge: Cambridge UP, 2011) lxxix + 312pp.

Mark Hussey's Cambridge edition of Virginia Woolf's *Between the Acts* (1941) does Woolf scholars a tremendous service, not surprisingly, coming from the man who gave us *Virginia Woolf A to Z: The Essential Reference to Her Life and Work*. This edition breaks new ground by giving us a completely new version of Woolf's posthumously published novel. It is based not on the first American edition (as is Melba Cuddy-Keane's Harcourt edition from 2008) nor primarily on the first British edition (as is the Shakespeare Head edition by Susan Dick and Mary S. Millar from 2002) but on the final typescript of the manuscript. In using the typescript as the source text (not the "authoritative text," Hussey says, because Woolf never saw such a text in print), Hussey seeks "to move the work closer to the state in which Woolf left it at her death" (lxiii). What is most "radical" about this edition, Hussey acknowledges, is his decision not to use italics to distinguish the words of the pageant from those of the framing narrative, as per Leonard's instructions to the printer. That momentous decision gives us a new novel, one that brings out its involuted structure and its allusive allure more vividly than any previous edition.

That crucial typographic choice is only one (though the most important) of the many noteworthy features of this beautifully rendered edition, compact and weighty, dense with information. Hussey's introduction provides an overview of Woolf's life and writings, of the composition and publication history of this novel, and of its contemporary reception and recent criticism, and a sustained reflection on theories and practices of textual scholarship that supply a rationale for his own editorial decisions. The explanatory notes number 530, more than twice as many as in the 2008 Harcourt edition, yet are never intrusive. Discretely noted in small type at the bottom of each page, these references are available, if the reader chooses to seek them out, in a section at the end. They cover London streets and landmarks; the flora and fauna in the novel; the names of historical and literary figures, cross-referencing them with Woolf's other writings; geographical, historical, literary and cultural references; and, "every character's name, shop name and every place name in the text" (159). The explanatory notes identify not only major historical events, such as the Napoleonic wars and King George VI's coronation, and key publications, such as *The Outline of History* that Lucy Swithin reads and the countless literary works whose phrases resound throughout the novel; but also such obscure, even odd references as the class significance of red villas and turtle soup, Mrs. Manresa's red nails and Mrs. E's red lipstick. The volume of notes, however, is not sheer pedantry; these notes tease out the literary and cultural palimpsest that is the novel itself and instance the critical tendency of the new modernist studies, to attend to minor details and the specificity of cultural and intellectual references (xvii).

In addition to the explanatory notes are two sections on editorial work, the textual apparatus that records variants between the typescript and the first British and American editions, and textual notes where Hussey "explain[s] and document[s] each instance of intervention" (lxiii) in keeping with the editorial ethic of the Cambridge editions: namely, transparency. Especially for a work that has no authoritative text—Woolf even stated explicitly that it was not ready for publication—the editor must make his choices explicit, whether he has relied on the author's words or those of other intervening agents, in this case the typescript Leonard prepared for the printer. Leonard's choice to italicize the words of the pageant constituted an interpretive act which has "influenced the reader's response to the text in a specific way" (lxiv). Hussey acknowledges that his choice to ignore Leonard's italics (except where clearly indicated in Woolf's typescript) also relies on a particular reading of the novel. And Hussey's reading is, for this reader at least, far more compelling than Leonard's. Indeed, this edition extends a prominent critical reading of the novel to the bibliographic codes of the text itself.

Unlike Leonard's, Hussey's editing is not intended to make the novel more easily consumable by the reader but to conform to the logic of the text itself. As Hussey notes, critics have long drawn attention to the blurring of boundaries between the pageant and the framing narrative as voices merge with one another, characters finish each other's thoughts, the narrator echoes the pageant's words, so that the reading audience is no more certain whether the play has begun or ended than is LaTrobe's audience. Leonard's use of italics for the pageant "has the effect of separating it from the narrative in a way the text itself undercuts" (lxvii). Hussey's version, on the other hand, makes "the subversive intent of *Between the Acts*" (xlvi) explicit. For scholars long familiar with this novel, the effect will not be the same as for first-time readers with no sense that the novel and pageant were ever clearly separated. Alas, most first-time readers, namely students, will likely never experience that effect due to the prohibitive cost of the Cambridge editions.[1] That, indeed, is a significant loss. For this version provides a dramatically different reading experience from those based on the first print editions.

For a scholar as meticulous as Mark Hussey, to find an error in an edition as otherwise flawless as this one must be galling, but it must be mentioned that on page 16, line 27, "The girls screamed" should be "The girl screamed."

But "we quit such odious subjects as soon as we can" (*O* 139) to end on a positive note. This edition of what critics call Woolf's last novel will be the

---

[1] Teaching the novel this semester, I have ordered the 2008 Harcourt edition (in a series edited by Mark Hussey) and placed the Cambridge edition on reserve, inviting students to compare the two versions.

definitive one for years to come. Not only are the notes, textual apparatus, and introduction as thorough as any to date, its typographic form mimes and intensifies the experience of reading that Woolf's experimental text sought to produce.

—Pamela L. Caughie, *Loyola University Chicago*

The Essays of Virginia Woolf Volume 5: 1929 to 1932 Ed. Stuart N. Clarke (Boston and New York: Houghton Mifflin, 2010) xxix + 705pp. *The Essays of Virginia Woolf* Volume 6: 1933 to 1941 Ed. Stuart N. Clarke (London: Hogarth Press, 2011) xxxi + 736pp.

In 1904 Virginia Woolf inaugurated her life as a professional writer with a review of W. D. Howells' *The Sons of Royal Langbrith* (written, she claimed, in half an hour) and a personal account of her visit to the Brontë parsonage at Haworth (this took longer—somewhat under two hours—to write). The enviable facility of these first ventures was not to last, of course, nor did these fledgling efforts seem especially precocious. Still, they are worth revisiting for intimations of preoccupations that would last a lifetime. The Howells review opens by making a workmanlike distinction between the novel of thought and the novel of action; her "pilgrimage" to Haworth, which she found "dingy and commonplace," causes her to wonder "how far surroundings radically affect people's minds" (*E1* 5). Thus are introduced two of the major themes that will dominate the great essays to come: one I might call, in my own workmanlike way, the aesthetic theme, in which Woolf explores and ultimately champions the inventive forms, the psychological emphasis, the uncensored subject matter that give modern fiction its power and distinction; the other the socio-political theme, which examines and often laments how baleful environments can affect people's minds, by which she means both their hearts and their imagination.

With the recent publication of the final two volumes of Woolf's collected and uncollected essays, reviews and occasional pieces, we at last have an indispensable chronological record of what and when Woolf thought what she did about art, about politics, about human character. Stuart N. Carke has taken over the editorial stewardship of this monumental project from Andrew McNellie, the impeccable, eloquent editor of the first four volumes. Clarke has proved a worthy successor, maintaining the same high standards and practices that made the previous volumes so pleasurable as well as informative to read and consult. Thanks to their exemplary work, we can survey Woolf's essays arrayed majestically from end to end and can appreciate anew and in greater depth how much the modern essay— at once relaxed and exacting—owes to her determination to record as honestly as she could her reactions to books, to social and political issues, to people and to places and to do so, moreover, while acknowledging the importance of mood—of bored or flagging spirits as much as exalted enthusiasms—in accounting for one's opinions, which were, she often reminded us, of the moment.

The mood deepens, as does the gravity of her concerns, in the works that make up these last two volumes. Volume 5 includes all the essays written between 1929 and 1932, years following the exhausting labor of *The Waves* and the impressive polemical achievement of *A Room of One's Own*. The essays from these years predictably reflect her feminist values and continue her critical assault on the generic boundaries traditionally separating poetry and prose. She is ardent in her appreciation of the vigorous colloquialisms and new coinages of American fiction, which she praises for capturing the freshness and impertinence of contemporary reality. But she continues to be adept at taking the long view, as exemplified in *The Common Reader: Second Series*, reprinted here in its entirety, which begins with "The Strange Elizabethans" and concludes by attempting to answer the rather timeless question of how one should read a book.

The sixth and last volume of the complete essays runs from 1933 to 1941, years that tested but failed to subdue her feminism and pacificism. *Three Guineas* belongs to this era, as do "Thoughts on Peace in an Air Raid" and "The Leaning Tower." Although these essays were written during wartime and while she was battling the debilitating depression that would finally cause her to take her life, there is very little of an end-of-the-world feeling about them. Among her last grand projects was a history chronicling the birth and social fate of "Anon" and "The Reader." Dangling over a precipice, Woolf managed to imagine the dawn of print culture and take comfort in the promise of the book, which "differs from the play in giving a different pace to the mind. We are in a world where nothing is concluded." This is the world, in which nothing was really finished, Woolf believed in and defended to the last.

These essays also reveal an aspect of Woolf's imagination that has not received the attention it deserves: her skill in delineating character from the outside in, rather than, as in her fiction, from the inside out. She did not have to enter into the consciousness of Beau Brummell, for instance, in order to capture the appeal and pathos of this improbable historical character. "Handsome and heartless and cynical," she writes, "the Beau"—(the Beau!)—"seemed invulnerable":

> His taste was impeccable, his health admirable; and his figure as fine as ever. His rule had lasted many years and survived many vicissitudes. The French Revolution had passed over his head without disordering a single hair. Empires had risen and fallen while he experimented with neck cloths and criticized the cut of a coat.

The years intensify her interest in eccentric characters and their relations to each other. She seems to relish telling the story of the stormy, vexing but undeniably affectionate and enduring friendship of Geraldine (Jewsbury) and Jane (Carlyle); in wondering at the warm, sensuous character of "Hazlitt, the Man," a man without reticence or shame whose "essays are emphatically himself"; or, at the opposite extreme, in appreciating the urbanity of Oliver Goldsmith, whose essays were marked by a "peculiar reticence which forbids us to dwell with him in complete intimacy," lacking as they do "the solitudes and sublimities" by which more confiding essayists, like Hazlitt, like Woolf herself, openly reveal themselves.

And then there is the sheer largeness of heart in her portraits of friends, as in her fond remembrance of Janet Case, her beloved Greek teacher, and, most notably, her obituary for Lady Ottoline Morrell. Woolf does not deny that those who knew Lady Morrell were generally amazed at her "strangeness, at the pearls, at the brocades, at the idealisms and exaltations," but she prefers to emphasize her "democratic spirit which led her not only to flout the conventions of the world, but to keep her house bravely open during the War to the unpopular and the friendless." It was her "inner freedom, that artist's vision," Woolf writes, that led Lady Morrell "past the decorated drawing-room with all its trappings to the actual workshop where the painter had his canvases, and the writer his manuscripts."

These essays take us into Woolf's own workshop, including as they do variants of several of her important essays, additional essays from 1906 to 1924, draft essays of such gems as the comical "Friendships Gallery," her homage to Violet Dickinson, and her wireless broadcasts, including the important piece on "Craftsmanship." The concluding volumes also attest to how generously she invested in the workshops of the future. Her sympathy for the young rarely deserts her, even when the young threaten to supplant her. This is the prospect she confronts in "The Leaning Tower," but she meets the challenge with great equanimity. She understood the peculiar emotional excitement that belongs to those just beginning their life as artists. In her charming "Letter to a Young Poet," she refuses the role of "nekrophilus," and warns of the fate of an "old gentleman" who in "the act of consigning all the arts to the grave choked over a large piece of hot buttered toast." The consolation that he was about to join the elder Pliny, she adds, "gave him... no sort of satisfaction whatsoever."

Woolf herself found satisfaction only in the living, not the dead past, in the vital and unconcluded present, in an open future. So much is attested in the somewhat astonishing prediction that appears in a late essay on Hugh Walpole of all people: "Whatever ruin may befall the map of Europe in the years to come, there will still be people, it is consoling to reflect, to hang absorbed over the map of one human face." The essay is called "The Humane Art," by which she means to honor the art (now nearing extinction) of letter writing. But humane also describes her essays, in which her generous, inquisitive, fearless, often humorous and crusading spirit is captured in all its varied life. Reading them, whether for the first or for the umpteenth time hardly matters—they continue to charm, disturb, challenge and, in their breadth of subject and sympathy, console us.

—Maria DiBattista, *Princeton University*

Modernist Commitments: Ethics, Politics, and Transnational Modernism. Jessica Berman (NY: Columbia UP, 2011). x + 372 pp.

In her earlier book, *Modernist Fiction, Cosmopolitanism, and the Politics of Community* (Cambridge: CUP, 2001), Jessica Berman critiqued a number of theorizations of community for their dependence upon a universalizable liberal subject, and drew on feminist theorists of justice to insist on specificity among the "web of stories we call our selves" (13). In this new work, she considers specific texts from a variety of locations to delineate an eclectic modernism, and also counters the notion that only realist writing can be politically engaged. Ranging from well-known texts by Joyce, Rhys, and Woolf, to works more recently familiar such as Mulk Raj Anand's *Coolie* and *Untouchable*, as well as to obscure and difficult to access works by Indian women writers of the early twentieth century, Berman argues that they all can be seen as examples of a transnational practice of modernist engagement with local political situations through the narrative creation of an "as if" world of imagined possibility. Although Berman does not go as far as some in her expansion of "modernist" (not as far, for example, as Susan Stanford Friedman), choosing to confine her readings more or less to the common temporal parameters of the interwar period, she does posit a "transnational optic" through which texts of quite different kinds might be united through social and textual relationships under the term "modernist." Casting so wide a net raises the question, for me, of whether thus establishing commonalities does not tend to flatten the world rather too much. If modernism's country is the whole world, whose modernism is it? These are ethical questions that Berman's thoughtful book takes to heart, but by finding a similar politically engaged purpose of aesthetic experimentation in all the texts she considers, Berman's readings maintain a paradigmatic modernism that can at times seem at odds with the effort to challenge the European and metropolitan bias of older definitions. It is eminently reasonable to say, as Berman does in her chapter on Spanish Civil War texts, that "if we restrict our gaze to a specific set of texts, formal attributes, or series of attitudes, we risk ignoring the various shapes and guises of modernism as it arises in response to aesthetic, social, historical, and rhetorical demands in a variety of locations" (185-86), but when that expansive gaze finds "modernism" almost everywhere it looks, its usefulness as a definition is weakened.

In pursuing her argument that "modernism brings to the fore narrative's role in helping us imagine justice" (7), Berman deploys philosopher Drucilla Cornell's concept of the imaginary domain, an intimate ethical space to which politics should be accountable. The Western liberal subject of the language of rights, for example, has been deeply problematic for those marginalized by its construction. Berman finds inherent in narrative the possibility of more just, more ethically responsive constructions. A theme of her book is that politically engaged writing does not necessarily have to eschew formal experimentation, a view that has made the 1930s seem anomalous in the history of modernism. She takes issue with critics who have read as realist writers such as Jack Conroy or Meridel Le Sueur, for example, and argues through close readings of Conroy's *The Disinherited* and Le Sueur's *The Girl* that their work is formally experimental in ways that intend to use aesthetic practices for political ends. "Commitment that seems to take precedence over form remains a sort of marker for 'that-which-is-not-modernism'" (27), she writes; she would like to bring such works into the modernist fold. However, the identification of "worldwide textual correspondences and intersections" (30) among the social and political commitments of texts from very diverse locations can risk imposing a kind of formal homogeneity on these chosen examples.

Having described in her introduction a tension between ethics and politics through a reading of Anand's *Untouchable*, Berman focuses in her first chapter on Woolf and Rhys. Woolf's often-stated desire to "know" others very different from herself (the urgency and frustration of which desire is expressed, for example, by the narrator of *Jacob's Room* in a scene at the opera house) is her starting-point. It's possible to see a similar desire motivating Berman's project in that in moving away from European and American metropolitan centers of modernism, she reads "mostly unknown," long out of print Indian women writers, untranslated and marginalized Spanish writers of the Civil War period, and obscure little magazines of the 1930s American left. Woolf's attempts to cross the gap between self and other have been the object of numerous critiques that seek to show how her class and race positions limit her ability to make that transit (and which also typically eschew any reference to Woolf's own considered recognition of those limitations). Berman suggests that Rhys's fiction undermines the possibility of achieving such a leap from a subaltern rather than dominant position.

What Woolf particularly understood and emphasized is the relational nature of reading and its analogous status with regard to the encounter of self and other. Berman links ethics and aesthetics in this way: "the connection between the maker and the perceiver that is essential to the aesthetic experience" is an ethical connection. The text asks the reader "Who are you?" just as the reader poses that question to the narrative. Berman draws on Mieke Bal's feminist adaptation of Deleuze's "fold" to explain how Woolf's narratives bridge gaps between subjects, and also how the folds of her texts enclose spaces of ethical significance. The fold can be quite literal: a folded-back curtain, for example, that allows Clarissa Dalloway to see her neighbor across the street. When this encounter is repeated just after Clarissa has heard of Septimus's suicide, at her party, it creates a moment of ethical awareness because Clarissa recognizes the subjectivity of the old woman looking back at her. Berman's reading of this scene as enabling "Clarissa to make sense of the importance of the death of Septimus" (61) underscores her argument that private moments can have public, social significance. Alternatively, the fold can be textual, as in *To the Lighthouse*, where the tripartite structure "folds" the first and third sections around the middle. In *Three Guineas*, however, Woolf disrupts this narrative practice to refuse the "forced fusion of sensibility that characterizes propaganda and serves to perpetuate war" (63). By manipulating the structure of address, Berman explains, Woolf refuses the identification with military figures or with the victims of war urged by propaganda.

Woolf's Society of Outsiders is a utopian "as if," a projection into the future of the world as it "ought" to be, as opposed to the world as it is—the distinction between "ought" and "is" constitutes the ethical field within which Berman's work is located. But Rhys's works make clear the constraints on Woolf's utopianism that are experienced by colonized subjects, situated as they are in marginalized spaces where possible futures are foreclosed by "the impasse of empire" (89). Although illuminating, this chapter would have benefited from a fuller discussion of the encounter between Woolf's and Rhys's texts. For example, in *Good Morning, Midnight*, Rhys's main character, Sasha Jansen, depends on marriage for a national identity, but Woolf's explicit discussion of marriage and nationality, and its implications for patriotism, in *Three Guineas* goes unremarked.

Geography becomes a central category in Berman's argument from the outset, and locating Woolf more specifically might have integrated her better into the discussion as it develops. If geography in the nineteenth century was an instrument of empire, an adjunct to exploration, then "modernist geography" produces a counter-politics through its emphasis on the bidirectional relations of human and landscape. Joyce's geography—"joggerfry" as Leopold Bloom names it to himself, hearing schoolchildren recite Irish place names—contradicts the simple identity of location and race or nationality, attuned as it is to migratory flows that create connections which undermine the center/periphery model of empire. In bringing together Joyce and Anand—the Indian novelist and activist whose encounter with Joyce's work profoundly affected his style—Berman "demonstrates the continuum of political engagement that underlies transnational modernism" (109). But again, if it is a similar politics that unifies such disparate texts, might this not risk a flattening of different locations into a kind of united states of modernism? Presumably, the rebuttal to this argument is that by attending to local differences, the understanding of modernism is itself complicated and extended across borders. Indeed, Berman calls for a modernism that is not an "established set of works" but a "global range of relationships, practices, problematics, and cultural engagements with modernity" (284). Her point is not that categories are mappable from one location to another, but that the relation, for one example, between Joyce and Anand is bidirectional, both of these writers similarly politically engaged. Thus *Coolie* challenges the developmental teleology of the *bildungsroman* and so changes the way we might read Joyce's *Portrait*.

At the beginning of the chapter on "Modernism in the Zenana" (i.e. in women's domestic space), Berman notes that several of the texts she considers are now very difficult to find. Many readers, therefore, will have to take on faith her accounts of works by Hussain ("the Jane Austen of India"), and Ishvani. Cornelia Sorabji, the third writer she considers here, has received attention from other scholars of modernism such as Sonita Sarker. In these works, too, Berman identifies "modernist" experimentation within the context of India's emerging political independence. Berman thus restores to the narrative of Indian literary engagement with modernity the voices of women who have been excluded from that narrative. This work of recovery does expand our understanding of modernism and its modes, but raises the question of the ethics of recontextualizing as "transnational modernism" what is simultaneously presented as a particular local instance of the encounter with modernity.

—Mark Hussey, *Pace University*

In the Hollow of the Wave: Virginia Woolf and Modernist Uses of Nature.
Bonnie Kime Scott (Charlottesville: University of Virginia Press, 2012) xi + 268 pp.

In her latest book, Bonnie Kime Scott joins the burgeoning conversation on Woolf and nature. Citing recent pertinent Woolfian events, including the 2010 Annual Conference on Virginia Woolf with its "natural world" theme and a *Virginia Woolf Miscellany* issue on "eco-Woolf," Scott greatly expands the scholarship on Woolf's experiences with nature and integration of it into her works. Touchstones throughout her study include Donna Haraway's term "naturecultures," which asserts the unity of what many hold to be separate entities, and ecofeminism, which examines how patriarchal concepts of power, dominion, and control affect the environment. While many earlier studies of Woolf viewed her primarily as a writer of the city, Scott finds Woolf firmly situated in the natural world as well, stating that "nature plays a significant part in both the external and the internal dimensions of her life and work, and that it is inextricable from her language and ethics" (10).

In Chapter One, "Toward a Greening of Modernism," Scott sees modernism developing in concert with writers' varying attitudes toward nature. She first discusses the men of 1914, including Wyndham Lewis, T. E. Hulme, and Ezra Pound, whose focus on urban settings in their art and writing is predicated upon their rejection of nature as feminine. Lewis, for one, "assigns masculinity and art to dry surface articulation and the feminine, as nature, to damp and chaotic depths of being" (16). Scott finds T. S. Eliot engaging the natural world more complexly, alternately depicting culture's dominance over nature, lamenting a lost natural world, or "refer[ring] to nature . . . to confirm the existence of God" (18). Childhood summers spent in Gloucester, Massachusetts, on the coast of Cape Ann, influenced him profoundly, Scott finds, "offer[ing] him experiences similar to those little Virginia had at St. Ives in Cornwall" (19). In Gloucester, Eliot "learned to identify seventy types of birds and various seaweeds . . . made an insect collection, combed through detritus on the shore, and examined crabs and sea anemones in costal rock pools" (19), drawing elements of these experiences into his works. James Joyce attended to nature in a variety of ways as well. In *A Portrait of the Artist as a Young Man*, the young Stephen undergoes influential experiences in the woods at Clongowes—or what he, lying sick in bed, imagines the woods may represent. Joyce uses bird imagery to depict character and has the mature Stephen experience a crucial epiphany at the beach. Dublin's River Liffey becomes a "female entity," Anna Livia Plurabelle, in *Finnegans Wake*. Numerous rivers course throughout modernism, Scott points out, such as the Congo in *Heart of Darkness* and the Thames in *The Waste Land*, signifying modes of being and consciousness.

Scott similarly writes of Gertrude Stein, H. D., Jane Harrison, D. H. Lawrence, Katherine Mansfield, and Djuna Barnes, noting how each adapted personal experiences in nature (parks, gardens, the woods, the seaside) into their writing and created innovative literature through metaphors and images taken from the natural world and its mythology. H. D.'s "explorations of the female body and sexuality approach ecstatic mysteries associated with goddess-centered religion at Elusis," for example (32), while Barnes "compared animals to marginalized sideshow performers, anticipating contemporary insights on commonly oppressive power structures" (39). A surprising omission from Scott's discussion is Jean Rhys, whose childhood amid Dominica's heady flora profoundly influenced her thinking and writing, particularly her 1931 novel,

Voyage in the Dark. Nevertheless, examining "Woolf's companion modernists" (13) demonstrates the significance of nature to modernist poetics and paves the way for further investigations into the topic.

Scott's second chapter, "Diversions of Darwin and Natural History," explores Woolf's late-Victorian and modernist experiences with taxonomy, botany, entomology, and related fields. In the early twentieth century, Scott reminds us, scientific pursuit and membership in professional societies were "off-limits to women and people of color" (42). Yet Woolf was fascinated with the natural sciences and scientists—often parodying egotistical male scientists, such as Mr. Pepper in *The Voyage Out*, and finding inspiration in the female scientists of her day, such as Eleanor Anne Ormerod. In addition, Woolf draws upon Darwinian theory in depicting characters and envisioning, notably in *Between the Acts*, not only a primitive but also a primordial world.

Scott devotes significant attention in this chapter to the young Virginia Stephen, her parents, and her siblings engaged in a variety of activities involving nature, including gardening, visiting parks, zoos, and natural history museums, collecting insects, botanizing, shrimping, bird-watching, owning pets, and going on long nature walks. In Scott's hands, the Stephen family comes remarkably to life, especially Thoby, "widely recognized as the model for the boy naturalists in [Woolf's] novels" (53). As a child Woolf parodied his nature exploits in the *Hyde Park Gate News* but later admired his dedication and skill, evident in his "notebook of natural observations," his writing displaying "his sensitivity to detail and movement" and his drawings of birds "remarkable for the precision and assurance of their strokes, and for the adept representation of movement, character, and groupings" (57).

Chapter Three, "Limits of the Garden and Cultural Space," details the impact upon Woolf of the many gardens she experienced throughout her life. Her description of her mother's garden at St. Ives in "A Sketch of the Past," for instance, presents a space free of fear, anxieties, and boundaries. As a teenager at Hyde Park Gate, however, she writes in her diary that "Father has taken up Doctor Seton's notion that I should be healthfully employed out of doors—as a lover of nature—& the back garden is to be reclaimed" (qtd. in Scott 74), a turn of events connecting gardening in Woolf's mind with patriarchal coercion and control. Scott also discusses Stephen family outings to Kensington Gardens, Kew Gardens, and Hampton Court—site of a dinner scene in *The Waves* (80), and the gardens of Caroline Emilia Stephen, Violet Dickinson, Ottoline Morrell, Vita Sackville-West, Vanessa Bell, and Leonard Woolf, all of which influenced Woolf's literary consciousness.

Similarly, Chapter Four, "The Art of Landscape, the Politics of Place," explores the various landscapes Woolf encountered, shaping her views on—and subsequent reworking of—England's pastoral tradition as well as her efforts to write about landscape without falling into sentimentality or cliché. In the same vein Woolf distrusted travel writing, seen in her critique of imperialist travel abroad in *The Voyage Out* and in the writing of Jacob Flanders in *Jacob's Room*, whose essay on Italy manifests the "colonial landscape of heat and dust . . . in his longing for tea and stiles, Jacob offers all the symptoms of 'Englishness'" (139). Certain landscapes, such as the moors, represent freedom for women, while others, like those encountered by Rachel Vinrace in *The Voyage Out*, represent patriarchal power and the interrelated subjugation of females. Tracing the character of Orlando throughout the centuries provides additional commentary on land and animal ownership, Romantic sensibilities toward nature, and the representation of the Victorian Age as vegetation run amuck.

"Animals have a pervasive, varied, and versatile presence throughout Virginia Woolf's life and writings," Scott states in Chapter Five, "Crossing the Species Barrier" (155). As in previous chapters, she first discusses Woolf's childhood influences, such as her mother Julia's stories for children, which invariably included injunctions to be kind to animals, and her father's animal drawings, enlivening the margins of his books. In addition, "Woolf exchanged animal nicknames through much of her life" (155), and the Stephens and the Woolfs kept pets. Moving into her mature writing life, we see that "[h]unting, herding, and fishing serve Woolf . . . as metaphors for mental processes and writing challenges" (156), including her recurring analogy of thinking as akin to fishing. The animal/human binary intrigued and disturbed Woolf in the same way as dichotomies involving female/male and nature/culture, all of which she opposed. Dogs, cats, horses, foxes, rabbits, birds, and insects roam throughout Woolf's writings as she sought to oppose the politically-motivated linking of animal abuse with women's vanity, "detect the hunt beneath the social fabric of British male privilege" (178), reflect on animals as commodities and pawns in colonial activities, and understand "the place of death in nature" (182).

In her final chapter, "Virginia Woolf and Ideas of Environmental Holism," Scott "considers whether an ordering approach to nature is decipherable in Woolf's work, [. . .] what her construction of such order might mean in facing trauma and environmental crisis," and how "Woolf's uses of nature contribute to or complicate feminist, modernist, and environmentalist understandings and agendas" (193-4). Scott finds today's feminist philosophers and ecofeminists countering persistent dubious agendas, including essentialist associations of female with nature, science's tendency to regulate, normalize, and oppress the environment, and "masculinist qualities" embedded in animal rights discourse (197). They strive instead for "improved models of sustainable environments," for example "highlight[ing] the roles of women in countering pollution and preserving traditions of indigenous agriculture" (197). In the same vein, Scott shows Woolf seeking throughout her works to include nature in epistemological frameworks, to adapt Mother Earth and goddess myths for cultural critique, to merge humans and nature, and also to grapple with discontinuities and disorder within the natural world. In sum, Scott's enlightening, highly readable book is sure to become a foundational resource for students and scholars of Woolf along with anyone desiring to cultivate a world "holding in high regard all living beings" (2).

—Kristin Czarnecki, *Georgetown College*

Thinking in Literature: Joyce, Woolf, Nabokov. Anthony Uhlmann (New York and London: Continuum, 2011) x + 164pp..

At a time when the humanities are increasingly under attack, Uhlmann's slender volume about *Thinking in Literature* is a much-needed study, as it intelligently defines the value of literature and literary studies. Central to the work is an expanded but rigorous definition of thinking, specifically "literary thinking" (5). It will probably strike readers as odd that Uhlmann would open a book about "the nature of thinking in literature" (4) with a chapter on the philosopher Spinoza, for the Enlightenment thinker is generally regarded as one of the founding figures of a reductive rationalism, which is usually considered indifferent to and many times hostile towards art. But one of Uhlmann's greatest strengths is to demonstrate how Spinoza's work on thinking, defined in terms of a relation and ratio that logically chart a causal nexus, can be used to illuminate modernist texts. Modernist literature frequently foregrounds gaps in plot, logic, and character. But instead of wallowing in the abyss of the textual gap, modernist writers, Uhlmann convincingly argues, expect and even demand that their readers apply a rigorous form of thinking in order "to bridge the gap" (15). Consequently, modernist texts simultaneously enact and habituate readers into the art of thinking, and it is a version of Spinoza's thinking that readers can and indeed must deploy in order to make the logical connections between seemingly disconnected parts.

To clarify how a version of Spinozistic thinking could be used to illuminate modernist texts, Uhlmann briefly applies it to the numerous gaps in the four narratives of Faulkner's *The Sound and the Fury.* For Uhlmann, in noting the gaps, "we are forced to make relations between the different fragments within the story to reconstruct the various lines of causation at play" (18). What enables readers to bridge these gaps is not a mode of thought intrinsic to the text, but what Uhlmann refers to as an "'external'" (3) mode of thought. This distinction is crucial, because it allows Uhlmann to expose the stream-of-consciousness approach as "narrowly subjective" (3), and, thereby, to justify his claim that modern literature does something much more important than offer an analogue of consciousness. It offers "an analogue of thought itself" (18).

On this topic of thought itself, however, Uhlmann is not as clear as he could be. He makes an extremely important argument about the way literary thinking enables us to bridge textual gaps. Using Spinoza, he claims that an idea exceeds what is contained within the word and "that one can link artistic thinking to this very excess" (11). Given the logic of this model, "art requires us to understand what is not present in, or goes beyond the linguistic signifier, what is in the idea rather than in the word" (11-12). But is the idea that Uhlmann has in mind a version of a Platonic Form, something that exists in the mind of God, so to speak? Or, is it something that is implied within the logic of a story or a text? Since he distinguishes the internal from the external mode of thought, one suspects that thought for him is a Platonic Ideal of sorts. This is especially the case as he bases his model on the work of Spinoza, for whom "ideas both exceed and precede the human signs that seek to relate them" (11). Plato and Spinoza certainly would not have agreed with Derrida, who claims: "To write is to know that what has not yet been produced within literality has no other dwelling place, does not await us as prescription in some *topos ouranios*, or some divine understanding" (11).

A similar problem appears in a chapter on Woolf. Uhlmann makes an extremely valuable distinction that seemingly allows him to escape the pitfalls of the traditional correspondence theory of truth. For his model to work, Uhlmann must expand the concept of thinking. Instead of being a colorless, cold, rigid, and distant abstraction, thinking presupposes and contains human sensation. In a very informative discussion of the painter Cézanne, whose work Woolf engaged when she wrote her biography of Roger Fry, Uhlmann argues that the "logic of sensations partakes of our human cognitive capacities" (88). Indeed, he later claims that sensation "is the very matter of thought" (147). But, again, his depiction of sensation raises some serious epistemological and ontological questions. Is sensation an external reality that contains a specific nature and/or a particular content? On the one hand, Uhlmann seems to say yes when he claims that "sensation is projected by an external nature and is then registered by an internal nature" (94). On the other hand, he seems to say no when he claims that "art does not represent nature; rather, it creates alongside nature" (105).

What causes the confusion is a slippage in what Uhlmann means by "an external nature," and, ironically, we get considerable insight into the nature of that slippage through Uhlmann's wonderfully insightful readings of *To The Lighthouse, The Waves,* and the essay, "Walter Sickert: A Conversation." External nature could mean an object in the external world, and as such, natural objects project, via sensation, their nature onto the perceiving subject. If this is what

Uhlmann means, then his model would be nothing more than a rehashing of the *liber mundi* tradition. The world contains a definite and readable content that humans can and must learn how to read correctly, though, in this updated model, humans must use a sensation-inflected version of thinking in order to read the book of nature correctly.

But given the examples that Uhlmann uses to clarify and justify his claims, it appears that external nature refers to art objects. He does excellent readings of Mr. Bankes engaging Lily Briscoe's painting, Bernard examining an art work at a gallery, and a group of people interpreting Walter Sickert's paintings. Within this framework, the external world projects a non-necessary and non-determinate sensation, which the artist organizes into a particular viewpoint. For the viewer of art, engaging the art object "both open[s] up and order[s] sensations in ways which are unexpected and revealing" (101). Therefore, what the artist replicates in the art object is not the nature of reality, as in the *liber mundi* tradition, but the artist's organized and codified sensations, which are an essential component of thought. These organized and codified sensations (thoughts) are not just subjective impositions onto the external world. True artists have a certain humility before the external world, which leaves them willing to modify their world view in relation to the external object. With regard to thinking, just as the artist uses sensation-thinking to organize impressions of the external world into a causal network, so too must the viewer use sensation-thinking to enter the artwork in order to tease out its causal network. Therefore, what the artwork incarnates is not a represented object but the artist's sensation-thinking about a represented object.

Uhlmann's expanded but rigorous concept of thinking is an essential contribution to modernist studies in general and Woolf studies in particular, as it provides a clear pathway for going beyond those deconstructive approaches that strand authors and readers in the abyss of the textual gap. There is definitely some confusion in Uhlmann's methodology and terminology, but this is not entirely surprising. Given the new model he is charting, there is a lot of work yet to be done. But Uhlmann has established an excellent framework that will enable scholars to think in new and more rigorous ways about literature and educators to teach students how to use modernist literature to refine their capacity to think.

—Michael Lackey, *University of Minnesota, Morris*

Work Cited

Derrida, Jacques. "Force and Signification," in *Writing and Difference*. Chicago: The University of Chicago Press, 1978. Pp. 3-30.

The Web of Sense: Patterns of Involution in Selected Works of Virginia Woolf and Vladimir Nabokov. Irena Ksiezopolska (Frankfurt am Main: Peter Lang, 2012) 247pp.

Irena Ksiezopolska's *The Web of Sense* makes a daring proposal: that by reading Virginia Woolf next to Vladimir Nabokov, we can gain insight into both idiosyncratic, experimental writers' techniques in constructing their novels. When we look at Woolf and Nabokov next to each other, we see similarities in their profiles: both writers construct their novels in layers of interpenetrating narrative, the interaction of which calls into question "reality" (a word Nabokov insists must always be put in quotation marks). Both writers rely on their readers to sort through those layers. Both, even more than most novelists, build their texts around networks of repeated images which become the emotional and philosophical keys to their novels. Both return to the same images repeatedly throughout their careers. And both, influenced by Bergson, treat time as the malleable product of human perceptions. Reading Nabokov next to Woolf and Woolf next to Nabokov helps us identify the structural devices and philosophical underpinnings of each, without diminishing the originality or uniqueness of either.

Ksiezopolska catalogues Woolf and Nabokov's shared structures in detail. The first section of the book examines various patterning devices, from repeated objects like Woolf's use of brooches in *Mrs. Dalloway* and *To the Lighthouse* or Nabokov's use of telephones in *The Defense*, to the writers' frequent use of "false doubles," paired characters whose similarities misleadingly appear to make them *doppelgängers*. These patterning devices, Ksiezopolska argues, center around a "pivotal point," the "centre of [the novel's] nervous system from which the lines of its subplots radiate" (74); these lines can extend still further, with a note sounded in one text echoing into the next.

The second section examines the writers' layered fictional worlds, in which incursions of the real world like sudden cameos by the author (Nabokov and his wife Véra dancing in *King, Queen, Knave*; the lady Bernard glimpses writing in *The Waves*) appear alongside apparently hallucinatory or imaginary characters. These texts foreground their narrators' unreliability and the texts' fictionality, and they cast the reader both as the detective responsible for unraveling the "truth" and as potentially yet another fictional character within a larger but still fictional universe.

The third section discusses Woolf and Nabokov's use of space and time, arguing that the apparent realism of their real-world settings (London, Berlin) is deliberately misleading, breaking down under scrutiny to reveal the essentially constructed nature of the fictional space and to call into question the linearity of time and "de-temporalize" the past (216).

Ksiezopolska's comparison of Woolf and Nabokov produces results on several different levels, from the individual novel to the field of twentieth-century literature as a whole. The sustained discussions of involuted space in the final section are particularly helpful in demonstrating both writers' blurring of boundaries between real and fictional worlds. The comparison of Woolf to Nabokov really does, as Ksiezopolska suggests, help illuminate the special features of each. (Ksiezopolska is careful to make no claims of intertextuality or influence, although, as she acknowledges, Nabokov did read Woolf. This may be a missed opportunity, but will probably help some readers accept the book's comparative argument.) The claim that both Nabokov and Woolf construct overall patterns not just in individual books but throughout their work, for example, helps show how important the techniques she identifies are for both writers, and also how unusual each writer is.

Most provocatively, while she distinguishes between Woolf's modernism and Nabokov's postmodernism, Ksiezopolska makes an implicit case for reexamining the boundaries between the periods. Drawing extensively on Pamela Caughie's *Virginia Woolf and Postmodernism, The Web of Sense* shows that the devices shared by Woolf and Nabokov—involuted narratives, *mise en abîme*, false endings, misleading plot elements, indeterminate outcomes, demands that the reader become a detective—are precisely the elements that critics identify as Nabokov's most postmodern. If Woolf makes similar use of these techniques, and if the novels under discussion were written at the same period, the division between modern and postmodern seems arbitrary, justified neither by style nor by calendar. *The Web of Sense* helps show that the web of twentieth-century fiction is larger and more encompassing than the established division between the modern and postmodern would have us believe.

If this summary of shared features initially sounds more like Nabokov than Woolf, it is in part because Ksiezopolska devotes more space to Nabokov. This decision may be motivated by his more overt use of the strategies she discusses: his patterning provides a clearer model from which to examine Woolf's than if the positions were reversed. This focus makes sense for the book's argument, but there are times when it might have been useful to discuss the precise differences and similarities between the two authors' use of the techniques further. If Nabokov and Woolf both use incidental details to build up larger patterns of reference within a novel or from one novel to the next, how is that different from the motifs and repeated images used by other writers? It seems true to say that their use of these images is different, but why? How similar is the payoff for each author? As Ksiezopolska mentions, Nabokov critics generally see his interest in design and patterning as part of the otherworld theme in his fiction, evidence of a supernatural world which influences our own. Since Woolf's attitude towards the supernatural was more skeptical, it would be helpful to discuss more directly what else the patterns Ksiezopolska finds in her work indicate.

A little more analysis, in fact, would be welcome throughout the first section. Ksiezopolska carefully provides a long list of objects which appear and reappear in works by each author, with little discussion of what the individual motifs are doing. The point of this book is not to provide individual close readings but to establish how networks of ideas are central to each writer's novels. Nonetheless, further examination of what those nets catch might also help show their nature. Ksiezopolska turns to this kind of analysis in the final section, when she offers sustained readings of individual novels, but at the beginning of the book, the lists of images can be a bit overwhelming. The book could also have used more systematic proofreading.

But perhaps that is the price of ambition. If *The Web of Sense* deals with individual images somewhat briefly or adopts rather a web-like structure itself, it may be because it covers a lot of ground in its 218 pages. The book concentrates on Nabokov's nine 1926-38 novels, particularly *Mary* (1926), *King, Queen, Knave* (1928), and *The Defense* (1930), written in Russian, and, his first novel in English, *The Real Life of Sebastian Knight* (1941), but it also mentions later works (the title comes from *Pale Fire* [1962]). The Woolf texts discussed in the most detail are *Mrs. Dalloway*, *To the Lighthouse*, *The Waves*, and *Between the Acts*, but the book also deals with most of the other novels, as well as short fiction and the diaries. *The Web of Sense* also includes a well-selected bibliography (though use of some of the critics listed is sparing). If some claims, like a suggestion that *King, Queen, Knave* is a parody of Theodore Dreiser's *An American Tragedy*, could use further elaboration, such moments also suggest the richness this kind of structural analysis can reveal.

—Rachel Trousdale, *Agnes Scott College*

Language, Time, and Identity in Woolf's The Waves. The Subject in Empire's Shadow. Michael Weinman (Lanham, MD: Lexington Books, 2012) ix +163pp.

The relevance of *The Waves* to deeply understanding the extent and complex implications of Woolf's experimentation is beyond discussion, especially in the light of the special position acquired by this text within her career, wherein *The Waves* proved both a climax in her incessant narrative quest ("I mean, I think I am about to embody the exact shape my brain holds" [*D4* 53]), and, simultaneously and in an intertwined manner, one of the works Woolf had to struggle more with, going through several re-thinkings and re-writings of it. This "play-poem" thus seems to request that the reader perform that same digging into consciousness, and, especially, openness to nuances and subtle perceptions which seemed essential to Woolf's conception and development of the work.

For this reason, one of the most striking features of Weinman's monograph is his level of awareness of the intricate and paradoxical dynamics which are active in this text and allow it perpetually to evade any fixed interpretation. It is in fact the ever-moving and ever-open nature of *The Waves* which motivates Weinman's choice of this text for his elucidation of how philosophical inquiry and literary theory may combine in the attempt to single out the dynamics at work between language, time and identity, a multi-directional and many-sided set of relations that the author aims to explore through the constant interaction between textual analysis and philosophical investigation. As Weinman clarifies in his introduction, his methodology does not entail a philosophical reading of the novel in the light of a specific theory, as one could initially infer given the prominence in his argument of Judith Butler's theory of performativity, nor is it "a Woolfian reading of Butler's thesis" (9); rather, the analysis is carried out with the purpose of a constant intercrossing wherein the literary text is seen as the space where philosophical dynamics can be explored at work, while, conversely, philosophy proves capable of enlightening the most subtle implications of the text. The relevance of a methodology based on interchange is evident also in the way the two main axes of Weinman's analysis, the Subject and the Empire, are brought to converge: the book's main assumption is in fact that a meaningful circular relation connects these two elements, insofar as *The Waves* is seen here as a text exemplifying how literary modernism may have resulted from the crisis of British Imperalism, but also as capable of revealing the "timeless" nature of the issue of subjectification, which cannot be exclusively explored as bounded by and arising from a specific historical period. In this sense, the challenge proposed by the author is that of bridging these temporal and a-temporal perspectives by taking into consideration the specific implications of the historical period from which *The Waves* arises, as well as widening this point of view through a philosophically informed analysis transcending period-bounded explanations.

In order to do so, Weinman proceeds through a strongly analytical method which clearly identifies, throughout the book, the purposes of the three sections which are meant, progressively, to lead to his concluding proposal to conceive *The Waves* as enacting what he calls the "conspiratorial intersubjective self": "a manner of being-together effected through the seeing together by two or more persons of the simultaneous stillness-in-singularity and multiplicity-in-motion of phenomena that genuinely are both single (and still) and multiple (and in motion)" (134). The development towards this complex and multi-leveled concept is carried forward through the analysis of the three chiasms which Weinman sees as central to Woolf's representation of the crisis of the subject, insofar as they point "to the impossibility of stable subjectivity" (23) The dynamics originating from the model of the chiasmus, with its relations of "mutual interdependence" (14), further clarifies the author's talent for investigations which attempt to go beyond given dichotomies and definitions to propose more integrated views of central issues such as the formation of individuality and its relation to body and language. One chief example of such open methodology can be found in the chapter examining the second chiasmus, that of "Time and Narrative," where Weinman's analysis of how the "interludes" sections work in *The Waves* develops by offering both a detailed examination of these specific parts (through the singling out of a set of "Imagic Themes" which are listed separately at the end of the book), and an analysis of how the interludes interact with the monologic parts, thus coming to represent less "the imposition of the novelist," but rather "the inherent tension between the cyclical directionlessness of time and the sequential character of narrative" which is "the epistemological condition for the experience of anything in language" (55). Equally careful investigation is offered on the two other chiasms proposed by the author, one between "identity and language," and another between "unity and diversity." In both cases, the analysis proposed by Weinman revolves around both the content and the style of *The Waves*, wherein, in line with the relevance acquired in the author's view by the ideas of identity and language in this novel, the characters' embodiment of the dynamics involved in the unfolding of such concepts (the different relations held with language by the different characters, and their connection with the body for the first chiasm, and the paradoxical merging of individuality and melting together for the second chiasm) are never disconnected from the specific linguistic features of the text. One good example of this textual yet theoretical methodology is the analysis of one of the initial scenes of the novel, that of the kiss between Jinny and Louis, in which all the details of the text (prepositions, pronouns) are carefully examined by Weinman insofar as they reveal the role of language within the dynamics of dialogue and exchange between different individualities.

The well sustained argument carried out in this book results from a solid textual and theoretical methodology, which is evident also in the accurate definitions that Weinman constantly provides of the terms he employs, a feature which proves fundamental when dealing with major conceptual issues wherein clarity of intent and terminology are most required. At the same time, as suggested, the monograph is all but an "arid" conceptual reading of Woolf's text. To the contrary, it exemplifies how the merging of philosophical and literary investigation proves essential for disentangling the complex matter at the heart of Woolf's writing, and how, conversely, her texts offer us the opportunity of re-discussing and, possibly, better understanding philosophical ideas. In this sense, one significant omission from the book's bibliography is Ann Banfield's pioneering monograph, *The Phantom Table* (2000), on Woolf's philosophical background, a text which may have offered further ground, especially, to the author's discussion of Bernard's wondering about "how to describe the world seen without a self." Apart from that, the book's background, ranging from an extensive use of Woolfian criticism to an acute mastering of philosophical pillars (Derrida, Habermas, Ricoeur, Searle, to name just a few) reveals the extremely original and important contribution offered by this text to Woolf studies.

—Teresa Prudente, *University of Turin*

Visuality and Spatiality in Virginia Woolf's Fiction. Savina Stevanato (Oxford: Peter Lang, 2012) xiii + 285pp.

In *Visuality and Spatiality in Virginia Woolf's Fiction*, Savina Stevanato takes seriously Maggie Humm's assertion that "Issues of vision and specularity haunt modernity" (1). With critics such as Humm, Diane Gillespie, Emily Setina, Karen Jacobs, Emily Dalgarno, and numerous others working on innovative approaches to Woolf and the visual, it is an exciting time to be writing on the subject. Stevanato's book contributes fresh, original readings of Woolf's fiction and the historical influences that shaped both the works and Woolf's conceptions of literary innovation. Her substantial volume most resembles recent work from Jessica Berman and Christine Froula in its impressive navigation of cultural studies, history, and new theoretical perspectives—an endlessly rich and dynamic combination of scholarly approaches to Woolf. But the book adds a new and productive voice to this interpretive landscape by insisting on an intentional formalism, which shapes fragmented perceptions into coherent systems of visual and spatial meaning.

Stevanato lucidly animates the historical situation of modernist aesthetic experiments by actively engaging with Woolf's contemporaries Roger Fry, Ezra Pound, Clive Bell, and Vanessa Bell. At the same time, she revisits with fresh focus Joseph Frank's traditional argument that modernist fiction should be understood spatially. Stevanato provides rigorous and sustained attention to aesthetics and aesthetic histories in demonstrating that "While visual artists were focusing their attention on formal arrangement and its relevant simultaneity, i.e. spatiality, verbal artists were doing the same" (39). In tracing this line from simultaneity to formalism, she reinvigorates well-worn aesthetic theories with impressive close readings and cogent formal analyses of Woolf's fiction. Privileging historicity and theory over engagement with the range of prior work on Woolf and the visual, Stevanato accomplishes the difficult task of both creating and effectively filling a gap that seems to overlook the important contributions of previous scholars. It is the volume's greatest strength and its greatest weakness. Stevanato's readings are freed by their originality and independence, but they can at some points seem ungrounded in the capacious archive of scholarship that explores the endlessly compelling dimensions of Woolf and the arts. Either way, Stevanato has certainly taken up Elisa Kay Sparks's recent prophecy that this field of study contributes "new theoretical perspectives [that] produce invigorating readings of particular texts," most forcefully demonstrated by the impressive new collection, *The Edinburgh Companion to Virginia Woolf and the Arts* (164).

Visuality and Spatiality in Virginia Woolf's Fiction is 23rd in a series called Cultural Interactions: Studies in the Relationship between the Arts (CISRA). As with other Peter Lang publications, Stevanato's monograph is theoretically dense and rigorously interdisciplinary—a distinction reflected in the book's organization and structure. In the preface, Stevanato highlights her primary objective: to show how the theme of the "cognitive quest" in Woolf's work (think of Bernard's quest to make sense of chaos through language in *The Waves* or Lily Briscoe's pursuit of the complete artistic vision in *To the Lighthouse*) is linked to "the role that artistic creation plays in the quest" (xiii). How Woolf's characters bring fragments into coherent wholes can be observed, she argues, through formal analysis of patterns, repetition, and symmetry in the works.

Stevanato examines a smattering of short fiction but focuses primarily on Woolf's later novels. However, readers will be surprised that Woolf is not mentioned in the first chapter, and the readings of the novels occur almost exclusively in chapter four. The cognitive quest and the spatial patterns of the author's thesis are effectively theorized and explicated, but this is not a book that benefits from selective reading; readers will find that it pays to read cover to cover rather than mine specific chapters for contained arguments or narrowly argued perspectives. Like Woolf, the reader will find the orts, scraps, and fragments coming together in the end—a readerly reward for imaginative and critical persistence.

The volume's primary concern is the nature of art and genre. Woolf and her contemporaries arrived at a fascinatingly hybrid way of seeing literature that resulted in painterly moments, photographic narrative frames, and the prosepoem/playpoem—generic amalgams most powerfully crafted by Woolf, Stein, and Joyce. In the first chapter, "An Approach to Interart Investigation," Stevanato contextualizes the literary tension between the visual and verbal arts through a series of debates about the real and the abstract, the material and the spiritual, and, of course, the visual and the spatial. She concludes that sight, especially in literary history, is a "double-sided source of knowledge"—a binate philosophy that produces a complicated paradox in Woolf's fiction (4). The simultaneous abstraction and immediacy of sight propels the author's inquiry into how this quest for truth might be inextricably bound up in the visual and artistic worlds.

The notion of the aesthetic and poetic is deliberately troubled and linked to cognition via concepts that do not fully surface until chapter three. However, the thoroughgoing biographical, philosophical, and historical accounts of Woolf and her circle lay the groundwork for the theoretical discussions that emerge in the rest of the book. The second chapter, "The Modern Age and the Arts," addresses the conversations between modernism's art theorists and writers, but Stevanato is careful not to collapse the two camps, suggesting that writers had a similar, but unique, agenda: "Literature…started investigating a new spatio-temporal dimension and exploring its own conventions following the experiments and achievements of the visual arts" (46). Readers finally hear about Woolf roughly halfway through chapter two in an exploration of Woolf's "own critical and personal writings" surrounding the subject of "her aesthetics and her poetics" (51).

The titular chapter three, "Woolf's Visuality and Spatiality," examines Woolf's short fiction and *Jacob's Room*, reserving for chapter four the later novels, which represent "her mature, spatial solution" to a literary representation of the cognitive quest (Stevanato 81). This section presents a compelling case that Woolf was not just a writer who appreciated art or had artist friends and relatives; rather, she was an art theorist in her own right, forging new perceptions of the visible world throughout her career. Departing from studies that have analyzed the work of art or vision in Woolf in order to think more deeply about how the artist interprets vision, grapples with, and ultimately shapes it into a spatial whole, Stevanato offers an exciting reading of "The Searchlight," a short story in which an elderly woman reminisces about a telescope-wielding great-grandfather as WWII searchlights probe the night air in preparation for the air raids. This example is one of several brilliant close readings in which the disparate narratives of visuality are woven through the fabric of a whole made manifest through the notion of cognitive contemplation—a concept defined as "Woolf's outwardly and inwardly directed visual compulsion…It involves seeing both the tangible surface and the inner depths which lie behind it" (111). Thus, patterns of vision and seeing in Woolf create many strands of attention that ultimately come together in the end, as the cognitive processing of sight is made whole in a theory of spatial arrangement. Stevanato's complex argument advances a new model for reading Woolf akin to the kind of linguistic, formal analysis practiced by Joyce scholars such as John Bishop and Fritz Senn.

Stevanato then delves into a series of close analyses, specifying that the fourth chapter, "*To the Lighthouse, The Waves, Between the Acts*: An Analysis," is "restricted to the thematized level alone. The formal level will be focused on in the following chapter"—a caveat that accurately characterizes the book's strict progression through various perspectives (125). Seeing and being seen—and the generative implications of sight that multiply as a result—characterize the readings that follow with special focus on mirrors, lighting, windows, and painting, making it my personal favorite section of the book. This constellation of material conditions hinges Stevanato's theories to Woolf's literary experimentation and leads to a productive rethinking of the nature of genre analysis altogether.

The final chapter, "The Remedial Implications of Spatial Form," is the most remarkable portion of the book as Stevanato narrows in on Woolf's poetics and demonstrates formal analysis with accompanying charts and diagrams of scansion. She parses Woolf's metrics to reveal the kinds of patterns, recurrences, repetitions, and variations surrounding the concept of vision that are central in the novels, a technique of formal prosody that produces "sound patterns" of meaning—verbal and literary patterns of expression, which complicate and finally give shape to space and vision (211). Thus, these complex layers of sound, sight, and cognition culminate in a unified spatial whole. This section of linguistic semantics maps a route through Stevanato's theories of visuality and spatiality, but it is undeniably dizzying at the same time. However vertiginous, Stevanato's theoretical rigor is precisely what makes the book both fascinating and forceful.

Visuality and Spatiality in the Fiction of Virginia Woolf is unconventional in its structure and ambitious in its scope and depth. Stevanato offers a systematic progression of aesthetic analyses, concluding with the formalism of narrative patterns. Although the book is largely disconnected from the work of other Woolf critics, its theoretical ingenuity and impressive historical scope make it a valuable contribution to ongoing conversations about vision, perception, space, and art in Woolf's fiction and circle. Taken as a whole, the book considers the biographical alongside the theoretical, and Stevanato achieves a nice balance that will certainly foster further research, analysis, and discussion on these issues.

— Amy E. Elkins, *Emory University*

Works Cited

Humm, Maggie. *Modernist Women and Visual Cultures: Virginia Woolf, Vanessa Bell, Photography, and Cinema*. New Brunswick: Rutgers UP, 2002.

Sparks, Elisa Kay. Rev. of *The Edinburgh Companion to Virginia Woolf and the Arts*. *Woolf Studies Annual* 18 (2012): 164-69.

Mourning Modernism: Literature, Catastrophe, and the Politics of Consolation.
Lecia Rosenthal (New York: Fordham UP, 2011) xii + 160pp.

In reading Lecia Rosenthal's *Mourning Modernism: Literature, Catastrophe, and the Politics of Consolation*, we might be forgiven for thinking of T. S. Eliot's question that haunted Europe's "lost generation": "After such knowledge, what forgiveness?" (*The Waste Land* 32). But for Rosenthal, in the wake of Lyotard's work on the postmodern and the sublime, it is now a matter of taking up an exhausting, and seemingly inexhaustible, question that persists in modernist studies: What (more) to say (once again) about all of modernism's paradigmatic ambivalences? The stakes of this inquiry are heightened as Rosenthal challenges any "periodizing frame that limits modernism to the period before the Second World War" (2); instead, she accentuates the affinities of the "modern" and "postmodern" as they converge in "the writing of finitude and catastrophe in the twentieth century" (1). Seeing in this writing a self-recriminating fascination with the "unprecedented" and an ambivalent investment in "futurity"—the "question of the future" and "of the end of the future" (32)—Rosenthal takes as her examples Virginia Woolf's *To the Lighthouse*, two 1932 radio broadcasts by Walter Benjamin, and W. G. Sebald's *The Rings of Saturn*. Concentrating on a handful of passages from these texts, and supplementing these readings with some rather dense theorizing (we encounter, among others, Adorno, Benjamin, Blanchot, Deleuze, Derrida, Freud, Kant, Lyotard, Marx, and Žižek), she locates the source of these ambivalences in the "drive for an aesthetics of the new and the utopian longing for catastrophe's end" (2).

In her first chapter, "Catastrophe Culture, Atrocity Supplements," Rosenthal borrows a key trope from Susan Sontag's *On Photography*, that of the troubling demand for "more—and more" engendered by photographic images of twentieth century atrocities. Much as Sontag explains how the shock value of appalling images (e.g., those of liberated concentration camps) soon gives way to an anesthetization of the viewer, and a demand for ever-greater stimulation, Rosenthal argues that modernism's insistent drive for radically new forms of (re) presentation enlivens a "demand for an addition in surplus," "a demand for more truth, for more than truth, for a form of representation somehow sufficiently self-critical of all preceding demands for and presentations of ostensibly new forms of truth" (9). While the prose, with its compulsion for (needlessly) tacking on modification after modification, can become wearisome, the extended analysis of modernism's prolepsis is compelling, showing how its poetics contains within it the avowal that it will never satisfy the desire, which it creates, for "more—and more." Rosenthal reiterates that this ambivalence and its conjugates—e.g., the tension between lurid fantasies of the end (of everything) and the drive for a regenerative aesthetics that might "make 'good' the encounter with loss" (12)—remain and, most likely, will remain, unresolved. Whether or not this constitutes a new insight is uncertain, but there is an unmistakable poignancy and vitality in her elaboration of the energy this poetics derives from the "rhetoric of the limit" (33), and all the ambivalences it generates.

"Virginia Woolf: Reading Remains," *Mourning Modernism*'s second chapter, begins by revisiting modernism's persistent obsession with war, and its ambivalent investment in the rhetoric of the "unprecedented." Particularly in the imminence of World War I (and its slogan "the war to end all wars"), much of modernist writing, according to Rosenthal, is mesmerized by "the fantasy of the unprecedented as both first and last" (42), and deluded by "a misleading *either-or*: either the end of the history of war or the end of history tout court" (45). Woolf, though, well-aware of the war's spectacular failure to purge humanity of its destructive impulses, confronts the alarming logic of this "either-or" by investigating what possibilities remain "for a more straightforward, less clumsy, perhaps more representative postwar aesthetic" (57). For Rosenthal, Woolf's essay "On Not Knowing Greek" highlights the desperate need to remedy the "affective fallout" of the age (57), the great incongruity between the war's unprecedented trauma and language's indirect, and often "clumsy," attempts to express it. The essay's reinvention, and troping, of the ancient "Greeks as figures of origin, of self-generating qualities and truths lost to history" (54), thus constitutes a provocation for postwar writers to, like these imagined Greeks, "step into the thick of emotions which blind and bewilder an age like our own" (*CR1* 34). What a "representative response" to all this might look like (57), Rosenthal admits, is unclear. But in reiterating Woolf's stakes in critiquing postwar art's "'clumsy' attempts to distinguish itself from the confusion of an age" (57), she returns us to a familiar topos in Woolf studies: the rejection of the "altogether inadequate, false 'consolations' of her own age" (58). Woolf's (mis)translation of a dead language and an irrecuperable past, then, constitutes a self-conscious turn away from her age's self-exculpating claims of exhaustion and insurmountable confusion, revealing that "what is truly felt remains to be said, at least if it is to be said 'simply'" (57).

Rosenthal's reading of *To the Lighthouse* is limited to "Time Passes." Here, she centers on the section's "'certain airs' and a certain 'feather'" (61) to demonstrate how Woolf's "interwar" writing tentatively enters the "thick" of an age "incapacitated before a density of affect" (57). These two figures, Rosenthal argues, "portray an allegory of war that is ominous in scale yet without clarity of end or meaning" (61). The gesture here is a familiar one, that of elucidating the relationship between art and war, between individual death—specifically the "bracketed death" of Mrs. Ramsay (60)—and the "general and vast catastrophe" of the war itself (61). Perhaps Rosenthal's most novel insight into this well-trodden ground is her application of what she calls the "late sublime": the simultaneous approach to, and deferral of, the end of sublimity. While "Time Passes" repeatedly writes, in her words, "a space on the precipice of the void" (61), it denies the reader "any figure of exceptional height, the triumphant verticality so often associated with the sublime at the brink of vastness and the void" (60). Instead, the "airs," as they circulate in the Ramsays' abandoned house, allegorize the failure to achieve sublimity by becoming a figure for "vision blocked and revealing" (62): "Nothing stirred in the drawing-room or in the dining-room or on the stair-case. Only through the rusty hinges and swollen sea-moistened woodwork certain airs, detached from the body of the wind . . . crept round corners and ventured indoors" (*TTL* 126). For Rosenthal, then, the partial, de-anthropomorphized perspective given by the "airs," along with the uncertain rhetoric of "allies" and "enemies" applied to the "torn letters," "flowers," and "books"—"How long would they endure?" (*TTL* 126)—denies the war any sublime figuration, and reiterates the fact that its effects are by no means finished. As such, the "stray airs" flutter between apocalyptic premonitions and moments of stillness and beauty, intimating, through their ambivalent and inhuman motion, a world that may come to be: "as if to suggest that the absence of life has brought an end to the discontinuities and ruptures of ending, the final forms of a world in an unchanging scene, a still life" (64). But precisely because this hypothetical peace could only exist with the extinction of humanity, Woolf is challenging her age's idealizations of the end, revealing the postwar peace to be "meaningful only as a fantasy, a story in which the postwar constitutes progress made and insight gained" (66). A different narrative of progress remains to be written, but what is even more distressing, in Rosenthal's reading, is the utter precariousness of even this "false" peace. The "feather," floating alongside Mrs. McNab and Mrs. Bast as they clean the house, becomes the arbitrary figure on which everything depends: "If the feather had fallen, if it had tipped the scale downwards, the whole house would have plunged to the depths to lie upon the sands of oblivion" (*TTL* 139). The feather, Rosenthal notes, does not fall. But in making the "apocalypse" hinge on this figure for "the utterly meaningless, aleatory, purely empty contingency of chance" (69), Woolf offers a poignant counterbalance to naïve, hopeful visions of the future, leaving us in a "now" with precious little to hold to.

Mourning Modernism refuses to console us. Instead, it emphasizes the tiresome persistence of modernism's ambivalences in our contemporary moment. "We live in an age of exhaustion" (112), Rosenthal writes, and this trope of exhaustion has itself become exhausting—without, that is, being exhausted. She does find something affirmative in Woolf's "in-exhausted aesthetics" (114), to the extent that it contests the notion we have said all that needs to be said, frustrating the fetishizing of limits and apocalyptic fantasies of the "promised end." But as long as the allure of "big" narratives, with their teleological insistence that profit can be wrung from catastrophe, endures, ambivalence is what will remain. After such knowledge, Rosenthal concludes, this is what we forget at our own peril: "the past that haunts us as the scene of so much unredeemed suffering . . . also presents the desire for catastrophe all over again, this time a new and more exhaustive catastrophe, the revolution of an apocalypse that would not fail to disappoint" (117).

—Kelly S. Walsh, *Yonsei University*

Works Cited

Eliot, T. S. *The Waste Land and Other Poems*. New York: Penguin, 2003. Print.
Woolf, Virginia. "On Not Knowing Greek." *The Common Reader*. San Diego: Harvest, 1984. 23-38. Print.
———. *To the Lighthouse*. San Diego: Harvest, 1989. Print.

Virgiia Woolf and the Theater. Steven D. Putzel (Madison and Teaneck, NJ: Fairleigh Dickinson UP, 2012) xxiv + 223pp.

Drawing on an extensive review of Woolf's personal and professional writing, Steven D. Putzel asserts that "drama, theater, and performance formed a continuous subtext in Virginia Woolf's art and in her life" (xiv), and moreover fundamentally shaped Woolf's experimental style. Her lifelong practice of theatergoing gave Woolf ample opportunity to investigate the complex relationship between audience and performance and to translate it into her own works. Woolf was, almost from the beginning, a "double audience...one reading between the acts, even as the performance unfolded before her" (109), conscious of the distance between and the intersections of dramatic literature and theatrical performance. While acknowledging Woolf's statements that she generally preferred to read drama rather than to see theater, Putzel clearly demonstrates that she nonetheless did see, review, and contemplate a wide variety of theatrical works. He argues that the particular relation between actors and audience that theater presents appears in Woolf's writing in various forms throughout her career. According to Putzel, the new form of writing for which Woolf sought is both inspired by and fulfilled through her engagement with theater. In turn, Putzel charts the influence Woolf's dramatic and performative but non-theatrical texts have had on the development of feminist theater.

Woolf's relationship to the theater is a neglected area of scholarly assessment. To contextualize his argument, Putzel fuses late nineteenth and early twentieth century theater history with Woolf's development as an audience member, critic, and occasional participant via extensive cataloging of productions Woolf actually witnessed in her life. Putzel documents some 183 plays, operas, and music-hall performances Woolf attended, from a magic show in December 1891 to village plays in the summer of 1940. For Putzel, the actual productions she saw provide a crucial window into the performative elements in Woolf's texts. He suggests we can trace her interest in and awareness of the complex relation between audience and performer, and by extension between reader and writer, back as far as her reactions to music-hall shows she saw as a child. Such an examination offers a more complete understanding of the place of the theatrical in her personal, critical, and fictional writing.

The book roughly divides after chapter three: the earlier section focuses primarily on theater history, documenting the changes on London stages through Woolf's eyes, while the later chapters turn more towards examinations of Woolf as a novelist and the afterlife of Woolf's narratives on stage. The first chapter, "Entertainment: From Music Hall to Opera," draws heavily on the *Hyde Park Gate News* and on Woolf's early diary entries to "explore how Woolf's own childhood experience as audience initiated her future explorations in the performative nature of narrative and reception" (2). Importantly, Putzel balances those personal accounts with detailed explanations of the structure and content of the late Victorian and Edwardian productions they reference. Putzel charts the ways Woolf's narratives of watching these performances demonstrate her awareness of her multivalent positions in the theater audience: engaged audience member, critic, 'performer' whose own entrances and exits would be witnessed by others in the theater, social commentator, and reader of plays.

"Bloomsbury Actors, Audience, and Playwrights" surveys private performance's role in Woolf's sense of the theatrical, from Clive Bell's Play-Reading Society to the informal tendency among Woolf and her Bloomsbury compatriots to assume characters and dramatic personae. Woolf's "involvement in the Play-Reading Society allowed her to take on multiple roles, to speak in multiple voices, and to be an interactive audience" (42); even after Woolf stopped participating in Society readings, private performances remained an important part of her life. Again, Putzel provides copious examples of Woolf's participation in these productions, including snippets of scripts written by Vanessa's children for family performances. Putzel steps back to consider the Dreadnought Hoax as a "not-so-private theatrical performance" (51): the hoax works because the "actors" make use of theatrical effects without the contextual cues that signal to viewers that they have become a theatrical audience. I found this line of discussion fascinating and wished that Putzel had pursued it further. Still, the broad context of private theater Putzel provides gives us a much clearer understanding of the place of *Freshwater* in Woolf's oeuvre. Rather than a generic outlier, the play instead emerges as part of a wide-ranging exposure to and experimentation with dialogue and drama, informed by Woolf's own experiences as a performer and audience.

"Pioneers and Their Uncles" examines women's status and position, both in the theater and in Woolf's critical and narrative writing, and investigates Woolf's contacts with modern drama. The title refers to Edith Craig's feminist-influenced Pioneer Players—few of whose productions Woolf ever saw—and the established male writers Galsworthy, Wells, Shaw, and Arnold Bennett whom Rebecca West called "the four Uncles" (a group that maps almost exactly onto Woolf's Georgians). Putzel notes with some surprise that Woolf shows "little interest...in the many plays written and produced by women she ought to have been interested in for various political, personal, and social reasons" (86). Woolf was drawn to female performers, whose perspective allows Woolf to "explor[e] the performative nature of all writing" (88), including her own. Woolf's interest in female characters leads to a discussion of the New Woman roles written by men and her particular enjoyment of and respect for George Bernard Shaw. Most importantly, Woolf's increasing attendance at and criticism of modern theater shows her becoming an equally "modernist audience" (103), aware of and resistant to the limitations of theatricality but also emotionally involved in staged works. A close reading of Woolf's review of *The Cherry Orchard* shows her at least temporarily "abandoning ... her lifelong belief that she was a better reader than viewer" (105).

The book's fourth and fifth chapters examine Woolf's narratives from two important perspectives. "Theatrical Theory and Narrative Practice" reads the influence of theater and drama in Woolf's developing theory and practice of narrative structure, while "Stage Adaptations of Woolf's Work" charts variously successful attempts to reimagine Woolf's novels as drama. Putzel quotes Woolf's lament in "Notes on an Elizabethan Play" that "'a play where nothing happens is an impossibility'" (114-15), an observation that signals the difficulty Woolf found in "incorporat[ing] the evocative power and the immediacy of drama into her own narratives" (115) and that experienced by theater artists attempting to re-present Woolf's texts as plays. Putzel mines Woolf's personal writings to show her recording her own experiences as if they were plays, setting down dialogue and positioning herself simultaneously as playwright, audience, and sometime performer. Chapter four focuses primarily on Woolf's late narratives:

The Years and, of course, *Between the Acts*. The argument that Woolf's theater viewing was fundamental to her experimentation would have benefited from more discussion of the experiments in earlier novels, such as *Mrs. Dalloway*: how do these perhaps less theatrical novels differ from the later works? Omitting in-depth discussion of the dialogue-driven form of *The Waves* seems like an oversight. While the earlier chapters do contain references to the other novels, including a link between the transformations in *Orlando* and the spectacular visions of staged pantos, the specific examination of Woolf's narrative practice could do more to discuss the earlier novels in detail—especially because these are the texts most frequently adapted for performance. Putzel lists no productions based on either *The Years* or *Between the Acts*, but ten adaptations of *Orlando* and six of *The Waves*. (While Putzel does refer to film adaptations he keeps his gaze squarely—and appropriately—on staged versions through the final chapter.) As he does with the nineteenth- and early twentieth-century productions discussed earlier, Putzel provides detailed descriptions of several of these adaptations, noting their successes and failures at translating Woolf's work to the stage. Noting that Woolf herself showed little interest in adapting her own novels, he suggests that postmodern theatrical innovation along with developments in stage technology allow for new ways to "tackle the omnipresent problem of staging interiority without making it bathetic or hyperbolic" (150).

As the book concludes, Putzel returns again to the space between audience and performance as the crucial one for Woolf or Woolf's works, explaining that successful stage adaptations must take into account Woolf's longstanding sense—derived from her own history with the theater—that the meaning of a production is actively created between the spectator and the stage. Putzel outlines the ways in which Woolf's nontheatrical writings—and the characterization of Miss La Trobe in *Between the Acts*—have given several generations of women playwrights the vocabulary and the inspiration to continue in theater spaces Woolf's experimental work in the novel.

As perhaps befits a book outlining new territory, its thesis and approach tend more to the observational than the argumentative. Putzel has a lot of ground to cover, and the transitions between theater history and Woolf studies are not always smooth. Occasional but significant typographic errors mar the text, most notably in the appendix charting the exhaustively researched and well-compiled list of theater productions Woolf saw in her lifetime, which is labeled "Chart of Plays Wolf Attended." Such unfortunate misprints, though, should not detract from the value of this book as a resource of historical and biographical information situating Woolf as a lifelong consumer of theater and drama. Putzel succeeds in establishing the ubiquity of drama, performance, and theater in Woolf's life and provides clear directions for future research that will extend his analyses of theater's intersections with Woolf's work.

—Mary Wilson, *Christopher Newport University*

Bloomsbury, Modernism, and the Reinvention of Intimacy. Jesse Wolfe (Cambridge, UK: Cambridge UP, 2011) viii + 264pp.

"High Modernism may or may not be a closed chapter in literary history," writes Jesse Wolfe in the conclusion to his subtle and informative study of how Bloomsbury's experimental ethos both participated in and helped to conceptualize a "reinvented" culture of intimacy. Wolfe's project tracks shifting representations of interpersonal relationships in the literary and philosophical production of the Bloomsbury group and its "satellites," and shows how the attempted reformulations of intimacy in their work—some revolutionary, some ambiguous, and some accommodating to the shape of tradition—interact with a similarly transforming social sphere. His seemingly uncertain pronouncement about high modernism is not simply an undecided question about literary periodization; instead it captures the particular legacy of Bloomsbury's writers, whose complicated responses to their own inherited past continue to stir a similarly productive ambivalence in their readers approximately a century later. In our contemporary attitudes regarding sexual partnership, romance, friendship, and marriage, have we progressed beyond the stage of reinvention experienced and captured by these writers, as they wrestled with a more limited range of options dictated by their Victorian forebears? Or is the reinvention of intimacy a perpetual process, always involving a complex negotiation between those forms of relationship that can be imagined and those that can be more sustainably lived—between, in short, theory and practice? Wolfe's study provokes these larger questions, about our emotional as well as historical relationship to modernism, as it carefully analyzes Bloomsbury's own negotiations of the creative possibilities of intimacy.

Wolfe's Bloomsbury is comprised of six major figures, three of them, as he says, "essential to the group" (Virginia Woolf, E. M. Forster, and G. E. Moore), and three "satellites" (D. H. Lawrence, Vita Sackville-West, and Sigmund Freud). The inclusion of Lawrence under this heading may be the most surprising, given Lawrence's expressed antipathy towards the kind of "intermediate" male sexuality practiced within the Bloomsbury circle, but he belongs in the study both because his "repulsion...indicates the important roles the Bloomsburian culture, including its unconventional masculinities, played in his imagination" and because he was "obsessed by similar questions" about how, and whether, the subject of intimacy could be creatively detached from the repetitive patterns of the past. Before turning to an exploration of novelistic reinventions of intimacy, though, Wolfe examines the philosophical background to this question as contemplated by the two thinkers most influential for Bloomsbury, Moore and Freud. The initial chapter on Moore's *Principia Ethica* should be of considerable use to students and scholars of the period, since this text is not frequently given the kind of close analysis Wolfe provides, despite functioning as a kind of Bible to Bloomsbury writers for its transcendent valuation of friendship and art as things that exemplify "good in itself in a high degree." Wolfe, impressively, makes sense of Moore's complicated treatise not by falsely resolving the gaps or idiosyncracies in its construction, but rather by fully revealing the tension between its apparent endorsement of new, seemingly rebellious formulations of intimacy and its ultimate orientation towards the ideal of a trans-historical and aesthetically "dehumanized" conception of love. Similarly, Wolfe makes the rather large subject of Freud's conceptualization of intimacy more pointedly relevant to the concerns of Bloomsbury by examining the logic, or illogic, of a single text, the case history of *Dora*, which exhibits "tensions between...theoretical radicalism and ethical conservatism" that are also, according to Wolfe, variously dramatized in the novels of Forster, Lawrence, Woolf, and Sackville-West.

The book's section on philosophical and psychological backgrounds also serves to introduce two key categories of analysis that structure its larger argument about Bloomsbury's advances and ambivalences regarding the culture of intimacy. Both Moore and Freud, Wolfe argues, were *anti-essentialist* in their theoretical orientation while providing *accommodationist* positions with respect to social and ethical practice. Wolfe puts the difference usefully in terms of two fundamental questions: both thinkers, he suggests, provided non-determinative, pluralistic, open-minded answers to questions such as "What are children, men, and women like?" while conceding to less radical, already existing conceptions of intimacy in answering the question, "How should we conduct our intimate lives, within and between families?" When the study turns to its readings of novelistic texts, this terminology allows Wolfe to inhabit critical positions that, for the most part, eschew the kind of dogmatic conclusiveness that is anathema to the Bloomsbury spirit. Wolfe further groups his writers by revealing some of the ways their texts navigate the tensions between theory and practice in a transitional age: in *Women in Love* and *Mrs. Dalloway*, Lawrence and Woolf exhibit an attitude of "anti-essentialist accommodation," revealing doubt about "Victorian theories of 'masculine' and 'feminine' essences" while retaining "faith in the practical value of marriage," while in *Howards End* and *All Passion Spent*, Forster and Sackville-

West articulate "essentialist rejection," through which they "largely reproduce Victorian treatments of gender" even as they condemn inherited marital tradition as constituting "prisons for women."

It is of course possible to quibble with some of these categorizations, but this is, in a way, a part of their utility for the book's reader, particularly because Wolfe's reasoning regarding each text's theoretical and practical attitude towards experimental forms of intimacy is clearly and intelligently made. The inclusion of Forster and Sackville-West as representatives of essentialist thinking regarding gender and sexuality seems counterintuitive to our usual understanding of these writers: Forster, after all, regularly champions an ethic of indeterminate "personal relations" above any claims to national or institutional identification, and Sackville-West, as Wolfe points out, is known for the "sexual iconoclasm" that inspired Woolf to write *Orlando*. Wolfe admits that neither *Howards End* nor *All Passion Spent*, in their essentialism, represent the larger oeuvre of their authors, but this is precisely why these texts deserve attention in the context of his argument. As illustrations of "ambivalence about the reinvention of intimacy," they remind us that the quick and easy equivalence of Bloomsbury with an unproblematic sexual adventurousness is a cliché that fails to capture the spirit of paradox built into the Bloomsburians' literary works. At times it does seem, though, that Wolfe arrives at his categorization by privileging plot mechanics over other aspects of novelistic expression. In the case of *Howards End*, his argument about Forster's essentialism revolves in part around Margaret Schlegel's failure to evolve into an exemplar of the New Woman that she appears to be at the novel's outset, and in part around the "missing figures" of men of intermediate sexuality, who are presented to us but ultimately negated in the form of Leonard (tragically curtailed) and Tibby (effete and ineffectual). One wonders if Leonard's death and Margaret's ascendancy as a Wilcox necessarily amount to "essentialism" regarding masculine and feminine gender roles, though: the experimental and queer potential of the novel can be said to be even more highlighted by a conclusion that noticeably fails to find a "flourishing" form of expression for either of these qualities.

In his discussions of *Women in Love* and *Mrs. Dalloway*, Wolfe suggests that both novels express a range of anti-essentialist positions regarding gender, sexuality, selfhood, and intimacy, even as they work their way towards a tense but seemingly necessary "peace" with the imperatives of companionate marriage. His readings of Lawrence and Woolf are absorbing and well written. In both cases it remains possible to ask whether the "accommodations" to marital culture are *endorsed* by Lawrence and Woolf simply because they are *represented*; Wolfe does discuss how each text evokes and contains queer or non-normative formulations of intimacy, but the shadow of these possibilities—sacrificed in

Women in Love, submerged into the past in *Mrs. Dalloway*—can be said to affect more significantly the relative peacefulness of each novel's compromise with conjugality. Nevertheless, Wolfe gives us much to respond to in his presentation of each novelist's consideration of the possibilities of intimacy, particularly in his exploration of the Dalloway marriage. The novel tempts us to pit Clarissa's ardent, sometimes tormented longings for Sally and Peter against the more contained and continuous satisfactions and dissatisfactions of her marriage to Richard. Wolfe importantly attests to the salutary benefits of the latter, which can easily be underplayed in critical accounts; he sees how the novel can exhibit a "prayerful gratitude" for the marital relationship that helps Clarissa maintain "her individual integrity, her grace, her material well-being," even as it registers the loss of alternative possibilities that feel equally essential to Clarissa's sense of self. Wolfe also highlights the largely unspoken nature of intimacy in the novel, noticeable as much in Clarissa's memory of her non-normative relationships as it is in her relationship with Richard. The inarticulateness of Woolf's characters on the subject of love, he argues eloquently, "implicitly chastens readers who would formulate definite distinctions between the characters' true, and their misguided, affections." Such nuanced insights about textual dynamics, along with Wolfe's deft interweaving of relevant historical, biographical, and sociological information, make this a worthwhile study for anyone interested in Bloomsbury's relationship to the transforming culture of intimacy.

—Erwin Rosinberg, *Emory University*

Contradictory Woolf: Selected Papers from the Twenty-First Annual International Conference of Virginia Woolf. Ed. Derek Ryan and Stella Bolaki (Clemson: Clemson U Digital P, 2012) iv + 310 pp.

In June of 2011, the Woolf community of scholars, creative writers, artists, dancers, and common readers gathered together at the University of Glasgow, Scotland for the annual conference, tantalizingly titled "Contradictory Woolf." But why? Why "contradictory"? Why Scotland? In her preface to *Contradictory Woolf*, conference organizer Jane Goldman asks similar questions, playing with the idea of contradiction in orienting readers to the magnificent versatility of the word "but" by beginning with the name of the central conference space, none other than "Bute Hall." It was within this room that conference participants listened to the plenary talks (and enjoyed one pageant play) offered by Judith Allen, Michael Whitworth, Marina Warner, and Suzanne Bellamy on the various if, ands, and buts that abound in Woolf's work and life, each distinctive presentation shifting the mood of the room. Readers of the collection will find the keynotes to be as varied and contradictory in tone as Goldman promises they were in life.

Contradictory Woolf as a volume is expansive. In addition to Goldman's preface and an introduction by the editors, Derek Ryan and Stella Bolaki, there are thirty-seven essays, a content bonus of about thirty-three percent more than past years' volumes of *Selected Papers*. Therefore, this review will attempt to point out a handful of highlights from the tome rather than exhaustively cover everything. As is evident by the varied work presented in the collection, Woolf studies as a practice continues to venture into new theoretical territories, offer up new methodologies in research and pedagogy, and reinvigorate older and longstanding debates. Michael Whitworth's plenary talk, "Woolf, Context, and Contradiction," especially brings the pull of the past and the push of the future into lovely, albeit contradictory, relief as he explores the implications of accepting newly annotated editions of well-worn texts into one's own teaching and research. Newly annotated editions, he argues, offer us the thrill of fresh contextual knowledge and, simultaneously, the embarrassment of having not already noticed particular allusions or historical markers as we dip into these resources (11). As he is currently annotating the Cambridge Edition of *Night and Day* (1919), Whitworth actively questions the contradictions inherent in being both an annotator/editor and a contextualizing critic, especially in terms of political, historical, and cultural readings of Woolf's work. It is his desire that the annotator provide *too much* information about locations and allusions within a novel such as *Mrs. Dalloway* (1925) so that readers far into the future will have enough context about interwar London to be able to imagine it as Clarissa experiences it. Whitworth's paper compels—no—implicitly demands us as scholars to maintain the connection between text and context within our own work and our teaching.

Suzanne Bellamy's keynote presentation put text and context into action in the form of a pageant play. One wishes the *Selected Papers* came with a bonus DVD or even a YouTube link to a video of what transpired as Bellamy, Krystyna Colburn, Gill Lowe, Jane Goldman, Jean Moorcroft Wilson, Cecil Woolf, Mark Hussey, Derek Ryan, Diane Gillespie, Leslie Hankins, Janet Winston, Judith Allen, Kathryn Simpson, and Robbie Goldman took to the stage in what appears to have been a great clamor of animal sounds and a good deal of improvisational acting. Readers will have to be content with the transcription that admittedly had the power to make this reviewer laugh out loud in a very quiet commuter train car.

While Bellamy's piece is a big, loud delight, there are quieter and surprising treats and gems interspersed throughout the book. Diane Gillespie's "'Please Help Me!' Virginia Woolf, Viola Tree, and the Hogarth Press" delves into the intricacies of class and snobbery by exploring the professional relationship between Woolf and Tree through Hogarth's publication of two of her manuscripts. Through her reading of Tree's book of manners *Can I Help You?* (1937), Gillespie draws productive comparisons to Woolf's own advice book, *Three Guineas* (1938), forging a contradictory, yet compassionate link between the somewhat gaudy stage actress and Woolf to reexamine the implications of snobbery and vulgarity. Gillespie includes lovely images from Tree's book illustrated by Virginia Parsons. Madelyn Detloff's "'Am I a Snob?'" follows and complements Gillespie's by deepening the discussion about Woolf's rather "irritating" class bias by offering a theoretical frame through which to understand the "pedagogy of disgust" that appears in myriad ways throughout Woolf's writing about class and access while she simultaneously distances herself from working class women (183-4). Kathryn Simpson's essay "'Come Buy, Come Buy': Woolf's Contradictory Relationship to the Marketplace" rounds out this cluster of essays on elitism by teasing out the complicated position in which Woolf found herself in the 1930s by being at "the peak of her fame but increasingly critical of the commercial world" with a reading of both the text of the short story "The Duchess and the Jeweller" and its position in the literary marketplace (186).

While there are many strong pieces throughout the book, the following are especially notable. The collection includes a selection of fascinating pieces on *Orlando* (1928): Leslie Kathleen Hankins' essay on Woolf's reception of travel film and its influence on the spectacular imagery of the novel, Rebecca DeWald's recasting of a fiery debate about Jorge Luis Borges' 1937 translation, and Katharine Swarbrick's Lacanian exploration of Orlando's *jouissance*. In their radically diverse approaches to the novel, these three essays provide a fine example of the interdisciplinarity possible in working with Woolf's texts and would have been well-suited to be clustered together in the book. Sowon S. Park's strong frame for a phenomenological reading of *Mrs. Dalloway* (1925) is useful to anyone working on bodies and the senses in Woolf's work. Additionally, Amanda Golden's piece on annotating and marginalia in which she explores Woolf's complicated relationship to and attitude about academia pairs productively (and beautifully) with Whitworth's plenary talk. Finally, not to be missed is Cecil Woolf's "Duncan Grant," reflections on his relationship with Grant given at the conference banquet. In the piece, Cecil Woolf remembers bumping into Grant "whose face was crowded with experience" in Piccadilly sometime in 1978 and being unable to resist remarking on the length of Grant's hair (293). In true form to Grant's memorable sense of humor, he says, "Yes, my barber has died, you see" (293). I am sure this elicited a laugh throughout the audience. Cecil Woolf's toast to Bloomsbury's "sole Scotsman" is a touching way to round out an impressive collection of creative and scholarly contributions to our ways of thinking and rethinking about Woolf's life, work, influence, and company. overt sense of thematic undergirding leaves the reader with the task of making connections among the essays rather than being guided by a structure determined by the editors. Those who did not attend the conference and are reading the volume in hopes of finding a narrative within the scholarship of the weekend's proceedings will need to invent their own own organizational signposts. BUT, in the spirit of contradiction, overall, I believe the breadth and scope of the work offered in this volume indicates that a healthy scholarly discourse continues to flourish within Virginia Woolf studies.

—Sarah E. Cornish, *Fordham University*

A Sense of Shock: The Impact of Impressionism on Modern British and Irish Writing. Adam Parkes (Oxford: Oxford UP, 2011) xviii + 284 pp.

At the Violet Hour: Modernism and Violence in England and Ireland. Sarah Cole (Oxford: Oxford UP, 2012) xiv + 377pp.

Violence pervades late-nineteenth and early-twentieth century Europe, so much so that we would be hard-pressed to find an arena of political or aesthetic life unmarked by its presence. In its horrifying material forms, anarchist bombings stunned people in metropolitan capitals, imperial violence scarred colonial subjects, and mass warfare took lives at the front and in civilian bombings during the Spanish Civil War and two World Wars. Critics have long seen the connection between these historical events and writing explicitly about war, or in selected avant-garde literary movements—like Vorticism and Futurism—that placed rhetorical violence at the center of their calls to BLAST cultural enemies or to find in art beautiful ideas which kill. But a far broader range of literature in the period attempted to come to terms with a culture defined through shock, trauma, and violence; this literature imagined the ways private life and aesthetic form engage with violence. Sarah Cole's *At the Violet Hour: Modernism and Violence in England and Ireland* and Adam Parkes's *A Sense of Shock: The Impact of Impressionism on Modern British and Irish Writing*—both virtuosic in their scope and in their close readings—trace the pervasiveness of violence and shock in the period. They frame their inquiries differently: Cole uses violence as a thematic frame for reading literary forms and Parkes takes a particular literary form, impressionism, as the context within which the shocks of perception register. But in doing so both explore the way form enacts, contains, and ultimately theorizes the relation between literature and violence.

Cole's *At the Violet Hour* asks how modernism imagines the capacities of literary form in direct response to the violence of its historical moment. Shadowed in large part by the presence in our own time of what Cole evocatively terms disenchanted violence—those dead or injured bodies that remain flesh, refusing symbolic or redemptive meaning—*At the Violet Hour* investigates the ways modernist forms can render death and violence meaningful or refuse to do so. In contrast, Parkes seeks the figure of violence within a more consistently aesthetic history. He traces the way fictional and visual impressionism embedded the impact of the outer world and the traumas of the psyche in a model of subjectivity as ruptured and dissolving. Both books read across different disciplines of writing, from revolutionary tracts to art criticism to poetry, seeing violence as a problem of aesthetic form as well as bombs.

Cole's magisterial study takes "violence in modernism [to be] so deeply embedded as to function almost as the literary itself" (26). She examines the work of a wide spectrum of writers and expands our sense of the links between modernism and violence well beyond those figures best known to have glamorized violence. Violence here is not only a historical force that modernist literature encounters; it also charges literary figuration so fully as to become entangled with symbolic potency and the possibility of meaning-making itself. *At the Violet Hour* uses a key scene from Joyce's *Portrait of the Artist as a Young Man* as a paradigm of the way modernism suggests violence allows literature to look inward at the private and bodily as well as expand outward toward the representative or allegorical. Cole analyzes the moment where the prefect of studies pandies young Stephen Dedalus, and shows how this scene not only offers an imaginary origin of language—Stephen's elemental cry—that moves outward into obtrusive literary patterning, but prefigures the way violence lets texts point simultaneously inward toward the body, "forc[ing] the imagination back to the moment of injury," and outward toward the symbolic and abstract, into an allegory of hierarchical power (10).

The heart of Cole's argument lies in another double movement: an ongoing tension in modernism between what she terms enchanted and disenchanted violence. Enchanted violence responds to the threat of what Max Weber termed a secular, disenchanted world by imagining that violence—as war, blood, or sacrifice—could be generative, prompting growth and redemption, and yielding spiritual plenitude. Disenchanted violence, in contrast, refuses to idealize the effects of pain or bodily suffering, strips symbolism from the violated body, and insists that this body repudiates systems of meaning that would recruit it. Cole's prolific, subtle readings show how closely entangled these two visions are, how even in the most hyperbolic versions of enchanted, transformative suffering, metaphors such as blood return us to a body never fully subsumed into symbol. Provocatively, she disentangles these accounts of violence from the political causes that appropriate them, the better to articulate the way individual aesthetic and political causes recruit violence to their ends. Drawing on this opposition between the enchanted and the disenchanted, she attends to the different patterns modernism uses to address violence, to aesthetically contain or pattern it, and to reflexively meditate on the effects of literature's patterning power.

Cole organizes the body of her text around three distinct historical periods in which modernism engaged with violence, each figuratively distinct, reading across literary, theoretical, and political texts. The first moment she discusses follows upon the invention of dynamite in the mid-nineteenth century, which led to a form of violence—the dynamite blast—that was embraced by anarchists and haunted the European cultural imaginary. Dynamite raised questions about meaning that fascinated both anarchists and novelists alike, visible in particular in Conrad's *The Secret Agent* and James's *The Princess Casamassima*. Both anarchists and novelists were compelled by the idea that a bomb blast might endow action with meaning, even as such violent blasts superseded any political meaning that might be attached to them. In her second example, Cole turns her attention to the tradition of writing leading up to and following from the Irish Rising of 1916, a movement best known for its commitment to enchanted figures of Christian sacrifice and national martyrdom. She reads across a trajectory of Irish writing about national community and revolution, weaving in and out of Yeats's poetry and plays, and tracing shifts between moments that fantasize generative violence and those that see instead only a cyclical pattern of reprisal. Finally, in her most extended section, she reads Virginia Woolf as a central theorist of violence in the 1930s. Analyzing the range of Woolf's novels, from *The Voyage Out* through *Between the Acts*, with *Three Guineas* as a recurring central text across the entire book, Cole sees Woolf's writing self-consciously absorbing violence into various formal, narrative terms: as interruption, bracketing off, repetition, or circularity. Woolf's narrative experiments thus both contain the violence she sees in the world and meditate on the implications of narrative as they do so.

A Sense of Shock charts a less material, but no less pervasive sense of rupture and dissolution in modernism by focusing on impressionist accounts of perception, which writers understood as a shock to the cohesive self. Parkes addresses the same historical span as Cole; however, he frames his account through the trajectory of literary (and to a lesser degree visual) impressionism, branching out from this core to a series of varied historical contexts that inform these works. *A Sense of Shock* begins with Ruskin's famous 1877 charge that Whistler's impressionist painting impudently flung "a pot of paint in the public's face"; the book ends with Ford Madox Ford's late writing of the 1930s, which dissolves its protagonists into types of their time (the Great Depression) so thoroughly as to make the category of the subject unrecognizable (qtd. in Parkes 21). In the course of this narrative—and through meticulous textual analysis—Parkes moves across a cluster of convergences between impressionism and other historical problematics in the period: addressing nationalism and cosmopolitanism in George Moore, anarchism and the press in Conrad, and the relation of external shock, internal trauma, and post-impressionism in Woolf's *Jacob's Room* and *Roger Fry*. As this range suggests, Parkes understands impressionism in capacious terms, which are well suited to his topic. For as he cogently analyzes, in one of the most interesting sections of the book, impressionism was often criticized at the time for a provocative messiness or vagueness; indeed, its practitioners often used such uncertainties for entwined political and aesthetic ends.

The central dynamic explored in *A Sense of Shock* is the way impressionism understands that the subject's inwardness has the potential to become mere outward-facing pose. Parkes introduces this dynamic through an engaging, compressed analysis of Jean Rhys's *Quartet*—an autobiographical novel that takes Rhys's former lover, the impressionist novelist Ford Madox Ford, as the basis for one of its characters. *Quartet*'s irony emerges as the Ford character's impressionist bafflement is revealed as a social and sexual strategy, a "discourse of self-presentation, or social surface" (4). This pattern—of inwardness that verges on publicity—emerges evocatively in the chapter on "Pater's Disciples," as writers influenced by Pater (Moore, Wilde, and Symons) offered competing public images of their intimacy with him, redefining both Pater and influence around the scandal of Wilde's trial and sexuality. For Parkes, much like Cole in reading Joyce, this turn both inward and outward leads to a critical methodology, as impressionism requires that its readers engage with historical problems as much as narrative strategies. The political and material resonances of shock enter the book most fully with its chapter on Conrad. Parkes, like Cole, focuses on *The Secret Agent*, where his interest in perception allows him to analyze the text's concern with the effect of shock on the person perceiving violent acts. This focus provides a good complement to Cole's attention to the body, and uses the problem of perception as a way to open up the novel's concern with narrative mediation—with the way both newspapers and novels filter and publicize violence.

Both *At the Violet Hour* and *A Sense of Shock* are expansive, ambitious books and scholars of modernism will appreciate their nuanced analysis of how literary forms engage with and even produce violent effects. This expansiveness can also pose a challenge to both books' cohesion and this difficulty emerges in particular in their readings of Woolf. Woolf is especially important for *At the Violet Hour*, where she occupies a welcome, justified place alongside other theorists of violence in the twentieth century. Cole's chapter does a particularly good job of placing Woolf among a cluster of writers in the 1930s and 1940s, including Sigmund Freud and Simone Weil, debating whether human aggression is innate. In this context Cole resonantly analyzes Woolf's interest in how narration itself may produce aggressive forms of disruption, although the distinction between violence and power, so useful in readings of the Irish Rising or Conrad, seems to fade here, perhaps appropriately, given Woolf's intense concern with power. The chapter has a wide scope, discussing the relation of violence to narrative form in all of Woolf's novels. While each reading is compelling, Woolf's accounts of violence shift often enough to require a somewhat laborious system of categories to integrate them. Parkes, too, writes well about Woolf, discussing *Jacob's Room* and *Roger Fry* as texts that dissolve their subjects and stage Woolf's engagement with Fry over the aesthetic principles of post-impressionism. The ambitious attempt to join these debates with categories of external shock and psychic trauma, however, leads to a schematic division between the forms of violence those categories might imply, where this intelligent book's own account of impressionism might suggest they intertwine more thoroughly. Such limitations are perhaps the inevitable result in studies whose rich readings offer insights that exceed easy categorization, and open new discussions about the relation between violence and the work of aesthetic form.

Virginia Woolf and the Literary Marketplace. Jeanne Dubino, ed. (New York: Palgrave Macmillan, 2010) xv + 263pp.

Jeanne Dubino's collection *Virginia Woolf and the Literary Marketplace* introduces readers to a wealth of resources examining Woolf's engagement with print culture. The volume's contributions reflect just how many dimensions there are to the literary marketplace and complicate existing conversations regarding publication history, composition practices, marketing, and modernism. Progressing from local to global contexts, the collection's four segments clearly organize a wide range of approaches to the development and reception of Woolf's *oeuvre*.

The opening section, "Woolf's Engagement with the Marketplace," investigates her reading, editing, and publication strategies. Beth Rigel Daugherty's "Reading, Taking Notes, and Writing: Virginia Stephen's Reviewing Practice" opens the segment with Woolf's apprenticeship as a book reviewer. Elizabeth Dickens in "Circulating Ideas and Selling Periodicals: Leonard Woolf, the *Nation and Athenaeum,* and Topical Debate," turns to the contexts shaping Virginia Woolf's work as she analyzes the publication's "Religious Belief Questionnaire." Vara Neverow examines Woolf's early response to contemporary audiences in "Woolf's Editorial Self-Censorship and Risk-Taking in *Jacob's Room*" (57). Considering her revisions of the novel, Neverow argues that Woolf "weighs every word and concocts an elaborate maze of coded and cross-referenced allusions" (68). Examining

Woolf's reading and other contexts informing her writing, in the final contribution to this section, Jeanette McVicker interprets "several moments in Woolf's lifelong engagement with the Greeks as crucial to her struggle to represent an ontological reality that would finally include truthful representations of women's material experiences, including her own" (74).

Woolf's rivalries with her female contemporaries and critiques of her predecessors provide the subject of the volume's second section, "Woolf's Relationship to the Marketplace." Katie Macnamara presents a lively account of the competition that fueled Woolf and Katherine Mansfield's fiction in "How *to* Strike a Contemporary: Woolf, Mansfield, and Marketing Gossip." As Macnamara argues, "Woolf understood that readerly curiosity about the lives of authors would continue to encourage textual circulation more than formal criticism ever could" (92). Heather Bean subsequently addresses the evolution of Woolf's response to the Brontës from her early piece "Haworth, November, 1904" to her later critique in *A Room of One's Own* (1929). In the final contribution to this section, "Virginia Woolf and Gertrude Stein: Commerce, Bestsellers, and the Jew," Karen Leick considers Woolf's response to Jews in such novels as *The Years* (1937) in which Leick observes that "the presence of Jews not only reveals, but also causes or is a catalyst for the new and changing marketplace that England has become" (128).

The third section, "Woolf's Marketplaces," turns to issues that have been at stake in the new modernist studies. Caroline Pollentier addresses Woolf's publication of "occasional, non-review essays" in "Virginia Woolf and the Middlebrow Market of the Familiar Essay" (138). In "Woolf Studies and Periodical Studies," Patrick Collier assesses the different foci of single author studies and "periodical studies," resolving that his essay "is more concerned with what Woolf can tell us about periodicals than what periodicals can tell us about Woolf; it advocates—and takes steps toward practicing—a scholarship in which we allow the periodical to upstage Woolf" (151, 153-4). The final two contributions in this segment address *A Room of One's Own* (1929). Melissa Sullivan argues that by publishing part of the essay in *Time and Tide*, Woolf "situated her work in a literary community of high and middlebrow women writers" and attracted a large audience (168). John K. Young, in "'Murdering an Aunt or Two': Textual Practice and Narrative Form in Virginia Woolf's Metropolitan Market," argues that *A Room of One's Own* reflects Woolf's "signaling [of] her own inevitable implication in the colonialist system by masking Hogarth's commercial success" (183).

The collection's final segment, "Marketing Woolf," examines Woolf's publication and reception history, particularly in international contexts. The first two contributions address Woolf's publication in Fascist Italy. Elisa Bolchi, in "The 'Grand Lady of Literature': Virginia Woolf in Italy under Fascism," begins in 1929 when Woolf's gave the rights to translate *To the Lighthouse* to Fratelli Treves, who did not ultimately translate it, and the subsequent Italian translations of Woolf's novels that followed (199-200). In "Translating *Orlando* in 1930s Fascist Italy: Virginia Woolf, Arnoldo Mondadori, and Alessandra Scalero," Sara Villa then analyzes the editing of *Orlando* as a case study. Villa observes that "[t]he first edition of *Orlando* in Italian is not only a key example of a masterful translation which managed to elude the censorship office, but is still one of the most faithful and accomplished Italian translations of all of Woolf's texts" (219). At roughly the same time, in "Appropriating Virginia Woolf for the New Humanism: Seward Collins and *The Bookman* 1927-1933," Yuzu Uchida addresses the ways that *"The Bookman*, a journal that promoted New Humanism, a philosophical movement endeavoring to return American society to certain humanistic values, used Woolf's works and name for this purpose" (223). In the collection's final essay, "Don't Judge a Cover by Its Woolf: Book Cover Images and the Marketing of Virginia Woolf's Work," Jennie-Rebecca Falcetta analyzes twentieth and twenty-first century Woolf covers, including a reader's cover image for *The Waves* envisioning six faces with different emotional responses as part of a "My Penguin" series in 2006 (248). Following Falcetta's example, future scholars could investigate Woolf's contemporary global web presence and the marketing of digital and print editions of her fiction.

Virginia Woolf and the Literary Marketplace provides a rich overview of the complexity of Woolf's publication history. The volume leaves readers with many new topics for future inquiry, including the role of the marketplace in the translation of Woolf's fiction in other countries, during her lifetime and after.

—Amanda Golden, *Georgia Institute of Technology*

Modernism and the New Spain: Britain, Cosmopolitan Europe, and Literary History. Gayle Rogers (New York and Oxford: Oxford UP, 2012) xvii + 283pp.

In 1929, when T.S. Eliot went looking for a way to bolster co-operation and "a community of interest" in Europe among post-war writers, thinkers and critics, one of the primary journals he chose for collaboration was the *Revista de Occidente*, edited in Spain by José Ortega y Gasset. Along with the *Nouvelle Revue Française* (France), the *Nuova Antologia* (Italy), and the *Europäische Revue* (Germany), Eliot's *Criterion* and Ortega's *Revista de Occidente* would offer a prize for a piece of short fiction that would be translated and published in several periodicals across Europe at the same time. The winning work would have to exhibit both local and international sensibilities. In the words of Ortega, it must be both "deeply rooted in the author's native land" and "have a European scope" (29). That Ortega and the *Revista* shared Eliot's vision about this project and became important partners in the quest to create a cosmopolitan literary Europe might come as a surprise to many English language readers, to whom the Revista is hardly a household name. Spanish writing in the early years of the twentieth century is too little known in its own right and too little acknowledged for its contributions to European modernism.

But as Gayle Rogers points out in his meticulously researched and fluent book, *Modernism and the New Spain: Britain, Cosmopolitan Europe, and Literary History*, Ortega and the *Revista* were at the center of an important and influential literary movement in interwar Spain, which helped nurture a cadre of important Spanish writers and circulate their work to Paris and London. These writers in the Ortega circle participated in a profound and wide-reaching aesthetic and critical conversation across Europe, and were significant, Rogers argues, in the development of English writing in the twenties and thirties. Critics, such as Antonio Marichalar whose 1924 essay "James Joyce in his Labyrinth" helped bring Joyce to Spanish readers (and is included in this volume), also wrote for Eliot's *Criterion*, helping to forge the links between Spain and England. They also helped create Ortega and the interwar Spanish vanguard writers as crucial interlocutors in the discussion about European culture and cosmopolitanism in England in the interwar years.

Rogers makes a strong case for the importance of Spain in the intellectual consciousness at mid-century. His chapter on the ties between the *Revista* and the *Criterion* make clear that the *Revista*'s version of vanguard writing was imagined in the context of a deep commitment to cosmopolitanism. Marichalar in particular served a role something like that famously played by Valery Larbaud in France, promoting and publishing in Spain "the first commentaries on most every figure of Anglophone modernism" and translating "Joyce, Strachey, Woolf and Faulkner into Spanish" (23). At the same time, Rogers argues that Spain begins to function as a productive site for reflection on Europe and on cosmopolitanism more generally. From Molly's Spanish roots in Joyce's *Ulysses* to Auden's "Spain," and—of course—Woof's concern with the Spanish Civil War in *Three Guineas*, the country figures as a point of reference, counterpoint and engagement for a generation of English writers.

Rogers begins with a fascinating chapter on Ortega's *Revista*, opening up a picture for English readers of the range of vanguard writing that was published in the journal between 1923 and 1936 when Ortega went into exile. Committed to a philosophy of cultural and political cosmopolitanism, Ortega consciously sought to join literary conversations across Europe and to bring innovative techniques and critical concepts to Spain. As Rogers claims, "British writers came to hold a privileged position as like-minded voices of the new cosmopolitanism that the journal articulated . . . the *Revista* soon became the first journal to publish in

Spanish works by Joyce, Virginia Woolf, and Lytton Strachey" and by 1936 it had also published essays on Eliot, G. B. Shaw, Aldous Huxley, as well as Katherine Mansfield, Eugene O'Neill, William Faulkner, Hart Crane, Langston Hughes and Jean Toomer (48). Though the politics of this cosmopolitan vision become more complex and more fraught for both Eliot and Ortega in the thirties, the significance of the journal and its engagement with Anglophone modernism is clear.

The chapter on "Joyce and the Spanish *Ulysses*" also focuses on a kind of reciprocity—that between the "Spain" in *Ulysses* and *Ulysses* in Spain. Joyce deploys Molly's past on the contested island of Gibraltar as an engagement with images and stereotypes of hispanicity as well as an encounter with Spain's modern history. In this guise as Rogers claims, the "collapse of Spain's empire functions functions as an analogue for the well-known critiques of British imperialism and Anglo-Irish politics that he articulates through his characters" (72).

In the following chapter, Rogers traces the influence of Lytton Strachey's Eminent Victorians and the "new biography" more generally, on the interwar writers who created a corresponding "nueva biografía" in Spain between 1928 and 1936. In this period "an array of Spanish writers produced biographies of figures ranging from a controversial nun, a famous boxer, and a famous robber; to Goya, Cervantes, and Isabella II" (97). By connecting these biographies, and particularly Marichalar's 1930 biography of the Duke of Osuna to Strachey's Eminent Victorians, Rogers is able to show how the "common hypocrisies of the British and Spanish states in the nineteenth century. . . provide [a] common text," calling for use of "irony, satire, comedy and impressionistic speculation" in the writing of historic lives (97). Though Rogers mentions Woolf's interest in renewing biography, and that of other British writers of this genre, this chapter might have held more interest, particularly for readers of Woolf, if it had ventured farther into that wider canon, rather than focusing primarily on close intertextual readings of Strachey and Marichalar.

However, the chapter entitled "Virginia Woolf and the Spanish Civil War: *Three Guineas*, Victoria Ocampo and International Feminism," offers a compelling new vantage point on Woolf's engagement with Spain and ought to become required reading for contemporary Woolf scholars. Rogers ties the analysis of Woolf's *Three Guineas* photographs, and the cosmopolitan vision she develops in the book not only to her sustained encounter with Spain, manifest in her Spanish travels (in 1905, 1912 and 1923), her early writings, such as "An Andalusian Inn," and her essay "To Spain," but also to her ongoing dialogue with the Argentine writer, intellectual and feminist, Victoria Ocampo, who translated and published Woolf's work. Ocampo's tireless efforts in the Argentine literary journal *Sur* (South 1931-1966), Rogers argues, pick up the threads sewn by the

Revista de Occidente. "The war displaced the *Revista de Occidente*'s circulation of British modernism into the hands of Ocampo . . . it endangered women's social gains under the second Republic; it created acrimonious political divisions among British writers; and, by Woolf's account, it exposed both the tyranny at the heart of English masculine society and the danger of foreign attacks on English liberal democracy. . . Ocampo's work in particular demonstrates that the cosmopolitan feminist community that Woolf articulates in *Three Guineas* as necessary to fight tyrannies was being animated throughout the 1930s by a sympathetic foreign colleague"(127). Ocampo sought out Woolf in 1934 when she traveled to London, and wrote an appreciative open "Letter to Virginia Woolf" (published in the *Revista de Occidente*). She was particularly drawn to Woolf's arguments in *A Room of One's Own*, placing herself in the line of descent from Shakespeare's sister in a letter she wrote to Woolf after their meeting. Though it is clear that their ongoing correspondence in the thirties was driven more by Ocampo than by Woolf, Rogers argues that Ocampo became an important interlocutor during the development of *Three Guineas* (142).

This tracing of the international connection to Ocampo's feminist literary work enriches Rogers's account of *Three Guineas* itself. He traces Woolf's engagement with the war in Spain, from attending a relief rally for refugees, signing a telegram to Chamberlain deploring his rapprochement with Mussolini, and helping to sponsor a showing of Guernica. He also shows the importance of Julian Bell's political engagement and death in Spain, pointing out that Bell is likely her addressee in much of *Three Guineas* and that she "uses the photographs [of ruined houses and dead bodies] to rhetorically position her addressee and her reader, next to her" (154). Rogers's reading, especially in the context of his broader argument, makes the Spanish and international situation of Woolf's powerful essay become far more complex than is usually described. One only wishes he had spent more time weaving this reading through a detailed encounter with Woolf's text.

Finally, the book reaches its close in a chapter exploring the role of Spanish writers, especially Federico García Lorca, in England in the 1930's and a Coda that treats the memoirs of the philosopher María Zambrano, whose lifetime and career touch on all the manifestations of Spain Rogers assembles in this capacious book. In pointing to the importance of translations of Spanish writers to Stephen Spender and other British writers in the 1930s, especially those collected in the 1939 Hogarth Press volume, *Poems for Spain*, Rogers claims, "to translate Lorca is to promulgate a reading of 'Spain,' and thus of Britain's relationship to both. . . [and] raises the questions . . . Who speaks for Spain and why? What is the relationship between poetry and modern war? The answers to these questions posited by the figures in this [book] represent a convergence of the modernist movements of Britain and Spain that culminated at a moment when Spain became the object of much of Europe's consciousness" (165). For these reasons along with its rich reading of Britain's encounter with Spain in the interwar years, *Modernism and the New Spain* is a fascinating and important new entry in modernist studies.

—Jessica Berman, *University of Maryland Baltimore County*

Charleston and Monk's House: The Intimate House Museums of Virginia Woolf and Vanessa Bell. Nuala Hancock (Edinburgh: Edinburgh UP, 2012) 226 pp

Virginia and Leonard Woolf knew they had taken on a challenge when they purchased Monk's House, in the Sussex village of Lewes, in a 1919 auction. Assessing the state of its facilities in her diary, Virginia Woolf wrote: "The kitchen is distinctly bad. Theres an oil stove, & no grate. Nor is there hot water, nor a bath, & and as for the E. C. I was never shown it" (*D*1 286).

Despite her cynicism, she was in love with the house, and remained so for the next twenty years; in her own words, "[E]very part of the day here has its merits – even the breakfast without toast" (*D*2 3). As a painter rather than a writer, Vanessa Bell may have waxed somewhat less eloquently about her attachment to her own nearby Sussex home, Charleston, but she showed her devotion exuberantly enough with her paintbrush, working alongside her companion Duncan Grant to festoon almost every surface in the house with gay colored patterns.

Both Monk's House and Charleston are today what Nuala Hancock calls "house museums," preserved, open to the public and drawing thousands of admirers every year. They are significant literary and artistic shrines, and provide a great deal of critical fodder. Hancock's own project in her book about these two houses was, she tells us, to develop "a different way of knowing Virginia Woolf and Vanessa Bell, through a sensory immersion in the intimate interiors of their former inhabitations" (11).

This book, then, does not pursue a number of lines of inquiry that one might expect in a work about Monk's House and Charleston. It does not provide any history of these two homes, both of which had stood for many years by the time they fell into the hands of the Stephen sisters. Nor does it tell the story of the houses during the time they were occupied by members of Bloomsbury, despite the numerous alterations and decorative schemes set in motion during their residence and the central importance of architecture, design, and interiority to both Virginia Woolf and Vanessa Bell's overall body of work. Finally, the book does not seek to catalogue or describe the houses in any systematic way; we do not learn how many bedrooms or water-closets each house held, how their out-buildings or gardens were planned, or even how the individual rooms of the houses were inhabited and used.

What Hancock does instead is to mount an investigation that takes as its guiding light Gaston Bachelard's magisterial 1958 work, *The Poetics of Space*. Bachelard's phenomenological approach to space examines how intimate spaces become invested with meaning that is bodied forth in poetry. Bachelard represents space as archetypal; following Carl Jung, he thinks about how we cathect to spaces like the home or the shell and in so doing create universal metaphors of attachment and belonging. Hancock is inspired by Bachelard, but her work is necessarily of a different order, dedicated as she is to two very particular spaces rather than to space as a universal domain of experience. Hancock's writing explores the hardy analogy between the house and the human body, a comparison in a Bachelardian vein, with its transhistorical cast and poetic potential. For Hancock, however, this analogy is localized and grounded in her own phenomenological encounter with Charleston and Monk's House. She takes the houses as an opportunity to reconstruct the interior worlds of their occupants, imagining Bell layering paint on the walls and Woolf's relying on Monk's House for a "second skin" to sheathe her own fragile embodiment.

Like Bachelard, Hancock writes in a style that is suggestive and questioning, seeking to explore rather than to deliver what Woolf in *A Room of One's Own* called "nuggets of pure truth." The feelings that come over us when we visit the house museum of a great artist or writer is chilly and ineffable, and it is Hancock's ambition to try and make sense of that encounter. More than anything, Hancock seems to want to look through the houses in order to connect back to their inhabitants and she grasps for traces as she wanders through the rooms, chasing ghosts and savoring the residual aura of the lives lived in Charleston and Monk's House.

She establishes a foundation for her work by showing how the creative output of both Woolf and Bell provides a basis for reading their respective biographies through their homes. The second chapter pursues the root claim of the book, that "the house museum offers an embodied encounter with the intimate inhabitation of the other" (30), here through the vehicle of choreography, or what Hancock calls the "place ballet." She wants to argue that their patterns of movement, discernible through their works and through clues in the houses themselves, permit the critic to "recast Woolf's and Bell's biographies as lives lived through movement and gesture" (53). From the metaphor of dance Hancock moves in the following chapter to embodiment, and a memorial reconstruction of how Woolf and Bell's bodies became imprinted on the surfaces of their homes. This liberally illustrated central chapter—though the reproductions are all in black-and-white—captures something of the quotidian habits of living associated with these locations.

In the second half of the book, Hancock transfers her attention from the house to the gardens. Both Monk's House and Charleston had corresponding and characteristic outdoor spaces, the former with its expansive view of the Sussex Downs, writing shed for Virginia Woolf, and rows of plants carefully cultivated by Leonard Woolf, and the latter with its painterly effulgences of color, dramatic statuary, and Impressionist use of water.

Once having compassed the grounds, in the fifth chapter the author goes to the heart of the experience created by the artist's house museum, looking into the ability of the material artifact to evoke its owner. Hancock pursues three case studies of such artifacts—Virginia Woolf's spectacles, a painted cabinet from Vanessa Bell's bedroom, and a dressing table in a Charleston spare bedroom. Her extremely close readings of these objects are set pieces in themselves, aimed to close the gap between the critic and her subject and to wrest every drop of meaning from the artifactual encounter. Though these passages are at times overwritten, they are full of a poignant critical yearning. About the spectacles, for instance, Hancock describes her own process of examining them:

> Within this casket, the spectacles lie. Disrupting their repose, I lift them from the case, disinter them from their place of attachment. As they emerge, they bring with them a rush of time – a repressed accumulation of memory – the space around them suddenly unbounded – blowing out emanations of the past – interspersing with the present – flowing into now. The more vividly they present themselves, the more far-reaching their source appears to be. (130)

Hancock is examining a pair of glasses, but her words suggest she is also engaged in an exhumation of their late owner. What secrets can a pair of glasses yield? Woolf recalled rummaging in the cupboards at 22 Hyde Park Gate and receiving "a terrific whiff of the past." Now the whiff is coming off her own spectacles.

Despite the powerful desire to reanimate her subjects, Hancock turns in her final chapter to an analysis of the inevitable gap between the museal reconstruction of Monk's House and Charleston and the homes actually inhabited by Woolf and Bell. Objects have disappeared or decomposed, records are incomplete, the interpretations of the curators intervene. Hancock does not emphasize the point, but I would add that Monk's House and Charleston were also homes in a constant state of transition while Woolf and Bell inhabited them. What day, what moment in June does the curator choose to recapture? There is no correct choice. At Charleston, the trustees have faced this issue in part by keeping the site alive as a place for making art, breathing a new gust of creativity and change through the grounds.

As a book founded on a belief in the singularity of direct experience, it may be inevitable that *Charleston and Monk's* House concludes without claims that greatly exceed its original thesis, that these houses "offer a richly modulated pedagogic medium— cognitively engrossing, imaginatively extending, emotionally affecting, sensorily awakening—opening up biographical possibilities, other ways of knowing Woolf and Bell" (173). Hancock has a stylistic habit of posing a pair of rhetorical questions at the beginning of many of her paragraphs, lending the book a tone that is questioning rather than assertive. This can leave the reader feeling unsatisfied, wanting more clarity—but perhaps it is part of Hancock's project to emphasize the final unavailability of definitive answers in this arena. Her sensory engagement with the house museums is an intriguing method of proceeding and recalls Diana Fuss's work in *The Sense of an Interior: Four Rooms and the Writers that Shaped Them* (NY and London: Routledge, 2004).

The historian Carolyn Steedman has written at length about what she calls "the historian's massive transferential relationship to the past," a relationship that pushes the historian in her impossible quest to recover and reanimate a subject that is, in irreducible ways, lost to time (*Past Tenses* [London: Rivers Oram P, 1992], 201) Hancock is not precisely an historian, but she is certainly on a quest to draw closer to Woolf and Bell by attending closely to their houses. She has that "transferential relationship to the past," that quality of a writer who longs to close the gap between herself and the elusive historical object of her investigations. The house museum, as described by Hancock, is part of this valiant quest.

—Victoria Rosner, *Columbia University*

On Being Ill. Virginia Woolf. With *Notes from Sick Rooms* by Julia Stephen. Introductions by Hermione Lee and Mark Hussey. Afterword by Rita Charon (Ashfield, MA: Paris Press, 2012) xxxiv + 118 pp.

Ten years ago the small non-profit Paris Press issued a lovely edition of Woolf's then little-studied essay *On Being Ill*, with reproductions of Vanessa Bell's original cover art and an insightful introduction by her major biographer Hermione Lee. Paris Press has now issued a tenth-anniversary edition which supersedes that earlier publication: By including Julia Stephen's *Notes from Sick*

Rooms, this new edition makes it possible for the first time to read Woolf's essay in dialogue with her mother's, hence providing an unparalleled opportunity to move between two very different experiences of illness, that of sufferer/patient and that of caretaker/nurse. Lee's introduction is now joined by Mark Hussey's introduction to *Notes from Sick Rooms* and an afterword to the whole edition by Rita Charon, clinician and founder of Columbia University's Program in Narrative Medicine. These three pieces provide different but complementary contexts for the two essays: Lee locates *On Being Ill* in the specifics of Woolf's personal and professional life at the time of its writing and publication; Hussey furnishes biographical background for Julia Stephen and *Notes from Sick Rooms;* Charon usefully juxtaposes the essays as each representing one of the two poles of illness which together "propel the reader toward the clinically powerful stance of radical ignorance" (115). All in all, this new edition of Woolf's essay affords rich ore not only for Woolf scholars but for scholars in a number of fields—Victorian and Modernist Studies, the history of nursing, narrative medicine—to mine.

Lee describes *On Being Ill* as one of Woolf's "most daring, strange, and original essays" (xiii). First published in the *New Criterion* under T. S. Eliot's editorship in January 1926, a shortened and revised version (with a different title) appeared in the New York magazine *The Forum* several months later. Woolf revised the essay yet again in 1930 and published it as a Hogarth Press pamphlet in a limited and signed edition of 250 copies. This 1930 version is the version reprinted here, but while Lee's introduction details the types of changes Woolf made in the essay's successive outings, this edition does not indicate those changes, nor does it include deleted passages or revised wordings (that kind of annotation is available to scholars in Andrew McNeillie's comprehensive edition of Woolf's essays). Woolf's continuing efforts to revise and republish the essay speak to her sense of its importance, a belief apparently shared by Leonard Woolf, who republished the essay in two separate collections of Woolf's essays after her death. The essay gives voice to what Lee calls "one of the main stories of Virginia Woolf's life" (xiv), illness and its transformative effect upon the sensibilities of the sufferer; in it Woolf lays claim to illness as constituting rich "undiscovered countries" for the writer (3). Along with such texts as *A Room of One's Own*, "Modern Fiction," and "Professions for Women," *On Being Ill* is a manifesto that insists on the importance of a perspective that has been marginalized and ignored.

Why, Woolf wonders in the essay's convoluted opening line, is the experience of illness so absent in literature when it is so common in life and so cataclysmic in the alterations it imposes? Considering it "strange indeed that illness has not taken its place with love and battle and jealousy among the prime themes of literature" (3-4), Woolf proposes two reasons for this glaring neglect: first, a pervasive mind/body dualism subordinates the "daily drama of the body" to the "doings of the mind" (5); second, the English language is poor in the language of illness, forcing the sufferer "to coin words himself, and, taking his pain in one hand, and a lump of pure sound in the other...so to crush them together that a brand new word in the end drops out" (7). Woolf implicitly challenges the binary that privileges the healthy over the ill: the healthy, "soldiers in the army of the upright," have neither the courage nor the time to face what the ill, the "deserters" from normal routine, comprehend all too clearly in their enforced indolence and bodily suffering: "It is only the recumbent who know what, after all, Nature is at no pains to conceal—that she in the end will conquer" (12, 16). Similarly, the heightened sensibilities of the ill make their approach to language more immediate and sensual than that of the well: whereas the "upright" approach reading with a view to meaning, the "outlaw" ill access "a state of mind which neither words can express nor the reason explain" (21). "In health meaning has encroached upon sound. Our intelligence domineers over our senses," Woolf explains. "But in illness, with the police off duty, we creep beneath some obscure poem...some phrase...and the words give out their scent and distil their flavour, and then, if at last we grasp the meaning, it is all the richer for having come to us sensually first, by way of the palate and the nostrils, like some queer odour" (21-22). As if to demonstrate this facility, Woolf ends her essay with an extended synopsis of an obscure biographical account of two Victorian women, a seemingly random inclusion that comes abruptly to a close with a stunning image of human suffering: an observer returns to the room where the new widow had stood at the window to see the hearse depart, and there finds an indelible imprint of pain where "the curtain, heavy, mid-Victorian, plush perhaps, was all crushed together where she had grasped it in her agony" (28). This closing image underlines the essay's two main assertions, that the physical body rules and eventually overcomes the mind, and that to express that servitude requires "crushing together" language with suffering until "a brand new word drops out."

Woolf conceals the steely logic of her manifesto of illness with a strategy of indirection that distances the essay from its author even as it reproduces the strange brilliance she attributes to illness. The essay proceeds through a process of free association that Lee describes as "shape-changing" (xiii): it deals not only with illness, Lee explains, but with "language, religion, sympathy, solitude, and reading," and it does so by touching on a bewildering array of subjects, "dentists, American literature, electricity, an organ grinder and a giant tortoise, the cinema, the coming ice age, worms, snakes and mice, Chinese readers of Shakespeare, housemaids' brooms swimming down the River Solent, and the entire life-story of the third Marchioness of Waterford" (xiii). But Woolf's conviction that the ill possess a passport to new territories inaccessible to the healthy emerges crystal clear: "We do not know our own souls, let alone the souls of others," Woolf declares. "Human beings do not go hand in hand the whole stretch of the way. There is a virgin forest in each; a snowfield where even the print of birds' feet is unknown. Here we go alone, and like it better so. Always to have sympathy, always to be accompanied, always to be understood would be intolerable" (11-12). Whereas the healthy delude themselves with the illusion that human experience is a collective and shared endeavor, the ill know otherwise, understanding in the "barracks of pain and discipline" (9) what American suffragist Elizabeth Cady Stanton termed in strikingly similar wording "the immeasurable solitude of self."[1]

Woolf's insistence on the unknowability of this "snowfield of the mind" (15) marks the clearest point of divergence from her mother's perspective as nurse and caretaker of the ill in *Notes from Sick Rooms*. Julia Stephen's manual on nursing is, as Charon notes, "radically 'patient-centered,'" whereby "the patient's plight is fully and sensually imagined and privileged...The nurse has access to the patient's experience, and it is this access that directs care" (111). In many respects, however, as Hussey points out, the two essays share a surprising number of parallels. Like Woolf, Stephen calls attention to the overlooked centrality of the experience of illness, and echoing Woolf's call for more attention to the "daily drama of the body," she directs attention to the myriad minutiae that can torment the patient: the smell of a candle, the incorrect placement of a pillow, the too-rough touch on sensitive skin, the scourge of crumbs, which the assiduous nurse must stamp out of the sick bed "as if it were the Colorado beetle in a potato field" (57-58). The care with which Stephen details the proper management of changing sheets, opening windows, using bed pans, and preparing food all speak to a sensibility exquisitely attuned to the suffering body in the bed. Stephen's is an attitude of profound respect and humility toward that body, and, again like Woolf, she appreciates the way in which bodily suffering alters the workings of the mind. Cautioning against the too-easy dismissal of patients' "fancies," Stephen asserts that "the patient's fancies are not absurd" (77); illness means that patients "can detect a draught or a smell where even careful and discerning nurses can find neither. The nurse must...not deny that the evil exists....The nurse must remove these evils should they exist, and thoroughly investigate the evil real or imagined" (77). Further, Stephen appreciates the constraints which illness imposes upon language: "The mind moves slowly to expression in illness, and the feeling that the words are impatiently waited for takes away the power to utter them" (78).

---

[1] Woolf's wording echoes that of Elizabeth Cady Stanton's "Solitude of Self," her last address to the US Constitutional Committee of the Judiciary on January 13, 1892. While numerous passages resonate with Woolf's, I am most struck by the similarity of the following: "think for a moment of the immeasurable solitude of self. We come into the world alone, unlike all who have gone before us; we leave it alone under circumstances peculiar to ourselves...in the supreme moments of danger, alone woman must ever meet the horrors of the situation.

The most striking parallel is stylistic. As Hussey notes, "This agnostic woman of the second half of the nineteenth century's gentle mockery of learned men's inability to account for the origin of crumbs foreshadows her daughter's feminist comedy" (44-45).

Taken as a whole, this volume has much to offer not only readers of Woolf but Victorian and Modernist scholars more generally, as well as those interested in the fields of narrative medicine and the history of nursing and medical practice. Hussey ably summarizes the importance of Stephen's essay thus: "Because it lets us hear the voice of the mother who Woolf tells us 'obsessed' her until she wrote *To the Lighthouse*, *Notes from Sick Rooms* is…an enlightening text to read with *On Being Ill*, an important piece of nursing history, a guide for care givers today, and also a fascinating document in the biography of one of the twentieth century's greatest novelists" (46). Charon outlines the importance of reading the two essays in tandem, for while they "support radically opposed conceptions of illness… both are required by the effective clinician" (114). The clinician hopes to put the knowledge acquired by experience to use "so as to ease the suffering of the patient who comes next into our care," but must at the same time "adopt the stance of radical unknowingness": "As long as I don't assume *anything* about a person in my care, I may learn something that will help…The more radical my humility, the more I will learn, and the more I can help" (114-115). In tandem these two essays spell out the inseparability of body and psyche and the heroism and courage needed to face the body's inevitable triumph over consciousness. Strikingly, both end with the agony of those left to confront the now-senseless dead: Stephen details the tender and calm care the nurse must use to lay out the body in order to spare the mourners "a terrible picture which will haunt them long and destroy the memory of what they held most dear" (105). Woolf ends with the imprint of grief, a curtain crushed in a moment of agony, recalling her own memory of standing at the window the morning after her mother's death and watching Dr. Seton "walk away up the street with his head bent and his hands clasped behind his back," leaving her with "the feeling that everything had come to an end" (*MOB* 84) and thereby inaugurating her own lifelong struggle with "the art of being ill" (54). From that "snowfield of the mind" she has sent back her findings.

—Patricia Moran, *University of Limerick*

The Angel of Death even makes no royal pathway for her…In that solemn solitude of self, that links us with the immeasurable and the eternal, each soul lives alone forever…there is a solitude, which each and every one of us has always carried with him more inaccessible than the ice-cold mountains, more profound than the midnight sea; the solitude of self. Our inner being, which we call ourself, no eye nor touch of man or angel has ever pierced. It is more hidden than the caves of the gnome; the sacred adytum of the oracle; the hidden chamber of Eleusian mysteries."

Dying For Time: Proust, Woolf, And Nabokov. Martin Hägglund (Cambridge: Harvard UP, 2012) xi+ 197pp.

Martin Hägglund's revolutionary new text, *Dying for Time: Proust, Woolf, Nabokov*, concerns itself with challenging various readings of Marcel Proust's entire *À la recherche du temps perdu*, Virginia Woolf's *Mrs. Dalloway* and *To The Lighthouse*, and Vladimir Nabokov's *Ada or Ardor: A Family Chronicle*, as well as specific texts of Freud, Lacan, and Derrida. As Hägglund notes in his introduction, all the modernist novels on which he focuses have been regarded by critics as texts that seek to transcend time, while his project instead rests in providing a "*chronolibidinal*" approach (his term), whereby he attempts to prove that instead of transcendence of time, these texts reveal a desire to "survive" rather than "transcend." Hägglund, the Swedish literary scholar and philosopher and author of the highly regarded *Radical Atheism: Derrida and the Time of Life* (2008), claims that we are all continually engaged in both "chronophilia" and "chronophobia," for the very aspects of life that we desire, and desire to keep and to which we are bound, require that we die:

> The key argument here concerns the co-implication of chronophobia and chronophilia. The fear of time and death does not stem from a metaphysical desire to transcend temporal life. On the contrary, it is generated by the investment in a life that can be lost. It is because one is attached to a temporal being (chronophilia) that one fears losing it (chronophobia). Care in general, I argue, depends on such a double bind. On the one hand, care is necessarily chronophilic, since only something that is subject to the possibility of loss—and hence temporal—can give one a reason to care. On the other hand, care is necessarily chronophobic, since one cannot care about something without fearing what may happen to it. (9-10)

To remain the same forever, embedded in the concept of and desire for immortality, would mean that we would not be bound to anyone or anything, for in order to experience desire we must also recognize that with it comes inevitable loss, and unless we experience the possibility of loss, we are not bound to life.

By structuring his text with an introduction that explains his theory of *chronolibido*, Hägglund considers a chronolibidinal reading of Socrates while challenging Plato and Epicurus and laying out his project concerning Proust, Woolf, and Nabokov. In Chapter 1, "Memory: Proust," his project is to debunk all readings of Proust's *Recherche* that perceive Marcel's focus on "involuntary memory" as a means of transcending time, while Chapter 2 focuses on "a chronolibidinal conception of trauma and mourning to give a new account of temporality in Woolf's writing," using "Woolf's aesthetics of the moment" as his point of departure (17). Chapter 3, "Writing: Nabokov," analyzes *Ada* in view of Nabokov's "aesthetics of time and memory" whereby Hägglund reads Nabokov's "persistent dramatization of the act of writing" as a culmination of Proust's "notions of involuntary memory" and Woolf's "aesthetics of the moment " (17). Chapter 4, "Reading: Freud, Lacan, Derrida," is, in the author's words, an articulation of "the double bind in a general theory of chronolibido," for "If one is bound to mortal life, the positive can never be released from the negative" (18). Thus he contests Freud's and Lacan's "theories of the death drive," arguing that his own theory involving the "chronolibidinal notion of binding allows for a better account of the trauma, violence, and repetition compulsion of psychic life" (18), while showing how Derrida "stages this double bind in his own text" and thus linking Derrida's writing to that of Proust, Woolf, and Nabokov (18).

Though all of Häaglund's chapters clearly further his theory of chronolibido, his analysis of Proust is perhaps the strongest given its wealth of pertinent examples. After closely examining Proust's depictions of involuntary memory, Hägglund states that it is, in fact, the "experience of involuntary memory [that] leads Marcel to pursue a chronolibidinal aesthetics" rather than "reveal the timeless essence of a true self" (22), as believed by such critics as Poulet, Ricoeur, Genette, Girard, and even Deleuze. Through involuntary memory, Marcel relives the past, recognizing that "the past is no longer and will never be again" (32); thus, "[w]hile a past self is retrieved through involuntary memory, the one who remembers can never be identical to the one who is remembered" (23). Whatever joy of resurrection occurs "is immediately traversed by the pain of mourning" rather than a "timeless essence" (33). Ultimately, Hägglund argues, it is not immortality but survival that Marcel seeks, including demonstrating that Marcel's desire to write the novel we have been reading is punctuated by his fear that he will not live long enough to do so.

In "Trauma: Woolf," Hägglund begins with a discussion of *To the Lighthouse*, arguing against Ann Banfield's thesis that "the fleeting world of temporal existence is opposed to the atemporal being of the moment" (57); rather, he writes, "precisely because Woolf seeks to convey singular moments, she has to convey that these moments are temporal rather than eternal. If the moment were not temporal, it could not be distinguished *as* a moment, since it would not be irreplaceable" (37). Hägglund's analysis of *Mrs. Dalloway* further delves into the themes of trauma and mourning, persuasively revealing over and over how "the threat of trauma, then, is latent in even the most precious experience" (73): "Beyond the depiction of specific traumas, however, Woolf displays how experience in general is characterized by a delay and deferral that can be described as traumatic. The characters' streams-of-consciousness convey how they are always in the process of comprehending past experience (delay) and how their present experience can be apprehended only in retrospect (deferral)" (63), as is seen in Clarissa Dalloway's early morning foray into the streets of London. While either a discussion of *To the Lighthouse* or *Mrs. Dalloway* rather than both would have been welcome, as the integrity of Hägglund's argument for a chronolibidinal reading of Proust and Nabokov is strengthened by his focus on one work, albeit a multi-volume one in the case of Proust, it is because every aspect of this author's brilliant discussion of each of Woolf's texts is illuminating that a more extended exploration of one or the other would be desirable, especially *To the Lighthouse*, with its own underlying consideration of the condition of temporality, yet it receives even less attention than *Mrs. Dalloway* and far less than Proust's *oeuvre* or Nabokov's *Ada*.

When focusing on Nabokov's *Ada* in "Writing: Nabokov," Hägglund maintains that Nabokov's writing also demonstrates chronophobia:

> It follows that chronophobia—in spite of what Nabokov sometimes claims—does not stem from a metaphysical desire to escape "the prison of time" (*Speak, Memory* 18). On the contrary, it is because one desires a temporal being (chronophilia) that one fears losing it (chronophobia). Without the chronophilic desire to hold on to the moment, there would be no chronophobic apprehension of the moment passing away. It is the chronolibidinal desire to keep temporal events that motivates Nabokov's autobiographic protagonists. They seek to record time because they are hypersensitive to the threat of oblivion. (82)

Thus, Van's and Ada's lifelong effort at constructing a dual autobiography, contends Hägglund, is also a product of the desire to survive in time rather than transcend it: "Even at the height of youth and in the midst of a summer day there is a sense of ceasing to be that induces the passion for the moment" (109), he writes, as we remember that Van and Ada are constructing their various versions of the moment only as death comes nearer.

In "Conclusion: Binding Desire," Hägglund returns to Proust, Woolf, Nabokov, Freud, Lacan, Derrida, and issues of binding and desire, in particular in Derrida's *Envoies,* seeing Derrida as staging "the double bind of survival in his own text and thereby pursu[ing] a version of the literary writing of chronolibido that is at the center of the preceding chapters"(18). As Hägglund demonstrates throughout this text, "*the same bond* that binds one to pleasure binds one to pain and the same bond that binds one to life binds one to death":

> To be invested in living on is therefore not only to desire but also to fear survival, since survival entails that one may be left to mourn or to suffer an unbearable fate. This condition of chronolibido cannot be cured; it is rather the source of hope and despair, compassion and aggression, protection and exposure. It follows that there is chronophobia at the heart of every chronophilia and chronophilia at the heart of every chronophobia. (167)

Dying for Time: Proust, Woolf, Nabokov ultimately convinces one of the validity of its author's Derrida-influenced challenge, as Martin Hägglund carefully refutes prominent critics, as well as Freud and Lacan, and consistently proves the validity of his chronolibidinal reading of these texts. Not only do we see how deconstruction is put to a new advantage via Hägglund's approach, but one is also moved by the elemental struggle to survive depicted in each of these three modernist writers. As the author reminds us in his conclusion, quoting Proust, "the true paradises are the paradises one has lost," for the true paradise is "here and now" for it can be enjoyed and appreciated only in retrospect, when it is *too late*" (154).

——Helane Levine-Keating, *Pace University*

Notes on Contributors

Michèle Barrett is Professor of Modern Literary and Cultural Theory in the English Department at Queen Mary, University of London, UK. She is the editor of *Virginia Woolf: Women and Writing*, published by Harcourt Brace in the USA and in print since the first edition in 1979, published by The Women's Press, London. She is the editor of the Penguin edition of *A Room of One's Own* and *Three Guineas*, under the general editorship of Julia Briggs. She is also the author of various papers on Woolf. Outside Woolf studies her books include *Casualty Figures: How Five Men Survived the First World War* (2007); *The Politics of Truth: From Marx to Foucault* (1991); and *Women's Oppression Today: Problems in Marxist-Feminist Analysis* (1980).

Denell Downum's scholarly interests include Irish literature and modernism. She has taught British and Irish literature at Suffolk University and Bay State College, both in Boston, and currently she is a faculty associate at Harvard University's Department of Celtic Languages and Literatures.

David Eberly is an independent scholar and poet. He is co-editor, with Suzette Henke, of *Virginia Woolf and Trauma: Embodied Texts*. In addition to his scholarship on Virginia Woolf, he has published many essays and reviews on gay male poets from Walt Whitman to Frank Bidart. More recently, he has turned his attention to narrative medicine and the rhetoric of trauma in the doctor-patient relationship. David has served in the nonprofit world for over thirty years and is currently employed at Boston Children's Hospital Trust.

Diane F. Gillespie, Professor Emeritus of English (Washington State University), is author of *The Sisters' Arts: The Writing and Painting of Virginia Woolf and Vanessa Bell* and of numerous essays, including most recently chapters for Maggie Humm's *Edinburgh Companion to Virginia Woolf and the Arts* and Helen Southworth's *Leonard and Virginia Woolf: The Hogarth Press and the Networks of Modernism*. She is editor of Woolf's *Roger Fry: A Biography* and *The Multiple Muses of Virginia Woolf* as well as co-editor of Julia Stephen's writings, *Virginia Woolf and the Arts* (selected papers), and Cicely Hamilton's play *Diana of Dobson's*.

Jamie Horrocks is Assistant Professor of English at Brigham Young University. She writes on late nineteenth- and early twentieth-century British aesthetics and the Victorian aesthetic movement. She has published recent articles in *Victorian Periodicals Review*, *Nineteenth-Century Prose*, and *Nineteenth-Century Gender Studies*.

Alice Keane is a PhD candidate in English Language and Literature at the University of Michigan, Ann Arbor. She is currently completing a dissertation on Bloomsbury's literature and economics.

Phyllis Lassner is Professor in the Crown Center for Jewish Studies, The Gender Studies and Writing Programs at Northwestern University. In addition to articles on interwar and wartime women writers and Holocaust literature and film, she has published two books on Elizabeth Bowen, *British Women Writers of World War II, Colonial Strangers: Women Writing the End of the British Empire,* and *Anglo-Jewish Women Writing the Holocaust.* She has served as Co-President of the Space Between Society and is Editor of the Northwestern University Press book series, "Cultural Expressions of World War II and the Holocaust: Interwar Preludes, Responses, Memory."

Monica Latham is a Lecturer of British literature at the English Department of the Université de Lorraine, Nancy, France, and a member of the Société d'Etudes Woolfiennes. She has published numerous articles on modernist and postmodernist authors. She has co-edited three collections of essays, *Left Out: Texts and Ur-texts* (Nancy: Presses Universitaires de Nancy, 2009), *The Lives of the Book: Past, Present and to Come* (Nancy: Presses Universitaires de Nancy, 2010) and *Book Practices and Textual Itineraries: Tracing the Contours of Literary Works* (Nancy: Presses Universitaires de Nancy, 2011). She is currently working on a book on contemporary authors who write in the wake of Virginia Woolf.

Patricia Laurence teaches in the City University of New York. Her teaching and research areas include twentieth and twenty-first century British, Sino-British and Irish literatures with a specialization in transnational modernism, Virginia Woolf and Bloomsbury. She is the author of *The Reading of Silence: Virginia Woolf in the English Tradition* and *Lily Briscoe's Chinese Eyes: Bloomsbury, Modernism and China.* Her current work, supported by Mellon and Fulbright grants, is a biography of Elizabeth Bowen. It includes Bowen's relationship with Virginia Woolf as well as with other women authors among its topics.

Maren Linett is an associate professor at Purdue University. Linett is the author of *Modernism, Feminism, and Jewishness* (Cambridge UP, 2007; paperback 2011) and the editor of *Virginia Woolf: An MFS Reader* (Johns Hopkins UP, 2009) and *The Cambridge Companion to Modernist Women Writers* (Cambridge UP,

2010). She has published articles about Woolf, Dorothy Richardson, Jean Rhys, Rebecca West, James Joyce, Henry Roth, and Elizabeth Bowen. Her current book project is entitled *Modernism and Disability*.

John McGuigan is Associate Professor of English at the University of Wisconsin-Whitewater, where he offers courses in modernism, British literature, composition, and screenwriting. He has published articles on Djuna Barnes, E. E. Cummings, and the film adaptation of Mark Bowden's *Black Hawk Down*, and is currently at work on "In the Anarchist Grain," which argues for the importance of nineteenth-century anarchism to the evolution of British and American modernist narrative.

Beth Rosenberg is an Associate Professor of English at the University of Nevada, Las Vegas. She has published *Virginia Woolf and Samuel Johnson: Common Readers* and co-edited *Virginia Woolf and the Essay*. She is currently working on a book about modernism, immigration, and the Jew.

Natania Rosenfeld is Professor of English at Knox College in Galesburg, IL and the author of *Outsiders Together: Virginia and Leonard Woolf* (Princeton UP, 2000). She publishes poetry, essays and fiction regularly in literary magazines and is at work on a novel.

Leena Kore Schröder teaches in the School of English at the University of Nottingham in the UK, specializing in twentieth-century and contemporary literature. She has published numerous articles on Virginia Woolf, as well as Herbert Read and John Betjeman. Currently she is finishing a commissioned monograph for the U of Edinburgh P, *Modernism and the Idea of Everyday Life*.

Mia Spiro received her PhD in English from York University in Toronto. She now has a postdoctoral fellowship from the Social Sciences and Humanities Research Council of Canada and is a Visiting Scholar at the Crown Center for Jewish Studies at Northwestern University. She is the author of *Anti-Nazi Modernism: The Challenges of Resistance in 1930s Fiction* (Northwestern UP, 2013) and winner of the Ontario Government's Polanyi Prize for Literature (2011). Her current project, *Modern Monsters: Golems, Vampires, and the Ghosts of War*, examines elements of the undead in cultural responses to migration and war.

Christina Svendsen is a Lecturer in Comparative Literature at Harvard University. She is currently working on a book manuscript titled *Stone, Steel, Glass: Constructions of Time in European Modernity*. Her translation of the German Expressionist Paul Scheerbart's *Lesabéndio: an Asteroid Novel* was published by Wakefield Press in 2012.

Lara Trubowitz is the author of *Civil Antisemitism, Modernism, and British Culture, 1902-1939* (2012). She is co-editor of *Antisemitism and Philosemitism in the Twentieth and Twenty-First Centuries: Representing Jews, Jewishness, and Modern Culture* (2008) and co-editor and co-translator of *Contemporary Italian Women Poets: A Bilingual Anthology* (2001). She is currently working on two new book projects: *Leonard Woolf in the Shadow of Empire: Modernism and the League of Nations* and *Selling Prejudice in Britain and America: Race, Religion, and the New Far Right*.

• HENRY JAMES • WILLIAM FAULKNER • *THE GETTYSBURG ADDRESS* • NEW YORK SCHOOL POETS •

—*linguae americanae*—

ARIZONA QUARTERLY

American literature, culture, and
theory, four times a year

1 year $20
3 years $40

1731 E. Second St. • University of Arizona
Tucson, Arizona 85721-0014

criticism

A Quarterly for Literature and the Arts
renée c. hoogland, editor

Criticism provides a forum for current scholarship on literature, media, music, and visual culture. A place for rigorous theoretical and critical debate as well as formal and methodological self-reflexivity and experimentation, *Criticism* aims to present contemporary thought at its most vital.

Subscriptions
- Institution: $172.00
- Individual: $61.00
- Student/Senior: $27.00

Back Issues
- Institution: $49.00
- Individual: $19.00

Recent Special Issues:
- 54.3: Shakespeare and Phenomenology
- 53.4: Transcultural Negotiations of Holocaust Memory
- 53.3: Open Source Culture and Aesthetics

Legacy
A Journal of American Women Writers

Edited by Jennifer S. Tuttle
Theresa Strouth Gaul and Nicole Tonkovich, Co-Editors

Legacy is the only journal to focus specifically on American women's writings from the seventeenth through the mid-twentieth century. Each issue's articles cover a wide range of topics: examinations of the works of individual authors; genre studies; analyses of race, ethnicity, gender, class, and sexualities in women's literature; and historical and material cultural issues pertinent to women's lives and literary works.

Coming in 2013: A special issue on "Women Writing Disability".

Legacy is the official journal of the Society for the Study of American Women Writers.

For subscriptions and back issues:
Visit **nebraskapress.unl.edu**
or call **402-472-8536**

Legacy is available online
on Project MUSE
bit.ly/LEG_MUSE
and
JSTOR Current Scholarship
bit.ly/LEG_JSTOR

 Follow us on Twitter @LegacyWmenWrite

Mississippi Quarterly

The Journal of Southern Cultures

Since 1948 the *Mississippi Quarterly* has published refereed articles on the life and culture of the South, past and present. Recent issues include essays on William Styron, Christine Wiltz, Arna Bontemps, Mary Lee Settle, Willie Morris, Lillian B Horace, Marsha Norman, Wendell Berry, and Forrest Carter. Recent special issues are devoted to Lewis Nordan, Faulkner and Labor, Lynching and American Culture, American Indian Literatures and Cultures in the South, the South in Film, and Southern Roots and Routes. The *Quarterly* is published by Mississippi State University's College of Arts and Sciences.

Subscriptions are $24 per year in the United States, $27 in Canada and Mexico, and $29 in all other countries. Back issues are available.

> *Mississippi Quarterly*
> P.O. Box 5272
> Mississippi State, MS 39762

missq.msstate.edu

Mosaic
a journal for the interdisciplinary study of literature

CALL FOR PAPERS
AN INTERNATIONAL INTERDISCIPLINARY CONFERENCE
A matter of *lifedeath*

The University of Manitoba, Winnipeg, Canada, October 1-4, 2014

Keynote Speakers: Andrea Carlino, Françoise Dastur, David Palumbo-Liu, H. Peter Steeves, Elisabeth Weber

Information on paper topics and submission details are available on the *Mosaic* website: **www.umanitoba.ca/mosaic**

Forthcoming Publications

- **BLINDNESS (September 2013).** This issue will bring together critical and disability theories to address historical and contemporary studies and interpretations of blindness across various genres, as well as studies of, to use Samuel Weber's title words (in *Institution and Interpretation*), "The Blindness of the Seeing Eye."

- **ROMANCE (forthcoming 2014).** This *Mosaic* special issue engages the rich history of the word Romance, with essays on "the Romantics," the roman, romantic fiction, Romanticism, the state of the love story in literature and film, and the figure of the "romantic."

Visit our website for current news, special offers and promotions.
www.umanitoba.ca/mosaic

Get Connected – stay abreast of *Mosaic* issues, news and events by having this information delivered to you via RSS news feed or by email.

Mosaic, a journal for the interdisciplinary study of literature
University of Manitoba, 208 Tier Building, Winnipeg, Manitoba, R3T 2N2 CANADA
Email: Mosaic@ad.umanitoba.ca   **Tel:** 204-474-9763   **Fax:** 204-474-7584

Tulsa Studies in Women's Literature

Eighteenth-Century Women And English Catholicism

Coedited by Anna Battigelli and Laura Stevens

www.utulsa.edu/tswl • tswl@utulsa.edu

Policy

Woolf **S**tudies **A**nnual invites articles on the work and life of Virginia Woolf and her milieu. The *Annual* intends to represent the breadth and eclecticism of critical approaches to Woolf, and particularly welcomes new perspectives and contexts of inquiry. Articles discussing relations between Woolf and other writers and artists are also welcome.

Articles are sent for review anonymously to a member of the Editorial Board and at least one other reader. Manuscripts should not be under consideration elsewhere or have been previously published. It is strongly advised that those submitting work to *WSA* be familiar with the journal's content. Among criteria on which evaluation of submissions depends are whether an article demonstrates familiarity with scholarship already published in the field, whether the article is written clearly and effectively, and whether it makes a genuine contribution to Woolf studies.

Preparation of Copy

1. Articles are typically between 25 and 30 pages, and do not exceed 8000 words. Inquiries about significantly shorter or longer submissions should be sent to the Editor at woolfstudiesannual@gmail.com.

2. A separate page should include the article's title, author's name, address, telephone & fax numbers, and e-mail address. The author's name and identifying references should not appear on the manuscript to preserve anonymity for our readers.

3. All submissions must include an abstract of no more than 250 words.

4. Manuscripts should be prepared according to most recent MLA style.

5. Submissions may be sent *either* by email to woolfstudiesannual@gmail.com *or* by mail to Mark Hussey, English Dept., Pace University, One Pace Plaza, New York NY 10038. For mailed submissions, please send **three** copies of the article and abstract.

6. Authors of accepted manuscripts are responsible for any necessary permissions fees and for securing any necessary permissions.

All editorial, review, and advertising inquiries should be addressed to woolfstudiesannual@gmail.com.

Inquiries concerning orders should be addressed to PaceUP@pace.edu.

Other Woolf titles available:

"The Hours": The British Museum Manuscript of Mrs. Dalloway, transcribed and edited by Helen M. Wussow (paper 2010).

Virginia Woolf, Jacob's Room: *The Holograph Draft.* Transcribed and edited by Edward L. Bishop (paper 2010)

Women in the Milieu of Leonard and Virginia Woolf: Peace, Politics and Education Ed. Wayne K. Chapman and Janet M. Manson (1998)

Virginia Woolf and Trauma: Embodied Texts Ed. Suzette Henke & David Eberly (2007)

Woolf Across Cultures Ed. Natalya Reinhold (2004)

Woolf Studies Annual 5 (1999)

Woolf Studies Annual 6 (2000): The *Three Guineas* Correspondence, edited by Anna Snaith

Woolf Studies Annual 7 (2001)

Woolf Studies Annual 8 (2002): The Fawcett Library Correspondence, edited by Merry Pawlowski

Woolf Studies Annual 9 (2003): *Virginia Woolf and Literary History Part 1*, edited by Jane Lilienfeld, Jeffrey Oxford, and Lisa Low

Woolf Studies Annual 10 (2004): *Virginia Woolf and Literary History Part 2,* edited by Jane Lilienfeld, Jeffrey Oxford, and Lisa Low

Woolf Studies Annual 11 (2005) - *Woolf Studies Annual 18* (2012)

Virginia Woolf and Communities: Selected Papers from the Eighth Annual Conference on Virginia Woolf edited by Jeanette McVicker and Laura Davis

Virginia Woolf Turning the Centuries: Selected Papers from the Ninth Annual Conference on Virginia Woolf edited by Ann Ardis and Bonnie Kime Scott

Virginia Woolf Out of Bounds: Selected Papers from the Tenth Annual Conference on Virginia Woolf edited by Jessica Berman and Jane Goldman

www.ingramcontent.com/pod-product-compliance
Lightning Source LLC
Chambersburg PA
CBHW061426300426
44114CB00014B/1566